CLOSING THE CIRCLE

A Memoir of Cuba, Exile, the Bay of Pigs,
and a Trans-island Bike Journey

To Jack & Beth
(more to Beth!)
Hope you enjoy this

Robert H. Miller

CLOSING THE CIRCLE:
A Memoir of Cuba, Exile, the Bay of Pigs,
and a Trans-island Bike Journey

Ebook & Paperback developed
by CognitioBooks.com

Cover illustration by GarrinchaToonz.com

ISBN 978-0-9990655-0-1
ISBN 978-0-9990655-1-8 (Ebook)

Dedicated to

Armando R. Lastra Faget

&

Ana Margarita Faget Otazo v/d Lastra

Orphan

What was I looking for in that room
Crowded with old books, shelves so full,
It seemed they could not hold another title,
Except where in places a weary volume
Leaned upon its neighbor's crooked spine?
Some dimly remembered novel or poem
I once read and loved, or dreamed of?
Either a real book or the book of dreams
A friend once advised me to record:
Write upon waking, the dreams will come
If you wait and listen, word for word.
And night and day must be reconciled
Like mother and father, parent and child,
Brother and sister, lovers who have quarreled.
Although I never did as I was told,
I have met the morning every day I could,
Shaken the darkness, come to the table,
Truly grateful for what fare was offered,
Bran or manna, ambrosia or bread,
A sentence, a tragedy, or a kind word.
And now, almost sixty and an orphan —
As nature would have it — I am the age
My father was when he died. Every day
Seems to me it might be the final one.
Pressed for time to make peace with the past,
I look for a book so broad-backed and strong
That it will stand up on the shelf alone.

Daniel Mark Epstein

Table of Contents

FOREWORD

Everyone in Cuba is related; we are all one big family. Even the descendants from the two continents—Europe and Africa—that provided the main source of settlers have interbred to such a degree that, unlike in the US, we all share the same cultural values, patois, styles of dress, music, etc. The only difference is religious, and even it is very syncretic, with Catholicism and *Santería* (in itself a syncretic practice based on indigenous Nigerian religions) coexisting quite tolerably within the same spiritual outlook. In Cuba skin color is just another physical trait; no different than weight, hair color, height or even disposition. My own DNA test reveals a 1% African origin within the past 500 years.

It's no surprise. My mother's side of the family came from the Canary Islands in the 1800s. The Canary Islands, a province of Spain, are geographically part of Africa. And the islands' distinctive Spanish accent—as unique and different as a Scottish brogue is to American English—is the source of Cuba's nearly unintelligible Spanish. Fidel Castro, famous for his eloquence and loquaciousness, practiced long and hard to acquire a more mainstream Spanish. Fidel's father came from Galicia, the northern, Celtic province of Spain fronting the Bay of Biscay. Galicians still play their bagpipes.

Francisco Franco too was Galician. Both he and Castro are very *gallego*: bull-headed and inflexible with a dedication to idealism, whatever the stripe. Vain, reserved and austere with strong characters and personality, neither has a well-developed sense of humor. Galicia's Premier, in a vain attempt at liberalizing Cuba, once invited Castro to retire to Galicia.

The Cuban people were never colonized—*they* were the colonizers *and* the colonized. Ignorant and intemperate, the Spanish colonizers inadvertently killed all the aboriginal inhabitants of the island: Caribs and Tainos. Most families retain strong atavistic links to the Old World regions from which they hailed: European descendants to their home provinces and African descendants to their tribes. These take the form of clubs or associations that meet often to promote old regional ties and values. During *carnaval*, groups parade in regional costumes and construct floats evocative of their heritage.

The other branch of my mother's family that plays a significant role in this family memoir hailed from Catalunya, the province on the northeast coast of Spain, on the Mediterranean Sea. Their way of speaking is so distinctive, it's considered a different language: Catalan. Italian and Catalan are the source of Buenos Aires' distinctive *porteño* accent, the butt of many jokes (but that's another story).

* * *

In 2016 I led a group of five friends, including my wife, on a bicycle journey across Cuba along the Carretera Central, or central highway. The Carretera Central was built in the 1930s, stitching the island together from end to end. My grandfather, a heavy projects contractor, was one of its builders. He was also a contractor on the capitol building in Havana and the Cárcel Modelo, or federal prison on the Isle of Pines (now the Isla de Juventud), where both Fidel Castro and my cousins Armandito and Cachorro all spent time—one for fighting Batista, the other two for fighting Fidel.

We were a diverse group: my Taiwanese college roommate, George Yen, recently retired as president of Toastmaster's International, but still running his industrial pipe fittings factory and import/export businesses in Taipei; Roy Smith, a Lancashire mountaineer and adventurer, with the first ascent of Alpamayo in the Andes under his belt, and many years running adventure education programs for American colleges; Roy's wife, Brenda Smith, a retired schoolteacher and trekking leader; and Tina Cobos, my lover—a biker, climber, kayaker, river guide and real estate agent.

The trip was nearly ten years in the making. With the deaths of my mother, uncles, cousin and the advanced age of other aunts and cousins who had played leading roles in the events recorded in this memoir—not to mention Fidel Castro's own advanced age, his close brush with death in 2006, and his transfer of power that year to his brother Raúl—something inside nagged me to go, to return to the land where I'd grown up.

In 2004, a cigar aficionado friend of the family's—we'll call him John—traveled illegally to Cuba via Cancun, Mexico. He'd been going to Cuba regularly and smuggling cigars back into the US. With the US embargo and the high price of quality Cuban cigars, this operation was a nifty source of supplemental income for him. We asked him, among other things, to drop by our old Havana home and take some pictures. He did. The house, looking quite a bit smaller—as adult realities always look compared to childhood memories—was noticeably run down and was now ringed by a concrete block wall that inelegantly severed the arching driveway in front. Being a pushy, libertarian sort of guy, he walked up to the front door.

We'd heard through the grapevine that our old house in Havana had been used to lodge visiting East Block dignitaries. After the fall of the Soviet Union and the ensuing Special Economic Period, our home—which we'd bought from the previous mayor of Havana—had been turned into a legal B&B. But the manager had been withholding taxes from the government— sometimes levied at over 100% of gross receipts.

The residence was later converted into a technical school guarded by a Kalashnikov-wielding militiaman. John engaged him and requested entry. The militiaman said that the house was now the property of the people and John wasn't welcome. John declared that he was "a people" and therefore could enter. The militiaman was taken aback by such logic but, still refusing John actual entry, allowed him to walk around the place and take photographs of both the outside and inside, through the windows.

I didn't want to go to Cuba illegally. Not only am I averse to lawbreaking, I'm temperamentally unsuited to lying. Until 2015, the only legal way for a US resident to travel to Cuba was to submit an application for travel, in an approved category, to the US Treasury Department and wait for permission to be granted or denied.

As a part-time, free-lance journalist, writer and a part-time educator, I had three categories open to me. Yet all presented problems. Neither journalists nor writers doing research are the most welcome species in Cuba, with many obstacles placed in their way. And my educational specialty was adventure education, Outward Bound-type courses with an academic component, nearly always run on a contractual basis as a self-employed provider—not a category-friendly designation for a bureaucrat to identify and approve.

Then in December of 2014, President Barack Obama announced that fitting a category for travel to Cuba would henceforth be on the honor system: no pre-approval from the State or Treasury Department required. I was all over that.

Cuba is a hot country. The weather is biker-friendly only between November and March. That meant that, with all the necessary preparations, my earliest possible date for travel was the following winter of 2015/2016.

Nearly a dozen friends wanted to accompany me, but only a few fit the still-extant categories and had the time, the money and the fitness to participate. The original five of us who committed decided on a February, 2016 date for the trip.

My next challenge was documenting the category we had chosen: Education. I had to write up a proposal and an itinerary to present to the institutions for which we'd worked in order to request their sponsorship; to present to the Cuban authorities—legal US travelers being subject to much more oversight than embargo-busting ones—and to present to US Customs and Immigration upon our return. We wrote letters to two colleges and a university requesting official—but not monetary (that would have been a deal-killer)—sponsorship for our project. We proposed to run an exploratory reconnaissance to determine the feasibility of running bike-based adventure-education courses focusing on the history, anthropology, and natural science of Cuba. We met with their staffers. We updated and submitted resumés. We promised not to embarrass them.

My friend John, the cigar smuggler, advised me to book lodging in Havana ASAP. Not only had European, Canadian, legal and illegal US travel—both individually and in organized, sanctioned tours—increased phenomenally in 2015, he suspected that President Obama's new dispensation on the "honor" system would flood Havana with tourists. In early October I began our search for a place to stay in February, still five months away.

We only needed a few nights in Havana to get oriented, register at the US Embassy, extend our 30-day visas, put our bikes together and catch a bus to Baracoa on the extreme eastern end of the island for the start of the bike trip. We also needed flexible lodging dates for our return to the capital after the bike ride. All hotels were booked solid for the 2015/16 season—not that we wanted to stay in overpriced tourist hotels.

Casas particulares, 'individual houses' (usually translated as *private* homes, a term I avoid because, so far, the concept of 'private' property rights is not fully developed in Cuba) is the cumbersome name for Cuban Bed and Breakfasts. In socialist and Communist ideology, everything belongs to the state—even the home one lives in. Residents can no more rent a room than they can sell their home; they live there at the sufferance of the state. But when the Soviet Union imploded and stopped subsidizing the Cuban economy, Castro was desperate for foreign exchange. Like Lenin instituting the NEP (New Economic Policy—free market reforms, which were later rescinded) after the Russian Civil War to increase production, Castro allowed B&Bs and small private restaurants, *paladares*, to open in order to draw more tourists and increase individual wealth—but not too much. Few, if any, employees were allowed in the new enterprises (for fear of 'exploitation'); and the restrictions and sliding tax scale made the businesses very unstable.

When conditions improved in the country, taxes on the little private enterprises increased, in many cases, to 100%. Many of the new entrepreneurial buds withered on the vine. But then Fidel retired. Raul, his brother, re-instituted the old reforms with more reasonable employee hiring rules and lighter taxation, and increased the legal self-employment categories to about 200. Cubans, in spite of having been burned once, jumped on the chance to go into business for themselves. Even Air B&B got in on the act.

So I began a search for a *casa particular*—preferably in my old neighborhood—that could accommodate 5 bikers in three rooms, with flexible dates, and store our bike boxes in the interim.

After many dead ends and failed communications, a Swiss *casas particulares* aggregator confirmed a booking for us in Havana's Vedado area and one in Baracoa in Oriente Province, where we would begin our bike ride. But then, in December, they notified me that the booking was no longer available. Would I accept a substitute? I answered *yes, anything*! But by mid-January, only three weeks before our departure date, they couldn't confirm the substitute.

It's not a good idea to arrive in Havana without a place to stay. Forget knocking on doors at random, begging for a corner of the floor to sleep on and flashing dollars. A Cuban can be put in jail for housing a foreigner without the proper permits and registrations. On top of that, licensed *casas particulares* must notify the police when they host Americans. So I took a back channel, grapevine approach.

Our travel arrangements routed us through Miami. I wanted to spend time before and after the bike trip with the Cuban branch of my family, and interview them for this book. I'd asked them for help finding a place to stay in Havana back in October. They promised to help, in that vague doesn't-have-to-be-addressed-yet-because-it's-months-away attitude. Now, in January, I relayed the urgency of our situation.

Alina, my cousin, came through. She said that Tondy, a very distant shirt-tail relative who worked in the government's tourism organization—gastronomy branch—had opened up a B&B back in November. She gave me his email address. I wrote him a lengthy request explaining our unique situation, hoping he'd be—if not able to accommodate us—at least give us a lead and help us find something.

Tondy didn't respond right away. By the time I was about to panic, Tania, his wife, responded. She apologized for the delay, explaining that their 3-year-old son had dropped their email tablet in the toilet and she had to scramble for other means to contact us. She was overjoyed to connect with a relative, no matter how distant, and that even though they only had two rooms they'd somehow accommodate us—and only charge $20 per room! I could feel the warm hospitality in her response.

After a few more exchanges to settle the deal, I asked if there was anything I could bring them from *Yuma*. Cuba is known for its shortages of basic household items: toothpaste, shampoo, toothbrushes, tampons and such. *Yuma* is a term used to refer to the better-off abroad. Tania demurred, probably thinking it inappropriate to ask for anything.

I persevered, saying not to be embarrassed for asking; if I couldn't bring something, I wouldn't. And if something was too expensive, I'd charge them—but to please ask. Finally, Tondy asked for a few gifts—such as socks or toys—for the boy who was going to turn three a day or two after our arrival. And then he asked for something that would put some skin in the game: a cheap laptop computer to replace the one his son had ruined—their only way of making bookings for their new enterprise.

His request was a bit of a minefield. I couldn't just bring in a laptop and sell it or give it to him. It had to be declared—a lengthy process—and a 100% tariff paid on it. A similar, used product on the Cuban grey market— if available, a BIG if—was more than twice the price of a new one in the US, putting it out of their financial reach.

Electronics for personal use by visitors, however, were allowed into Cuba as long as they were taken back out. One way or another, I was determined to bring Tondy, Tania and their son toothbrushes, toothpaste, an Etch-a-Sketch, a Slinky, cumin seed, ball point pens—and a Lenovo Chromebook.

One week before departure we received sponsorship letters from Yavapai College, Bloomsburg University and Prescott College. I even received a sponsorship letter from *Liberty* magazine—for which I often wrote—to present to US Customs on our return, just in case additional documentation substantiating a legal category might be helpful. Separately, our charter flight tickets and Cuban visas arrived in the mail. We were set to go.

* * *

This memoir is divided into three parts. The first part covers my immediate family's saga in Cuba, from our roots to our exile in 1960. The second part tells the story of my extended family, focusing on the experiences of my cousin Armandito Lastra, and a cousin-in-law, Carlos "*Cachorro*" León, who were key—albeit minor—players in the Bay of Pigs invasion and subsequent counter-Revolutionary infiltrations that continued until 1967.

Today, the Bay of Pigs affair is remembered—if it's remembered at all—as an ill-conceived fiasco engineered by a rogue CIA under vague US government approval against the legitimate Cuban government of Fidel Castro. But then, history is usually written by the victors. Fidel Castro described the Bay of Pigs as a US invasion staffed by mercenaries. Cuban expatriates, on the other hand, prefer to describe it as a civil war in which one side was helped with money, expertise, and armaments by the USSR, East Germany and Czechoslovakia, while the other was similarly helped by the US, Guatemala and Nicaragua.

In spite of at least half-a-dozen excellent books on the Bay of Pigs in English, misconceptions persist. Perhaps the most prevalent, albeit perfectly logical misconception is that since the overall planning and execution of the invasion was so badly conceived, the same held true for the action on the ground—with the implication that the invaders were poorly trained and didn't perform well. Two close friends of mine, from opposite sides of the political spectrum, both refused to believe that Castro's forces suffered 4,000 to 5,000 casualties in the affair compared to 67 combat deaths in Brigade 2506, the free Cuban invasion force.

Those figures strain credulity. They imply a motivation and performance on the part of the free Cubans that beggars the imagination; after all, they ran out of ammunition and they lost. And they imply, correspondingly, an incompetence on Castro's troops that is unimaginable in light of his later extraordinary success against the apartheid South African army in the Angolan civil war. Castro admits to only 176 deaths on his side. The 4,000 figure comes from *U.S. News & World Report*, April 22, 1996. The 5,000 figure from Jim Rasenberger's *The Brilliant Disaster: JFK, Castro, and America's Doomed Invasion of Cuba's Bay of Pigs*.

Compared to Viet Nam, Afghanistan and Iraqi war veterans, whose post-traumatic stress syndrome (PTSD) levels hovered around 30%, Bay of Pigs veterans suffered almost no PTSD. Humberto "*Chino*" Díaz Argüelles, president of the Casa de la Brigada, the Bay of Pigs veterans' association and museum, attributes Brigade 2506's low incidence of PTSD to their idealism and absolute dedication to their cause. Though the actual battles at the Bay of Pigs lasted only three days, they were the full measure of all-out war: extremely high casualty rates and operational field conditions that could drive a soldier from duress to despair to madness. Add to that the 20 months of incarceration by the Castro regime with death an ever-present threat, and the Bay of Pigs experience becomes a more conventional PTSD scenario.

I have relied consistently on Haynes Johnson's *The Bay of Pigs: The Leaders' Story of Brigade 2506* as an outline for much of this section. And I often quote him at some length, especially when I don't have an insight, an eyewitness account, or a better way of phrasing his information. But this memoir is the "grunts' story"—my family's "grunts," plus a few of their close intimates.

I have also depended heavily on Bradley Earl Ayers' *The War That Never Was: An Insider's Account of CIA Covert Operations Against Cuba*, Peter Wyden's *Bay of Pigs: The Untold Story*, and Pablo Pérez-Cisneros', John B. Donovan's, and Jeff Koenreich's *After the Bay of Pigs: Lives and Liberty on the Line*. I mention these here because without them, this book would have been nearly impossible. My cousins, like the blind men and the elephant, experienced limited aspects of the entire Bay of Pigs saga. Additionally, being lowly grunts, they weren't privy to the bigger picture. Finally, they never discussed their experiences after they returned, mostly because they'd been told to keep mum with the press.

But I don't want to minimize all my other sources, both written and oral. They are fully credited in the acknowledgements at the end of the book.

The last third of the book is a travelogue of our bicycle ride across Cuba.

* * *

Cubans dub everyone with a distinctive nickname. With so many characters in this memoir, I've mostly refrained from using whole names and stuck simply to nicknames or, in their absence, first names only (unless they're historical or well-known characters, in which case I use either their full name or simply their last name), to avoid tripping into a *War and Peace*-type confusion. But there are two additional reasons for this simplification.

In Spanish and Latin American nomenclature—for example, Fidel Castro Ruz—names follow a different form from US or British custom. The last name in Castro's name is his mother's name, while "Castro" is his father's name. When referring to Fidel, either Fidel or Castro will identify him. Calling him Ruz implies that he's illegitimate and would be very confusing. Alphabetical lists use the penultimate or father's name. Ernesto "*Che*" Guevara Serna is another example. "*Che*" is the nickname; Serna his mother's name; Guevara his father's name.

When a woman marries, she usually retains her maiden name and does not take on her husband's name (unless he dies, in which case *v/d*—followed by the husband's name is often appended; meaning *viuda de* or widow of).

Sometimes, when the penultimate and last names are common, both are always used together, sometimes hyphenated. To complicate matters further, many exiles became Americans and adopted American customs in rendering names. Some Cuban-Americans use both styles, depending on context.

Finally, some names have been changed to protect the guilty. Cuba is, after all, a police state and the revelation of some names could imperil people still in Cuba.

I know someday, that will change.

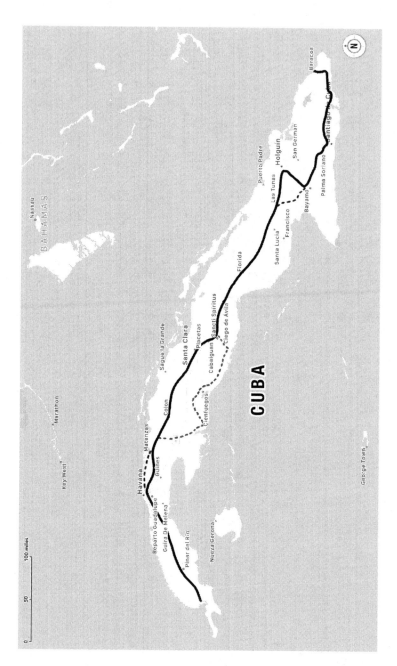

Cuba. The solid line is the Carretera Central, route of the author's 2016 bike ride. Built between 1927 and 1931 by the author's grandfather, John Maurice Fitzgerald, one of its contractors, it remains the primary trans-island artery. The dashed lines are the author's divergence from it to visit Playa Girón and the Bay of Pigs, and the author's family's confiscated beach homes between Havana and Matanzas.

PART I
CUBA CALLS

1

The Archaic

"Fidel does not have cancer. I'm very well informed….Nobody knows when Fidel is going to die" —Hugo Chavez

My mother, Ana María Flora Minerva Fitzgerald y Díaz, died on the 14th of July, 2000 at 78 years of age. For 40 years, ever since our flight from Cuba in 1960, she'd clung to the hope of outliving Fidel Castro Ruz, a man 4 years her junior. Almost more galling than having Castro outlive her was having her saint's day fall on July 26, the anniversary and official title of Fidel Castro's revolutionary movement. To a Cuban, one's saint's day—the birth date of the Catholic saint after whom one was named, in this case Santa Ana—is a personal holiday second only to one's birthday. After our flight following the Revolution, first, tentatively, to Mexico and then to the United States, she never again celebrated anything on that day.

My family has deep roots in Cuba. My maternal grandmother, Ana María de la Caridad Díaz y Otazo, was a third-generation Spanish émigré from the Canary Islands. John Maurice Fitzgerald, my maternal grandfather, was an American contractor in Aguascalientes, Mexico when the 1910 Mexican Revolution erupted, so he fled for Havana where prospects seemed better.

Both were stern and imposing, with bulldog jowls, sharp, no-nonsense eyes, Grecian noses, and thin, locked lips, ever-vigilant against any whiff of impertinence. Nonetheless, it must have been love by-the-by because they married in 1914.

Ana María Díaz y Otazo, grandmother (abuela) of author, about age 26. Date: Circa 1910. Source: A. R. Hatch-Miller collection.

John Maurice Fitzgerald, grandfather of author, about age 26. Date: Circa 1911. Source: A. R. Hatch-Miller collection.

A massive man, rigid disciplinarian, and heavy drinker and gambler with a streak of willfulness that could turn violent, John Maurice was also an ambitious wheeler-dealer. He soon worked his way as a primary sub-contractor into Cuba's biggest construction projects under President Gerardo Machado.

Nineteen-fourteen Cuba was caught in a time warp. It had achieved independence only 12 years before. Tiny next-door Haiti had been independent since 1804, besting what was then the world's most powerful army, the Grande Armée of Napoleon. Since Cuba's independence from, first, Spain and then, in 1902, from the United States—a facilitator in the first effort—it had experienced only five chief executives, two of whom were governors appointed by the US during post-independence interventions. Only three were duly elected presidents. And only one, Tomás Estrada Palma, the first, was considered uncorrupt.

In some ways 1914 Cuba was like the US in 1804, when the War for Independence was a relatively recent memory, and its heroes still played a significant political role. But unlike the US in 1776—a thriving outpost of a British Empire that was nowhere near its potential peak—Cuba was a distant province of an increasingly decrepit, inept, and corrupt Spanish empire. Slavery had only been abolished in 1886. Spanish investment in Cuban infrastructure was nearly non-existent. There were no paved highways, and dirt roads were impassable after rains. What few railroads existed charged exorbitant monopoly prices for ox cart-speed delivery of agricultural produce and freight. Cuba was a faded canvas awaiting, if not a Michelangelo, at least a Jackson Pollock. But first it needed re-framing, re-stretching, re-starching, stapling, and a solid foundation up on a hardwood easel.

The not-yet-thirty-year-old John Maurice began to specialize in big works. He partnered up with an R. Plowman and founded Fitzgerald & Plowman, General Contractors. Their first major commission was the *Teatro Nacional*, or National Theatre, adjacent to Cuba's inchoate capitol building. Today, the National Theatre—renamed in 1985 the *Gran Teatro de la Habana*—is probably Cuba's most impressive building, especially at night. Renovated in 2013-14, it re-opened on January 1st, 2016.

The core of the theatre was built in 1838 as the *Teatro Tacón*, but acquired by the Galician Social Club—Cuba's oldest provincial roots organization—and re-developed as the *Centro Gallego* beginning in 1907. The architectural specifications required the preservation of the *Teatro Tacón's* magnificent interior. John Maurice's challenge was to build the steel skeleton to support the neobaroque building of the new National Theatre around the existing theatre. The project was completed in 1914. Unfortunately, the magnificent new shell did no favors to the *Tacón's* excellent acoustics.

Ana María Díaz y Otazo & John Maurice Fitzgerald, author's grandparents, ages early 30s at Varadero beach, Cuba. Circa 1920. Source: A. R. Hatch-Miller collection.

In 1925, Brigadier General Gerardo Machado, a hero of the War for Independence from Spain, ran for President under the slogan "water, roads, schools," promising to end corruption while serving only one term (as the 1901 Constitution dictated).

When he was elected, Machado kept his promise, building a beautiful new capitol building in Havana, with rotunda and wings modeled on the US capitol, a paved trans-island highway, an enlarged and modernized University of Havana, a modern, progressively designed federal prison, the Hotel Nacional and Hotel Presidente, the Asturia Building (today the National Museum of Fine Arts), the Bacardi Building, and an expansion of health facilities. But he was not as successful in attacking corruption. In 1927 he pushed through Congress an amendment to the Constitution that allowed him to run for a second, successive term—a term his opponents condemned, and a term that turned out as clean as the still undependable Havana tap water.

John Maurice was a beneficiary of the Machadazo, as Machado's steam-roller public works program was nicknamed. His first commission under Machado, the capitol building, was completed in a scant three years. Initially begun in 1912 under President Menocal, it was completely redesigned during the Machadazo, partially demolished, and restarted in 1926 by the Purdy Henderson Co. It took 8,000 men and 25% of the national budget to complete by 1929.

Capitol building and Gran Teatro, Havana, Cuba, two of the author's grandfather's first commissions. Circa 1954. Credit: Rolandez. Source: A. R. Hatch-Miller collection.

Gran Teatro at night, 2016. Credit: Roy Smith.

Gran Teatro detail. Credit: R. H. Miller.

He then joined the big push to complete the Carretera Central, Cuba's main trans-island artery; also built all at one go between 1927 and 1931 by a consortium of the Associated Cuban Contractors, Inc. and the Warren Brothers Co. of Boston, Massachusetts. Except for engineers, supervisors, and technical experts, the contract stipulated that 70% of the workforce had to be Cuban, a requirement that was strictly enforced.

The highway begins at the Capitolio in Havana, with one branch heading east and the other west. It touches the coast in only three places, Havana, Matanzas, and Santiago de Cuba. Straddling the island's spine—what, in effect, is the north-south watershed divide—the highway is an engineering marvel in that bridge crossings—only 536—were relatively unnecessary. Though no grade-level railroad crossings were included in the design, many granite-paved ox cart crossings dot the highway. All 705.6 miles (by 20.66 feet wide) are asphalt-topped concrete. At a price of over $107,000 per mile, there was much skimming involved. But when the highway opened in 1932, Alberto Casas, a schoolmate of Fidel Castro's and scion of one of Oriente's largest cattle growing families, remembered the occasion as one of his childhood's most momentous events. The concrete artery opened a flood of commerce into Santiago de Cuba and created quick links with Havana for the first time in 400 years.

According to Sergio Díaz-Briquets and Jorge Pérez-López, corruption on a grand scale through highly inflated costs, dogged both the Capitolio and Carretera Central projects. The allegations against authoritarian President Gerardo Machado and his cronies also included kickbacks to the

Warren Brothers contractors, and even to Chase Bank of New York, which had provided critical financing. Whether John Maurice was a beneficiary of what, at the time, were common practices, the record remains mum.

Carretera Central stratigraphy: Two layers of asphalt over a concrete base, 2016. Credit: R. H. Miller.

Lest anyone jump to any conclusions about 'graft' and 'corruption' in the scions of the Roman Empire, a short detour for context is called for—not that Cuba was colonized by the Romans. But it was colonized by the Spanish who, in turn, had been colonized by the Romans.

Modern political systems that evolved from Roman tradition—a tradition based more on personal loyalty, patronage, and nepotism than ideology—is often perceived as corrupt by those wholly nurtured within Enlightenment political tradition. In many modern countries descended from the Roman tradition, both systems vie for supremacy and are often in conflict.

The Roman tax code during the height of the Republic (roughly the 1st and 2nd centuries BC) was devilishly complex. Instead of independent accountants and friendly IRS agents to help decipher it, a class of public contractors called *publicans* was authorized to enforce it and collect the taxes. To ensure a steady stream of revenue to the Senate, the right to collect taxes for a particular region would be auctioned every few years for a value that (in theory) approximated the tax available for collection in that region. The payment to Rome was treated as a loan and the publicans would receive interest on their payment at the end of the collection period. In addition, any excess (over their bid) tax collected would be pure profit for the publicans. The principal risk to the publicans was that the tax collected would be less than the sum bid.

Under this system, publicans tended not only to bid as low as possible, but also to squeeze as much tax out of the populace as they could, not only to increase their profit but to ensure no losses on their investment.

The system inadvertently created an attitude toward public service that was to permeate the scions of the Roman Empire down through the centuries: Providing a necessary service to the state successfully, on time, and efficiently, warranted a commission—much like modern American waiters and waitresses expect a good tip for good service. Working such a system well—and, yes, honestly—was possible, and in no way considered 'corrupt'—a word reserved for taking money while not fulfilling one's duties, or engaging in outright fraud or deceit. Still, publicans, as the New Testament mentions, were feared and hated.

The Carretera Central didn't reach Baracoa, Cuba's easternmost and oldest city. To reach Baracoa, the road had to cross the eastern escarpment of the Sierra Maestra Mountains. Castro made much of this, calling it capitalist fraud. After coming to power, he pushed the road from Guantanamo to Baracoa, claiming that only Socialism fulfills its promises. But he did a good job. As per the original, the Carretera Central over the mountains has properly segmented concrete under asphalt.

Family lore holds that John Maurice also worked on the Cárcel Modelo (or model prison), the federal penitentiary on the Isle of Pines (the insular comma off the south-east coast of Cuba). Built between 1926 and 1928, at the same time as the Capitolio and the Carretera Central, the three projects must have been a logistical challenge for the 41-year-old contractor. How he juggled these many responsibilities remains a mystery, though it is not uncommon for contractors to spread themselves thin by taking on multiple projects (often to the irritation of their employers).

Little did Jeremy Bentham, the 18th century English philosopher and advocate of Utilitarianism (the philosophy whose fundamental axiom is that the measure of right and wrong is the greatest happiness for the greatest number), suspect that his design for the perfect penal institution—a Panopticon—would be built by Gerardo Machado in mid-20th century Cuba. The Cárcel Modelo was an adaptation of a progressive, Benthamite concept intended to help rehabilitate prisoners while treating them more humanely. It incorporated a novel design: four six-story, round and squat silos later nicknamed the *circulares*. Each floor had 93 cells designed for single or double occupancy arranged around a commons with a single guard tower in the center manned by one guard invisible to the prisoners. The low supervisor-to-prisoner ratio would save money, while the constant supervision and inability of the prisoners to observe the guard would encourage good behavior all the time.

Under President Fulgencio Batista, the *circulares* housed only common criminals; political prisoners were kept in separate small apartments where many privileges, including conjugal visits, were allowed. Fidel Castro, captured after his abortive Moncada Army Barracks attack on July 26, 1953, spent time there—as did my cousins, Armando Lastra and Carlos León, after the Bay of Pigs invasion—the former in the conjugal barracks; the latter, in a completely different area and, for a short time, in the conjugal barracks (without the amenities the name implies).

Following the 1959 Revolution and anticipating a decline in prisoners due, either to the new regime dedicated to social justice or, more cynically, to make a stay there more memorable, the revolutionary government removed all but one toilet per floor in each *circular* (these were impressed for ballast on a Russian cargo vessel). Later the entire prison was closed down after the prisoner-for-medicine exchange with the Kennedy administration following the Bay of Pigs invasion. To eliminate any vestige of the prison's infamy, the island was rechristened Isla de la Juventud (Isle of Youth), and the prison was turned into a museum.

* * *

When my mother turned 13 she was shipped off to a Louisiana Sacred Heart convent to learn English. After graduation she was offered a full scholarship to a Sacred Heart college in Missouri. It was not to be. With the Great Depression in full swing and the war in Europe about to break out, her father, John Maurice suddenly died of a kidney infection, leaving the family nearly penniless and saddled with his gambling debts. So instead, Ana María attended secretarial school, graduating quickly and putting her new earning power immediately to use as a bi-lingual telephone operator back in Cuba.

Ana María (Mina), aged 14, and Ana María, age 51; daughter and mother; author's 'mama' and 'abuela'. Date: 1935. Source: A. R. Hatch-Miller collection.

Sometimes she'd field long distance calls from Ernest Hemingway whom she always recognized by his unintelligible Spanish. He insisted on using it anyway. When my mother, in turn, insisted that he speak English so she could understand him, he'd demand to know if she was aware of whom he was. "No," she always answered tersely.

"I'm Papa," he'd impatiently retort. When no acknowledgement was forthcoming, he'd testily add, "Papa Hemingway!"

My mother's answer, "I don't know who you are," was always followed by a torrent of profanity. Ana María not only didn't care, she disliked arrogance, pretension, the concept of celebrities, Hemingway's writing, and Hemingway himself.

With time these outbursts became more frequent. It seemed—to her anyway—that her imperious prudishness egged him on, something that gave her great satisfaction. With time and little patience, she took to hanging up on him—another 'no' he interpreted as a 'yes'.

Ana María had developed into a strikingly beautiful, statuesque woman. Tall for her times, with a ready laugh, she was indispensable in her social circle. Nicknamed Mina—a practice universal in Cuba (and probably derived from her middle name Minerva)—her friends called her Minita, the diminutive being more expressive. Nonetheless, she was not frivolous and had inherited her parents' sedateness and instinctive disgust toward all manner of filth and uncouth behavior, *malas palabras* (obscenities) and the bodily functions to which they referred, including bodily odors. She always accused anyone who sweated profusely as stinking like a *"guaguero de la Ruta 43"*, a Havana Route 43 bus driver.

Ana María (Mina), 'mamá', aged 24, just before meeting her husband-to-be, Howard, the author's father. Date: 1945. Source: A. R. Hatch-Miller collection.

Fully bilingual and a product of the nuns of the Sacred Heart, Mina had a particular aversion to the word *coño*. While the word's literal meaning translates to 'cunt' in English, in common Cuban parlance it peppers nearly all animated conversation—mostly as a mild, intensifying interjection akin to 'damn' in English. Her knowledge of the former precluded her acceptance of the latter. Mina's older brothers, John and Robert, well aware of her discomfort with the word, never ceased to exploit it, teasing her no end and reveling in her vexation. (In contrast to Cubans' quibbling use of *coño*, the word *papaya* was never uttered lightly. In a visual and olfactory onomatopoeic allusion, *papaya* was the word for the female sexual organ.

The papaya fruit, on the other hand, was always called a *frutabomba*—a bomb fruit.)

During WWII, Mina worked for the US Office of Censorship in Miami. After the war she returned to Havana and got a job with the recently founded American International Company (now American International Group, or AIG). The Havana AIC branch was established in 1946 by my father, Howard Wesley Miller, who had been a principal in the founding of C. V. Starr & Co., the parent company of AIG in New York.

In need of a bilingual secretary, Howard was assigned Ana María. A trusting man of few words and a forced smile, he found Ana Maria's regal reticence attractive (not to mention, as they say in Cuba, that she was *"más bella que pesetas"*—more gorgeous than dollars) so he immediately fired her. Already married, he didn't quite trust himself. When his wife unexpectedly died the following year, Ana María was rehired. They were married in 1948.

* * *

Howard, born in 1897, 1898, 1899, or 1900—the uncertainty being due to his forging of papers in order to enlist in the Navy during WWI (a ruse Mina was later to use to obtain a driver's license before her time)—was more than 20 years Mina's senior. He had already packed a lot of living into those years.

After two years as a gunner's mate in the Atlantic theatre, he was discharged in 1919. The war had kindled a spark for adventure. With an Irish Belfast buddy from the Navy, he bought a used Model-T Ford and crossed the United States along the old Lincoln Highway, part of the National Trails roads network; a disjunct network of pioneer trails, of-times poorly maintained state highways, municipal streets, unmarked rural roads, and confusing and braided connecting easements—the majority consisting of unconsolidated sand and dirt that turned to mud after rains.

One particularly gnarly section in Arizona, between Williams and Ash Fork, which would later become the path of Route 66 and, even later, Interstate 40, required extraordinary effort and planning to traverse. Ash Fork Hill was steep and consisted of unconsolidated volcanic sediment and ash which, after nearly any rain, turned to mud so thick, greasy, and bottomless that not even a tank could stay above ground much less make progress. Road traffic queued up at the Ash Fork train station for ferrying up to Williams.

Howard wasn't the only veteran planning to travel coast-to-coast after the Great War. Dwight D. Eisenhower, a Lieutenant Colonel in the war, and a motorized vehicle aficionado had spent his tour of duty stateside training tank crews for the newly developed technology. After the war, he was demoted to Captain. Discouraged at the few opportunities in peacetime service, he thought of quitting. Until he heard about the US Army's 1919 Cross-Country Motor Transport Train.

The plan was to send a convoy of 80 or so trucks and other military vehicles across the country on the most famous section of the National Trails road, the Lincoln Highway, which ran between New York City and San Francisco, California. The Army wanted to know if motor vehicles which had been used in combat only since 1916, could stand the trip.

So Ike and a buddy, Major Sereno Brett, volunteered to go along to observe the operation of the one tank in the convoy.

Every day, a scout would drive ahead to find the road and mark it so the military vehicles wouldn't get lost. Many bridges were just barely able to carry cars, so the Army had to strengthen them, build new ones at some locations, or ford the streams. The bad roads were tough on tires, axles, motors, and anything that could be shaken off as the vehicles rumbled over the bumps and ruts in the road. Mechanics, who had been trained to repair horse-drawn wagons, were kept busy learning about a new type of vehicle.

Many years later, Howard offhandedly mentioned seeing a tank on that adventure, but since I didn't know about Ike's convoy at the time, I never thought to probe his memory further. With little cross-country road traffic of any sort (in 1914, only about 50 "tourists" had made the trip), it was doubtless the US Army's 1919 Cross-Country Motor Transport Train that he crossed paths with.

After 62 days and 3,000 miles of atrocious conditions averaging 5 mph, Ike became convinced of the need for a high-speed road network to lace the nation. In his memoir, *At Ease: Stories I Tell to Friends* Ike summarized the trip as, "difficult, tiring, and fun." In 1956, as President, he signed into existence the Interstate Highway System.

Still restless, Howard then headed to Havana to learn Spanish and serve an apprenticeship in public accounting, a trade he'd briefly studied in Chicago. In 1921, immersing himself deeper in the Latin American milieu, he went to Buenos Aires, rooming—by chance—with Aristotle Onassis, another ex-pat also looking to make his fortune. Both applied for jobs with Standard Oil of New Jersey, then just starting to exploit possibilities in Argentina and Bolivia.

Howard W. Miller (Pop), on left, aged 20-2, at a Havana beach. Date: 1920. Source: R. H. Miller collection.

Onassis didn't make the cut: his language skills—in either English or Spanish (I never got that straight)—weren't up to snuff (not that Howard's Spanish merited any gold stars). Still, for some unknown reason, Standard Oil hired Howard, assigning him his own mule as an exploratory geologist's assistant, prospecting for promising deposits across South America's Chaco region. Eschewing traditional gaucho garb (or even a hat), and parting his hair straight down the middle, Howard, a native New Yorker and third-generation German immigrant, donned Wellies, jodhpurs, a white dress shirt, and wire-rim glasses. Though he stood out for his mildly eccentric outfit among the Chaco gauchos, it was his brains that were soon noticed. In no time, he was promoted to field clerk in a drilling camp in Patagonia and, before his 30th birthday, became Officer and Director of Standard Oil's Argentine and Bolivian subsidiaries. That was when his earlier acquaintance with Onassis came into play.

Not one to pass up a good grudge, Onassis—by then well on his way to acquiring the world's largest, privately owned shipping fleet—had refused to carry Standard Oil products because of their earlier rebuff of him. But Howard needed tankers, and only Onassis's fit his needs. Over a meeting I can't possibly imagine—my father being neither garrulous nor guileful, and neither a big eater nor drinker—the two men sat down to resolve the problem. What was said, promised, or done, only the two men knew, but, their differences resolved, Onassis added Standard Oil to his list of potential clients.

Howard Wesley Miller (Pop), aged 24-6 with native workers, while working for Standard Oil of New Jersey at a drilling camp in Patagonia, Argentina. Date: Circa 1924. Source: A. R. Hatch-Miller collection.

Twelve years in Latin America—10 with Standard Oil—had taken their toll on Howard: he had contracted malaria, a condition that would bedevil him for the rest of his life. However, more importantly, he was still restless. Although Standard Oil had treated him well, and his position there had honed his managerial skills, there was little opportunity for him to exercise his more creative ambitions combining management, negotiation and deal-making, creative accounting, and tax and regulatory law into complex finance.

He decided to call it quits and returned to the states. The Great Depression and FDR's New Deal regulatory environment were the perfect challenge for him. If he could turn a profit under such adverse conditions, imagine what he could do in boom times. For the following 10 years he became, successively, Comptroller of the Sphinx Trading Corporation, then Treasurer of Bush Terminal Buildings Company—a commercial property developer—and then Controller of the Oxford Paper Company of Rumford, Maine, at the time the world's largest paper company under one roof, in the world, now the MeadWestvaco Paper Company.

Although in his early 40s when the Japanese bombed Pearl Harbor, Howard immediately volunteered for the Navy, his old service branch. He was given a desk job, this time as an auditor. But for some unknown reason—perhaps his recurring malarial attacks, he served for only six months before being discharged. In 1942 he joined Starr, Park & Freeman, Inc., the initial precursor of what would much later become AIG, as Assistant Treasurer. It was at this time that his talents really skyrocketed. In his new capacity, he took over the complicated job of setting up a centralized accounting control for all the many companies in the American International groups (American International Co. (AIC), American International Underwriters Corp. (AIU), C.V. Starr & Co., et al.)

Howard W. Miller (Pop), aged 45-7. Portrait proof for C.V. Starr & Co. and American International Underwriters, just before meeting his Havana secretary and wife-to-be, Ana María, the author's mother. Date: 1945. Source: A. R. Hatch-Miller collection.

In 1946 he returned to Havana as president of the American International Company, which supervised American International Underwriters operations throughout Latin America. That's when he met my mother, Ana María.

Howard and Mina got married in Manhattan on August 1 of 1947, only five months after his first wife's death (reportedly by suicide: she was plagued by a terminal condition). They took separate honeymoons, Howard immediately leaving for Manila, Shanghai and Hong Kong to nurture the

AIU branches he'd established there six months previously; Mina returning to Havana.

It was in no small part due to Howard's pre-Revolution business initiatives in Shanghai that opened the door for AIG's re-entry— prestigiously, one of the very first foreign firms allowed—into the Middle Kingdom after the free-market reforms instituted by Deng Xiaoping in 1980.

But by December the newly weds reunited in New York. Howard had returned to a promotion: Treasurer and Director of AIU, soon adding Director, Vice-President and Controller of C.V. Starr & Co. to his positions.

In 1948, a *controller* was also known as a *comptroller*. Today the position is more commonly referred to as a CFO, or Chief Financial Officer. Though technically an accountant and by no means as prominent as a CEO, the CFO wields wide-ranging powers exercised behind the scenes. Finance chiefs play a fundamental role in shaping the scope and direction of a company; they are deeply involved in setting corporate strategy by allocating capital to bring a company's vision to life. Their detailed knowledge of the corporate landscape increases their influence.

The best use the ever-increasing set of rules in the tax code to their advantage, even finding profits in losses. It was Howard who built the foundation that made AIG the largest, most profitable insurance company in the world. What he would have thought of AIG's insuring CDIs (consolidated debt instruments), those barely-examined financial instruments at the heart of the 2006 Great Recession, remains a mystery. But I suspect he flipped over a couple of times in his grave, first, when someone decided to underwrite CDIs without adequate risk evaluation, and then again when the crash hit—in spite of having my mother buried on top of him.

Howard and Mina settled in Massapequa, Long Island. The newlyweds planned on having children, adding some siblings to Howard's 13-year-old son, John, from his first marriage. Howard was in a position to call his own shots, so the return to the United States had an ulterior motive: my parents wanted to ensure that their children were born in the US, in case they ever wanted to run for President.

2

Wet Behind the Ears

I, Robert (soon to be nicknamed Baten, in the Cuban fashion), was born on November 19, 1949, proving (contrary to some opinions) that I am not a bastard. Though I was born in the US, my mother couldn't wait to turn me into a Cuban. At two-and-a-half months of quivering bundle, she wrapped me up, flew me to Havana, deposited me in the care of her mother—my *abuela*—and flew back to New York alone.

Two months later, perhaps coinciding in part with Easter vacation, she nabbed her 14-year-old stepson John and drove to Miami where they boarded the ferry to Havana. After a short visit with her mother (which included a stay at a spa), she returned to New York with the two of us.

What possesses a 27-year-old first-time mother to, more-or-less, abandon her newborn for a couple of months? She was certainly overwhelmed. At the time, child care was mostly intuitive and passed on from one generation to another. Dr. Benjamin Spock had only just published his baby book in 1946. Had she read it? What was she thinking when she removed her newly-acquired stepson from school to drive cross-country with him—before interstate highways and modern credit cards (other than gasoline company cards)? Was he included for her safety? Was the road trip supposed to be a bonding experience?

I don't know. Mina was self-confident, headstrong and very independent—though she always deferred to my dad, an extremely tolerant and permissive individual. I never heard her recount that story or a few of the others related here. Many of the events that I recount left absolutely no trace in my memory, either because I was too young or because memories, like stratigraphy, get jumbled, and are subject to uplift, unconformities and erosion—difficult to reconstruct. Old photos and vague recollections of jumpy, scratchy home movies left behind in Cuba stimulate traces of lost realities. Neither my father nor my mother kept a diary. However, they kept—and periodically reconstructed—time-lines of their lives, with intriguing but forgotten details such as "Sutton Place" in NY and a "glass farm" in Pennsylvania (to which Howard makes more than one reference and visit).

Their *extreme* peripatecticness boggles the mind. Their travels, as revealed in their notes—and from today's perspective of crowded airports, interminable lines, TSA indignities, scarce parking and all the other hassles that make air travel a major undertaking—are amazing. They were caring (as it turned out), albeit not doting parents.

My sister Anita (Naná—from *hermana*, 'sister' or Nani, in diminutive) was born in December of 1950. For the blessed event they stayed home for nearly eight months. Mina had to. Labor was long and difficult, and there was great loss of blood during the breach birth. It helped that they had brought along Cuba with them in the form of Mina's mother, our *abuela*, a Cuban *tata* (nursemaid) to take care of us and a Cuban cook. Mina's gynecologist advised her *never* to get pregnant again.

But then they took off on a business trip to Buenos Aires, Montevideo, Rio de Janeiro, Caracas and Havana. In June of 1952 they took Naná on her first trip to Cuba. Howard, Mina, Abuela, Naná and I spent a month at our family beach house in Boca Ciega, just outside Havana. Again, we were abandoned to our grandmother. From Havana, Howard and Mina left on a trip around the world: San Francisco, Seattle, Tokyo, Manila, Hong Kong, Bangkok, Karachi, Tel Aviv, Rome, Paris, London, Reyjkavik, Bermuda, Havana—to pick us up—and back to New York (if only Pan American Airlines had provided frequent flyer miles).

Less than a year later, with Mina regally pregnant and only a month away from giving birth a third time, she and Howard flew off to Buenos Aires, Rio de Janeiro, Sao Paulo and Havana.

They returned just in time. On October 4, 1953 Patsy was born. When Mina returned from the hospital with the baby—my earliest solid memory uninfluenced by photos or stories—she placed Patsy on the sideboard of the foyer, called Naná and I over, and introduced her as our new sister.

How I marveled! She was so novel, helpless, and intriguing, but immeasurably cute. I had never seen a baby. I stood staring, transfixed for what seemed an eternity, completely ignoring Naná, who seemed unaware of the import of the occasion. I resolved then and there to always be a protective brother to little Patsy.

Howard, now Pop to us, and Mina (*mami, mamá* or *mima* to us) lived in a Tudor mansion on a magnificent estate with an enormous lake behind it—or so it seemed to this 3-year-old kid. Our *tata* would often take us to the lake for an outing—in the summer, to pretend to fish; in the winter, to pretend to ice skate, an undertaking so thoroughly befuddling to her, and one that scared her so much, that she always invoked the saints and cut it short. Few Cubans had ever seen ice *in situ*.

Exposed fitfully to my parents, my first language became Spanglish, with a bias toward Spanish. We had a Dalmatian named Freckles (nicknamed Paca) who had his own fenced mini-estate. My brother John—at this time strictly an English speaker—and I loved to play with Paca. John had just graduated from a military boarding school and, with his sharp uniform, impressed me no end. Like his father Howard, John was a man of few words.

* * *

In the spring of 1954—nine months after Fidel Castro had launched his first failed coup on July 26, 1953—and when Patsy was just barely seven months old, Pop and Mina moved the family to Havana, first via Pan American Airways to Miami, then on the *S.S. Guadalupe*. It was the first plane ride that I remember and one that I thoroughly enjoyed, pampered by the beautiful stewardesses and immersed in an illustrated book on American Indians and one on the animal kingdom. On the ferry, also my first, I became violently seasick.

Howard and Mina settled in Alturas del Vedado, one of Havana's poshest neighborhoods, in a two-story concrete house near the dead end of Calle 43, next to a tributary gorge of the Almendares River. Terrazzo-floored throughout, the salmon colored house was high-ceilinged, spacious and airy. My sisters shared a room, while my brother—whom I seldom saw—and I shared another room. Pop had gotten him an accounting internship at AIC's Havana office. John would invariably come home late and leave early. When he reached majority, John left Cuba to seek his fortune in the US.

Our first home in Havana on dead-end Avenida 43, Alturas del Vedado, later to be rented out to CIA agent David Atlee Phillips. Photo taken in 2016. Home has been well-maintained and renovated. Credit: R. H. Miller.

Nineteen-fifty-four was a hectic year for our family. Pop became the C.V. Starr & Co's. senior executive in Havana. No sooner had we moved to Havana than he and Mina flew back to New York and on to San Francisco, Hong Kong, Tokyo, and back to Havana. Later, both went off to Bermuda. In August Pop took me to New York to arrange the sale of our Long Island house, after which he took another trip to Bermuda. In October he was off again, arranging the transport of our furniture and personal belongings to Havana via the *S.S. Guadalupe.*

We children were strangers in a strange land. Soon after arriving, our parents engineered a birthday party to end all birthday parties, in order to introduce us to every possible playmate available in this new country. Every little cousin—no matter how distant (even in-law cousins)—every child of Mina's or of Pop's friends, or business colleagues, or friends'-of-friends' kids—every kid in the neighborhood was invited. They all came. Pop and Mina hired a mini-amusement park, set up in our large back yard, with an electric train, a *mini-montaña rusa* (roller coaster), ponies in a circle, a petting zoo—mostly goats and rabbits—and who knows what other childish delights. It was all meant to be a surprise—and it was.

There were 30 children there—not a single one smiling in surviving photographs. I well remember my own reaction: resentment at sudden, forced fun, friendship, and camaraderie. What were all those people doing there? Why did I have to "enjoy" myself? I had always been the master of my days, each one an empty vessel that I filled creatively according to my whims and plans. When someone imposed an agenda on me, it was a violation of my autonomy (which, I must admit, was a bit presumptuous for a 4-year-old, but nonetheless true). Naná, even more sour-looking in photos than nearly all of the other children, particularly resented having to share a birthday with *me*, older and a boy to boot. I tried to hide, but someone dragged me out (in a not unkindly fashion). A gift of cowboy cap guns with holsters cheered me up, so I donned an Indian headdress and shot little girls at close range.

One of those little girls was Sara María, the skinny, curly haired daughter of Mina's best friend. She and Naná had become friends. Sari, as we called her, wasn't your typical doll-clutching, let's-play-house little girl, so I put up with her. After immigrating to the US, we kept in touch. She was to marry Luis R. Luis, an academic, who was later to become the Organization of American States' (OAS) chief economist, and whose insightful studies of the post-Castro Cuban economy became the basis for many of my later articles about the island.

Kitty-corner across the street lived the just-deposed ex-mayor of Havana, Nicolás Castellanos, with whose children and grandchildren I'd later come to hang out with. Directly across the street lived Luís Echegoyen, the star of *MamaCusa*, one of the top-rated comedy shows on Cuban TV, somewhat reminiscent of Jonathan Winters' "Maude Frickert" character. His sons, Yoyi and Luís, about my age, became frequent playmates. One block away stood the Mexican Embassy, and two blocks away, the Peruvian Embassy.

1953 joint birthday party for the author and sister Naná. Only individuals mentioned in this memoir are identified. Top left: Abuela; next to her, held in tata's arms, 13-month-old little sister Patsy; front row left, fourth little girl in looking directly at the camera, MariCris Casanueva, daughter of Cuca and Pillo; sixth girl in from left, front row at the corner of the table, Alina Lastra, daughter of Tita and Armando, and sister of Armandito Lastra (to whom this book is dedicated for his service in Brigade 2506); little girl in center of picture between both birthday cakes, sister Naná; immediately behind her to the right, cousin Johnny Fitzgerald, son of Marta Lopéz and John Fitzgerald, brother of my mother; next to Johnny in front row, the author; directly behind the author (and the only kid smiling), cousin Richard Fitzgerald, brother of Johnny Fitzgerald; next to the author, Sara María Bellini, who would later marry Luis R. Luis, chief economist for the Organization of American States (OAS); next to Sara María is Marianito Faget, son of Mariano Faget, head of the Foreign Counter-espionage Activities Department for the Batista administration; last kid on the far right, Pedrito Casanueva, brother of MariCris Casanueva. Credit: Bodas Erenio; Source: A. R. Hatch-Miller collection.

1953 joint birthday party for the author and sister Naná. Left to right, Naná, Pop, Mina holding little sister Patsy who had just turned two, author.
Credit: Bodas Erenio; Source: R. H. Miller collection.

More ominously, Rafael Salas Cañizares, Batista's brutal Chief of the National Police force, lived a stone's throw away. Cañizares, a fat sadist who targeted student dissidents, invaded the Haitian embassy when he heard that four student revolutionaries had sought asylum there. Never mind diplomatic immunity—Cañizares burst in, guns drawn, shooting. But he got more than he expected. Inside, along with the students, were 6 survivors of Fidel Castro's assault on the Goicuría Army Barracks, an attack that had occurred only 6 months before. One rebel was armed. As the Chief was bending over to administer the coup de grace on the one fatally wounded survivor, the rebel fired one shot right into Cañizares' gut. Cañizares died instantly.

Since the shootout wasn't in the neighborhood, we experienced no consequences, although the incident no doubt must have affected Pop and Mina, who must have known where Cañizares lived.

* * *

Second in power only to the president, the mayor of Havana was also one of the richest men in Cuba. Nicolás Castellanos controlled the most lucrative sources of illegal income on the island. As a child, I'd often hang out at the Castellanos' home playing with whatever children of the large extended family were present. When his daughter Irma got married at one of Havana's colonial cathedrals, I was the ring boy at the ceremony. Castellanos, head of the Nationalist Party, had been the principal power broker in the jostling for the presidency at the run-up to the 1952 election.

Wedding of Irma Castellanos at Havana cathedral, 1956. Irma in the center; groom next to her; author, ring boy, at far right.
Credit: Omar Llaguna. Source: R. H. Miller collection.

Now, at the time, Cuban elections had always been relatively free, that is, when compared with voting practices in countries such as Mexico or Guatemala. Nonetheless, the most ambitious party could always find ways of digging up dependable votes: union leaders controlled their workers; businessmen squeezed their employees; ministries rewarded civil servants with illegal bonuses; plus a high percentage of voting cards lacked the requisite photographs and so could be used by anyone. The system had produced only one laudable administration, the very first one after independence, that of Tomás Estrada Palma. And at that, only his first term. By his second, he'd been soured by the lack of reciprocal idealism and turned vengeful, venal, greedy, and power mad.

The 1952 election started out no differently than any other: in Cuban-cigar-smoke-filled rooms with Mayor Castellanos cajoling together a grand coalition of anyone and everyone who had a claim on a piece of the action. Together they would apportion power and spoils uncontroversially and multi-partisanly. But this time Fulgencio Batista, one of the primary contenders—who didn't stand a chance of winning—didn't want to share.

Batista was a tragic figure. He was nicknamed "the Okie from Banes" (*el guajiro de Banes*) and "*el negro*" because of his modest education, lack of sophistication, and dark complexion. According to the scuttlebutt of the time, he was one of the last surviving mixed-blood, indigenous Carib Indians—noteworthy because the Spanish *conquistadores* had—unwittingly—almost annihilated Cuba's entire aboriginal population (Cuba was now European, African, or mixed). Batista had only risen to the rank of sergeant when, in 1933, he stepped into history. That year, during the unrest that followed the overthrow of Gerardo Machado, who had become a dictator, he led a popular, behind-the-scenes, intra-army "Sergeants' Coup" that wrested power from the commissioned officers and, in an absurd reversal of traditional chain-of-command logic, conferred power unto the lower non-commissioned ranks—the sergeants themselves.

Prior to the coup, the army had been kept out of politics through a spoils sharing program whereby politicians paid off the higher officer ranks to secure their loyalty. The sergeants wanted a fairer redistribution of the loot. After the insurgency, Batista turned the government's loyalty-buying racket into an overt army-extortion racket that benefited all ranks. Now that he ruled the armed forces, he promoted himself first to colonel and later to general. Batista, in effect, yet behind the scenes, ruled Cuba for seven years. In 1940 he ran for president, won, and ruled more-or-less competently—competently according to the standards of the time, with economic development programs, infrastructure improvements, and health and education investments.

While Fidel Castro's reforms are usually touted as a response to criticism of his brutal rule, Batista's are seldom mentioned. During his tenure in power the Okie from Banes strove to do good while doing well. The Cuban legislature was dominated by reformist representatives. Batista worked with them. First off, he instituted a fifty-fifty employment law that reserved half of the jobs in any foreign-run enterprise for Cubans. According to Patrick Symmes in *The Boys from Dolores: Fidel Castro's Schoolmates from Revolution to Exile*, Batista "launched the first national campaign against illiteracy, a 'civic-military' campaign that used teachers from the army and was funded by a military budget. Between 1936 and 1940, the Batista government constructed 1,100 new schools...illiteracy dropped by about 10 percent." Additionally, curricula and grading norms were standardized.

After being elected president in 1940, he worked with labor unions, the socialist and communist parties to ensure good wages for Cuban industrial workers, which rose to become the world's eigth highest by 1958 during his usurped term, while agricultural wages also increased becoming higher than some European countries'. Batista's public health and sanitation reforms led to very low rates of typhoid and diphtheria.

At the end of his term in 1944 he had become immeasurably rich but his marriage was falling apart, his popularity was at an all-time low and he still hadn't been asked to join the exclusive Havana Country Club. More importantly, his party surprisingly lost the election. In the midst of a mid-life crisis, the Okie from Banes divorced his wife of many years, married a young socialite and fled to Daytona Beach, Florida, into self-imposed retirement to enjoy his wealth and new-found connubial bliss.

Then, in 1948, restless, ambitious, and more popular than ever in his own mind, he decided to run for senator of Las Villas Province, a campaign which he won in spite of contesting the election from his home in Florida. But Batista had his eye on higher office.

Nicolas Castellano's coalition could easily have defeated Batista in the 1952 presidential elections, but on March 10, 1952, he staged a coup at the behest of the Cuban armed forces. Discontented with the way President Carlos Prío Socarrás was neglecting the army and disturbed over rumors about Prío's tolerance of organized crime, the Cuban military requested Batista's assistance. The coup cost Castellanos the mayoralty. More importantly, it was the *casus belli* that launched Fidel Castro on the road to the revolution that rules Cuba to this day.

Cuba's two main parties at the time were the *Ortodoxos* and the *Auténticos*. Castro was running for Congress as an *Ortodoxo*, the party that was sure to win the presidency and control of Congress. But Batista's coup spoiled all that.

On July 26, 1953, and just before our new, 5-member family had moved to Havana, Fidel Castro—precipitately, unprepared, and with a handful of loose cannons (both literally and figuratively)—attacked the Moncada Army Barracks in the province of Oriente. Some of his contingent even traveled by public bus. They were quickly defeated and brutally rounded up. Most were shot on the spot. Castro escaped with his life only because he'd married into the family of one of Batista's ministers. Imprisoned for fifteen years in the Cárcel Modelo on the Isle of Pines, he declared that, "History will absolve me," his famous closing arguments speech before the tribunal that sentenced him. That speech referenced Carlos *Cachorro* León's grandfather, a

War of Independence hero, three times. Carlos, or *Cachorro*, as I'll refer to him throughout this memoir, is my ex-cousin-in-law, and will play a central role in the second part of this book.

* * *

We didn't last long at the house on 43ʳᵈ street. Pop was doing well and, feeling a bit restless, cramped, and ambitious (he rued being from Brooklyn, at that time a run-down, unsavory neighborhood), approached Mayor Castellanos with a business proposition. He and Mina bought the ex-mayor's residence in March of 1955. Castellanos in turn built himself an even bigger house on the empty lot next door.

Our new house at 130, Calle 36, was located on what, arguably, was Havana's highest terrain. All the land around it sloped down. No wonder it was called Alturas del Vedado (Vedado Heights). It had all the amenities one might expect from the residence of the second most powerful man in Cuba.

Home at 130 Calle 36, esquina 43 that we bought from Havana Mayor Nicolás Castellanos. Date: 1955. Credit: A. M. Miller. Source: R. H. Miller collection.

Along with 4 bedrooms and bathrooms (all with bidets), one of which, the master suite, had a large adjacent make-up room lined with mirrors on every wall, the house boasted the following: A banquet-sized dining room (also lined with mirrors); a spiral terrazzo staircase leading upstairs from a grand entry foyer; four living rooms, one upstairs, and one with a 6-foot aquarium; a small upstairs kitchen; a large office; a main kitchen with a built-in breakfast counter island which could sit 12 people, and a built-in, industrial, 6-door, stainless steel refrigerator with an additional 2 doors facing the opposite room—a bar with curved counter adjacent to a patio; a multi-car garage with chauffeur's quarters; an attached L with maid's, cook's, and *tata's* quarters; and, finally, a small, triangular chemistry lab, one which I soon put to good use with a 1950s-vintage, definitely-not-child-safe, riddled-with-warnings, skulls-and-crossbones chemistry set. Not good enough for Pop, he immediately added a swimming pool with adjacent shower and changing room next to the already existing wading pool.

And the grounds! Three large, fenced yards, each with a patio; the yards thick with bougainvillea, hibiscus, and all sorts of flowering tropicals only adults could identify; a breadfruit tree, a mango tree, and a flamboyant tree, with its huge, distinctive seed pods, and overarching, protective canopy. The breadfruit tree, next to the *columpio*, or swing set, was a disgusting botanical specimen.

The breadfruit—large, flesh-colored, wrinkled bombs, like a fat, old woman's oversize breasts—would drop to the ground when overripe and plop open disgorging a viscous, off-white, vomit-like, foul-smelling interior. It was unimaginable as a food source, but wonderful for mortifying my sister, whom I would try to push into the putrid glob. I had once tried to pick up a portion of a felled fruit, carefully holding it by its skin, to lob at her, but the glutinous mass had no integrity and I ended up covered in breadfruit glop.

In one corner sat 2 giant clay *tinajas*, surrounded by *malangas*, broad-leafed taro plants. These became our hiding places. Crawling inside shut the world out. Not even Mario the gardener could find me or Naná when I disappeared into them.

But the mango tree was my favorite. Of climbable proportions with delicious fruit, it was one of my preferred hang-outs. Adults would warn me not to climb, in case of a fall—one that could result in broken bones, even death. Of an empirical frame of mind even at such a young age (I must have been about 7 or 8), I decided to jump down from the tree on purpose. I didn't die or break any limbs, but I lay splayed, dazed, and reflective for a long interlude. I never climbed that tree again.

Years later, after the triumph of the Revolution, after our home had become the property of the *Controlaria Nacional, Dirección de Capacitación e*

Investigación (a ministry that one respondent, when asked what the name meant or what the ministry did, said, "Who knows? The government has more ministries than it has soldiers"), I made my way to the house on a bike. The house was now surrounded by a tall concrete fence with a guard at its gate. The guard, about my age, had been in the neighborhood since my own childhood. When I told him I'd grown up in that house, his official reserve melted and he did everything he could to welcome me, sharing stories of the neighborhood. He said Blás Roca, head of the Cuban Communist Party under the Batista government *and* under the Castro government, acquired (I hesitate to say 'bought' as that implies a voluntary exchange between buyer and seller) a house close by. The neighborhood still has cachet.

* * *

Afraid I'd lose what little English I'd acquired, Pop and Mina enrolled Naná and I in Ruston Academy, an American school. The arrangement didn't last. Mina was disgusted with their low academic standards with an emphasis on drawing, naps, and play time. It seemed that we were learning nothing and paying a high price for it. After a short while, she transferred Naná to the local Academy of the Sacred Heart, while I was transferred to La Salle, a Catholic school run by the Christian Brothers, many of whom were Spanish (at the time, Cuba had been independent from Spain for only 53 years, and the ties were still strong). President Fulgencio Batista's children attended La Salle at the same time, but whether I was aware of this, knew who Batista was, or might have cared, I don't recall. The students would ceaselessly ridicule the Brothers' (to our minds) effeminate Castilian pronunciation of 'Ds' and 'Ss', always lisped in the most affected manner. But they got back at us: their fire-and-brimstone approach to catechism instilled the fear of God, hell, and sex in me for the next 20 years.

Catholic school didn't quite have the same effect on Fidel Castro, who attended Belén, a Jesuit school in his time. The boilerplate catechism instilled in him the virtues of sacrifice and a strong empathy for the poor. As for sex…Castro hasn't been nicknamed *El Caballo* (the stallion) for nothing. *El máximo* philanderer's sheer number of affairs, assignations, and marriages rivaled the length of his speeches, the longest of which, delivered on January, 1968, was 12 hours long.

* * *

Pop rented our first house in Havana to an American by the name of Phillips, whom my mother said was a CIA operative. Naná, my sister, recalls, "All I remember about the Phillips family is that there was a girl close in age to me who spoke very little Spanish and that one Easter they invited me over for an 'Easter Egg' hunt, a bizarre concept to me at the time, and even weirder because the eggs were NOT CANDY but REAL HARD BOILED EGGS! YUCK! These Americans are CRAZY!"

Pinpointing the identity of that Phillips is a hit-or-miss affair, based on a last name, the memory of a little girl's playmate, and my dead mother's off-hand remark made years ago. Luckily, a David Atlee Phillips, CIA operative in Havana at the same time, wrote a memoir, *The Night Watch*, with many details that can be cross-checked against our meager bits. If Pop's renter isn't David Atlee Phillips, the coincidences verge on the miraculous.

Phillips, a failed cemetery lot salesman and a not-too-successful actor, decided to try his hand at writing, a craft at which he at first modestly succeeded, and much later excelled. But his $200 a month retainer from his publisher was a meager subsistence for a new family. So he decided to move to Chile where the money would go much further. After investing his savings in a failing Santiago-based English-language newspaper, he was approached by the CIA and offered a part-time job as a "dangle", false bait to entrap a KGB operative. It was easy work and paid moderately well. Phillips accepted.

In 1954 he became a full-time operative and was assigned to *Operation PBSUCCESS*, the clandestine effort to overthrow the regime of Jacobo Arbenz in Guatemala. Although Arbenz had been democratically elected, his regime had become increasingly oppressive and he'd promised the Soviets a military base in Central America, something the US wasn't ready to tolerate. So President Dwight D. Eisenhower ordered the CIA to help the opposition overthrow Arbenz.

Phillips's job consisted of setting up a secret radio station that would be used to bypass official censorship regulations in order to broadcast reliable news, to disseminate propaganda beneficial to the opposition, and to engage in psychological warfare. The operation succeeded beyond anyone's wildest dreams with little bloodshed on either side. Unfortunately, the successor regime of Carlos Castillo Armas led to a series of military dictatorships. The hapless Castillo Armas was assassinated in 1957.

Phillips's next assignment the following year was in Havana, Cuba, under deep, deep cover, an operation he doesn't describe at all in his memoir, other than to comment that it "was routine, leaving time for golf and the beach." He rented a house in central Havana to be, I suppose, close to the action, perhaps too close:

"One morning I took María (his 5-year-old daughter) *to the front door to wait for the school bus. Before she could get out the door, I grabbed her quickly and escorted her through the kitchen, the back door, and the yard to wait for the bus on another corner. I didn't want her to see the body hanging from a tree in the front yard."*

Phillips figured his cover had been blown. But after a thorough investigation, it was determined that the event had nothing to do with him; his tree was just a convenient place for the regime to dispose of a political enemy. Nonetheless, Phillips decided to move to a better neighborhood—ours.

As tenants, the Phillips family didn't last long at our old house. A few days into 1957, Phillips was reassigned to Beirut, Lebanon (although his account relates being in Havana during the March, 1957 student assault on the Presidential Palace). But he didn't last long in Beirut either. By November of 1958, he was back in Havana as a private citizen, working only part-time for "the Company." But by then, Pop had sold the old house. Phillips was certain of Castro's upcoming victory, and knew the new regime would swing far left, but thought there was money to be made by starting a public relations firm. The new administration would need to present its best profile to the populace. What better cover for a CIA operative than to become Fidel Castro's PR firm?

Phillips was the first to notify the US Government of Batista's 1959 New Year's Day flight out of Cuba, spotting the presidential plane flying east at 4 am, a time when no commercial flights were scheduled.

Phillips stayed in Cuba another year-and-a-half, while our immediate family didn't cut all physical ties with the island until nearly 2 years later. But his situation was much more precarious.

His public relations firm—real, but still a cover for his clandestine activities—was in shreds with the cover becoming gossamer thin. All the nationalizations and confiscations of properties, and the centralization in government of anything having to do with "public relations," turned Phillips into an advocate representing clients trying to salvage investments. In this new role he was able to turn sympathetic bureaucrats into informants.

By mid-1959, only six months after Castro's victory, a strong but disorganized anti-Castro and anti-Communist resistance movement had taken root. Phillips was asked to monitor it. It was much larger than he imagined—so large, that he feared infiltration by Castro's secret police. He feared for his life after several men were arrested and one assassinated.

Phillips, his wife Helen, and his four children left Cuba on the Havana-Key West Ferry in March of 1960, one month before we left. But he wasn't through with Cuba or our family—yet. That would have to wait for the Bay of Pigs fiasco.

* * *

Pop and Mina were hands-off parents. Besides their constant travels—together or separately they went twice to Mexico City, once to Guadalajara and Merida and once to San Francisco in 1956—Pop worked every day. But he had also taken up golf at the Havana Yacht & Country Club, where I'd occasionally accompany him on rounds. In the locker room, it was my first exposure to naked men, something that made me feel very uncomfortable and inadequate. As for naked women, they were completely imaginary. The thought of what they might look like had never crossed my mind—until I noticed a black-and-white picture of a nude on my parents' bedroom dresser.

Once, finding myself alone in their bedroom, I studied the photo closely, not pruriently, but curious about the overall anatomical differences. I can't remember why I didn't think twice about whatever was hidden between the tightly crossed legs; that, anyway, wasn't the focus of the photo. The lady—I believe she was carrying an urn—had, like men, hair under her armpits and at her crotch, but nowhere else. Her breasts were large, with a noticeable overlap at mid torso. I craned my neck from every angle trying to glimpse behind those big breasts. I was certain that, just like the hidden crannies at the armpits and crotch, the little caves behind the large breasts contained hair, perhaps homologous to men's chest hair. Though I wasn't able to confirm my hypothesis, I remained convinced for many years that women had chest hair behind their breasts.

Neither Naná nor I remember spending any time with *mamá*, with one exception. Later, after we'd moved into the mayor's house, my bedroom connected to my mother's dressing room through a common door. Most non-school mornings I'd hang out with her while she "put on her face" applying make-up and becoming a sounding board for whatever outfit she tried on. Mina's vanity, L-shaped and entirely mirror-lined with decorative smoked edges, was extensive, and it was packed with brushes, lipstick, curlers, mascara, talcums, creams, lotions, and myriad unidentifiable devices and concoctions. Mina was an excellent amateur painter and she approached her face as she would a blank canvas. The conversation flowed easily and we enjoyed each other's company. Intermittently, she'd get up and head for the walk-in closet to try on an outfit. She never directly asked my opinion as to how it looked. To this day we still wonder how our mother passed her days in Cuba. Mostly, our *tatas*—now two, one for baby Patsy and one for Naná and me—took care of us.

* * *

By the age of 5, I wasn't fully toilet trained. Of course, I didn't wear diapers or let loose without warning, but I hadn't yet learned to wipe myself, and always notified an adult when venturing on the toilet. Now…for some inscrutable reason, Cubans are fixated on bodily functions: eating, defecating, and sex.

The fixation on defecation is particularly acute. Armando Valladares in his prison (Cárcel Modelo) memoir, *Against All Hope*, recounts at least 2 instances of ordure torture. While in a punishment cell, he was regularly doused by guards with half-buckets of urine and excrement diluted with water, and not allowed to bathe for three months during the ordeal. "Chunks of excrement fell in my mouth", he writes. Another time he describes one of his most excruciating ordeals as having to wade in a *cloaca*, an open cesspool of settling septic waste. Carlos Eire, in *Waiting for Snow in Havana*, also mentions the fixation.

My own uncles, Mina's brothers, John and Robert, had a favorite prank. They would collect feces (from god-knows-what source), dig a shallow hole in a public beach, and wait at an unsuspicious distance for an unsuspecting mark to dig in the sand to build a sand castle or playfully bury a companion. They would squeal with delight when someone made contact with the turds.

Abuela was not immune to the obsession. I will never forget the day she finalized my toilet-training. She was an imposing third-generation Spanish émigré whose sense of duty and propriety left little room for humor but plenty for nurturing. I don't remember what precipitated the lesson, but that morning at the new house, we ended up together in the upstairs, salmon-tiled bathroom we shared. First, she established a proper etiquette by washing her hands, leaving the door ajar and adopting a particularly stern manner. Down went my pants and up onto the toilet went my butt. She was all business detailing proper toilet comportment and procedure.

Now, little boys have little penises and they tend to stick straight out rather than arc down. So I instinctively pressed the little protrusion down into the bowl to keep the urine from spraying out between the rim and the seat. Abuela would have none of this, instructing me that it was unnecessary to touch my penis.

She was doubtlessly concerned that any unnecessary touching might lead to arousal, masturbation, and, ultimately, eternal perdition. She probably pictured in her mind an adult-sized, dangle-down penis (her sense of shame and modesty precluded any prolonged look at her naked little grandson's private parts).

Abuela turned away, walked outside the room—staying close enough to monitor my progress—and waited a decent interval for me to evacuate my bowels. She then came back in and instructed me on how to wipe my bottom: triple-fold the double-ply TP, reach in behind the back and apply a pinching motion to catch any cling-ons, the procedure then followed with more TP arced in a front-to-back swipe. Repeat as necessary until the paper turned up unsoiled. The subject never surfaced again.

It was the one and only time Mamá ever spanked me. And what a spanking it was! Not limited to my buttocks, but an all-over pummeling. I had soiled my underwear. I was so mortified, so riven with shame, that I didn't put the briefs in the hamper. Instead, in a futile attempt to hide them, I stuck them in a dark corner of a chiforobe. When my mother found them she asked me to explain. I temporized and prevaricated. That's when the beating began. She made sure to emphasize that the punishment was not related to the fouling, but rather to the lying.

It was a lesson that, to this day, has kept me honest.

Cubans are also obsessed with butts—and are not shy about it. Carlos Eire, in his memoir, dedicates an entire page to the description of one phenomenally impressive derriere wrapped in sheer, skin-tight red fabric. Many years later, when I'd married a Mexican-American by the name of Tina, with buttocks round as two basketballs, I took her—as a sort of rite-of-passage—to Miami's Little Havana to meet the extended family and sample the culinary fare. Walking down Calle Ocho, we stopped at a sidewalk expresso stand for a demitasse of the strong, sugary Cuban staple. Tina was the target of every eye.

While waiting for our coffee, up ambled an unsavory, disreputable character with a pencil-thin mustache who presumed a confidence with me he'd never established. Eyeing Tina, he pointed to a buxom, 60ish blonde sitting next to her and confided that he trailed the blonde because…(at this point he circled his index finger with his thumb and inserted his tongue into the little orifice). Undoubtedly, he thought he'd found a kindred soul.

I was appalled. But I wasn't threatened, and peremptorily dismissed him with a short lecture on sidewalk propriety.

3

Pura Vida

Life in the new, big house—especially now that I was a bit older—was an opportunity of possibilities. Pop would, on occasion, read me to sleep. His staples were Zane Grey and *Winnie the Pooh*, about the only English I was exposed to, but one that paid a dividend. Our home office contained a full set of the *Encyclopedia Americana*. Mamá had told us that encyclopedias contained the entire world's knowledge in one set of books. It was an incredible assertion. Though she'd added that the *Americana* was a distant second to the *Encyclopaedia Britannica*, which, to her, was the gold standard. Nevertheless, I'd spend hours reading random articles in random tomes, always keeping in mind that I was only ingesting second-best.

One of Pop's business associates from the US would occasionally come to visit. He'd always bring his little daughter, Kathy, with him. For some strange reason—in spite of little boys' general aversion to little girls—we took a shine to each other. Not more than 6 or seven years old, Kathy and I would seek nooks and closets to hide in and kiss—kisses that were no more than chaste pecks. Our favorite hide-away was the home office closet, a spacious walk-in where we kept home movies, photos and the complete works of José Martí. We were not overly concerned with being discovered—other objectives being more pressing at the time—except by my sister Naná, who would try to exploit the knowledge to tease me (to no avail).

We acquired a black Chrysler limousine with fold-out middle seats, and a black chauffeur, Jesús, to match. And yes, it's true, Cuban chauffeurs always had a great collection of dirty magazines. Jesús and I became buddies. For some unknown reason, I never saw the rest of the household staff associating with him. He and I would take to hanging out, talking about absolutely nothing of consequence. His strong and unaffected, easy Cuban Spanish entranced me. It flowed so unencumbered and atonal. All the Ds and Ss, and many of the Rs became slight aspirations, or just vanished. The Vs and Bs became indistinguishable. Most GUs became Ws. All fricative and lingual obstacles somehow disappeared. Even the consonants seemed to slouch. One commentator quipped, "If Cubans dropped any more syllables, they would be speechless." I came to idolize Jesús and, when asked what I wanted to be when I grew up declared, *"un negrito chusma del solar"*—a black bum from the sticks.

Cubans talk to each other directly, informally, usually without tact, but always with respect, referring to each other with nicknames that reflect physical characteristics: *El Chino, la mulata, gordo* (a nickname I bore for a while), *flaca* (skinny), *chato* (squished nose), *negro de pasas* (negro with raisins—a very black man with kinky hair), *rubio* (a blonde), *leche con una gota de café* (milk with a drop of coffee—a very light mulatto), *negro azul y trompúdo* (blue-black and thick-lipped), *bárbaro* (extreme, in either a good, bad or eccentric way), *flojo* (lazy), *cojo* (lame), *bigotón* (big mustached), *barbudo* (bearded)—the possibilities are endless, and due to the absence of racism, lacking the pejorative overtones similar racial expressions might conjure in the US.

And Cubans, like the Irish, cherish word play, including Monty Python-esque non-sequiturs, absurd associations and sassy nonsense, where the sound of Cuban Spanish—every bit as sonorous as a brogue—is enjoyed for its own sake. During the Pope's 2016 visit to Cuba, orange traffic cones along the *Malecón* marked his route. I asked a traffic monitor whether *el Papa* had passed by yet. He answered, *"El Papa y la malanga!"*—a double entendre, *papa* also being the word for potato, and nonsensically coupled with *malanga,* another root vegetable that tastes like a potato on steroids.

After recounting or listening to a story or anecdote that leaves one without a response, either because it includes no denouement, moral or even recognizable climax, a listener or narrator might conclude with *que le zumba el mango* (roughly, that his mango be tossed—in effect doubling the absurdity of what was recounted). With a little creativity, no one is easier to befriend than a Cuban.

One day, stuck in a traffic jam on the way to the Barnum & Bailey circus (a rarity in Havana), right at an intersection, a car in the cross street T-boned into our limousine, scaring us all to death. *"Ay, Dios mío!"* exclaimed Abuela. It was our very first car crash and proved to be the end of both the limousine and the chauffeur. Jesús, who knows why, was let go, even though the accident was not his fault. I suspect Pop and Mina weren't totally accustomed to being chauffeured people. Pop then bought, in quick succession I think, first a Cadillac, then a Ford Fairlane.

Other changes ensued. Mama and Pop enrolled their youngest daughter Patsy, still only 2-years-old, in a convent school, the Colegio Lestonnac. She'd expressed a desire to "be like the big kids." Mina took her seriously. The first time the school bus came for her, *tata* René walked her out holding her hand—she was still unsteady on her feet—and relayed her to the bus's monitor. Naná, Abuela, and myself stared wide-eyed, uncomprehending, as if she were being sent to the gas chambers. She seemed much too young to be going off to school. The impression was confirmed when, on the bus's return in the afternoon, Patsy was delivered to our door, cradled in the monitor's arms, fast asleep, clutching her security blanket and sucking her thumb.

Tatas Carmen and René with the author's little sister Patsy on the steps to the entry of our new home in Havana. Date: 1954.
Credit: A. M. Miller. Source: R. H. Miller collection.

After only one year at La Salle, Pop and Mina transferred me to the St. Thomas Military Academy, another Catholic school. Since I was a little angel, I can only surmise their reasons for the transfer. For one, it was a partial boarding school, in that I left home at 7 am and returned at 7 pm, was fed 3 meals a day, and showered. Additionally, it was an arrangement that had suited my brother John so well when he was in grade school, that he chose it willingly when he entered high school. Finally, Mina's brothers, John and Robert, had both gone to military school. But they were scamps of the worst sort and needed discipline like a broken bone needs a cast. Looking like twins, they'd often cover for each other when one got into trouble.

St. Thomas was located outside the city, in the middle of manicured parade grounds, athletic fields, and open space all surrounded by giant trees that blocked any outside view. Its focus was discipline, and it was instilled under many guises. Students were assigned a number; mine was 119. Woes betide him who forgot his number. Marching drills with rifles alternated with kickball played on a baseball diamond. Students wore starched white shirts with sharp, grey and black uniforms topped by either a crushable garrison cap or a billed dress winter cap—and black patent leather shoes shined and buffed to perfection, set off by brass belt buckles and buttons, which, if not properly polished with Brasso once a week, loaded the cadet with multiple demerits.

I don't remember how the subject came up. Perhaps shining those shoes was more than Mina wanted to burden our staff with; perhaps I was feeling 'grown up', wanting to assume more responsibilities, but somehow, it fell to me to shine my own shoes. Mina got me a can of Kiwi or Shinola, some rags, a brush, and newspapers upon which to spread the work. She explained that the purpose of shining shoes wasn't only to make them look good, but also to preserve and rejuvenate the leather. I listened intently and took the job very seriously.

When she left the room, I set about the task with alacrity. To reach all the interstices of the tongue, I removed the laces; to reach between the welt and the uppers, I grabbed a toothbrush. But I didn't stop there. Reasoning that if the shining was to preserve the leather, and the part of the shoe that got the bulk of the wear and tear was the sole, I lathered the soles with the black wax.

Beaming with pride, I called out, "*Mamiii!*" She came right away. When she saw what I'd done, she smiled, and praised my reasoning. But then she sat down and pointed out the impractical side of my effort. Finally, she told me a story about my uncle John.

John and Robert were trouble looking for opportunity. Their father—my grandfather John Maurice—was a bull of a man who saw red capes everywhere. After performing some unspecified assault on the walls of his bedroom, Uncle John was ordered to paint his room. Instead of asking his father what color, he asked his mother—my Abuela—if he could paint it any color he wanted. Abuela said any color was fine. So John painted his room black—including the ceiling.

But John Maurice had the last word: steely silence. And so began another—one of many—test of wills. He made no comment on the prank, forcing Uncle John to live in a black bedroom until he humiliatingly had to ask if he could re-paint it.

Robert and John Fitzgerald, brothers of Ana María, the author's mother, and the author's uncles at military school in Havana. Nine years later Robert was to immigrate to Venezuela.
Date: 1935. Source: A. R. Hatch-Miller collection

Uncle John, a big, dark, jowly man with a pencil thin mustache, receding hairline and slicked-back black hair, had married Marta Lopéz, one of Mina's childhood friends and next-door neighbor. She was a short, vivacious woman, addicted to playing the lottery, who chased John and insinuated herself into his life until he surrendered and married her—by proxy.

John wasn't much on tradition, much less convention. He wrote his own rules. At the time of his formal, every-member-of-the-family-attending church wedding, he ran off to Texas. Unwilling to reschedule (and perhaps even lose John), Marta went through with the ceremony. John didn't object. Pancho, her brother-in-law, stood in for John and declared his vows. Such an arrangement was not without precedent. In the Catholic Church it's called marriage *per procuram*, though traditionally it was the exclusive privilege of royalty.

While in Texas for some WWII related tasks, John drove a battered old pick-up truck. Driving down a deserted road, John spotted a black man with his thumb extended. He stopped to pick up the hitch-hiker. The black man stepped up on the running board and made as if to jump in the bed, but John stopped him and told him to ride in the cab. The man refused, warning John that riding in a vehicle with a white man could get both of them killed. John didn't argue.

Aunt Marta Lopéz and Uncle John Fitzgerald after their marriage 'per procuram' (by proxy). Date: Circa 1945. Source: A. R. Hatch-Miller collection.

John and Marta had 2 boys, Richard and Johnny, one a year younger than me, the other one year older—a minor difference that forever marked our lives. Richard and I learned to speak English without a trace of accent. Johnny, well into puberty when the family escaped to the US, always retained an accent.

Uncle John ran a jute factory, Sakoyute, S.A., outside the city, owned by his in-laws. He loved to tinker with motors and solve mechanical problems. But he never smiled. When he laughed, the laugh was rooted in irony, sarcasm or, more commonly, schadenfreude—opportunities he eagerly savored and went so far as to concoct. He was obstinate, argumentative, and didn't suffer fools; quick to criticize and slow to praise.

I idolized my uncle John. Sometimes my family would visit his family on weekends, on his days off. He spent these lying in bed, in his pajamas, drinking beer, chain smoking unfiltered Camel cigarettes, and reading comic books. While everyone else pursued their interests, I—and sometimes Richard—would laze on the giant bed with him reading the comics and commenting on the folly of everyone else, sharing his dry humor and wry perspective.

He was the only person I knew who could win a test of wills with my mother. Once, when they were entangled in an intense discussion, eyes locked on each other, John angrily warned her, "*No me mires!*" (Don't look at me!). She averted her gaze. It was the only time I ever saw her back down from a confrontation.

Staring became a teasing tactic I adopted: just looking intently at my sister. It worked beyond my wildest dreams. Naná would notice me staring at her and become unnerved. She would appeal to whatever adult was around, "Tell him to stop looking at me!" Of course, it never worked. Buck up, Naná.

Sometimes, just to up the ante—especially on long car rides—I'd extend a finger and slowly advance it toward Naná, as if I were going to touch her. It drove her absolutely bananas. She'd scream, "Baten's going to touch me!" But I seldom did, as that would have been an actionable infraction.

My caginess and Naná's hyper-sensitivity were a combination that stumped our logical parents. Some degree of frustration must have built up in Pop because he disproportionately walloped me the one time he actually caught me actionably teasing Naná.

It was a Saturday, a day off when he liked to enjoy a full American breakfast out on the patio reading the newspaper. Then, *wham! bang!* out the sliding glass door burst Naná, screaming at the top of her lungs, hotly pursued by me waving a plastic, grey King Arthur's sword. She ran circles around the patio table, mutely looking to Pop for salvation.

Without saying a word, Pop got up, grabbed the sword, bent me over and beat my butt repeatedly until I cried. It was the only time he ever disciplined me. I looked at him uncomprehendingly, but he didn't say a word and never explained himself. Then he sat down and resumed his breakfast.

Our entire clan had communal beach houses in Boca Ciega, a beach community with unpaved streets just east of Havana. Pop's and Mina's were separate (though only a block away) from the giant compound of the extended family. If I remember correctly, ours had been in the family since Mina's childhood, but now proved too small for a family that had metastasized. It was Uncle John who came up with the idea to build a block-sized compound with accommodations for all the existing and future nuclear families in the clan. For some reason, Pop didn't want to participate and retained the old family dwelling.

Uncle John owned an inboard fishing boat that he kept at the harbor. Fishing was his passion. Every so often he'd take Richard and me—and anyone else who wanted to come along—on overnight fishing trips when, he swore, the fishing was best. And it was. We never came home empty handed.

My favorite fish was *pargo*, red snapper, fried and eaten with lemon and salt. Richard and I, when we craved fishing but didn't have the means, would head for the nearest pier and gig for *jaibas*, purple crabs common in Cuba. Supposedly, they were good eating; though I never ever even touched, much less tried one.

* * *

My father had retired from AIC in 1955 because of failing health. It wasn't just the malaria. He returned home one afternoon looking very serious. Mamá told us not to disturb him; he'd been diagnosed with a heart condition, angina pectoris, and would henceforth have to take dynamite pills. I was incredulous that dynamite could be used as a medicine. He was also advised to give up smoking.

I watched Pop go into the living room farthest from the center of the house, sit down, and pull out his pack of unfiltered Pall Malls. He stuck a cigarette in his mouth, lit it with his Ronson pocket lighter, and took a big drag.

I didn't understand.

"He's enjoying his last smoke," my mother whispered. After he was done, he got up, threw the remaining pack away, and became his old, cheerful self. He never smoked again. It was a lesson in self-discipline I never forgot.

Retirement didn't slow his travels. In 1957 Pop flew to NY to dot the Is and cross the Ts on his retirement with AIC, while Mina went to her Sacred Heart high school reunion in St. Louis, Missouri. Both then met up in Phoenix, rented a car and drove to San Francisco to visit their son John who not only had completed his first year with the companies that would later become AIG, but had become engaged. Later, in August, Pop and Mina— this time separately—again flew to New York, and then together to Los Angeles where they rented a car and drove to San Francisco.

Pop was only 57 (or 58 or 59 or 60) when he retired from AIC, but he was full of dreams still unfulfilled. Politically he was a moderate social democrat. He was one of those extremely successful capitalists with a strong sense of *noblesse oblige*—he wanted to do good while doing well. So he introduced the 1950s version of the Model-T Ford to Cuba: the Volkswagen bug.

VW's first Latin American foray had been in Brazil, where the bug became very popular. Pop's Autos Volkswagen de Cuba S.A. building, a combination showroom and mechanical plant, was outside Havana, near Rancho Boyeros, the airport (now José Martí), and Mazorra, the insane asylum. Pop was proud of his new venture and took us all to tour it. In the spirit of things, he sold our Ford Fairlane, and brought home a red and white VW microbus. Such a strange-looking contraption! And so much fun! We loved to ride around in it. In no time he had orders from tour companies who wanted to use the multi-seated vans with sun roofs for sight-seeing groups. Even Fidel Castro got to test-drive one of these new "People's Car" after he grabbed power.

Early after the triumph of the Revolution, before the sugar cane curtain descended, before the endless rationing queues and shortages taught Cubans the lost virtue of patience, before the busybodies of the neighborhood Committees for the Defense of the Revolution killed all spontaneity and much of the humor, before physical and moral despair enveloped the island—while he was still popular, even idolized, Fidel Castro liked to appear in public unpredictably, followed—of course—by his retinue of guards. It wasn't just vanity; he wanted to keep his finger on the pulse of the progress of the Revolution.

Dropping into a restaurant, he struck up a conversation with a pretty girl nicknamed Kika. One thing led to another, and he ended up going home with her in her VW bug, surrounded by his caravan of vehicles full of guards.

"You're a very good driver," Fidel told her, but added that the Bug was uncomfortable for anyone over six feet tall. The *primus inter pares* was too big for a proletarian car. Nonetheless, he was impressed. In the famous speech he delivered in March of 1959, the one during which a white dove alighted on his shoulder, Fidel promised every Cuban a Volkswagen Beetle. Whether potential windfall or possible confiscation disaster, Pop's reaction to Castro's pledge went unrecorded.

* * *

Meanwhile, Batista, to improve his poll ratings, had decided to amnesty all political prisoners. On May 15, 1955 the Castro brothers were released. In June they flew to Mexico to lick their wounds, reorganize, and plan their invasion of Cuba. One year later, on November 24, 1956, they sailed for

Cuba with 82 men aboard the critically overloaded yacht *Granma*. A week later they landed on the south-west coast of Cuba. Only a dozen survived or evaded capture. Those 12 men made their way into the Sierra Maestra mountains, regrouped, and rebuilt a force that would soon become a minor thorn in the government's side. That thorn slowly infected and spread rot to the entire island.

But I wasn't aware of any of that. I was now old enough for my First Communion, a Catholic ritual that marked entry into the age of reason, when a child was old enough to cope with the mystery of transubstantiation and understand that the bread and wine ingested at Communion were the body and blood of Christ—literally. It would be many years later when, as an anthropologist, I would interpret Communion as ritualized, symbolic cannibalism, a practice shared by many religions. But for now, I was torn by conflicting emotions.

Wine! I'd get to drink wine! At dinner, Pop already let me sip his Hatuey beer, a bottle of which always accompanied his meal. I was ambivalent about its taste, mostly just wanting to imitate and bond with my father. But wine! That was some real grownup stuff.

Author's First Communion at St. Thomas Military Academy. Author is second from left, first row. Date: 1956. Source: R. H. Miller collection.

On the other hand, I was filled with foreboding at the gravity of the holy sacrament and my responsibility to do my best in the eyes of God. Unfortunately, that required participation in another sacrament: confession. I'd been taught that, when confessing one's sins to a priest, two things were essential: full disclosure and full contrition. It was never easy for me, especially if I thought the priest knew me. I didn't mind God knowing my sins, but another person? Especially one who was my teacher at St. Thomas Military Academy, where the event would take place? It seemed an undignified violation of one's sovereignty, but one which I soldiered up to…

…Until I came up with a brilliant idea for my Confirmation a year or two later, an idea somehow, no doubt, inherited from Pop's (and manifested in both my brother John and later Patsy) number-crunching affinity for accountancy.

Confirmation, a rite-of-passage meant to ratify and seal the Catholic faith in the recipient, is an acknowledgement of the child's doctrinal maturity. I was going to become a foot soldier of Christ, and I took my prospective responsibilities very seriously, especially since the sacrament was going to be administered by a bishop, my first ever contact with a Prince of the Church. The ceremony took place at our parish church, Our Lady of Perpetual Help of the Redemptorial Fathers.

For that confession, instead of divulging every sordid detail, I'd tally the number of violations against each commandment and present the results as if they were on a ledger:

"Bless me father, for I have sinned," I'd begin, followed by:
1st Commandment: no sins
2nd Commandment: no sins
3rd Commandment: no sins
4th Commandment, "Honor thy father and thy mother": no sins

(Had I known that Catholic doctrine includes, by extension, siblings, a confession of these transgressions would have been in the double, perhaps triple digits.)
5th Commandment: no sins
6th Commandment: 20 sins
7th Commandment: no sins
(As already noted, I was scrupulously honest.)
8th Commandment: no sins
(Ditto, as per the 7th)
9th Commandment: no sins
10th Commandment: 2 sins

(Not being able to distinguish between greed, envy, and admiration, I always admitted to a couple of sins in this category, just to be sure to cover all my bases.)

Notice the 6th Commandment.

Little boys, especially little (and big) Cuban boys, are obsessed with sex. I was no exception; to some, I would set a high standard in high school and college, where I was to be nicknamed "Dirty" Bob. Conflicting signals of imminently raging hormones, extreme curiosity, spontaneous sexual climaxes often due to nothing more than daydreaming or, even, muscular exertion, all pitted against the Catholic doctrine of eternal damnation in hell fire for even contemplating the pleasure of sexual arousal twisted me into knots of guilt, sophistry, rationalization, and utter emotional and intellectual confusion. Best to just give a number and not reveal the gory details, details no priest ever asked for. The new system worked so well, it became my confession formula until I lost my faith many years later.

* * *

Life was perfect. It was a timeless time, a time to explore life. The hands-off parenting really suited me. No rules were imposed other than being home for dinner on time, never lying or stealing, and getting As in school. I had the run of the neighborhood, and it was the perfect neighborhood for a kid to have the run of. Four parallel dead-end streets, accessed from a marginal avenue with little traffic, butted up to a tributary *barranca* of the Almendares River. A continuous concrete wall, doubled at the street ends with a smaller concrete barrier, separated the 200-foot precipice from the homes, empty lots, and dead-end streets atop the highest ground in the city, Alturas del Vedado. Kids didn't stray far. All the routes on the other three sides out of the neighborhood led downhill and into congestion.

Three blocks away stood the *Parque Zoológico*—the zoo, actually the zoo *park*, because it wasn't just a zoo; it included large playgrounds with swing sets, slides, and sandy play areas. Carmen, our *tata*, would often take us there to pass the time. Those times always included the awkward experience of 'making friends'—meeting up with kids you didn't know, or barely knew; kids you hadn't been introduced to; little strangers whom you didn't know whether you wanted to know at all; little kid bodies that hid cruel little bullies inside that were impossible to escape from once engaged; but whom, if you didn't make some sort of connection with, you'd be stuck playing with your sister or, even worse, stuck playing with your sister and the little girls *she'd* managed to befriend. Anyway you looked at it, it was pure hell for a shy, private little boy.

The author, age 7 and sister Naná, age 6 at the Havana zoo.
Date: 1956. Source: R. H. Miller collection.

A giant entry moat full of fat, catatonic crocodiles guarded the park entrance. We'd throw *kilos*—pennies—onto their hides to get them to stir. None ever did. One could roughly estimate a croc's last move from the number of pennies on its back. Once we spied one so laden that the *kilos* added up to near a *peso*, so we alerted the keeper that he was dead. The keeper laughed, saying that that giant was particularly lazy.

Zoo visits were always a treat, in spite of the disconcerting social scene. The roasted peanuts vendor sold a hot, paper cone-full for *un medio*—a nickel. Once, when Pop took me there, he stopped at a roadside *cafecito* stand for a sweet Cuban expresso on our way back home. The attendant eyed me to see if the order was for two. I looked at Pop silently asking if it would be alright if I had a demitasse. He ignored the silly question. Today we were two men, sharing a drink. Though my siblings and I, seven-, six-, and three-year-old children already drank *café con leche* for breakfast, it was my first shot of 100-proof Cuban expresso. We each had two.

Coca Cola was popular in Cuba at the time as it was in the US, a staple of Cuba Libres—rum and cokes—but kids gravitated toward Malta, a thick, rich, very sweet, carbonated malty soft drink—somewhat like a Guinness without the alcohol and lots of sugar—or Ironbeer, a soft drink still very popular in Latin America. Coke was, however, reserved as a special treat when mixed with condensed milk—a nectar imbibed only at home or when one was a guest.

After the US embargo was instituted and Coke was no longer available, the Cuban government created TuKola, bottled and sold by the Cervecería Bucanero. Someone ought to have been investigated for subversion, or excessive sense of humor. *Tu cola* means, literally, your tail, or more accurately, *your butt*. Because of the Cuban obsession with glutei, it has become an endless source of catcalls, inuendos, and, now, very old jokes.

I learned to ride a bike quickly, but was more enthralled by cars. At 8 years of age I decided to build a go-cart. It wasn't solely my idea; many of the neighborhood kids my age were working on home-made go-carts. We emphatically did not work together. Like separate manufacturers working on original designs, secrecy was paramount. The competition was fierce. My mechanical savvy was limited to a top-of-the-line Erector Set, at that time quite a sophisticated and expensive toy, so I figured I could build anything.

Pop, Mina, and anyone I could finagle helped in bits and pieces: how to use tools, finding scrap lumber and wheels, and, most importantly, encouragement. The finished product worked—high praise indeed, and the most that could be said of it. Its minimal performance standards were its primary safety features: it couldn't go fast, had no brakes, wobbled, steered spastically, and fell apart easily. Good thing, too, since all the neighborhood streets inclined down. We of course chose the steepest for our test runs. All of us lost control instantly and crashed spectacularly. There were few injuries other than completely totaled go-carts.

When Elvis Presley hit Cuba's airwaves Naná went gaga, a condition I missed no opportunity to ridicule. If I happened to catch Naná playing a record and enjoying herself, I'd demand equal time on the record player. Our tastes in music were opposite extremes. Naná adored Elvis, Sarita Montiel, Ramoncito Veloz, Pedrito Rico, Doris Day, and musicals, a genre I found particularly insipid and offensive. Sometimes she'd sing along softly or sway to the rhythm, responses I couldn't bear to watch or hear for their undignified uninhibitedness. As soon as her record was over, I'd put on Tchaikovsky, Rossini, or whatever else our parents had collected that Naná never played, and listened intently, up close, cross-legged, impassive—except when she wasn't around when I'd sometimes try *trepaking* through a mazurka.

After the Revolution triumphed, Ramoncito Veloz recorded "El Cielo Es Más Azul", a rebel hymn that had become very popular and every kid knew by heart. Naná developed a burning crush on the 15-year-old Veloz, and decided to call him. She enlisted the help of Marci, the Castellanos' niece. Even at such a young age, it was such open-ended, spur-of-the-moment, hair-brained ideas hatched—like a Lucy and Ethel scheme—without a follow-up plan, and based on a spontaneous impulse wrapped up in unbounded enthusiasm that irritated me no end. It was an irresistible dare to meddle and ridicule—had I known about it.

She and Marci looked up Veloz' phone number in the directory, finding—to their surprise—that his listing was printed right there, available to every pre-pubescent girl in Havana.

They dialed.

Veloz did not answer; someone else did. Whoever it was didn't call Ramoncito to the phone. It was just as well. Naná's and Marci's plan hadn't gotten beyond the point of getting the heartthrob on the other end of the line. Having then achieved a measure of success, they just hung up and reveled in an ecstasy of shivers.

A cast of colorful characters plied their trades on our streets, either with horse-drawn carts or push carts. *"Granizado, granizado!"* The shaved ice vendor would clarion. He was my favorite, followed by the ice cream man. *Un medio*, a nickel, was always forthcoming from Abuela, and would buy anything I wanted. We ignored the tamale man, Cuban tamales being somewhat bland, with the pork chunks mixed in with the corn meal.

Early in the morning—earlier than I was usually up—the bread vendor would come by. Little Patsy's preferred breakfast was a fresh roll smothered in olive oil accompanied by *café con leche*, hot milk and coffee, in equal amounts, with lots of sugar. Naná and I, introduced to scrambled eggs, wouldn't eat them without ketchup (a condiment we also liberally poured on black beans and rice).

The produce cart appeared in mid-morning, with mostly local produce· *"Malanga! Boniato! Mamey! Mango! Guanábana! Frutabomba! Yuca! Plátanos verdes y maduros! Piña! Kimbombó!"* The vendor would shout, never missing an item, sometimes peppering his *pregones* with simple rhymes or double entendres. Oftimes I'd accompany the cook out to the cart to watch the transaction and help carry the produce in.

I remember the lottery vendor, a staple of the Cuban street scene, appearing at our back door only once. He never returned. Either the gambling bug hadn't hit our household staff, or he was asked not to come back.

During mosquito season, a fumigating jeep plied the neighborhood roads, fogging entire blocks with the sweet-smelling DDT. I was fascinated by the process, knowing that the fog was poisonous, yet widely and regularly used. At night, we slept under white mosquito nets, made bearable when the new, window-model air conditioners were installed.

The local cop, a pasty-faced, pudgy cherub with the ubiquitous pencil-thin mustache, made no enemies, but he kept a sharp eye on the neighborhood. He once picked me up after dark—I must have been 9 years old—during that fateful week in 1958 between Christmas and New Year's when Batista was about to capitulate but the rebels hadn't yet reached Havana. For those few days Cuba had little government. I'd been out late with my pellet gun gunning for electric wire birds. It wasn't a good time to wander the streets after dark with a gun.

But not everyone on the streets was, to me, a welcome sight. Gerardito was my neighborhood *bete noir*. A bit older than I was, he always approached with a wry smile, a con man's smile; engaged me with some line or other until he could trip me up. Then he'd pounce. The first time he tried talking me into tasting an Habanero pepper right off the vine, saying it was delicious. Since Cubans don't eat and are not familiar with chilies—Cuban cuisine being more Spanish than Mexican—and at 8 years of age I wasn't a fan of raw vegetables, I didn't bite. When he became pushily insistent and wouldn't take a bite himself, I suspected something was up. Finally, he grabbed a pepper and squished it all over my face, concentrating on my mouth and eyes.

He didn't laugh. He just watched me scream and run away. Secure bullies simply enjoy the quiet satisfaction of success.

The next time I saw him, he had a broom stick in his hand. One end was whittled to a dull point. I immediately ran away. But being bigger and older, he caught up with me. As I struggled to escape, he rammed the stick into my right nipple, repeating "See what happens when you run away from me?"

The injury soon festered and grew so large that Mamá called our doctor. Dr. Ferrara came right away, diagnosed a cyst, and declared it had to be removed in a hospital. It was my first operation with full anesthesia. Years later, in American schools, I'd be asked why I had only half a nipple. "I was caught up in a street fight in Cuba during the Revolution," I'd respond.

Later, after the Revolution had triumphed, Gerardito adjusted well. He was the only kid we knew with an electric toy car, one you could actually ride in. Carnival, at the beginning of Lent, was a big affair—as it still is in New Orleans and Brazil. In Cuba, where ancestral Spanish ties were still strong, clubs and associations based on the region of Spain from which one's family hailed—Asturias, Valencia, etc.—would sponsor Carnival floats, marching bands, bagpipers, commercial displays, dance troupes, and just about any home-grown spectacle that would instill pride and provide delight. Children would dress up in regional Iberian costumes, complete with mantillas, castanets, and painted-on mustaches.

In 1959, Gerardito broke with tradition. Riding solitary between floats in his little electric car, he'd dressed up as Fidel Castro, with a fake white dove of peace attached to his epaulet, a vain, arrogant smirk on his face. Fidel wouldn't have objected.

Our household staff managed to be more inconspicuous yet more informal than most servants in more temperate climes. Carmen, Naná's and my *tata*, was thin as a sugarcane stalk, dark haired, and with a face lined by country living that did not reveal her age. She was very relaxed but very serious. After Pop, Mina, and we kids left the country, our house became the property of "The People." It was deemed too large for Abuela, the single resident—according to the new regime's housing laws. So our grandmother invited Carmen and her entire family—mother, daughter and niece—to move in. They did, and were allowed to remain. Carmen sent us letters every month or two, keeping us informed on the condition of Abuela and the house. As conditions on the island deteriorated and food became scarce, Carmen obtained chickens from her extended family in the countryside and raised them in the back yard.

Ana, our elegantly beautiful mulatto maid, was always cheerful and transparent. Once, when she was walking up the stairs with open slippers, I noticed the soles of her feet and mused out loud, to no one in particular, "Why are the soles of her feet white, but the rest of her brown?" An uncomfortable moment suffused the room. Ana stopped dead on her tracks, smiled awkwardly, and responded with an appropriate platitude that managed to be straight from the heart.

4

1958

When January of 1958 dawned, it only hinted at what the future held for the island. The previous year, 1957 had been pretty uneventful, except in two important respects.

Throughout 1957, Fidel Castro's 12 men—reduced to 9 soon after landing—had managed to entrench themselves in the Sierra Maestra mountains (in Oriente Province, on the western extremity of Cuba's easternmost province), grow to a respectable force, and even win a few skirmishes—but they had gained little ground.

They were lucky. Batista had been tipped off about the landing and had sent the army and air force to welcome them. With a casualty rate of 73 men out of 82, armed forces commanders were convinced that the invaders had been neutralized. They radioed headquarters that Castro and his men had been annihilated. As far as the government was concerned, no follow-up action was required, and Castro was left alone to reorganize.

Two weeks later, Herbert L. Matthews of the *New York Times*, made his way into the Sierra Maestra and interviewed Castro in his redoubt. The interview and story brought Fidel Castro to the attention of the world with both print inchage and television footage. It was the moment when Castro stepped onto the world stage—and into people's hearts and imaginations. Matthews portrayed the bearded rebel as serious, humble, honest, and idealistic, a role Fidel fit—or played—to a tee.

Various previous—and independent—attempts at widening the struggle had failed. In 1957, first, the *Directorio Revolucionario* led an assault on the Presidential Palace, hoping to catch Batista. The July 26 rebels were supposed to participate, but said that they "missed the bus." Other sources dispute this weak excuse and attribute their no-show to the fact that the assault wasn't led by Castro's organization. Later that same year, an expedition organized by the *Organización Auténtica* landed a group of rebels in the yacht *Corinthia* in Oriente Province. But they were soon surrounded by Batista forces, taken prisoner and summarily shot.

Fidel Castro, Commander-in-Chief of the 26 of July rebel forces.
Date: 1959. Credit: Felices Company. Source: R. H. Miller collection.

The failed rebellion with the most impact took place in September of 1957 at the naval base in Cienfuegos. Navy sailors mutinied and took over the naval yards. Encouraged by their success, the city's civilians followed suit. But Batista counterattacked, deploying the air force with bombs and strafing, and sent in loyal troops from nearby Santa Clara. Survivors were tortured, killed and, in some instances, buried alive.

The next year, however, was another story.

On January 31, 1958, an expeditionary force of 16 men and one woman, with a large quantity of arms, left Miami in a small yacht, the *Thor II*. They landed near Nuevitas, in Camagüey province, in the middle of the island, where Cuba's northernmost coast protrudes up like a dowager's hump. They broke up into smaller units and, with the aid of supporters and new recruits, began the arduous, 120-mile trek into the Escambray mountains, due south, near the southern coast of the island. Along the way they engaged two army units, one by ambush.

Under the joint command of Eloy Gutiérrez Menoyo, a Spaniard whose family were Republican veterans of the Spanish Civil War, and William Morgan, an idealistic American soldier of fortune, the men reached their new base of operations in the mountains within a few weeks. At the end of

February they published their *Escambray Manifesto*, laying out the objectives of their movement.

A second front, unrelated to Castro and his July 26 Movement—but with common cause—was now established. It was the only successful uprising against Batista that was completely independent of Castro's forces.

Eloy Gutiérrez Menoyo, Commander of the Second National Front of Escambray rebel forces, which were independent of Fidel Castro's 26 of July Movement. Date: 1959. Credit: Felices Company. Source: R. H. Miller collection

"Aquí, Radio Rebelde, la voz de la Sierra Maestra!" The voice of the Revolution, set up by *Che* Guevara, began broadcasting in February. Between 5 pm and 9 pm, all of Cuba listened in to the daily battle accounts and Fidel's speeches. Rumors that anyone listening would be arrested and tortured dissuaded no one, and only titillated audiences. Listening in made everyone feel like a participant in the Revolution; it made people feel that they were getting away with something—a hard-to-resist guilty pleasure.

We didn't need Radio Rebelde to tell us about M26's—as Castro's rebel movement was known—bold incursion into central Havana that February. It was all over the news. Two men had gone into the Lincoln Hotel and kidnapped Juan Manuel Fangio, the Argentine Formula One world champion race car driver. Although semi-retired, he was in Cuba for the island's Grand Prix. Fangio had dominated the first decade of Formula One racing, winning the World Drivers' Championship five times, thus establishing a record that stood for 47 years. To the boys at St. Thomas, he was a BIG celebrity, and it was all we could talk about.

Dr. Ernesto Che Guevara, Commander of the 8th Column, Ciro Redondo, of Fidel Castro's 26 of July rebels. Died leading a guerrilla group in Bolivia in 1967. Date: 1959. Credit: Felices Company. Source: R. H. Miller collection.

The kidnapping was meant to embarrass the Batista regime by canceling the Cuba Grand Prix. But Batista insisted that the event go on. Police set up roadblocks and checkpoints everywhere, but Fangio could not be found. The rebels treated Fangio well, installing him in comfortable quarters, and allowing him to monitor the race on the radio. They tried to win him over to their revolutionary plans, with very limited success, since the Argentine was apolitical. After twenty-nine hours Fangio was released, after forging friendships with the young idealists.

The publicity stunt was a great success. Fidel Castro and the July 26 Movement were on everyone's lips—and not just as a distant guerrilla effort. The kidnappers were never found, adding to a growing perception of the regime's incompetence. Public opinion sensed that Batista was losing his grip on power.

In March, Fidel Castro took another big gamble: he divided his forces and opened up another front in Oriente. Raul Castro, with a force of 67 men, marched east of the Sierra Maestra to the Sierra Cristal on Oriente's north coast, opening up the Frank País—a third front—in the war against Batista. The revolution was morphing into a real war.

Raúl Castro, Commander of the 2nd Front, Frank Pais, of the 26 of July rebels. Date: 1959. Credit: Felices Company. Source: R. H. Miller collection.

* * *

Pop was a fan; Mina was a sceptic. Optimistic about Castro, he was later to contribute money and property to the Revolution both before and immediately after its victory. But revolutions, no matter how well-intentioned, are inherently disruptive and unpredictable. This didn't stop Pop. The urgency of his ambitions was fueled by the specter of the grim reaper. With the addition of rheumatoid arthritis, a crippling and disfiguring disease, his chronic malaria and angina pectoris became a threesome.

After the Bug took root, he partnered up with a German colleague from Volkswagen, and launched a brand new enterprise in early 1958. Though he'd been Controller of the Oxford Paper Company for only a short time back in 1940, he must have felt confident in opening Cuba's first big paper products factories, Envases Modernos S.A. and Industrias Cello-Pak S.A. He wanted to give Dixie's and/or Lilly's (I don't remember which) de facto monopoly a run for their money. When the paper cup assembly line became operative, he proudly took the family out to the factory to watch the process, and presented us each with a waxed paper cup as if it were a votive offering.

Less than one month after Castro's victory, when euphoria and grandiose schemes still permeated the Cuban atmosphere, Fidel proposed planting a thousand trees along the avenues that had hosted the rebels' triumphant procession. Pop immediately offered to donate 1,000 paper cups to hold the seedlings. Not only did he not receive an answer, no trees were ever planted.

Nineteen-fifty-eight also brought television to our home. Instantly it became hypnotic. *Rin-Tin-Tin, Annie Oakley, Sea Hunt, Bat Masterson, Gunsmoke,* all dubbed in Spanish, became staples, keeping us kids indoors in the evening, sitting cross-legged on the floor, as close as Abuela would let us. Years later, in an unexpected turn of events, I'd end up with Craig Arness, James Arness's (Marshall Matt Dillon) son as a classmate at Prescott College.

TV was however, in a very early insight, mostly limited to evenings for us kids. I don't remember Mina or Pop ever watching. Abuela, on the other hand, always tuned in to the new soaps format—*Mamá, La Novela de Las Diez,* and others. Sometimes some of the household staff, Carmen, René, and Ana would join us.

After Castro's victory, however, all broadcasting became live news, 20/7, way before CNN. Though initially spellbinding, Fidel's speeches soon tired us: the endless narration; the panoramic shots of crowds supporting this or that, or protesting this or that; the mass televised trials; and the endless coverage and speculation over the explosion of the *La Coubre* in Havana Harbor in March of 1960, a ship bearing an arms shipment, with Fidel's endless rhetorical question, *"Armas, para que?"* "Arms, for what?", we sought more entertaining distractions elsewhere. The arms were intended for the new revolutionary government, but Castro spun the sabotage to his advantage.

* * *

Halfway through 1958, in May, with four active guerrilla fronts operating on the island, Batista finally decided to get serious. He dispatched 10,000 troops to destroy Castro's 300 guerrillas in Oriente Province, and the *Directorio Revolucionario's* Escambray front, now also numbering in the hundreds.

But it was not to be.

Throughout June, July, and August government troops suffered defeat after defeat, surrendered en masse, or switched sides. Huge amounts of equipment, including tanks, fell into the hands of the rebels. By September 1st, two of the Oriente fronts, one under the Argentine Ernesto *Che* Guevara Serna, the other under Camilo Cienfuegos, had begun a two-pronged advance westward, toward the center of the island. It would be only a matter of time before they reached the capital.

Camilo Cienfuegos, Commander of the 2nd Column, Antonio Maceo, of Fidel Castro's 26 of July rebels. Died in a plane crash after returning from being ordered to arrest Commander Huber Matos. Date: 1959. Credit: Felices Company. Source: R. H. Miller collection.

With the steamroller now nearly unstoppable, Cubans began letting down their guard. No longer was *Radio Rebelde* listened to clandestinely; it was openly monitored and discussed. Young men—and some women—from all over the island rushed to join the advancing rebels, jumping on the bandwagon as it picked up momentum.

Headed over to the Castellanos', in search of distraction, I ran into one of the young guys—associated somehow to the ex-mayor—who were often there. He was a guy who had actually paid attention to me, shown friendship, and kindness even—behavior that, to a 10-year-old boy, instantly made him a role model. Now he was dressed in full olive green army fatigues, with backpack and sidearm, and was walking down the street nonchalantly. Since the regular army wore khakis, either this guy was foolish or fearless, or the risk was minimal.

I stopped dead on the sidewalk in front of him, speechless, eyes bugging out. The only soldiers I'd ever been this close to were my little toy soldiers. He said he was off to join the rebels. I asked if I could go with him, even though I knew that was impossible. He smiled, metaphorically (or perhaps actually) patted my head, and kindly said no, that I was too young. When I told my parents about the encounter, they shuddered, grimacing that his behavior was beyond foolish.

Events in Cuba didn't curtail our parents' travel. In late summer Pop flew to Pennsylvania and then New York on business. From there he flew to Phoenix and on to Los Angeles where he rented a car and drove to San Francisco. Concurrently, Mina flew to Merida to visit friends, and then joined Pop in San Francisco. John's first son, Howie, was due and, I surmise, they wanted to be there for his birth in early September. From San Francisco they flew to Mexico City from where each took separate flights at different times back to Havana.

* * *

Whatever possessed Pop and Mina to enroll me in English saddle equestrian lessons, I'll never know. For one, the lessons took place at the Havana Yacht & Country Club, requiring their presence and thereby impinging on their busy life. Mina was a city sophisticate with absolutely no horse background and Pop had only ridden mules in Patagonia on a purely utilitarian basis. He never expressed an interest in horses—other than reading me to sleep with Zane Grey. Naná burned with jealousy. It's not that she, like so many little girls, was smitten with horses; it's that it was something I got to do and she couldn't.

I had no interest in riding horses, much less dressage or hurdle jumping. Unlike dogs, with whom one can see eye-to-eye, assess each other for compatibility and choose—or not—whether to establish a relationship, horses' eyes—those erstwhile windows into the soul—are inaccessible jointly. They're disconcertingly far apart, off on the verges of the skull and at an awkward angle for a face-to-face sussing up. Even if, standing on a step ladder at close range, a person and a horse were to look into each other's eyes, the horse wouldn't be able to see you and react with a facial expression (not that they're endowed with a sophisticated set of facial muscles with which to express subtle sentiments): their eyes are so far apart and on the side of their heads that they have a blind spot right in front of their face. In an attempt to compensate for this, horses' eyes bug out like a toad's, as if trying to reach around the front of their muzzle to eliminate that blind spot. It's impossible to read a horse's thoughts by looking at his face and therefore, for me, an impossible animal to trust, establish a relationship or bond. Why put oneself at the mercy of a large, emotionally opaque, and therefore dangerous and unpredictable beast weighing at least ten times a little boy's weight? Still, it was new, I trusted my parents' judgment and I didn't completely object.

Cuban horse culture existed mostly in Camagüey province where herds of beef cattle roamed the mid-island plains. The cowboys all rode Western saddle, a tradition directly descended from Spanish horse culture. Perhaps it was all a nouveau riche exercise in introducing their children to high society pursuits now that Pop was far from Brooklyn and we'd bought the Havana Mayor's house. Naná enrolled in ballet and Spanish dance classes while I also signed up for fencing at St. Thomas.

It was all for naught. I don't know how long I lasted at that. I remember learning how to control the horse, a terrifyingly large animal that I needed help mounting. The "control" was more faith-based than actual. I could walk, trot, canter, gallop (very scary), stop (essential), and turn the horse. I also remember being prepped with the courage talk facing my first jump. Not that I needed it; I was good at following directions and the results were always as expected.

With Mamá and Pop watching from the bleachers, the trainer led me and my horse to the far end of the arena. My first—and only—hurdle, perhaps halfway down the course, couldn't have been more than two feet high. The trainer said the horse didn't need any special signals to jump the hurdle; just aim him at it, tap his flanks and go fast: the horse would automatically jump the hurdle. As for me, he instructed me to lean forward and hold on tight, especially during the jump.

What a disaster! As the horse flew over the hurdle I flew off the horse. Mamá, Pop and the trainer rushed to my side hovering as if I were a disfigured newborn. I wasn't hurt, but I declined to ever ride a horse again.

* * *

In September, Guevara's and Cienfuegos's troops, advancing separately, met up in Camagüey province and continued their westward march as one large force. Government resistance to the advance was mostly limited to aerial bombardment, intermittent at best because of the heavy rains of the fall hurricane season.

On October 7, the now-combined Castro forces crossed into Las Villas province and encountered the forces of the *Directorio Revolucionario* in the Escambray Mountains under the field command of Faúre Chaumont. Though Castro's 26 of July Movement and the *Directorio Revolucionario* had heretofore been completely independent enterprises, Chaumont, after protracted negotiations, agreed to a coordinated offensive. The news ignited Cubans; hundreds of men volunteered to join the rebels.

In November, government forces concentrated behind defensive positions in the cities of Las Villas province. Rebel forces, meanwhile, worked out operational plans for the new joint command, planned the next offensives, trained new recruits, and awaited drier weather.

Fidel himself remained ensconced in his headquarters in the Sierra Maestra, coordinating military and political strategy, while his brother Raúl secured eastern Oriente Province. Fidel's physical seclusion in the mountains but unquestioned leadership and tenacity gave him an Olympian air, abetted by his curly Greek beard—one he would never again shave.

Nearly all the rebel forces sported beards and long hair, starting a sartorial trend, with philosophical implications, that would take the world by storm in the 1960s. Raúl Castro, with his skimpy fuzz of a beard, gave rise to rumors that he was either homosexual or illegitimate—or both. Camilo Cienfuegos, on the other hand, hirsute as a Tolkien character in *Lord of the Rings*, with a beard that made one wonder whether it housed legions of unidentified critters, was beginning to upstage Fidel. Handsome, with a seductive and ready smile, and a twinkle in his eye under his black cowboy hat, he would later die in a suspicious plane crash in 1959 on a fool's errand for Fidel.

On December 20, the rebel offensive began. In quick succession, the cities of Cabaiguán, Placetas, Remedios, Cruces, and Sancti Spíritus fell to the onslaught. Two days later, Camilo Cienfuegos, began an assault on the army garrison at Yaguajay; while Guevara's and Chaumont's combined forces attacked Santa Clara, capital of Las Villas province.

After nearly two weeks of intense combat and aerial bombardment, 250 government soldiers surrendered Yaguajay to Cienfuegos on New Year's Eve, and 1,000 more surrendered to Guevara and Chaumont on New Year's Day, 1959.

5

1959

"New Year's Eve 1959 was a memorable one and not soon to be forgotten! Word passed around like wildfire that Batista and his cronies had fled, throwing in the sponge at last. The island had been cut in half at the now famous Bay of Pigs and the Escambray rebel troops were headed for Havana. On New Year's Day it became a reality and while many mobs roamed the streets seeking revenge against the hated dictator's cronies who had not as yet left, we were not molested. I personally did not leave the house, carefully following the advice given over the local radio."

So begins my father's account of those fateful days between Batista's exit and the rebels' arrival, an account he wrote for *Time* magazine but that was never published.

When Batista fled the country at 2 am on New Year's Day 1959, Havana erupted into an orgy of celebration. The metropolitan police, technically members of the old regime, kept a low profile. We children weren't allowed to get near the windows much less leave the house. All the prisons were thrown open and riotous mobs roamed the streets wreaking havoc on anything associated with the old regime, especially casinos. Another favorite target was parking meters, a hated source of government income. My sister Naná remembers one passing car peppering our living room with bullets. My mother, ever cautious, concocted a Molotov cocktail "just in case".

The next day when Castro's tanks rolled into the city, mobs lionized the long-haired, bearded rebels. Contingents of the olive-clad, Thompson sub-machine gun-wielding soldiers ringed all the embassies to prevent "enemies of the people" from escaping. With the Mexican ambassador's residence only a block from our house, I couldn't keep away. Armed with my pellet gun—for solidarity and fun—I'd hang out for hours with the militiamen target shooting at birds and passing the time. For a 9-year old kid, it just didn't get any better. As I'd later say when I learned English in Mississippi, "I was shittin' in tall cotton".

CMQ, channel 6, went to round-the-clock programming. Though I preferred outdoor activity, the novel, continuous TV coverage of events mesmerized us. Abuela, us kids, and the household staff—whenever they managed time between chores—gathered in the TV room to watch the Revolution unfold.

On January 2nd Manuel Urrutia, the judge who had tried Castro sympathetically after his July 26, 1953 uprising, became President of Cuba. He was appointed to the post behind the scenes by Castro, no doubt because his reputation for probity and his spotless record wouldn't cause any ructions domestically or internationally. José Miró Cardona became Prime Minister. Days later the US recognized the new government, and appointed a new ambassador, Phillip Bonsal.

I asked Abuela how Urrutia became president without an election. She shrugged her shoulders and mumbled something I can't remember. She'd seen so much. It would have taken too much effort and too long a time to try to explain it all to a nine-year-old kid.

Then on January 8, Fidel Castro, with his now-mechanized No.1 José Martí Column rolled slowly into Havana amidst a stately procession of troops and army vehicles. It was beautifully scripted to appear spontaneous which, to some degree, it was. *Not* riding atop a tank—as has often been reported—along Havana's Malecón seawall and waving to the ecstatic crowds, Castro seemed to have turned out all of Havana—along with busloads of provincials—to line the streets. Luis R. Luis, who was later to live across the street from Castro's mistress, Celia Sánchez, and much later became chief OAS (Organization of American States) economist (and our childhood friend Sara Maria's husband-to-be was there):

"I was present at Fidel's triumphant entrance into Havana on January 8, 1959. A friend and I wanted to see the revolutionary motorcade and we persuaded a caretaker of a building at La Rampa near the malecón to give us access to the roof from where we would have a prime viewing site. There were a handful of people on the roof alongside a miliciano with an M-1 rifle guarding the strategic location and watching nearby buildings. La Rampa street was packed with onlookers. We waited a long time, perhaps close to two hours before the first vehicles of the column arrived. Many vehicles came by with bearded folk toting M-1s, Thompson's and what looked like World War I era Springfield rifles. At last a couple of jeeps emerged followed by a Sherman tank atop which was a bearded man in green olive fatigues. The crowd rushed towards him thinking it was the conquering hero himself. I recognized the bearded warrior; it was Juan Nuiry an old friend of my family and president of the University Students Association (FEU) who had joined Fidel at the Sierra Maestra. Many vehicles followed and perhaps some 30 minutes later Fidel

approached on a jeep with two or three escorts and a bearded man that looked like Camilo Cienfuegos. The pace of the motorcade was very slow and the crowds had plenty of time to contemplate the visage of the aspiring tyrant who would become ubiquitous for decades to come."

Flanked by Comandantes Camilo Cienfuegos and Huber Matos, Castro stopped in front of the Columbia Army Barracks and ceremoniously approached the podium and microphones that awaited him. It was the biggest crowd ever to line the streets of Havana. After he'd begun talking, three white doves alighted on his podium, one landing on his shoulder. The crowds went absolutely wild. Most thought it was a sign from Providence: Fidel was "untouchable." We were glued to the TV, in spite of just being little kids listening to a politician.

Mina's cousin Eddy, a mostly unemployed *bon vivant*, was there also. Afterward he set out to regale the extended family about the event—to little response. He'd make the rounds of relatives ingratiating himself and cadging what he could. Mina didn't care for him and called him a Communist. Chuchu, just a kid at the time but later to marry into our family, got to watch the procession from the balcony of his nearby home.

In three days the TV spectacle switched to military tribunals set up to deal with members of the old regime, followed by executions before firing squads with screams of *"Al paredón!"* (To the firing wall!) This prime-time TV *tableau vivant* continued through January and into February, and trickled into March with a break during Easter Week, by which time 483 "war criminals" had been executed—a little over half the total number of war dead on both sides during the two-year Revolutionary war. Near the end of January, 100 "women in black" demonstrated against the executions. As many as 500 *Batistianos*—Batista partisans—were executed, with the US calling it a "blood bath." Had we not lost interest in the repetitive, propagandaish, and predictable drama, I sensed that Abuela might have tried to distract us with a game of cards.

In spite of this—after all, the nuances of the rule of law and due process were slippery to non-existent in 9-year olds, and excused by most adults in the excitement of a well-intentioned revolution—all my family were middling-to-sympathetic Castro supporters. But one detail nagged me: Castro held no formal role in government. How did he wield so much influence? Perhaps it was a naïve question for a 9-year old, but it was prescient.

On February 16, Fidel replaced Miró Cardona as Prime Minister with himself. With Castro now holding a formal government post, things started to make sense to me. Kids just don't understand power without position and titles. Twelve days after his appointment, Castro announced that, "Elections could not be held now because they would not be fair. We have an overwhelming majority at present and it is in the interest of the nation that the political parties become fully developed and their programs defined before elections are held."

* * *

The Revolution did not interfere with school—much. Cuban Christmas vacation extended beyond January 6, *El Día de Los Reyes Magos*, the day the Magi visited the newborn Christ child bearing gifts. This was the day most Cuban kids received gifts. But Cuban families with an American influence double-dipped, getting gifts both on Christmas day from *Santiclós* and from the Magi on the Feast of the Epiphany. It must have been stressful on those parents. Ours chose squarely Christmas Day; though sometimes adding token gifts on the Epiphany to go along with the presents from outside the immediate family marked for unwrapping on the 6th (some people could be quite ideological about the gift-giving days).

St. Thomas Military Academy opened on schedule, without skipping a beat. No changes, except a few, sometimes subtle and voluntary ones, were evident, but none as radical as the ones that convinced Mina and Pop to later remove me from school. Naná's school, on the other hand, suspended bus service for the students a few times, calling on parents to provide transportation to-and-from school during the initial phases of the regime change.

Revolutions, no matter how radical, always provide opportunities for profit. Sometime that winter or spring, the Felices Company, a sweets and canned guava producer decided to sponsor a new idea—a set of 268 "baseball" cards that commemorated the Revolution and its leaders. The events depicted on the cards were rendered in colored line drawings, while photographs—like real baseball cards—depicted the Revolution's leaders. Fidel was number 126; Raúl, 127. The full collection, pasted into a bespoke album, traced the Revolution from 1952 to 1959. Production of the individual cards was dribbled out, both in time and quantity, to create a sense of drama and expectation. A flat slab of bubble gum accompanied each little packet of cards, the exact content of which was always somewhat indeterminate.

This indeterminacy was a stroke of genius on the part of the Felices Company. Kids might end up with many duplicates of the same card or a few hot-off-the-presses new cards. The resulting oversupply and scarcity created a hot trading market among kids, who were all racing to be the first to fill their albums and complete their set.

"I'll give you two Almedias for one *Che* Guevara!"

"No way! *Che* is worth much more. One Almedia, one Chibás, and one Cubelas, and you can have *Che*."

"OK, deal."

Kids who had absolutely no interest in baseball—me included—became avid collectors of the Revolution cards. Recess at St. Thomas became a swap meet for cards. Fights and impromptu games ceased. I don't remember anyone not participating. Even my nurdy, chubby, reclusive, almost-albino friend, Urzurrún—nicknamed *bola de nieve* for his glaringly white complexion—started collecting the cards and pasting them in his album.

But it was the educational (some might say propaganda) benefit that these cards provided that was most overlooked. Little kids don't read much; and what they overhear adults saying about current events is discreet, discontinuous, out of context, usually boring, and often misunderstood. These cards made history and current events come alive. Some of us memorized the names of all 16 Rebel *Comandantes*. We'd argue about the cause and effects of the events depicted on the cards, marvel at the deeds and atrocities, and elaborate speculatively about the events given short shrift.

Some of us even went so far as to read Castro's "History Will Absolve Me" speech—his defense summing-up at the end of his trial in 1953—that was printed in full on the inside back cover of the album. Had the speech been assigned reading for an 8th grader, eyes would have glazed and rolled, homework would have been put off, and stern admonitions from teachers would have poured forth. But the Felices Company managed not only to make 4th graders read and re-read the speech, but to do it voluntarily and with enthusiasm.

I have no idea how much the Felices Company profited from this venture or even if they ever got to keep their profits as money and property were confiscated bit by bit. But a recent Google search for *Album de la Revolución Cubana* revealed that one leather-bound, mint condition, completed album sold for $100,000 at Sotheby's. An old, ratty one like mine goes for about $1,500 on EBay.

Other games at St. Thomas, while still innocent—these were, after all, 9 and 10-year-olds—were edgier, like a scene out of Reinaldo Arenas' *Before Night Falls*. As related before, St. Thomas' student schedule went from 7 am to 7 pm, with three meals *and* a shower. Showers were supervised by Captain Garcia, a pear shaped, neatly mustachioed man with a pasty complexion. Captain Garcia was neither mean nor nice, but he *seemed* sympathetic.

The locker-shower room complex was one long, rectangular room. The lockers ran back-to-back, three-quarters of the way down the middle of the big room. The showers, one big square area at the far end of the room, were tiled white and divided in half by a partition that provided for plumbing with more shower spigots on both sides. There were no individual cubicles; the showers were all open. There was no one position where Captain Garcia could monitor the entire room; it was either one half or the other. Captain Garcia favored a position near the entry door. Intermittently, he'd decide to look around the end of the lockers to the other half, and he'd walk over, lean out, and glance at the little boys on the other side.

And these little boys could be mischievous. In what seemed in retrospect a primitive expression of dominance or an exuberance of testosterone—or both—some boys would pounce on an unsuspecting, naked mark by attempting to pretend-copulate with them from behind. At times, this turned into a veritable Conga Line, with constant pretend couplings and uncouplings. Nicknames, such as locomotive and caboose, were coined for the more aggressive boys and for the more passive kids, usually those that tried to be oblivious to the whole thing. I tried to ignore all the goings-on, but, when I became a target, I was reluctant to pull away from an assaulter too fast, in case I might be singled out as a particularly sensitive mark, one ripe for this sort of teasing.

This didn't last long.

One day Captain Garcia glanced around the corner of the lockers and caught the Conga Line. With his face revealing no emotion, he ordered us all—pointing individually to those caught in the act—to immediately get dressed and report to Lieutenant Martinez' office.

Martinez was Garcia's bulldog, a man who'd punish a kid with 3 hours of parade march simply for asking a question to which Martinez believed the boy ought to know the answer. For worse infractions, the Lieutenant would unhesitatingly lay on the strop. As if not already absolutely mortified at being caught in such a disgustingly depraved act, one for which we'd certainly burn in hell for eternity, facing Lieutenant Martinez guaranteed something much worse than eternal damnation—*right away*. A stern, unkind martinet of a disciplinarian, the Lieutenant was a man to be avoided at all costs. Martinez was clean shaven with a closely cropped crew cut. He was tall and thin and exuded military vigor. Still, facing Lieutenant Martinez was preferable to being immediately expelled and facing our parents—fates that inexorably awaited us.

I thought of running away, but there was nowhere to go. As a Catholic, almost nothing was worse or generated more guilt than a sin involving sex, particularly homosexual sex. As a Cuban, absolutely nothing was more degrading and shameful than being a *maricón*, a queer.

We lined up in front of Lieutenant Martinez' desk, Captain Garcia standing unobtrusively behind him and to the side. Martinez stared at each of the dozen or so of us, individually searing his contempt into our consciences. One little boy wet his pants. I don't remember the gist of his lecture; we were too impatient for the sentence. When it came we nearly fainted.

Perhaps these men had the wisdom to understand the context: Nine and ten-year-old kids, not actually copulating but just going through the motions, mortifyingly ridiculing each other, counting *coup* and laughing—however inappropriately—were not engaging in "the love that dare not speak its name." Or perhaps they didn't want to face outraged parents with the news of rampant buggery at St. Thomas; or imperil the reputation of the school, especially during those unpredictable revolutionary times. Whatever the case, we were given a stern warning with the threat of disclosure if it ever happened again. We were then dismissed.

* * *

In mid-April Pop flew to the US, going first to New York and Pennsylvania on business, and then on to Atlanta, Albuquerque and San Francisco to see his newborn grandson.

Castro, too, visited the US on a ten-day trip in mid-April, where he was greeted everywhere by exuberant crowds. TV had more or less returned to normal broadcasting, but special events always received full coverage. Because the month before Castro had expropriated the properties of ITT (International Telephone and Telegraph Company) in Cuba and had taken over control of its affiliate, the Cuban Telephone Company (CTC), some of the reporters of the American Society of Newspaper Editors, his hosts, asked him outright whether he was a Communist. Castro publicly denied the allegations.

Pop must have been somewhat reassured in spite of owning 50 shares of CTC valued at $5,000 (about $50,000 in 2010 dollars), shares in which he still held ownership. The Cuban Telephone Company was, after all, a public utility with a de facto monopoly—to many, an excusable target for government takeover. Telephone rates dropped.

But then, in mid-May, Castro signed the Agrarian Reform Act, which, in a little over one year, expropriated nearly half the land in the country, forbade foreign land ownership, and nationalized cattle ranches. Farms were restricted to 13 km^2 with other real estate holdings limited to 993 acres. The majority of expropriated property was retained by the government for state-run communes, while the remainder was redistributed to peasants in 67 acre parcels.

To implement the new law, Castro established the National Agrarian Reform Institute and named *Che* Guevara as its head. Expecting some resistance, Guevara created a special militia to enforce the reforms. Though he supported agrarian reform, Pop began to worry about the foreign ownership bit.

We owned a small 13.75 acre piece of rural land, Finca León, valued at $7,000 (about $70,000 today). It was well below the maximum allotment and was not a farm, but it was definitely foreign-owned.

By this time, Pop was hedging his bets—probably a strategy he would have used no matter how confident of the future he was. As a good businessman, he tended to minimize risk by not putting all his eggs in one basket. This took the form of creating diverse partnerships, limiting capital outlay, never becoming the official CEO of any enterprise, etc. Howard relied on talent instead of subterfuge to pursue his objectives.

Meanwhile, President Urrutia, to allay growing fears of Communist infiltration of the government, declared himself a strong anti-Communist and began attacking the ideology. In response, Fidel Castro theatrically resigned as Prime Minister, demanding Urrutia's resignation. In mid-July, Urrutia and his entire cabinet, pressured by Castro, newspapers, and a 500,000-strong protest march, resigned the Presidency. A week after his own resignation, and in the presence of great public consternation, Castro resumed his post as Prime Minister, giving long speeches both when he resigned and again when he resumed the office. He replaced Urrutia with Osvaldo Dorticós Torrado, an obscure Cuban Communist Party lawyer, again without a vote.

Six months after gaining power Castro made his first foreign revolutionary foray, in part to distract public opinion from the Urrutia cock-up: He attempted an invasion of the Dominican Republic. But it was an ill-planned, pathetically executed affair. Rafael Trujillo, the Dominican dictator—and a truly sadistic butcher—was perceived in Cuba as the twin of—the much more benign—Batista. Castro proudly declared that it was his duty to extend his Revolution over to the sister republic. It was a wildly popular move, because Trujillo had helped Batista in every way he could. But the real reason was revenge. Trujillo had done everything he could to derail Castro's revolution and, as the future would later reveal, Castro's grudges would rival his speeches in endlessness.

Castro's expeditionary force of 200 men was wiped out by Trujillo's army, which had been tipped off and was awaiting them. What few survivors remained were soon dispatched when Trujillo offered $1000 *per head* for the fugitives. The *campesinos*—the peasants—took him literally. Farmers started showing up at Dominican army posts with burlap bags of bearded heads to collect their rewards. Trujillo ended up paying more than $250,000, according to CIA operative Félix Rodriguez, because a lot more bearded heads were being turned in than there were Cuban invaders. (The ancillary irony is that when Batista fled, he sought refuge in Santo Domingo from Trujillo; but Trujillo held him hostage for months until Batista paid him a ransom of many millions of dollars from his ill-gotten gains. Only then did the Dominican President allow him to fly into permanent exile in Portugal.) Undeterred, a month later Castro launched an identical operation against Haiti's dictator, Papa Doc Duvalier. There were practically no survivors.

More troubling than the Agrarian Reform Act was the establishment of the ironically titled Ministerio de Recuperación de Bienes Malversados (MRBM), or Ministry for the Recuperation of Ill-Gotten Gains. Established in January of 1959, it at first focused on the recovery of the previous regime's illicit proceeds. But it didn't hit full stride until later that year when it began going after exiles' property. Its remit extended over every type of private property, owned by just about anybody, down to personal jewelry and silverware. Historian Herminio Portell-Vilá says that, "it functioned capriciously, without the rule of law, anarchically, settling cases hastily…and without the protection of (the courts)." It even ransacked banks' safe-deposit boxes—without warrants—for loot. By the end of 1959, the MRBM had confiscated 58 million dollars' worth of property, a figure that would, by 1961, rise to over 400 million.

* * *

Pop hadn't quite become like the proverbial slowly-boiled frog, but he decided to take a break from the increasingly bad omens in Cuba and take an old-fashioned two-month car trip in the US with the family.

Mina and we three kids flew to Merida, Yucatan from Havana while Pop flew in from New York, where he had probably been hedging his financial bets for possible exile. It was Naná's, Patsy's and my first trip abroad to a country other than the US or Cuba. And what a trip it was.

Mexico was a huge shock. Hot Yucatecan fare—to a Cuban about as strange as eating turnips and mud—was the first salvo. Hot, in the sense of *picante*, was an unknown concept to us. Chilies are not used in Cuban cuisine, which is primarily Spanish based. But it was a sensation for which I soon developed a taste. We couldn't decipher Mexican culinary terms. *Refried* beans in the Yucatan consisted of a turd-shaped and sized, crusty 4-inch serving of *fried* black beans—a source of unending adolescent glee at mealtimes. In Cuba, that was a rare and exotic side dish simply labeled 'fried beans', and shaped rather differently. It made no sense to call something that was fried once, *re*fried. And then there was that pancake, a *tortilla*. We had never seen such a contraption. In Cuba, a tortilla was a Spanish omelet with potatoes and onions, and sometimes Spanish sausage. The Mexican version, a flat, unleavened bread, though totally different, was good. We never liked Cuban tamales, made of bland corn mush with a dollop of pork mixed in and wrapped in banana leaves; so we avoided the much tastier Mexican tamales—until years later when we discovered how delicious they were.

Montezuma's Revenge laid me and Naná up for a week. When not sick, we spent a lot of time in the hotel's pool, since we were not allowed out on the streets of Merida, and Yucatan at that time, lacked TV signals. But it took a while to get us into that pool. Though the water was clear and clean, the sides and bottom were lined with slippery green algae, an extremely uninviting prospect. Pop led the way.

And the Mexicans! All dark and Indian-looking—very strange coming from Cuba, where the Spanish had exterminated the indigenous population and the only Indian visage we were familiar with was Hatuey, the Taino chief who'd led a revolt against the colonizers and now graced the brand of Cuban Hatuey beer. We were shocked at the number of beggars—young and old; fit and missing limbs that frequented the sidewalks. As the second wealthiest country in Latin America, Cuba had few beggars, and we never passed by one without contributing something. But in Mexico, that was impossible.

In Cuba, no one had ever given us a second look, but in Mexico, we stood out and were perceived as strange—a very uncomfortable experience—not just because of our looks, but also because of the way we spoke. Cuban Spanish is to Mexican Spanish as Brooklynese is to Liverpudlian Scouse. Mexicans spoke eccentrically, in sing-song cadences with unintelligible constructions, peppering their utterances with filler words that had no discernible meaning, such as *órale pues*, Mexico's answer to Canada's *eh?*, and using words for which they'd creatively discovered new meanings; or vice versa, inventing odd words for simple nouns, such as *canche* for *rubio*, or blonde; or *cuate* for friend. We soon learned, when attempting to find out when something was scheduled to happen, that *ahorita*, the diminutive form of *ahora*—meaning "now"—did not necessarily mean *now*; it instead often meant "soon." It was an adverb that, to a Mexican, was unconstrained by any time frame. While Cubans were always fashionably late, or just running late—in spite of wearing watches—Mexicans seemed to have absolutely no concept of time and wore watches strictly as jewelry—if at all. Additionally, Mexicans seemed reserved and deferential, always addressing everyone with the formal *usted* instead of the more informal *tu*. But they were always relaxed, unlike hyper-active Cubans.

One day we went to visit a Mexican acquaintance of Mina's, probably a schoolmate from her time in Louisiana. The concrete house, a combination of interior and exterior space full of foliage, included a crocodile for a pet. The croc had its own space, enclosed on three sides but open to the rest of the house on the fourth side, with a small, shallow pool, about 6 inches deep and just barely large enough to contain the 6-8 foot beast. It was a Morelet's Crocodile, common along the Caribbean coast of Central America, and only occasionally aggressive.

We were aghast. Naná and I recoiled reflexively. The croc ignored us. It was inconceivable to entertain a crocodile for a pet. Petting it? Cuddling with it? Impossible! What was the attraction? Might it not turn on its owners? Did it have the consciousness to know and appreciate its owners? Our host answered all of our feverish questions but took advantage of our naiveté, toying with our disquietude by always subtly alluding to some risk by, for example, saying they usually fed it raw meat, but sometimes gave it a live shoat—and that it was important to keep it fed. And yes, the croc sometimes wandered about the house at will—just like a *real* pet.

We also visited Yucatan's Maya ruins, another otherworldly experience for us. In 1959, none of the structures were cordoned off, and we could stroll around at will. Pop hired a guide to help us make sense of it all and, knowing Pop, contribute to the local economy. My immediate response, probably an omen of my future addiction to mountaineering, was to climb Chichen Itzá's grand pyramid. Even with the small feet of a 9-year-old, the tiny steps intimidated me; but no one stopped me, so up I went—my first notable summit.

I don't know how long we spent in Merida. Time, to a kid, is now, forever, soon, and whenever—and it always seems longer than it actually is. We left the Yucatan for Mexico City, where Mina had another school friend. All I remember was that she was very well-off and we stayed at her family's mansion. Whether it was more than one night, I have no idea. We had to be very polite.

From Mexico City we flew to Albuquerque, New Mexico. Pop's three brothers and one sister lived together there. The brothers had never married. They grew a large truck garden and ate plain New England fare. Quiet, reserved, stuck in their ways, they were very kind. They sipped their Miller's Specials, a concoction of soda water, gin, and grapefruit juice, ceremoniously at calibrated time intervals. Mina couldn't find commonality with them—and never quite did.

Pop bought a VW microbus (as a dealer, he got a discount) in Albuquerque and we drove it to San Francisco to see John. Either on the way there or on the way back, we visited the newly-opened Disneyland and afterwards Yosemite, Yellowstone and Grand Teton National Parks.

All I remember of Disneyland was the ride through the Matterhorn. The artificial mountain intrigued me no end. Riding through it I ignored the euphoria of the roller coaster and concentrated on examining the mountain's skeleton. The seemingly higgledy-pigledy girders made sense, but I couldn't figure out how they'd constructed the Matterhorn's skin.

Driving through Yosemite I was gripped by an uncontrollable desire to get onto the sensual granite slabs of Tuolumne Meadows. The urge was so strong that I begged my parents to stop and "do something" out of the car. However, nine-year-olds are clueless and tactless. I pouted, and quietly deeply resented my parents' physical shortcomings. Pop was 60 plus, suffering from arthritis and a heart condition; Mamá was becoming increasingly overweight—she'd never been physically active. Anyway, we had miles to go and parking along the winding, 2-lane road was scarce. Finally, at one pull-out, we stopped. I ran my fingers over the smooth salt-and-pepper rock and then ran a short way up the slabby apron. I didn't get nearly enough of the experience, but at least regained my good humor.

In Yellowstone we could all enjoy the improbably predictable geysers, bubbling chocolate-pudding mud pots, pie-crust terrain, stinky tea-kettle boiling pools and soda water fountain springs that were all adjacent to the roadside. The begging bears, bison herds and elk were animals we had never seen. At one car back-up a mama bear with a cub was working the sedans, going from one to another hoping for a handout. Little Patsy was mesmerized, until the bear came to our micro-bus window. Patsy panicked. In a fit of ecstacy and fear, she dropped the tid-bit she had on offer.

When we reached the Tetons, it was I that did an emotional somersault. The atavistic urge I'd experienced in Yosemite possessed me. Parked in front of the range at Lupine Meadows, Naná and Patsy fed the begging squirrels, while I stared entranced at the serrated summits. The air was so clear and crisp I could smell the peaks; they seemed so close I could reach out and touch them. The meadow, an intense, emerald green, seduced me. I took my shirt off and rolled in the grass, oblivious to the mosquitoes. I asked Mamá if I could climb the mountains. She said they were farther away than I realized. However, ever since Yosemite, she'd come to some sort of realization about me. "*Como no* (of course)," she said.

It was a lesson I never forgot and, as a teacher later in life, often applied. I was back within the hour, deterred but not disillusioned. The unconditional support she offered became a lifelong reservoir of tenacity and hope.

We spent most of August at the Indian Arms apartments on Indian School Road in Phoenix—most of the time immersed in the pool to mitigate the 120 degree heat. Pop then flew to New York while Mina drove us to New Orleans, where she picked up Pop on his return from New York. From there we drove to Miami to take the ferry back to Havana.

How we managed to get out of Cuba for this little vacation was probably due to our American citizenship. By this time, leaving Cuba was already becoming difficult. The first US Coast Guard rescue of refugee Cubans escaping in a small craft across the Florida Straits occurred on July 22, 1959. Nine men were picked up off the Dry Tortugas near Key West. "During the first six years of Castro's revolution, the Coast Guard rescued almost seven thousand Cubans attempting the journey in makeshift craft," writes Lily Prellezo in *Seagull One: The Amazing True Story of Brothers to the Rescue.*

* * *

The fall school term at St. Thomas began unremarkably. Discipline was strict. All meals were eaten in silence at round tables covered with white tablecloths, four cadets to the table. The boys were expected to eat everything served. No metal trays for these little soldiers; meals were served on chinaware accompanied by glassware for beverages, with cloth napkins and metal silverware at the side. Lieutenant Martinez, the humorless martinet, served as proctor, hands clasped behind his back, rigid as a Titan II missile, walking slowly among the tables ensuring compliance with all the rules. Captain Garcia often stood by the door, keeping a disinterested eye on the proceedings.

One day polenta was served. It was steamy, greasy, yellow and very cheesy. I wouldn't touch it—I could barely eat the rest of my food for the penetrating smell of melted cheese. I hated cheese. The very thought of it caused olfactory nausea, gastro-intestinal ructions, and extreme mental distress. I was later to suspect that I suffered from lactose intolerance.

On his rounds about the tables, Lieutenant Martinez spotted the untouched luteous blob on my white plate from across the room. He made a beeline for my table and ordered me to eat. I tried to explain my aversion, but he ignored me, sternly whacking the table with his riding crop, indicating that the next whack would be on me.

So I ate.

Three forkfuls into the mush, it all erupted out onto the plate, now tinged with green bile. Lieutenant Martinez wasn't moved. He whacked his crop again, this time across my chest, and ordered me to eat my vomit.

I did.

But the now-recycled glop made a second curtain call. At that point, Captain Garcia came over and had a quiet word with the Lieutenant. Martinez excused himself, Garcia walked away, and I was left to ponder the finer points of discipline. I told no one about the incident.

* * *

Next to Fidel, 27-year-old Camilo Cienfuegos was the most popular Comandante in the Revolution—and he was probably more trusted, because of his unassuming, transparent demeanor. *Che* Guevara wasn't even in the same league. Though popular, not only was he a foreigner, he was also an ideologue who wasn't affected by the limelight. Raúl had power due to his position as Fidel's brother, but he wasn't popular. Fifth down that line—though third in command after the Castro brothers—stood Comandante Huber Matos, who had been made military commander of Camagüey province.

Cuban military ranks had been subjected to curious political manipulations ever since 1933 when Sergeant Fulgencio Batista led his non-commissioned officers' coup against both the higher echelons and, by later behind-the-scenes machinations, the government. He'd then promoted himself incrementally to colonel, then general.

Throughout Latin America, rank inflation since the wars for independence had gotten out of control, like incontinent old men engaging in a pissing contest. Titles such as Field Marshal, Emperor, Dictator-for-Life, and Most Serene Highness, all self-conferred and bandied about to a degree that relegated the rank of General to dog catcher proliferated. Probably the most absurd stretch of military rank protocol was Mexican President Antonio López de Santa Anna's conferral of a state funeral with full military honors to his amputated leg.

Fidel Castro took a different approach, even though his rank of *Comandante*, Commander, was also self-conferred. Comandante was the highest rank in the Rebel Army. There were only 16 Comandantes including Fidel. It was a stratagem that implied humility and equality, a fiction that didn't take long to evaporate, with the *primus inter pares* becoming simply *primus*.

In late October of 1959, Comandante Huber Matos, along with 14 of his officers, resigned citing the appointment of Communists to key positions of power in the government. Matos had declared against Batista the very same day, March 10, 1952, that the ex-President grabbed power, by leading a protest at the school at which he taught.

After joining Castro's forces, Matos was put in command of Column 9 and tasked with securing Oriente Province and its capital, Santiago de Cuba, Cuba's second largest and most important city after Havana. Success, which he achieved through heavy combat and artfully deceptive stratagems—with a minimum of casualties—united Fidel's forces in the western Sierra Maestra with Raúl's forces in the eastern Sierra Maestra, the Sierra Cristal. Matos fought alongside his men and became a well-seasoned combat veteran.

Huber Matos, Commander of the 9th Column, Antonio Guiteras, in the 26 of July rebel forces. Arrested by Camilo Cienfuegos on orders of Fidel Castro in October, 1959 for wanting to resign his commission in protest to the Communization of the Revolution. Sentenced to 20 years imprisonment, Matos served 16 in solitary confinement. He was released in 1979 and exiled to Miami.
Date: 1959. Credit: Felices Company. Source: R. H. Miller collection.

There was already some bad blood between Castro and Matos. Matos had risen through the revolutionary ranks for his dedication, bravery, organizational ability and principled stands. But he wouldn't kowtow to Castro. Fidel had a penchant for dressing down and humiliating his officers in front of their men for no reason other than to turn them into sycophants. When his turn came, Matos would have none of it. He respectfully called Castro on that manipulative gambit and left the guerrilla leader speechless. Additionally, Matos publicly proved himself braver than Castro.

It happened during a planning conference at Fidel's mountain redoubt. Batista planes were strafing the area. Castro and his entourage immediately retreated into a purpose-built shallow cave. Matos perceived little danger. He'd lived through so many straffings and bombings, he could discriminate between general aerial terror and targeted attacks. This was just part of the aerial melee that was mostly ever-present throughout the Sierra in rotating sorties. Castro ordered him into the cave but Matos refused, standing outside a few feet away and continuing the conference: Matos thought the confines of the little cave stuffy and smelly. It was a snub the *máximo líder* never forgot.

Using the pretext that Matos was organizing counter-revolution, Fidel dispatched Camilo Cienfuegos to arrest him. But Camilo didn't want to arrest Matos—the two men were close and shared similar misgivings about the course the Revolution was taking. He argued with Castro that Matos was an honorable man and should be allowed to resign for reasons of conscience, that Matos was no danger to the Revolution, that he was not planning an uprising, and that he was a man who kept his word, that arresting Matos would be "a sticking of one's foot in one's mouth." But Castro wasn't moved. He'd already sidelined and disparaged the popular Camilo within the inner circles of power. What's more, according to Matos, Raúl despised Camilo, jealous of his popularity and lack of nomothetic ideology. Matos speculated that sending Camilo to arrest him was a set-up to rid the Revolution of both men. With luck, Matos and his men would resist arrest in a shoot-out. But Matos didn't resist. So Camilo arrested all fifteen men and incarcerated them.

Days later, Camilo set up an escape plan for Matos with a plane and pilot to fly him into exile. Matos refused on principle. Afterward, when Camilo was returning to Havana, his plane, a Cessna 310, disappeared.

Some believe Castro ordered it shot down, perhaps because Camilo was becoming too popular or because he questioned Castro's orders. Others think it simply disappeared over the ocean during the night flight. A few days' search yielded nothing but speculation; speculation that, to this day, has only caused both sides to reach for more tenuous extremes of supporting evidence. However, according to Carlos *Cachorro* León, my cousin (of whom we'll hear more in the second part of this book), recalls that the Castro government refused an independent search by the Cessna Company, which was skeptical of the government's conclusions. The Cessna 310 was designed with sections that would float *no matter what*. Cessna wasn't interested in embarrassing Castro, only in correcting possible flaws in their plane's design.

Though others were questioning Castro's intentions, it was the Cienfuegos-Matos affair that put the first doubts about the Revolution in my ten-year-old mind. Matos was sentenced to 20 years imprisonment in the Cárcel Modelo on the Isla de la Juventud (Isle of Pines). That he wasn't executed Matos attributes to the many rebel soldiers loyal to him. He served his full sentence, much of it in solitary confinement, subjected to multiple beatings and torture. Afterward, he joined the Miami-based anti-Castro CID, *Cuba Independiente y Democrática*.

I wasn't the only doubter. Matos' conviction marked the end of the "revolutionary coalition" between moderates and radicals, and put the great Cuban exodus that continues to this day into high gear.

* * *

By mid-December, only nine of the original 21 ministers of the revolutionary government remained. With Raúl Castro as Minister of Defense, Dorticós in the presidency, Guevara in charge of the Central Bank, and himself as Prime Minister, Castro had concentrated all the reins of power in his hands.

Money, instead of being the root of all evil, is the tangible, distilled essence of a person's best efforts; a repository that allows him to store his labor and talents in tiny bits of otherwise useless paper and metal for later conversion to food, housing, clothing, transportation, dreams, and even love. For safekeeping, once the reservoir exceeds, say, a month's earnings, people usually resort to the safety of a bank, where funds are guarded and insured. It is a sacred trust.

How *Che* Guevara, an Argentine doctor, became head of the Cuban National Bank owes more to ideology than to expertise. Soon after taking power Fidel had to transition his confidants from military duties to civilian appointments. During one brainstorming session—according to a story Guevara told David Atlee Phillips (Pop's CIA tenant) at a popular Cuban coffee house—Fidel asked who among them was a dedicated economist. *Che* Guevara, for some unknown reason, heard 'dedicated communist'. His arm shot up, so Castro appointed him first, Minister of Industries, then Finance Minister, and finally President of the National Bank in November of 1959.

The Argentine immediately began a series of draconian currency controls that, in effect, stole depositors' money. But he did it incrementally, so that depositors wouldn't withdraw all their money and run. Much later, between June and October of 1960, these controls culminated in the nationalization of all the banks. And then, on August 4 of 1961, in a quick sleight-of-hand move, he announced the introduction of a new currency, convertible only in limited amounts. Most Cubans' life savings suddenly shrank or even disappeared. Here's how it worked:

1. Law No.963, covering currency change is passed. The law states that as of August 6, a new currency will be introduced and the old currency will

be retired. The exchange rate will be at par, and exchange is mandatory during August 6 and 7, starting at 8 am. Past bank closing time on August 7, the old currency will no longer be valid or exchangeable.

2. During those two days, each nuclear family can only change $200 pesos ($200 dollars). Any amount in excess of $200 will be deposited in a "Special Account" in the name of the depositor. Any currency remaining outside of Cuban territory after August 7 will become null and void.

3. Those who fail to declare their fungible assets during this period will lose them and be subject to 6 months to 5 years imprisonment.

4. During those two days, all boats and planes traveling to and from Cuba were suspended.

5. On August 9, Fidel Castro declares Law No.964 whereby anyone presenting more than $10,000 for the currency exchange/"Special Accounts" program will have the excess confiscated, while sums below $10,000 will only be available at the rate of $100 per month. Confiscated funds will be used to reduce the government's debt to the National Bank of Cuba.

6. Fidel Castro netted $462,100,000 in old bills not exchanged, with another $35,500,000 in restricted "Special Accounts."

Two months later, in a macabre twist, the National Bank of Cuba took out a full-page ad in the newspapers inviting the populace to deposit their savings: "Moneys deposited in the Banco Nacional is guaranteed safe and free of all risks."

Guillermo Vicente Vidal, a Pedro Pan evacuee and much later to become mayor of Denver, describes the currency transformation in his memoir *Boxing for Cuba*:

> *"Then, in an effort to end the distinctions between Cuba's economic classes in a single astonishing move, Fidel announced that the nation's longstanding currency henceforth would have no value, meaning that stocks, bonds, savings, and financial instruments of every kind were suddenly worthless. In place of the old currency, every Cuban now would receive a one-time payment of 200 new Cuban pesos—no more and no less. Every one of us were suddenly economic equals...robbed of the results of their life's work. Papi was beside himself with anger, loss, and the deepest kind of desperation. Everything he strived for—and the very work that had proved his worth as a man—now were gone."*

I cannot begin to imagine the stress Pop and Mina were undergoing towards the end of 1959, but I'm certain they were no longer at all sanguine about the direction the Revolution was taking. I seldom saw either one—not that they'd confide their worries and troubles to us kids. In his action against the Cuban government, filed under the International Claims Settlement Act of 1949, Foreign Claims Settlement Commission of the United States, Pop would file a sub-claim of $24,219 for "Impairment to health & loss of ability to work."

It wasn't just his immediate family that Howard was worrying himself sick about; it was also his employees, their families, their livelihoods; the employees of his enterprises and their families. These were people who depended on him and his businesses for a living. He was concerned about all of them equally. Pop came from a family that took in stray cats; that, upon encountering an upside-down beetle, would stop to right it; that shooed away flies instead of killing them; that wrote poetry to pass the time—a family so shy, sensitive, quiet, and self-effacing that few of his siblings ever married, preferring to continue living together for the rest of their lives.

Christmas of 1959 revealed little of the brewing storm. The big public controversy was Castro's suggestion that true Cuban patriots should decorate a palm tree as a Christmas tree instead of an imported pine tree, and should relegate *Santiclós* to the dustbin of history. We stuck to a locally grown pine tree.

Pop and Mina went all out. When we kids awoke at 5 am and tip-toed down the stairs to see what *Santiclós* had brought, there were more presents under that tree than I had ever seen. But the *piece de resistance* was the elaborate, full-scale, Lionel train set with my name on it; one which, when it came time to leave the island, I was forced to leave behind. By the end of the year, more than one-hundred-thousand Cuban refugees had gone to the US.

I well remember New Year's 1960. Alone, at the end of one of the streets that butted up to the Almendares Barránca, I reflected on my life thus far, and on the new decade and the changes it might bring. As I sat on the inner barricade, when midnight struck, I said goodbye to the '50s, realizing in amazement that they were forever gone and would never return—their events now part of the past. And I wondered what the new decade, the '60s, would bring. It was so curious, so concretely surreal, to stand at the exact threshold between my first and second decade. At the moment the clock struck twelve (not that I had a watch; the instant was marked by distant bells, bangs, and fireworks) I felt the pang of the irreversible passage of time, forever irretrievable.

A few minutes after midnight, I wandered home. No one questioned my whereabouts.

6

1960

Not everyone welcomed the New Year as contemplatively as I had. Now that *Che* Guevara held the three most important economic portfolios in Cuba—President of the National Bank, Minister of Industry, and head of Agrarian Reform—he began to rapidly extricate the Cuban economy from world markets and bring it into dependence on the Soviet Bloc. His first moves, to sever Cuba's ties with the Inter-American Development Bank and from the International Bank for Reconstruction and Development aka, the World Bank, were coupled to a sweetheart trade agreement with the USSR.

On February 6, Soviet Deputy Prime Minister Anastas Mikoyan visited Cuba and signed a preferential Trade and Payments Agreement worth $100 million in oil, petroleum products, wheat, iron, fertilizers, and machinery for…sugar. With the exits from the I-ADB and the World Bank, the Castro regime destroyed its traditional geo-political ties between Cuba and the Western World. Full diplomatic relations with the USSR were established in May after having been severed by Batista seven years previously after his coup in 1952. Ironically, it had been Batista who first established diplomatic relations with the USSR back in 1943, and who had brought a number of Communists into his government, albeit without voting rights.

Unites States responses to these moves began as early as October of 1959 with preliminary studies, and took actual form in January of 1960. Concerned about the possibility of another attempted Soviet military base in the Western Hemisphere only 5 years after the overthrow of the Marxist Arbenz regime in Guatemala, President Eisenhower ordered the CIA to create a Cuba Task Force to draft overt and covert response scenarios to the deteriorating diplomatic and human rights situation.

There are many misconceptions surrounding the US Central Intelligence Agency. Its basic remit under the Executive Branch is to gather information about foreign governments in order for the US to design an effective and appropriate foreign policy. Since the US cannot depend on CNN and Fox News for its information, it must rely on on-the-ground, on-the-spot sources abroad, along with satellite and electronic surveillance.

This is called "spying"—an essential operation for a practical and engaged foreign policy. The CIA is not a 'government onto itself', is not a military organization, does not have any law enforcement capabilities, took no part in Watergate, and is very limited in its domestic intelligence gathering. Its operatives have a GS 1-15 government employee rating and are subject to normal federal regulations.

The CIA, under specific executive branch orders, also promotes democracy in its wider sense: not just electoral democracy, but also individual rights and free markets. As to "overt" and "covert" actions, the first refers to US military operations; the second to aiding and organizing home-grown resistance against despotic regimes. Covert operations are impossible without credible and widespread domestic opposition within the target country. Since 1960, counter-terrorism and non-proliferation of nuclear weapons have been added to the CIA's priorities.

We kids had no inkling of the gravity of the impending changes until Naná, after playing at a neighbor's house, came home one evening with trivial gossip. Marcia, her friend, had sat her down conspiratorially on the bed to confide something her mom had told her: that "everyone will soon be leaving Cuba by boat because of the Communists."

When Naná told Mina about her talk with Marcia, it was more a shotgun shell of hidden queries than a comment: What did Marcia's mom mean? How could everyone leave Cuba by boat? Were *we* going to leave Cuba in a boat?

Mamá approached her response slowly and thoughtfully, first saying that talking politics was impolite, but then, after a long pause, adding that it was "dangerous to talk politics."

Whether nine-year-old Naná could make the connection between politics—as in elections and voting on the one hand—and leaving Cuba by boat on the other hand, as both being 'politics' is questionable, though she already had a healthy fear of Communism, not just from her catechism classes but from watching movies about the Spanish Civil War. At that age Naná was too slow and shy for follow-up questions. Nonetheless, Mamá's response and the way she delivered it made a deep and lasting impression on Naná.

As for me, an even more blatant incident went completely over my head. I had been assigned a poem to memorize and recite at an upcoming public forum at St. Thomas, celebrating something I can't recall. When the day arrived, Mina was present, sitting with all the proud parents and attendees on movable bleachers. In between presentations, the St. Thomas Military Academy brass band played martial music. For a short while, I took center stage.

I don't remember being nervous or even the gist of the poem, but there was only perfunctory applause afterward, even though my recitation had been flawless. At the close of the ceremonies, Mina was nowhere to be found. I waited patiently by the car for her appearance. After a while I spotted her marching around the corner, headed for me, all four horsemen of the Apocalypse in one big bundle of angry woman. Steam was coming out of her head but she said nothing during the drive home. I retreated into inconspicuousness, unwilling to experience any collateral damage from that critical mass.

Later, I overheard Mamá and Pop discussing the incident. Mina thought the poem was un-American. But not just 'un-American'—it was a load of scurrilous lies made to be delivered by a 10-year-old American kid to a Cuban audience. Mina took it personally. But she also didn't take it as an isolated incident. She was connecting dots that led all the way up from a poem at St. Thomas, through the new public policy ukases now filtering into education at even private schools, to Fidel Castro himself.

I was later to glean that it was this incident that, for Mina, sealed our exit. Trivial as it seemed, compared to the conflicts Pop must have been struggling with, forthcoming events were to indicate that Pop was doggedly insisting on reconciling irreconcilable views. His concern for the family butted up against his optimism that everything would not turn out as bad as the Cassandras perceived. Mina's insistence convinced him to leave, yet he remained frustratingly diffident. He took no concrete steps to divest himself of Cuban assets, thinking that his businesses and expertise would be beneficial to the new order—or, since I'm trying to delve into a mind long gone—he did not want to raise any red flags with the regime by appearing to be about to leave the sinking ship.

But a sinking ship it was. By March of 1960 the *New York Times* reported five "serious" anti-Castro groups—out of a recorded 184—operating out of Miami, supporting a revived guerrilla resistance force in the Escambray Mountains. Soon after, President Eisenhower—who continued the arms embargo of 1958, begun so as not to take sides in the Revolution— authorized a "Covert Action Plan Against Cuba," which included the organization of a paramilitary force of Cuban exiles to overthrow Castro— what was to become the Bay of Pigs invasion.

One week after Eisenhower's authorization, David Atlee Phillips, our old tenant, was appointed Director of Propaganda for the Cuba Operation. He immediately began the project to set up and run Radio Swan, the disinformation arm of the operation. The powerful CIA anti-Castro radio campaign was based on Swan Island, an uninhabited tiny dot in the Caribbean halfway between Nicaragua and Cuba, but claimed by Honduras. Starting out with 40 CIA operatives, nearly 600 US non-combatants were to be involved in the entire Bay of Pigs operation—as trainers, organizers, technical experts, and all-round fixers.

Mamá and Pop flew to New York that March, then to Westchester, Pennsylvania on business—and to lay the groundwork for our exile. They'd come up with a plan.

Part of that plan was boarding schools for Naná and me once the summer of 1960 was over, so our parents could remain "nimble" in case they had to act quickly due to changing circumstances (I can't help but also think that it might have been to ease Mamá's transition into "homemaker"—a role she'd never played—since she'd only be taking care of little Patsy once we other two were away at school).

From Westchester they flew to New Orleans, rented a car and drove to De Quincy, Louisiana, where Mina had cousins. While in De Quincy Mina contacted the convent she'd attended back in the '30s at Grand Coteau, Louisiana. They agreed to take Naná. The problem was that their grades began with the 5th grade, and Naná would have only graduated 3rd grade. The problem was quickly solved, no doubt with Naná's math grades and a little alumni pressure. Skipping a grade right into the grade I, who was one year older, was in became a source of endless superiority for Naná—to this very day. In her mind it was a triumph of talent over expediency.

But then there was me. Grand Coteau was a girls' school. What to do with Baten? Grand Coteau suggested St. Stanislaus, a Brothers of the Sacred Heart boarding school in Bay St. Louis, Mississippi, right on the Gulf Coast. St. Stanislaus already hosted a small variety of Latin American students, including a handful of Cuban refugees. Pop and Mina drove to the school. St. Stanislaus was glad to accept me for the upcoming school year.

Afterward Pop and Mina flew to San Francisco, then Atlanta, finally Miami and back to Havana to arrange our affairs. Being able to leave quickly had become imperative.

Just before the Easter holidays of 1960, Castro ordered an island-wide strike against foreign-owned businesses. My father arrived at his Envases Modernos paper factory to be welcomed by big red graffiti on the yellow walls urging "Miller *al paredón!*" (Miller to the firing squad wall). He knew it hadn't been painted by his workers; he knew them all too well and shared a mutual trust and affection with them. To him, it looked more like Fidel's handwriting on the wall—a much more troubling scenario. His diffidence disappeared.

Pop drove to the AIC offices downtown and told Hilda Navarro, his secretary, "I've got to leave".

Hilda, a large, fun-loving, twinkle-in-her-eye woman was incredulous. She responded, "Nonsense, I can live under any government", and agreed to hold down the fort for what they both believed would only be a temporary interlude. Later, after the 'temporary' became wishful thinking, she was to write Pop asking for help in seeking exile.

Two days later, under the guise of going on vacation, my father, mother and we three kids left for Ft. Lauderdale, Florida carrying a suitcase apiece and $25 each. My grandmother, Ana María Díaz y Otázo, stayed. She was too old and too Cuban to leave; and too parsimonious to abandon our grand mayoral residence to the clutches of Castro, as the new revolutionary laws was very soon to require.

We didn't stay in Florida, but instead immediately left for De Quincy, Louisiana, where Mina's American cousin, Frances, taught at the public school, a fine old brick building surrounded by Spanish moss-laden oaks. Her husband Cecil was the principal. We rented a house and settled there temporarily to—according to Mina—allow us kids to finish what remained of the school year. However, our family needed a respite—a time to rest, gather our thoughts, and think through our next move. Was going back to Cuba in the cards? If we stayed in the US, where should we settle? What would Pop do for a living?

Frances and Cecil were the epitome of southern hospitality. Besides finding us a place to rent and enrolling us in school, we were dinner guests nearly every night, after which the adults would endlessly discuss our options, possibilities, plans, politics, and future scenarios. Bored with the adult angst, we'd go outside and catch fireflies in Mason jars. Frances and Cecil had two daughters, slightly older than us. They were somewhat reluctant—in that haughty southern way—to play with younger kids. This was exacerbated by our talking in Spanish, which they countered by talking in pig-Latin, to our great frustration—especially since I was developing a crush on the younger blonde.

Mina had never kept house before. Cooking, cleaning, taking care of three children overwhelmed her, though she seldom showed it. She enlisted us kids to help by assigning chores—another concept we were unfamiliar with—in a typical American fashion: Baten on garbage duty, Naná doing dishes. Six-year-old Patsy got off easy pretending to help Mamá clean. I remember sliced white bread being a mealtime staple. It was there that we discovered peanut butter. At first, thinking it was a dairy product due to the word "butter" in the name—something all three of us kids detested—we refused to try it. Assured that it wasn't, we gingerly tasted a spoon-tip of it. Soon we couldn't get enough of it. Later, when hordes of Cuban refugees flooded Florida, peanut butter was one of the staples handed out by the US government as assistance to tide over refugee families in their transition. It was just as strange to them. My aunt Marta accumulated shelves full of #10 cans (creamy style), which she hoarded in her garage. She scorned the stuff but knew it was valuable and refused to part with the cans.

De Quincy's elementary school was worlds apart from St. Thomas Military Academy. The teachers were kind and helpful, making sure our language shortcomings were not an impediment. Math was a breeze; Cuban schools were way ahead in that department. But Naná found spelling, which had an entire class period dedicated to it, quite incomprehensible. In Spanish, almost all words are spelled exactly as they sound, so no formal course in spelling is needed. English sound and spelling are historical and retain vestigial elements of the language's evolution, so until we could figure out their abstruse logic, we resorted to memorization. Still, to this day, we pronounce English words we see for the first time as if they were in Spanish.

The kids neither shunned nor befriended us—it was up to us to make acquaintances. The boys played a running competition of counting coup by attempting to land a kiss on a girl. The girls reacted with disgust. Some kids came to school barefoot and shirtless, outfitted in denim cover-alls or a jump suit—like characters on *Hee Haw*—all grimy-faced and dirty. "They're just poor," our teacher said when we asked. At the end of May, I graduated 4th grade and Nani 3rd grade, after which we hit the road again, this time continuing our plan—however dubious and flexible.

The second part of Pop and Mina's plan was to settle in Miami—for the time being. Not only to better monitor the situation in Cuba but also to be near family and friends.

The drive along the Gulf Coast was dominated by the 1960 Nixon-Kennedy election, ever-present on the radio. The kids plumped for Kennedy: he was young, Catholic, handsome, and promised change—at least in style. Mamá was skeptical. She said Kennedy was inexperienced. She had a lot more confidence in Nixon.

Eight months later Mina was proved right. During the campaign, Kennedy had talked tough on Cuba, going so far as to imply armed intervention. Nixon had responded by calling him irresponsible. The irony was that Nixon, as Vice-President, knew about Eisenhower's Covert Action Plan Against Cuba—what would become, at the very last minute, the Bay of Pigs invasion. But the plan was top secret and Nixon didn't want to let the cat out of the bag. It was a very awkward moment for him.

With the invasion scheduled approximately sometime between elections and inauguration, President Eisenhower decided to postpone the operation until the new president would have the opportunity to review and approve it. After Kennedy was elected, he was finally briefed about the proposed invasion on January 28, only 10 weeks before D-day was actually launched—not enough time to carefully consider the plan and all its ramifications. Consequently, he was indecisive, relied on conflicting sources (the previous administration had been Republican), and made spur-of-the-moment decisions.

When we reached Miami Pop bought a modest house in a suburban neighborhood. In a vain attempt to salvage some of his business interests, my father flew back to Havana in late June. He carried six-year-old Patsy with him. Why, I can't fathom. Either Pop was still in a state of partial denial as to the danger he was in, or it was a temptation to draw Abuela into exile with us. Either way, it was foolhardy.

Pop didn't even leave the airport (according to some accounts). An associate who met him there warned him to leave immediately as there was a warrant out for his arrest. For what, we never found out. Instantly he made a crucial decision: he left Patsy with Blake, his associate, and got back on the plane. I surmise that if he'd been arrested *with* Patsy, she would have passed into the hands of Castro's government. Better to leave her with friends who could later repatriate her to the US. Pop was unable to salvage anything in Cuba. Later, he was to successfully lobby the Kennedy administration to pass legislation to allow the deduction of Cuban property losses through the federal income tax.

How he financed the initial stages of our exile will forever remain a mystery—but he did. I don't remember asking where we were going or what our plan was, probably because the adventure of going from one exotic place to another on short notice was too much fun and kept us entertained. But, looking back on it, I realize we were connecting refugee dots, going from one friend or relative to another until we could figure out our next move.

* * *

Over the course of the spring and summer, Cuba nationalized all US companies and properties, singling out oil companies and banks. Meanwhile, Eisenhower's Covert Action Plan Against Cuba went into full swing. Work began on a 5,000-foot runway at an airfield at Retalhuleu in Guatemala to deliver and supply the Cuban exile force that was to begin training in the nearby mountains on the Pacific coast of Guatemala.

Although the entire operation was meant to be top secret, almost from the start it became an open secret, with both Castro's secret police and even journalists discovering and reporting on the operation. But I doubt that Pop was aware.

On October 13 the Urban Reform Act took effect. The legislation effectively outlawed the sale or rental of residential property. Existing rents that were not covered by the act were cut in half. Additional protocols stipulated ratios of inhabitants to floor space. To hang on to our big house—and to avoid eviction—Abuela invited the remaining servants' relatives to move in with her. Most of Carmen's immediate family took up the offer. Other, separate legislation nationalized nearly 400 Cuban companies and the three American-owned oil refineries. In retaliation, President Eisenhower extended the arms trade embargo to include US Cuban sugar purchases, US oil deliveries to the island, and various other items.

The by-now 55-year-old US trade embargo against Cuba first established by President Eisenhower was further broadened by President Kennedy and then made punitive under President Clinton through the Helms-Burton Act. The embargo wasn't just a retaliatory measure; it was a defensive measure. How could you trust a trading partner to pay his bills when at the same time he was stealing your property, to the tune of over $700 million by mid-1960?

* * *

Uncle John was more bullheaded. In spite of Aunt Marta's persistent nagging about the fact that Howard and Mina had left, that Howard was smart, that Mina wouldn't do something stupid, that he didn't want his sons to come to any harm, and that blah, blah, blah...John wasn't ready to leave Cuba. He was a tough operator, and took pride in obstinately resisting Marta. In October he finally relented—partially—and sent Marta and his sons Johnny and Richard off to the US. He, however, stayed behind, hoping to salvage something of his rapidly disappearing life's work.

What he thought of Operation Pedro Pan, I'll never know. Over the course of the summer and fall of 1960, the Castro regime had closed all parochial schools and expelled the nuns and priests who ran them, taking over the operation of all primary and secondary schools. Cuban parents were aghast. They feared the indoctrination of their children by the government; they feared that the Castro regime would take away their parental authority.

Remembering the airlift of Spanish children to the USSR during the Spanish Civil War for 'safety and education', and paying heed to the alarming rumors going about, over 10,000 worried parents, organized by James Baker, the headmaster of our kindergarten alma mater, Ruston Academy, and with the help of the Catholic Church and the US government—to the tune of a million dollars and visa waivers—organized an airlift of 14,000 children to Miami the day after Christmas.

Their fears turned out to have been altogether too true. Under the guise of the Literacy Campaign of 1960 and School Goes to the Countryside, thousands of kids were removed from their homes for 45-day periods to camp with their teachers in farming cooperatives, combining education with productive work. According to Flor Fernández Bárrios in her book, *Blessed by Thunder*, the abuse and punishment for non-conformity at the camps was nearly as bad as having to eat your own vomit. Even worse was the shipping of 1,000 kids to the Soviet Union in January of 1961 for schooling. Then, on May 1, Castro nationalized all private schools.

When, on January 3 of 1961 the US severed diplomatic relations with Cuba, Uncle John finally left, at the vanguard of what was to become an exodus of over one million Cubans during the next two decades.

Meanwhile, Pop still held illusions of returning to Cuba. These dreams were finally dashed in April of 1961 with the Bay of Pigs invasion. Mina, echoing Pop's sentiments—with just a dash of hope still expressed—wrote: "Invasion. Now chances of return very slim."

7

Exile

I had my own troubles. At the beginning of September Mina put me on a Greyhound bus bound for Bay St. Louis, Mississippi, my new home at St. Stanislaus boarding school, 900 miles away from Miami. Now nearly 11 years old, I boarded the bus stoically never questioning my parents' plans. Mina took the driver aside for a quiet word; she didn't want to lose me.

But drivers get relieved, and she did almost lose me. In Tallahassee I missed a connecting bus to New Orleans. Without any concept of American geography or Greyhound bus routes, I remained on the bus I was seated in because its destination, St. Luis, Missouri, sounded very much like Bay St. Louis. Somewhere in Tennessee, in the middle of the night, someone discovered that I was headed in the wrong direction. It was as close to total despair as I'd ever been—utterly alone, lost and forlorn, nearly English-less, penniless, and now suitcase-less.

At the next stop, lacking a proper verbal explanation, I showed my ticket to the driver when I was about to re-board after a rest stop. He looked troubled. Escorting me to the ticket window, he explained my situation while I nodded approvingly. The attendant escorted me to a bus headed in the right direction, explained to the driver what had happened, and made sure that driver personally passed me on to the next driver at my next connection. Tired, barely able to keep my eyes open, and trying to be as inconspicuous as I could, I headed for the back of the bus.

After sitting down, all the passengers turned and stared at me. When the driver noticed, he came back and moved me a few rows forward, explaining that the back of the bus was reserved for Negroes. I didn't understand—there were plenty of empty seats at the back. But I didn't argue.

At the New Orleans bus terminal I noticed the 'Colored only' signs at the rest rooms and water fountains. I wondered impishly what would happen were I to drink from a 'Colored only' fountain, but decided not to test my luck.

The Deep South in the early 1960s was in turmoil over civil rights. Coming from Cuba where there was no overt racism, the confrontations were inexplicable and terrifying to me. The segregation regime had the insidious effect of intensifying itself, like an evil feedback loop. Normally receptive to interacting with anyone, I began avoiding Negroes, perceiving them as unapproachable, exotic, and even dangerous—not that they themselves were dangerous, but for the wider consequences of associating with them.

It even affected Mina, as racially unprejudiced—albeit opinionated—a human being as ever existed. The only color she was concerned with was green, the color of money—essential for rearing children, caring for a sick husband and paying the bills. Shortly later, when we were managing apartments in Phoenix, civil rights groups would randomly target businesses to test their racial tolerance, subjecting those that failed their test to protests and demonstrations—definitely not good for business. Hotels, motels, and apartment houses would get either a visit or a phone call from a black couple inquiring as to availability. Mina instructed us to confirm that yes, we rented to colored folk, but that at that time we were full; or to quote them an almost absurdly high fee to discourage them—tactics that would later be laughably transparent.

I was aghast, angry, and contemptuous. How could my mother collaborate with such racist practices? How could she so blatantly lie, manipulate, and dishonor our high moral standards? What sort of example was she setting for her children? I argued with her, but at cross purposes— she arguing from practicalities; I from idealism.

It would be many years later that I came not to condemn her approach; and even later when I came to appreciate the tough position she was in. And only when Arizona Senator Barry Goldwater voted against the 1964 Civil Rights Act (the one that outlawed private businesses from discriminating) after having voted for the first two in 1957 and 1960 (which outlawed government discrimination)—commenting that the law can't see what's in a person's heart—that I realized that the connections between intent and action are more complex than I ever imagined and not easily reducible to a facile platitude. At the time I couldn't imagine Pop going along with that, but he did—quietly. Except in a letter to then-President Lyndon Johnson, about to present the 1964 Civil Rights Act to Congress, where Pop echoed Goldwater's concern:

"Certainly this law may have moral force; but…there are sections that are obviously unconstitutional; housing, for example. When I arrived in Phoenix, I had one #$@& of a time renting a 3 bedroom apartment (I have three children). I was met with "no children, no pets." And, while it did not make me happy, it is certainly the landlord's right. I let off steam by observing, "Oh, so you are against children, don't believe in them, eh?" Now, the Civil Rights Law will attempt to deny the landlord his rights!

"Let's face facts, when the Civil Rights legislation is being implemented, there is little doubt in my mind that nobody but a philanthropist will open housing to Negroes without committing economic suicide!

"I now own apartments here in Phoenix, and I certainly cannot afford to go bankrupt after the severe losses I suffered in Cuba!

"We should be on the road to an intelligent program to implement the Civil Rights law without impoverishing another section of our society."

We never saw Pop and Mina argue or fight: as far as we knew, they were always of one mind. On the other hand, besides being hands-off parents, Howard and Mina were hands-off partners. We never saw them being lovy-dovy with each other, holding hands or flirting—though they did call each other "darling" and "honey." Both of their many siblings also shared a reticence for physical contact; all implicitly demanded ample personal space. Perhaps, to make up for this reservedness, they instituted ritualized kissing. Every night before going to bed, and every morning after getting up, we children even—and especially—into our teen years were required to kiss each parent goodnight or good morning; otherwise, we might all have lived our lives without ever touching each other. Unlike many couples who bandy about the term 'love,' I never recall them saying they loved each other. However, they always expressed the greatest respect and admiration for each other, emotions infinitely more meaningful than the cliché 'love.'

* * *

St. Stanislaus was located right on the Gulf of Mexico, with a huge elevated pier extending out into the water from which the students were allowed to fish and, during the warmer months, to swim. Founded in 1854, the U-shaped, 3-storied brick complex retained the whiff of a Dickensian orphanage, with stationary, ink-well flip-top oak desks in giant study halls monitored by a proctor's desk, raised even higher than a judge's dais; pre-World War I, white-tiled lavatories topped with wire cubbies; rusty, coiled spring beds in three vast dormitories housing 11 to 18-year-old boys; always-cassocked clerics with heavy, ostentatious crucifixes dangling from their necks; and unquestioned discipline and regimentation enforced by example, penetrating gazes, razor strops, and wooden rulers. There were no colored students or faculty, except for one Osage Indian, one East Indian, and a couple of Hondurans, all of whom were darker than a pair of brown Oxfords.

Waterfront Bay St. Louis was both the business district and the white part of town, built primarily out of masonry. Inland, the roads turned to gravel, then dirt; the buildings to clapboard-on-stilts; and the skins to black. My classroom was somewhere in between, halfway to 'niggertown.' It was a one-room, white clapboard building, three blocks from the main campus on a dirt road. It was St. Stanislaus' only outlier—the archetypal one-room schoolhouse—and housed the school's 5th grade. Overarching the small structure was a giant oak tree with thick, extensive, and sinuous surface roots among which we'd play marbles at recess, each radiating pair of roots creating separate play areas. Kids would line up to challenge the winners of each round.

Lunchtime required a trek to the cafeteria, one of two more modern buildings back on the main campus. Meals were scheduled in three tranches, for Junior, Middle, and Senior Halls, and were served cafeteria style on partitioned metal army trays. It was my first exposure to grits, Kool-Aid, and SOS, which I soon learned meant shit-on-a-shingle. Unlike at St. Thomas, meals were unregimented, all-you-could-eat (or not eat) affairs. I didn't know what to make of grits and was flabbergasted that they were a daily breakfast staple. I tried salt and pepper like the other kids; sugar (they thought I was nuts); and even maple syrup. Nothing made them edible.

* * *

By the 6th grade, now in a classroom on the main St. Stanislaus campus, I became a philatelist. Perhaps it was to replace collecting Revolution bubble gum cards; perhaps only because I was a bit of what was to be termed OCD, obsessive compulsive disorder—a pretentious term for diligent behavior. Close by, St. Augustine's, an integrated Catholic seminary hosted a small stamp shop. Brother Joseph, a mulatto, tended the little outlet on weekends, the only time grade school boarders were allowed off campus. A friend and I regularly visited Brother Joseph's shop to ogle the available offerings on our $1-a-week allowance. It was our only sanctioned interaction with a colored person. After a while, I broached the subject of race with him. Brother Joseph breasted his cards, but not without sympathy. It wasn't a subject he wanted to pursue with us. A quarter would go a long way in a small Mississippi Gulf Coast town seminary stamp shop, and we kept going back.

St. Joseph's Girls' Academy was next door to St. Stanislaus. Nothing intensifies the hormonal surges of a pre-teen's and teen's development than the unavailable proximity of the opposite sex, coupled with the intimate proximity of your own sex. It was all we obsessed about—fleeting glimpses of the girls, imaginary trysts with stolen kisses and hands under blouses, wet dreams, wetting the bed, erections, masturbation, boys who liked boys (or were accused of liking boys), the morphology of each boy's genitals as espied during showers, and every imaginable prurient connection a pubertal boy could make. Nothing was too crass or out of bounds for these little crackers.

My constant struggle to balance these all-encompassing urges with the certitude of the raging fires of hell they guaranteed, never let up, and I found solace in greater piety. I took to attending mass every day and became a voracious reader of the lives of the saints, in the form of a Catholic book series the school library carried. Though nearly all the saints I read about were martyred in gruesome and horrible ways, the stories were really stories of triumph, since the saints never broke, always attained eternal glory, and became beacons of behavior and faith. When I'd read every last one of them, I began reading about the Holocaust and the Gulag. I found it easy to put myself in those shoes. Again, these were stories of incredible triumph against overwhelming odds, paeans to the human spirit—after all, they were mostly written by survivors. These, in turn, led to books with identical themes but in radically different genres: adventure books of survival, mountaineering, seafaring, and polar exploration—exploits that were all monuments to indomitable will, and which deeply influenced my later pursuits in life.

But it wasn't exultation I needed; it was the fear of God. So I turned to the tales of H. P. Lovecraft, Guy de Maupassant, and other masters of terror based on the supernatural. And I needed isolation from temptation (not realizing that one can't isolate oneself from oneself). So, in 7th grade, I decided to enter the religious life. I asked Brother Valery, fat and always jolly (he'd dress up as Santa Claus at Christmas), young and approachable, what it took to become a Brother of the Sacred Heart. He told me their seminary took candidates in right at high school. But he also admonished me as to what a serious decision entering Orders was, and what the wider consequences entailed. Practical as ever, I asked him what options one had when second thoughts impinged. I had a year in which to think things over, so I simmered the prospect indefinitely.

Friday nights Brother Ephrem, Junior Prefect of Discipline for the 5th, 6th, and 7th grades, would take us to the nickel movies. Brother Ephrem was thoroughly inscrutable and ageless, declaring silence at study hall with a sharp rap of the ruler on his desk. On miscreants, the rap would land on an open palm. He'd patrol the theatre aisles with a flashlight to deter any hanky-panky in the same manner that he'd patrol the dormitory after lights out. But he wasn't as vigilant on the grounds of the school, an open field with three brick handball courts on one side and two tether ball poles under the nearby oak trees.

Though I liked hand ball, I wasn't any good at it. Instead, I loved tether ball, queuing up for a match every chance I got. The biggest kid in Junior Study Hall, Vogel, was a passive bully. He was seldom aggressively intimidating but he always got his way, forcing his will through sheer presence. Once, playing Ponce, a small Guatemalan student, Vogel humiliated him for no reason at all. Ponce was a wide-eyed, squished-face and homely, socially inept waif with nearly no English and without any friends—except me. But Ponce never backed down, doggedly pursuing whatever he'd set his mind to, which is exactly how he befriended me—by sticking to my side and constantly engaging me.

When Vogel hit Ponce, I stepped in to defend him. It was a bad call. Not only did we have different fighting strategies—he a boxer, I a wrestler—but he was much bigger with a much longer reach. Try as I might, I couldn't get close to him. Every time I tried, he'd land a punch on my face. Still, I wouldn't give up. By this time we'd gathered a small crowd. Ponce kept to the margins. Finally, either by charging him and being overcome or by being pummeled, I found myself on the ground, nose bleeding, with Vogel on top demanding I say "uncle," an admission that had not quite yet become a cliché.

I was loath to give in, but when Vogel resumed punching me, I said uncle. Humiliating me further he admonished me, "that'll teach you to mess with me."

Yet it wasn't the last time I came to Ponce's aid. Finding out I'd acquired an off-campus pass, Ponce decided to accompany me on the outing. I asked him if he'd gotten a pass since he wasn't one to always color within the lines. He assured me he had, but his assurance was so fuzzy it was unconvincing—

and unconvincing to the Brother that discovered his absence. Through a combination of misunderstanding compounded by a language barrier and wishful thinking, Ponce was deemed in violation of the off-campus rules, a transgression considered so serious, it bypassed the principal and went right to Brother Hugh, President of St. Stanislaus, to whom he was called to account. Afraid of more misunderstandings, I insisted on accompanying Ponce.

Brother Hugh, usually a fair-minded and business-like man, had no time for complicated explanations during this inquisition. He limited me to translating his simplistic questions to Ponce and Ponce's naïve responses. Ponce looked terrified (but then he always did). Wasting no time, Brother Hugh made up his mind and asked me to translate the sentence. Down came Ponce's pants and out came the razor strop. Ponce bent over Brother Hugh's desk and took his undeserved wallops with equanimity and just a few tears. On the way out, there was little I could do to console him.

Although an honor student and serial awards recipient, I too once suffered the welts of the strop. All our clothes had to be tagged with our assigned number—mine being 60—so Brother Ramon, in charge of laundry, knew in whose bin which clothes belonged. One T-shirt Mina had overlooked marking had a Cuban clothes tag on it. Since I was the only small-sized Cuban, Brother Ramon tagged me. But his heart wasn't in it; three whacks to the bum, lest standards decline.

My $1-a-week allowance was just enough incentive for me to strive for more, even though there were few opportunities for money-making for a 13-year-old in boarding school. Like a fish facing tasty bait, I eagerly bit the first morsel offered. Fall football season in the Deep South was a particular American mania to which I'd never been exposed. Though St. Stanislaus hosted inter-high school sports, I wasn't even aware of them, most of the games being played off-campus. But one day, posted on the Junior Hall bulletin board, was a notice announcing a poster competition with a $5 first prize to the winner. The posters were to depict the inter-collegiate football matches between the regional universities, such as Ole Miss vs. LSU.

I had never drawn a thing in my life, but that didn't stop me. Gathering paper, tracing paper, pens, coloring pencils, two rulers, a protractor, a compass, stencils, perspective guidelines, and renditions of what I wanted to draw, I sat down to create spirit-enhancing football posters. To my complete surprise, I won. Afterward, for every weekend contest, the St. Stanislaus Junior Hall hosted a poster competition. I won every one. Unfortunately, football season only lasted through fall so, with part of my winnings, I invested in a shoe-shine kit. Upperclassmen, especially the dozen Latin Americans—Cubans, Costa Ricans, Hondurans, Panamanians, Mexicans— were natty dressers, always concerned with their appearance—though the upper crust Louisiana creoles weren't far behind. Without competition, I was soon raking in riches in nickels and dimes. Ponce, inspired by the easy money, quickly followed suit, but with his slapdash approach, few chose to get a shine from him. I'd begun an entrepreneurial trend that didn't quite fit into St. Stanislaus' regimen. To their credit, the Brothers of the Sacred Heart didn't interfere.

Most Latin American boys had traveled too far to leave campus for holidays, except perhaps for Christmas, which even some spent at St. Stanislaus, their parents having scrimped and saved just to send them to a good school in the US. I, at least, got to go home for Christmas, Greyhound bus and all. But other breaks were too short. We Latins informally clubbed together, the upper classmen looking out for and encouraging the younger set. We were all over-achievers, over-represented in school government, honor societies, awards, and even baseball. By Thanksgiving I'd been recruited to one more money-making scheme: selling personalized mail order Christmas cards door-to-door. Not really a "people person", I nonetheless managed to sell enough to repeat the effort in subsequent years.

The holidays gave us an opportunity to interact with the Brothers in a slightly more familiar way, as did hurricane threats, which always occurred during the fall. Sometimes the storms were imminent and powerful. At those times we'd be herded into the newest campus building, the infirmary. Deep in its bowels, we'd camp out with Mrs. Thames, the resident nurse—a jolly, cumbersome woman with squinty eyes, squeezed close by her fat.

As a toddler, I'd been a thumb sucker, a habit I retained longer than was probably healthy. At some point the habit had morphed into obsessive nail biting, which sometimes got a bit out of hand (so to speak). One particularly deep avulsion at my cuticle became infected. The pain, swelling, and pus were such an inconvenience, I visited Mrs. Thames at the infirmary. After kindly lecturing me in her clipped Cajun accent on the harmful consequences of nail biting, she washed the finger and then scooped up a spoonful of her breakfast oatmeal, wrapped it around the fingertip and contained it with gauze and a bandage.

I couldn't believe this was modern medical treatment from a registered nurse. It seemed more like *Santería*, a potion out of Afro-Cuban syncretic practice, which, come to think of it, Afro-Cajun culture wasn't far removed. But Mrs. Thames reassured me that the oatmeal would draw out the infection very effectively, and that I should return every day to change the poultice. Of course, she turned out to be right.

* * *

During the summer of 1962 Abuela died and our home in Havana was confiscated. Abuela's death affected Mina deeply. We moved to Arizona, far from the Cuba obsessions and speculations. But that wasn't the only reason. The hot, dry climate was just what Pop's arthritis and Mina's asthma required. The move only affected my summers; my school terms were still spent as a boarder in Mississippi.

At first, Pop and Mina managed an apartment complex in Scottsdale. Later, Pop went into partnership with a Mr. Clark, and then bought his own complex in Phoenix. Finally, he leveraged us into another apartment complex nearby—this time as a sole proprietorship. It was a full-time, full-family job, one that taught me many useful skills, most of which I acquired reluctantly and gracelessly—perhaps because they consumed my summers, which in Phoenix were already a miserable 110 degrees plus.

In 1964, now well settled in Arizona, Pop and Mina brought me home to begin high school at Brophy Prep, a Jesuit academy in Phoenix. Brophy took boarding students, and I chose to board in spite of our home being only 4 miles away. It was a strictly academic choice; fewer distractions from the challenging Jesuit education I expected.

The change from St. Stanislaus to Brophy redirected me from pursuing a life in a religious order. I still attended mass every day and decided to become an altar boy, figuring that being fluent in Spanish and having signed up for Latin and Greek classes would simplify the vocation. But I found myself overwhelmed by the intensity of the participation in such a solemn rite and immobilized at the prospect of making any mistakes. Lost in their own reveries, the old priests whom I served weren't very helpful. Prior to the mass, we were expected to lay out their garments and refill the cruets. One day at dawn I caught kind old Father Sturtzer nipping the sherry. He explained that the wine had to be tested periodically to make sure it hadn't turned. When he wasn't looking, I too tested the sherry. It tasted good. That was the high point of my faith.

I didn't last long as an altar boy; the job proved too stressful. I was always discombobulated by performance anxiety. On top of that, Father Burke's freshman catechism class was the antithesis of Jesuit dialectics: rote memorization without elaboration or discussion, out of a question-and-answer format book. Father Burke was a paunchy, dark little gnome of a man with black-rimmed glasses that made his eyes pop out. He never showed any emotion and answered all questions by repeating the catechism answer he'd just recited. Years later, at the age of 80, he was convicted of the sexual abuse of a retarded 51-year old man the Jesuits had given a home to, in return for kitchen chores, at a retirement home for old Jesuit priests. Luckily, we weren't exposed to any of Father Burke's ministrations.

The next year, expecting more of the same, we dreaded sophomore Bible study class. But Father Sullivan, somewhat of a mystic and a tall, lanky golf fanatic, was everything for which Jesuits had gained an unmatched intellectual reputation. On the first day of class Father Sullivan began a summary of the Old Testament—but with a twist. His narrative was ironic and sarcastic with a condescending tone toward Holy Scripture, implying (but not actually stating) that it was all ridiculous. He even made us laugh at the absurdities in the Bible with a chum snicker or two to get us going. And he didn't stop until the entire class was at least chuckling. Everyone was so stunned; no one had the presence of mind to ask any questions. After class, it was all we could talk about for the rest of the day. What was Father Sullivan up to? Whatever it was, how could he do that?

The following day he laid into the New Testament, making fun of the virgin birth, the miracles, the crucifixion, the resurrection—in a word, of Jesus Christ Himself! We couldn't figure it out. Our minds were in turmoil, experiencing multiple crises of faith. We couldn't wait for next day's class, hoping Father Sullivan would clear things up.

He did. But he took his sweet time about it.

He primed the first five minutes of the class with an unnerving, pregnant silence. Then he looked at each of us in turn before summarizing his previous two days' presentation, emphasizing that the only difference between his account and the Bible's was *tone*—the "facts" were no different. And then he presented us with a challenge: Did we or did we not believe the founding premises of our Christianity? It was a question we each needed to ask ourselves, irrespective of the tone in which those tenets were presented. They weren't meant to make sense; their acceptance required faith. Without faith, those tenets made no sense at all. It was an admission that was obvious, but only through critical thought. Unlike Emmanuel Kant, Father Sullivan didn't believe faith and reason could be reconciled.

Father Sullivan treated us like grownups, presenting us with a choice that required deeper study, reflection, and intellectual commitment. I will forever be indebted to him for helping me understand that if something is too implausible to be true, it probably isn't.

* * *

Perhaps it was the racial conflicts, or the strange new foods or, maybe, the English-language school system, but I slowly ballooned to morbid obesity weighing over 200 lbs. by the time I was 14 years old. Mina also struggled with a weight problem, as did both my sisters. However, the events in our life took a much bigger toll on my father. Already in bad health, he was to deteriorate acutely and die in 1967.

Weighing in at 203 lbs. was not a big disadvantage; I was the biggest kid in the freshman class. Everyone urged me to join the football team—I'd be a shoe-in. So I did, even though I knew nothing of football (in spite of the posters I'd drawn at St. Stanislaus). So I did.

Coach Allender had me anchor the team in the center. As an offensive center, I wasn't required to do anything other than snap the ball and hold my ground no matter what. It was a good thing. No one ever explained the rules of the game to me and it remained a mystery until I quit in disgust as a varsity player. Were American football's rules genetically transmitted only to Americans? I of course understood the gist of the game, but esoterica such as "ineligible receivers" or even "clipping" was cryptic knowledge I couldn't intuit.

One year before I lost my father—as a junior in high school—I lost my Spanish accent. My cousins, Johnny and Richard—uncle John's and aunt Marta's sons—fared divergently. Johnny, one year older than me, always retained a Spanish frisson in his English. Richard, one year younger, lost it. Apparently, learning a new language before, during, or after puberty influences the loss or retention of one's mother tongue's inflection in the second language.

The year before he died, Pop taught me to drive. It was a labor of love that I hope didn't hasten his demise, for he did not respond with equanimity to my leaden clutch foot, lugging, popping, and stalling our little white VW bug as we first made our way around the next-door Episcopal church parking lot, and then the streets of Phoenix. But we both persevered until I got my license. Still, he never quite relaxed whenever I got behind the wheel.

With my newly acquired driver's license, I took to the lecture circuit, giving presentations on the Cuban Revolution. With an oversize, homemade map of the island illustrating the key events in the Revolution awkwardly slipped into the back of Pop's VW, photos of the main characters, notes for my talks, and usually accompanied by a friend, I headed to whatever grade schools, high schools, and private organizations such as Chambers of Commerce, Kiwanis Clubs, and even the John Birch Society—some as far away as Montana—that took up my offers.

Pop was too sick to attend any of our football games. The few he did attend made me very proud. By senior year he was in and out of hospitals. I hadn't lost much weight as much as grown into it. But I had become a fast sprinter. Coach changed my position and trained me to be something called a "pulling guard". After 3 years of playing football, I still didn't know the finer points of the game, having joined the teams primarily for exercise and weight loss. A pulling guard's job, he explained, was an offense position. After the ball is snapped to the quarterback, the pulling guard hits his opposite on the other team, the defensive guard facing him, hard enough to take him out—so he can't get to our quarterback—and then pulls either far left or right and runs downfield to provide blocking for whomever the quarterback has given the ball to, taking out any opposing team members nearby. That was all he said.

By 1967 Brophy had adopted video technology to record games, the better to engage in analysis after matches. At one post-mortem, after a particularly bad loss, Coach Aldrich told us to focus on the next play up on the screen. The camera at first panned the entire scrimmage line, but then zoomed in on one lonely figure running downfield with all his might. But then that figure slowly and anticlimactically decelerated near the end zone and turned around, walking listlessly back. Where was the ball? Had the cameraman royally goofed up?

"Who is that?!" screamed the coach, and before anyone had a chance to answer, he added, "Miller!!! You dumb cow! What did you think you were doing?"

"I ran downfield to block as you'd told me to do", I sheepishly answered.

Coach Aldrich ranted—incomprehensibly and lividly—why what I'd done was wrong, and that we'd been penalized for "too many downfield receivers" or something like that. I didn't understand and retorted, "No one explained the rules of football to me."

The room fell completely silent. To them, that answer was more incomprehensible than Coach's explanation was to me.

But Coach didn't give up on me. I was big, powerful, and fast. He trained me to hit hard and low, following through as if my opponent weren't even there, and made me sprint the 100 yard dash over and over. To solve the problem of my incomprehensibility, he decided to put me in only when a pulling guard play was to be executed, that way I couldn't screw things up. He was getting me ready for the tough match against Prescott High, an away game 100 miles north of Phoenix.

It was a cold, mid-October weekend evening, perfect for filling up the stands—which they were—with spectators, Prescott being a big booster of high school football and the stadium being right on Gurley, the town's main street. Prescott's team was full of cowboys, miners, and ranchers; Brophy's with altar boys, sodalists, and forensic society debaters. Prescott was favored.

I don't remember how close a game it was, but when Coach sent me in it was because he needed the play I was primed for. I didn't let him down. As soon as the ball was snapped I laid such waste to my opponent that he never got back up. Meanwhile, I ran downfield hitting everyone I could see allowing our ball carrier to score a touchdown. With the opposing guard still on the ground, the referee blew his whistle putting a stop to the play. The team doctor ran out, followed by a stretcher. I don't know what happened to the kid, but he was removed and taken to the hospital by ambulance. Off at the sidelines I tried to remove my helmet but couldn't. I had hit the kid so hard my helmet bent in on itself. I needed help removing it.

The rest of the evening was a blur. I don't even remember the drive back to Phoenix, but I know we must have arrived late. I carried the misshapen helmet home—empirical evidence of my success—and fell dead asleep. The following morning I got up early and headed for the hospital to see Pop, helmet under my arm, to recount the game. When I got to his room the door was locked. Posted on it was a sign, "Patient in Isolation: Please see Nurse." Still half asleep, I walked over to the nurses' station and asked about Pop.

The nurse fixed me and said, "Mr. Miller passed away last night."

"Oh"

I was dumbfounded, numb, lost all peripheral vision, pulsating and in a trance, putting one foot in front of the other to get to the car, to drive home, to see Mamá, to make some sense of this. She told me she'd woken me up to tell me at about 2 am when she'd gotten back from the hospital, and that I'd acknowledged the bad news, albeit somewhat nonchalantly. It had been a sleepwalker's response; I had no recollection.

My father's death on the same day I'd sent a kid to the hospital put an end to my football phase—it was just too much; it didn't seem worth it and my heart had never really been into it. All that "teamwork" stuff, pointless aggression, elaborate outfits, injuries, and false camaraderie meant nothing to me. When I told Coach that I quit, no one questioned me.

* * *

After Pop's death, team sports seemed almost a sacrilegious assault to the human spirit, nothing but meaningless, trivial distractions without any redeeming value. I was primed and ready for a big change. On the surface, it had nothing to do with Pop's death, but in some vague, atavistic way it connected to Pop's early, adventurous exploits prospecting for oil in the Chaco, sailing and fighting in the navy, and crossing the US in 1919 in a Model-T Ford, all of which packed more meaningful punch than any number of Packers vs. Steelers games. In college I discovered alpinism, kayaking, deep-sea diving, long-distance biking, trekking, and running, and every other sort of adventure sport that made a mockery of organized team sports, focusing on the challenges of overcoming objective obstacles as opposed to pitting one group of people against another in a contrived mini-war.

When in 1974 I was offered a place on—what was then considered—an "expedition" to climb Mt. McKinley (as it was then known), I accepted, volunteering to ferry all the expedition's food and equipment—nearly one ton—up to Alaska. In my mind, this was *real* sport, right up there with the accomplishments of Shackleton, Amundsen, Mallory, Hillary and Norgay.

At that time, not many attempts on McKinley (20,320') were successful and many climbers perished. Though I'd always been an American by birth, a Cuban by early upbringing, and a skeptic by design, I determined that, if successful, I'd be the first Cuban-American to plant a Cuban flag on North America's highest peak.

Our group of eight included an Englishman, an ex-US Special Forces trainer, and a woman with a chip on her shoulder who detected slights in every interaction with her fellow climbers. For the duration of the climb, she kept shuttling between tents in a mutual intolerance for each other's company. Don Sheldon, the noted bush pilot—over the course of two days—flew our party and gear up onto the 7,500 foot level on a spur of the Kahiltna Glacier, where we organized and packed gear for the climb.

Each morning (in mid-May, that far north, daytime lasted the better part of twenty hours) we'd first melt snow for breakfast, then pack our 180-pound load allotments, half into a backpack and the other half onto a sled to be pulled by a chest harness; strap on our snowshoes, rope up (as protection against falling into hidden crevasses), and begin the arduous trek to our next camp destination. At the lower elevations, the mid-day sun was brutal and we'd strip down to T-shirts and broad-brimmed hats. Up at 16,000 feet, temperatures plummeted to way below zero, making toilet excursions excruciating endeavors.

During the first half of the climb, each succeeding camp was defined by how far we'd gotten by lunch that day from the previous camp—often a dishearteningly short distance, the first day, only 3 miles, onto the Kahiltna Glacier proper. Lugging 180 pounds seems, in retrospect, an incredible exaggeration, one no one would believe. However, our loads had been sorted and pre-weighed back at Sheldon's hangar.

At one point on the second day, when the tedium and exhaustion breached our limits, Roy Smith (the Englishman) and I accused each other of shirking our fair share. In the spirit of fairness and to quell our grousing, but probably just for a break, we decided to switch backpacks, he donning mine while I strapped on his. After no more than half-an-hour we both simultaneously asked for our own backpacks back. To this day we still laugh about that.

At lunch we'd drop our loads and return to the morning's camp with empty packs and sleds, strike the tents and the camp, load up again, and move camp to where we'd dropped our lunch loads. Exhausted, we'd pitch the tents; dig a latrine and build a group kitchen, both protected by walls made from cut igloo snow blocks; melt snow for dinner and to drink through the night; eat and pass out.

The next day, repeat. After three or four days we desperately needed a rest day. But the more experienced of us nixed it. The weather was uncharacteristically perfect and it was decided that making progress while the weather held was essential. However, we did leave a small cache of food, duplicate equipment, and extra ropes marked by a tall flagged wand, for our return trip. All the food had been packed into 5-gallon metal tins to protect it from marauding ravens, the only other higher life form to visit these frozen white deserts. All along our route up, we'd cache some food, fuel, and gear.

It took a week to get up to Camp VII at 14,300 feet. On the way up, not all loads had seamlessly reached each camp, some having been prematurely dropped from exhaustion and requiring a bit of catch-up the next day in spite of load-carrying beginning at 6 am and usually continuing past 8 pm. During that first week three climbers had fallen into crevasses (and been rescued), and one big earthquake had triggered avalanches all around us in a spectacular display of giant gossamer veils whipping through the air.

Finally—a rest day at Camp VII! Double rations and extra sleep for everyone. From here on up the real climbing began. Off with the snowshoes and on with the crampons. We'd carry single loads from here on up, without sleds—impossible anyway as we were facing a 50-55 degree thousand-foot face. Thankfully, the previous party had left their fixed ropes in place.

The next day, we jummared up the big ice wall onto a narrow ridge and Camp VIII at 16,300 feet (Jummars: self-locking mechanical rope ascenders). The weather was holding. Sheldon dropped 5 gallons of ice cream down to us, but 3 missed our narrow isthmus and fell down the wall. Breathing was difficult and sleep nearly impossible without pills. Though 16,300 feet is no great altitude, near the poles it's akin to being much higher up due to the earth's and its atmosphere's not-quite-round but rather squat shape. For sleep, we each took two Seconal, which threw us into paroxysms of giggles at first, but later worked their magic.

It only took half a day to reach Camp IX at 17,300 feet, a broad col between McKinley's North and South summits. The evening was clear, sunny, windless, and cold—50 degrees below zero—perfect for a first-light summit attempt.

Carrying loads up the West Buttress headwall on Camp VIII at 16,300 feet on Mt. McKinley to Camp IX. Credit: Roy Smith.

Camp VIII at 16,300 feet on Mount McKinley (20,310'), Alaska. Credit: Roy Smith.

Camping out in temperatures that cold required special preparations. All metal objects that might come in contact with bare skin were covered with a layer of duct tape. Pee bottles for nighttime relief were essential. Nighttime and breakfast water—including the water for our summit attempt—had to be melted from what was now, up here, very hard and compact frozen snow—perfect for making igloos. Furthermore, each of us had to sleep with about 2 gallons of the water so it would last the night without freezing. Mummy sleeping bags aren't roomy. In addition to the water and pee bottles, we had to sleep with our boots inside the bags, otherwise the sweat they'd absorbed during the day would freeze and they'd be impossible to put on.

As the official expedition chronicler, I recorded our summit attempt on the log the NPS (National Park Service) required us to keep. It is worth quoting at length:

"Roy wakes us up at 5 am, says we'd better give it a go—good weather! All of us set out at 7 am with 4 sleeping bags, 5 gallons of water tied around our necks and shoulders and under our coats to keep them from freezing, one pot and one stove and a gallon of fuel—hope we don't have to use that stuff. We crossed the basin separating us from Denali Pass just above the Peter's Glacier bergsrund. It was steep and icy, though some steps had been carved into it. The morning was very cold and we were moving slowly. I dropped my ice ax but Roy was able to recover it before it fell too far. From here on I tied a line of cord to it. Up to now our Dachstein mitts had kept our hands quite warm, but the cold was such that those who had them put on their down expedition mitts. I had some MSR wool expedition mitts which kept my hands both cold and useless. Stoller only had his Dachsteins, and with a hole in them at that. By the time we reached Denali Pass he had contacted a case of frostbite on his thumb and forefinger. We rested at the Pass while Watkins passed around some brandy and we ate a bite. My water had frozen solid. It was too cold to take out the thermometer to measure the temperature.

"It was here that the Wilcox party had set their last camp, and a small igloo with a food cache was the only shelter available. We often thought of the Wilcox group because Sheldon had spotted an arm sticking out of the ice clutching an ice ax the day before our arrival on the mountain. Many of their bodies lay scattered between Denali Pass and Archdeacon's Tower. I, for one, did not wish to encounter even the merest sign of their passing, much less a body.

"Halfway up to Kahiltna Spur (19,100'), Allen lost his crampons. Roy had to come and help him as only his hands were tough enough to endure the cold and secure his spikes. The going was steep and icy in places—very hard breathing. Watkins, Ossorio, Allen and myself were on a rope. Ossorio's beard was covered in rime condensed from his breaths. Allen felt bad but improved after a short rest. He and McIlwaine are really feeling the altitude. Roy, Ossorio, and Watkins are going very strong. I was in top shape though began to feel quite weak much later on the way down. The day was still holding miraculously clear, sunny, and windless. We had a short rest and a bite to eat at Kahiltna Spur. We regrouped and moved on across the South Peak dome. At a shallow basin next to Archdeacon's Tower and at the base of the final summit rise—another 1,000 feet—we left our bivouac gear and waited while Watkins took care of a slight case of the runs.

"We never did see the summit until we were right on it at 2:30 pm. I pulled out the Cuban flag, took pictures, ate, joked, peed. It was one small step for a climber; one giant step for a Cuban. I don't think I'd do it again! We were all nearly in tears. The weather was still unbelievably beautiful and we wallowed in our success.

Summit of Mt. McKinley, 20,310'. L to R: Bob Allen, author with Cuban flag, Leonard Ossorio (on knee), Bob Watkins. Credit: Roy Smith.

"The descent to Camp IX was long and arduous. We were back at 8 pm thoroughly beat, tired, and exhausted and not still quite believing our good fortune. We all had a bit of a hard time sleeping due to exhaustion and headaches."

Our retreat was a rout. The following morning dawned windy with the promise of a storm—snow, sleet, and whiteouts. To aggravate things, the previous run of good weather had melted much of the glacier's snow cover, exposing many crevasses, and weakening what few snow bridges were left. Much probing followed by many falls became the rule, all the way back to Camp I. Due to the awful conditions Sheldon was unable to pick us up. We waited nearly a week subsisting on dehydrated mashed potatoes. At the merest hint of clearing, we'd march out of the tents and stomp a runway for the plane on the fresh, unconsolidated snow—day after day.

Finally, early one morning, we heard Sheldon's plane. He made one pass to check out our landing strip. He tipped his wings to indicate it was OK and for us to keep our distance. Then he landed and took half our group out, returning the next day for the rest.

PART II
INTO THE MAELSTROM

8

War & Peace

Ana Maria's cousin—and best friend—Tita, is still a contender for outliving Fidel. Both shared the same dream of witnessing Castro's demise—a tiny but immensely satisfying symbolic victory for two old women over the 20th century's deadliest ideology. A flirtatious ball of energy and Bette Midler look-alike, she can reduce you to stomach-cramping laughter within minutes of meeting her. Everyone is her instant friend. Though 3 years older than Castro, she can still run circles around Fidel's hospital bed—even in her wheelchair. For Tita, outliving Castro is an intensely personal goal.

Tita Faget, author's mother's cousin and best friend, and mother of Armandito Lastra. Date: 1939. Source: A. R. Hatch-Miller collection.

Tita's paternal side of the family hailed from Camagüey where her father had managed a sugar cane refinery for an American company. An intensely patriotic Cuban, he lied about his daughter's January 24 birthday.

Tita's birth certificate is dated January 28, the birthday of Jose Martí, Cuba's greatest independence hero. Her great-grandfather emigrated from Catalunya in Spain—exactly when and why are memories that remain unreachable.

She and her brother Alfredo attended the University of Havana with Fidel in the mid 1940s. Alfredo studied law with Fidel. While Alfredo joined the basketball team and later represented Cuba—twice—in the Olympics, Fidel chose a more dangerous sport. Both remember him as a pistol-wielding political gangster-type (a common phenomenon of the times) with an emphasis on action rather than ideology. What little there was of the latter came from José Antonio Primo de Rivera, the founder of Spanish Falangism with a dollop of Benito Mussolini thrown in for broader appeal. While Tita got her doctorate in *Filosofía y Letras* (roughly, philosophy and liberal arts), both Alfredo and Castro became lawyers.

In Cuba everyone is connected by only 4 degrees of separation instead of the proverbial 6. While at the University, Castro married into the Batista political family and, unknowingly, into what would later become the George W. Bush administration. Mirta Díaz Balart, Castro's first wife, was the daughter of Rafael Díaz Balart, a prominent Batista cabinet minister; and the sister of Rafael Díaz Balart (junior), another cabinet minister in the Batista administration. It was Castro's in-laws that saved his butt after the abortive Moncada Army Barracks attack, pleading for his young life. The latter Rafael Díaz Balart was the father of Lincoln and Mario Díaz Balart, at one time long-serving Florida Republican Representatives for the 21st and 25th Congressional Districts respectively. But that was to be way in the future.

Tita's uncle, Mariano, also worked in the Batista administration. A law enforcement professional—and a martinet of the first degree—he was in charge of the important sounding Foreign Counter-espionage Activities Department. Not that Cuba had any foreign enemies. Having been a loyal albeit minor member of the Allied contingent in WWII, Cuba became a dutiful cold warrior in the 1950s refusing diplomatic relations with the USSR and establishing the Departamento de Actividades Enemigas to exercise solidarity with the free world. Mariano was a conscientious bureaucrat but, like the Maytag repairman, had little to do.

When Castro triumphed, Mariano, reading the writing on the wall, hitchhiked out of Cuba on the plane that flew Batista into exile. His secretary, a man by the name of Castaño and a strictly career civil servant, wasn't so lucky. Castaño landed in La Cabaña, the jail adjacent to Morro

Castle. Pulling every long distance string available, Mariano got the US ambassador to intervene. The ambassador personally extracted a promise from Ernesto *Che* Guevara to release the hapless secretary for immediate flight out of the country. When, the following morning, the ambassador showed up to take charge of his charge—in a scene straight out of Andy Garcia's *Lost City*—Guevara declared that an enemy of the people had been liquidated. According to Tita, Guevara bragged that he himself had pulled the trigger.

* * *

In 1943 Tita married Armando, a larger-than-life character and had two kids, Armandito and Alina. The marriage only lasted a short 10 years, when Armando died unexpectedly of a heart attack, leaving everyone disconsolate—especially 10-year-old Armandito. Tita's family lived next to the Aisa family compound near the center of Havana in Santos Suarez. Little *Chuchu* Aisa, two years younger than Armandito, but 7 years older than Alina, was their best friend and confidante. Alina was later to marry *Chuchu*. Armandito, on the other hand, made him his co-conspirator, concocting daring escapades no adult countenanced.

Armandito was impetuous, curious, and single-minded to a fault, all of which made him impervious to adult admonitions. He was a boy with no boundaries; it wasn't that he couldn't 'color within the lines'; he contemptuously ignored 'the lines' as arbitrary nuisances. He wasn't disobedient or rebellious for its own sake, but rather, he needed to find things out for himself. When, as a little child, Tita told him that Habanero chilies were dangerous, he looked her straight in the eyes and proceeded to investigate them for himself, suffering a burning tongue and a torrent of tears. A troublesome student, who incurred a stint in military school, he nonetheless became a voracious reader, absorbing as much as possible on his own.

Tita, an auburn red-head, had a dark-haired, near-twin younger sister, Cuca, with whom she was very close. Cuca was small and, on first impression, not one to make waves. But behind Cuca's impassive smile hid a steely determination and a gyroscopic character that kept her family on a steady course through the storms of revolution, prison and death that lay waiting in ambush.

Cuca married Pillo Casanueva, a serious and quiet man of boundless tolerance, with a silly and whimsical sense of humor. He was not a typical Cuban. Pillo thought religion was a scam. He didn't dance, drink, gamble or womanize; hated motorboats and loved salads—a dish as rare as peanut butter in 1950s Cuba. His in-laws thought he was a Martian. Pillo's command of English was excellent, but his precise pronunciation, as if it were Spanish, was laughably incomprehensible to the untrained ear. When I heard him say 'beaRd', with an exaggerated rolling R for the English word 'bird', I had to ask him what it meant. Like my own dad, Pillo became an accountant with a creative streak: he managed the Central Toledo, Cuba's largest sugar refinery, and later the Topper factory, where Tappan ranges and ovens were manufactured.

Pillo and Cuca sired two kids, MariCris and Pedrito, both of whom recognized few constraints—little rascals no one would ever describe as team players. They lived in the Reparto Náutico (Náutico Neighborhood) of Marianao, a swank Havana area right on the waterfront, where Batista owned property. Close-by lived the prominent León family, whose patriarch had been mayor of Marianao. It was a close-knit community. The León's son, *Cachorro* ('cub,' hence 'lion cub', but with overtones of 'spiteful pistol' also) became close to Armandito, who was his same age, albeit considerably smaller, going to the same parties and hanging out with the same group of girls.

Cachorro went to school with Jorge Luís Batista, the President's son, throughout grade and high school. Poor Jorge Luís. The boy was gay and stained by his father's regime—two strikes that condemned him to contempt. But Cachorro remembers him as a stand-up guy. One day, when little Batista was absent, their civics teacher, a muscular, flat-topped, French Foreign Legion veteran-turned priest, warned the class never to make any critical remarks about the President in Jorge Luís' presence or "they'd have to answer to him"—this in spite of the teacher's aversion to the regime.

Cachorro wasn't the loose cannon Armandito was becoming; and, unlike MariCris and Pedrito, who saw a world without rules or fences, Cachorro approached life more cautiously, with the thoughtfulness of a novice chess player. His comparative reticence was the ideal complement to Armandito's and MariCris' lack of inhibitions, and they soon formed bonds that only death would sever. A young Tony Curtiss look-alike, Cachorro took a shine to little MariCris, an irresistible copper-toned princess (and closer cousin to me than was appropriate), initiating a very long and tempestuous relationship. They were later to marry, an ill-conceived venture that would last only ten months—plus another couple of years in limbo due to his obstinacy to sign the divorce papers.

Girls' 'Quinceañera' (coming out party) with their dates in Reparto Nautico, Havana Cuba, 1959. Carlos 'Cachorro' León is at top left, Armandito Lastra is next to him. Notice the slightly crazed look in Armandito's eyes. Both boys had just turned 16. Next is Manolo 'Croqueta' Rodriguez-Aragón, who later became an infiltrator on Cachorro's team.
Source: Carlos León Acosta collection.

After their travails following the Revolution, Cuca, Pillo, MariCris and Pedrito were to immigrate to Guatemala, where Pillo was to revive Tappan's dilapidated, shuttered, and leaking facility in Amatitlan full of rusted and dismantled machines into a working, productive enterprise with nothing but his resourcefulness and a laughable budget.

Tita and Cuca became inseparable after Pillo died. With piercing eyes and much less of a cut-up than Tita, Cuca still had a keen sense of humor. While Tita was all hustle and bustle—a red-headed tornado cooking, entertaining, and racontouring—Cuca made sure food got stirred, the table got set, and Tita didn't exaggerate too much. Many years later, when living together in Miami's Little Havana, Tita liked to recount their doctor's nickname for them: *Teta y Caca*—tit and shit—beaming with glee at the over-the-line naughtiness and her own lack of inhibition. Cuca quietly went along, wanly smiling—it was an anecdote *she'd* never recount, a nickname *she'd* never accept, but a situation she gladly went along with because Tita infused such delight into the retelling.

* * *

145

While by the end of 1960 my immediate family had left, our extended family got a bit more caught up in events inside Cuba. Cousin Eddy, an old-line Commie, stayed, as did Tita's and Cuca's families, hoping for better times—a prospect 15-year-old Armandito didn't see. With his great-uncle Mariano's exit, the execution of Castaño (Mariano's secretary)—not to mention the hundreds of others who had also been peremptorily executed— the violation of his friends' and family's property rights, the increasing radicalization of the regime, and his strong Catholic faith, Armandito was nearing critical mass.

Cuba was falling apart, morally and politically, and *he* had to do something about it. Armandito had become a gasoline-drenched tinder pile awaiting a spark. A hot-headed, idealistic naïf, it didn't help that he didn't have a father to temper his macho teenage excesses or model thoughtful reflection with effective action. Not that his father Armando was any sort of paragon of restraint. Armando *père* had once, in a fit of frustration and anger at his car's refusal to start, retrieved his pistol, opened the hood, and with legs apart—firing squad-style—emptied his chamber at the recalcitrant V-8 motor.

Armando Lastra, Armandito's father, shooting the motor of his car because it wouldn't start. Date: Circa 1948. Source: MariCris Casanueva collection.

Sometime in late 1959, while Armandito was attending Catholic services at the Jesús de Miramar church, a group of newly-installed Castro policemen approached the church. Feeling their oats, testing their new-found anti-clerical indoctrination-turned-into-idealism—and perhaps following orders—they entered the church and disrupted the service with ridicule. The congregants resisted, with Armandito, a very strong and large 15-year-old, in the vanguard. A fight, involving over 200 participants broke out. Armandito's tinder was lit and, Armandito being Armandito, his bonfire was soon out of control.

He developed pretensions of joining the counter-revolutionary movements already inchoate in the Escambray Mountains. Instead, he used his wits and guile right at home, in Havana. Counter-revolutionaries had been landing armaments on isolated beaches outside the city. Armandito volunteered to locate the caches and transfer them to secure locations. For a 15-year-old kid this was heady stuff, albeit very dangerous. But he wasn't alone. Cachorro, although a month older, followed his lead.

The two had a third accomplice, Ricky Casanueva, a cousin of MariCris' who lived at her house in the Reparto Nautico. Between the isolated beaches and the secure locations, those armaments ended up being temporarily cached in the Casanueva's garage. Pillo was aware of what the boys were doing, but he probably didn't tell Cuca, a practical woman through and through who would not have approved.

All three boys had been inspired by Bebo, Cachorro's uncle, who'd been a professional revolutionary ever since both boys could remember; first against Batista and then, since January 4, 1959—only four days after his triumph—against Castro.

To save him from himself, Tita shipped Armandito off to the US, while she remained to care for her mother who was too sick to travel; as did her sister Cuca whose husband Pillo still held hope that things might not turn out as bad as they seemed.

Unbeknownst to Tita, Armandito was already way deeper in the resistance than she realized. The boy didn't want to leave Cuba. Once in Miami, he tried to join the resistance-in-exile but was rebuffed due to his age. So his family shipped him off to New York, as far from rebel activity as they could manage. There he worked odd jobs, learned English, acquired a Social Security number, and networked with whatever counter-revolutionaries he met.

* * *

And there were plenty. One old saw states that wherever there's two Cubans, there are four political factions. Jim Rasenberger, in *The Brilliant Disaster*, reports that there were 184 different anti-Castro groups in the US in 1960. By 1961, Jay Gleichauf, the CIA's intelligence man in Miami, reported almost 700 counter-revolutionary groups in Miami alone. These straddled a spectrum from old-line Batista supporters, to Constitution of 1940 advocates, to disillusioned Castro revolutionaries, to Escambray revolutionaries sidelined by Castro, to free-market liberals, to Christian Democrats, to democratic socialists, and to every finely parsed philosophical and political distinction one could imagine slicing and dicing into ever finer sub-sets of conviction.

One of them, the *Movimiento de Recuperación Revolucionaria* (Movement to Recover the Revolution), or MRR, grew to become the principal counter-revolutionary movement with supporting members in Miami, Mexico, Venezuela, and other countries. It organized infiltration by guerrilla groups into Cuba, arms drops, communications, sabotage missions, dissident extrications, etc. with assistance from the CIA after 1959.

The irony is that the MRR was created in Cuba, in late 1959, by Dr. Manuel Artime, a professor at the Havana Military Academy and a psychologist and medical doctor. In addition to those duties, he'd volunteered to implement the Agrarian Reform law for the National Institute of Agrarian Reform (INRA) in Manzanillo, Oriente province. But Artime's idealism took a dive following the Huber Matos affair on October 19 and the wave of arrests that followed.

Manuel Artime, political leader of Brigade 2506. Photo of photo credit: R. H. Miller. Source: Casa de la Brigada, thanks to Humberto 'El Chino' Díaz Argüelles, President of the Brigade 2506 Veterans' Association.

What finally turned him 180 degrees against the regime was a secret meeting of the INRA a few days later in which he heard Fidel Castro personally outline a plan to Communize Cuba within 3 years. Artime's tentative suspicions were confirmed and he decided to take action. He resigned his position at the Academy and at the INRA to organize his co-workers into a resistance movement, what would ultimately become the MRR. With the help of students and peasants, he marshaled the core for an underground movement in every province in a scant three weeks.

But by late November his life was in danger, so he sought asylum. In December he escaped Cuba on a Honduran freighter with the aid of the CIA. Artime would rise to become the political leader of Brigade 2506, the name the Bay of Pigs resistance fighters would adopt.

The idea for the Bay of Pigs was conceived on January 18, 1960 by Jacob Esterline (aka Jake Engler), CIA Caracas Station Chief, and J. C. King, chief of the CIA's Western Hemisphere Division, as a "relaxed guerrilla venture" in case the situation in Cuba worsened and the US government decided to take action. Initial training of thirty Cubans would begin in the Panama Canal Zone.

Four months later, in March of 1960, President Dwight D. Eisenhower made what would later be called the Bay of Pigs official. He ordered the CIA to produce a covert action plan against Cuba that included the organization of a paramilitary force of Cuban exiles to be used against Castro. The Escambray Mountains already nurtured counter-revolutionary guerrillas, many of whom had been part of Eloy Gutiérrez Menoyo's *Directorio Revolucionario*, the revolutionary movement—independent of Castro's M26 group—that Castro had sidelined when he took power. Eisenhower's paramilitary force would join forces with the existing guerrillas.

By April the "covert action" got into in full swing. First, the CIA approached a group of prominent Cuban exile leaders—including, among others, a former Prime Minister, a former Minister of Foreign Relations, and Manuel Artime, leader of the MRR, the largest resistance group—to offer its assistance in organizing military action against Fidel Castro, letting them know that the US government was fully committed to the success of the operation with money, training, planning, ships, airplanes, logistics, and arms, but that the operation would be manned strictly by Cubans.

The Cubans thought they'd won the anti-Castro lottery. Still, they were skeptical. Plus, they needed a professional *Cuban* military leader. Artime suggested *Pepe* San Román, a twenty-nine year old graduate of Cuba's military academy who had also trained at Fort Belvoir, Virginia and Fort

Benning, Georgia. San Román was already planning a campaign against Fidel from Mexico with a group of ten ex-army officers, among them Hugo Sueiro who would become Armandito's 2nd Battalion commander.

José Alfredo Pérez Pepe San Román, military commander of Brigade 2506 at his graduation from Cuba's Military Academy in 1953. Source: Casa de la Brigada, thanks to Humberto 'El Chino' Díaz Argüelles, President of the Brigade 2506 Veterans' Association.

Tall, slender, dark-haired, quiet and reserved, San Román had served under Batista, then revolted, been imprisoned, released, served Castro, was again imprisoned, again released and finally escaped to the United States. Artime's men and San Román's officers had been enemies in Cuba—they still distrusted each other. After many lengthy meetings and a reconnaissance of the CIA training camp on Useppa Island, a CIA golf course in the Gulf of Mexico off central Florida, San Román and his officers agreed to join the effort. They could sense the depth of commitment from the personnel they met and the money that was being spent.

Second off the starting line was David Atlee Phillips, my family's old Alturas del Vedado tenant, who was put in charge of organizing, equipping, and programming Radio Swan, an anti-Castro radio station transmitting from Swan Island, a tiny islet 90 miles off the coast of Honduras. The CIA station went on-air on May 17.

Next up was the recruitment of a nucleus of resistance fighters for training, volunteers for which there was no shortage. Most were students from the *Agrupación Católica Universitaria*, with a few ex-Batista and ex-Castro soldiers thrown in for diversity. These few dozen early recruits began training in late May on the Useppa Island golf course. But that wouldn't last.

Useppa was US territory and training of foreign nationals on US soil for a military action against a foreign power was illegal. So the CIA moved the training to the Panama Canal Zone—in spite of it being territory still legally under US jurisdiction—where the recruits trained for two months. They then approached Guatemala seeking a training base on foreign soil. The Guatemalans agreed. Construction of a training facility, the 5,000-acre Camp Trax, and an airport at Retalhuleu, both in the western sierra, was well underway by late May. The first 50 trainees, which soon grew to 150, were tasked with building the seat-of-the-pants facilities: a 4-hole privy, 12-man tents and leaky barracks without foundations, and separate quarters for the American trainers. Showers weren't built until October. It wasn't until November that the force grew to 300 men. One single, tattered issue of *Playboy* constituted the library. Home-grown pot was popular. One man developed a relationship with a mule. It rained constantly.

With the US government now joining and coordinating the fray, ensuring that success might be a real possibility, the five major anti-Castro groups in Miami—including the MRR—joined forces in June. The coalition became known as the *Frente Nacional Democrático*, or simply, the *Frente*.

Restless, frustrated, feeling isolated from where the action was happening, and privy to the exile rumor mills, 16-year-old Armandito was soon back in Miami pulling every possible scam to get him into the Frente, its offices now located in a big house at Twenty-seventh Avenue and Tenth Street Southwest.

And Cachorro was right there with him. His dad had left Cuba first, in 1960, to test US waters. Once settled, mom and sister soon followed. Unlike Armandito, whose revolutionary spark was lit by a rumble in a church, Cachorro's revolutionary trajectory was evolutionary; a slow and deliberate process inspired by the idealism and example of his uncle Bebo, who was already in Miami, deep in the *Frente*.

Neither boy, at 16, with their birthdays only one month apart, could join up. The Frente only accepted 18-year-olds and older—17 with parental permission. In September of 1960 Cachorro turned 17, followed by Armandito in October. Immediately, Cachorro asked his dad for permission. "No way," he said, "If you died or came back maimed, your mother and I would never be able to live with ourselves and would regret the decision for the rest of our lives."

Unable to get parental permission, they turned to uncle Bebo, who immediately forged "parental" permission for both. Subjected to a thorough interview followed by a lie-detector test, the boys—the third and fourth youngest combatants in the entire Bay of Pigs effort—were in.

Chuchu, Armandito's other childhood co-conspirator and future brother-in-law, didn't stand a chance of joining: at 14 years of age, he was just too young. His contribution to the anti-Castro cause would come later, after the Bay of Pigs prisoners had been repatriated.

9

Guatemala

In December of 1960, my cousins Cachorro and Armandito landed at the CIA air strip at Retalhuleu, deep in the western sierras of Guatemala, after a 6-hour flight whose destination was kept mum. At least they could smoke. They were part of a 430-man cohort of Cuban exiles headed for boot camp to train for an invasion of Cuba. This second cohort followed the pattern of the first: Most were students from the *Agrupación Católica Universitaria* (Catholic University Group), or ex-Cuban military.

At the Retalhuleu air strip, little was disclosed. A select few were given the opportunity to volunteer for paratrooper training. Cachorro signed up. The remaining cadets were convoyed to distant Base Trax for infantry and artillery training. For some reason Cachorro can't recall, Armandito didn't join the paratroops; he and Armandito—against their instincts—found themselves inadvertently separated.

The Guatemala training bases were scattered along the length of the Pacific coast Sierra Madre Mountains, with the Retalhuleu Air Base more or less centrally located among the other bases at an altitude of 650 feet. Guatemala was well disposed to help the operation, even volunteering Guatemalan military personnel for security. It helped that the 1954 US-aided coup against authoritarian President Jacobo Arbenz had been spectacularly successful. Retalhuleu was the central access point for the other bases and the main entry and exit point to and from Guatemala for the CIA operation. It is where the Brigade's Cuban pilots underwent flight training from Alabama Air National Guard volunteers.

Only a few miles away, under the shadow of Santiaguito volcano, but 7,000 feet—and 3-4 hours away—up in the mountains, camp Base Trax became the main infantry and artillery training center. Close by, the paratroopers trained at Halcón Base. Farther south, almost at sea level, camp Garrapatenango (literally, *tick-town*), was also used for paratrooper training, flying out of nearby San José airport on the coast, a location that would also be used for amphibious landing and joint operations training.

Apprehensive and lonely, Armandito and Cachorro soon found older classmates and acquaintances from Cuba that made the rigors of training by US military personnel on loan to the CIA more bearable. Armandito hooked up with *El Chino*, a slightly older boy he'd known since he was 14. They were fortunate. They were better prepared—being young and athletic—than most of the other volunteers for the upcoming operation.

Upon arrival in Guatemala the men were asked what positions they wanted to train for. Mario Martínez Malo, a law student, asked what positions were available. When he heard 'forward observer,' he asked, "What's that?"

The instructor explained that a forward observer had to be an expert with map, field communications and codes. An FO approached the enemy as near as possible—usually with a radio man—under cover. The two would pinpoint the enemy position and radio back coordinates for artillery fire. An FO is a particularly vulnerable target from both enemy and friendly fire: from the enemy because of their proximity; from friendly fire, for their proximity to the target. The instructor revealed that FOs in the Korean War sustained a 95% casualty rate.

Martínez Malo immediately volunteered. It wasn't that he wanted to die for Cuba. It was that, with such a high casualty rate, he figured not too many men would volunteer; and that, in order for them to succeed, essential— albeit extremely vulnerable—positions had to be filled. Martínez Malo wanted, more than anything, to free Cuba from Castro.

Armandito ended up in the 2nd Infantry Battalion (numbering 183 men) under the command of Hugo Sueiro Ríos, at twenty-one years of age the youngest Brigade officer; Company E, led by Oscar Luis Acevedo; 6th squad. Second Battalion was full of close relatives. It contained two groups of three brothers, five groups of two brothers, one father and son, four cousins, two sets of brothers-in-law, and many who'd known each other since infancy.

Each recruit was assigned a number beginning with 2500 to make the force seem larger than it really was. The Cubans honored soldier number 2506, who fell to his death in a mountain training accident by using his number to name the brigade: Brigade 2506. Armandito's number was 3386.

Cachorro was assigned to what Eli César, author of *San Blas: Ultima Batalla en Bahía de Cochinos*, called "the most elite unit of Brigade 2506": the 1st Battalion of paratroopers under the command of Alejandro del Valle, a seasoned jump instructor in the Cuban army. Cachorro was part of Company A, Squad: Escuadra de Armas, a unit composed of 9 paratroopers. Three were riflemen, with at least one operating a .30 caliber machine gun and another either a bazooka or a recoilless rifle. As Cachorro recounts, "I was the *cargador* of the .30 caliber on my squad. I would carry the bullets for the shooters of the machine guns and pinpoint with my M1 tracers where they should aim. There was absolutely no one lower than me."

Alejandro del Valle, Commander of the Paratroopers Battalion of Brigade 2506 and Erneido Oliva, overall second-in-command of the Brigade. Source: Casa de la Brigada, thanks to Humberto 'El Chino' Díaz Argüelles, President of the Brigade 2506 Veterans' Association.

Full-on, intense physical fitness and military discipline training began at 5 am the day after their arrival at the camp. Forced marches interspersed with 2-mile, double-time runs lugging full packs were only the beginning. To this was added basic small arms handling, along with training on the 4.2 mortar, the 57mm recoilless rifle, the 3.5 bazooka rocket launcher and the .30 and .50 caliber machine guns. Due to his size and strength, Armandito was trained to operate a .30 caliber machine gun. Close quarters combat exercises with and without bayonets added a personal touch. Crawling on elbows and knees with rifles (or much heavier machine guns), cradled on biceps, under live rounds fired 3 feet above ground—toward the bullets— acutely seared the sacrifice of life and honor the recruits were vouchsafing.

The training took its toll on the men, weakening their immune systems. Many suffered from dysentery and other maladies; some caught malaria. Second Battalion's medic injected the worst cases with doses of gamma globulin to strengthen them for the invasion. Mario Martínez-Malo, having volunteered as a forward observer, took his training very seriously. Weighing in at 171 pounds, he'd dropped to 96 pounds when he set sail for the invasion.

Still, this was only the beginning. After some sense of esprit de corps had welded the men together and their physical fitness allowed, the training regimen became mobile, taking place at night and, at times, in torrential weather. Finally, at Garrapatenango, when the entire Brigade assembled for comprehensive exercises, water training was added: amphibious landings in heavy surf, swimming in shark-infested waters, underwater distance swimming—all under fire. One unfortunate recruit, a man nicknamed *El Cabito*, became shark chum.

The disruption of quotidian habits took their toll. Plagued by piles, Armandito underwent a hemorrhoidectomy at boot camp. With so few toilets, and all in full view, personal habits were disrupted, and even became group theatre, albeit more comedic than dramatic (except when pit vipers, scorpions and poisonous spiders were involved).

Cachorro's training included parachute jumps, er…jump. Though successfully completing preliminary parachute training, for some reason he can't explain even today, he performed only one practice jump, and at that, *without* carrying the hundred pounds of .30 caliber bullet cans it was his job as a *cargador* to carry. "If I didn't release it properly, it would have crushed me at landing. Never trained for it," he told me.

And that one jump was a near disaster. Cachorro landed in a ceiba tree and ripped his uniform. Tony Zardon, another paratrooper, wasn't so lucky. The hapless jumper was swept by a violent gust of wind and smashed against a giant tree trunk that broke his back.

The paratroopers had some of the typical fly-boys' disregard for rules and protocol. Two, J.J. and Maqueira, had secretly purchased a piglet from a local farmer, which they set out to fatten for a *Noche Buena* (Christmas Eve) feast in case they were still in Guatemala the following Christmas. Maqueira warned J.J. that the piglet needed to be watched closely. He'd heard from a credible source that a group of chuters were conspiring to steal the shoat.

One afternoon the Garrapatenango camp was disrupted by a big commotion. *El Negrito* William was found hanging from a tree, apparently a suicide. His body was lowered and taken to a tent where medics attempted resuscitation. Right away, one medic emerged to announce that *El Negrito* was dead.

It suddenly hit Maqueira. He turned to J.J. and said, "This is a trick! Everything is faked. They're stealing our piglet!" And Maqueira, with a lightning-quick response, ran and caught the thieves red-handed with the piglet. But with their secret out, Maqueira and J.J., reconsidered. A few days later, they put on a big feast, roasting the pig for all the paratroopers—and nominating *El Negrito* William for an Oscar.

* * *

Not all disruptions ended in a party. Over the course of the Brigade's training period, 66 recruits were sentenced to the stockade. They included a wide assortment of miscreants; from AWOLs, deserters, Castro agents that had infiltrated the camps, to the leaders of the leadership mutiny, led by twenty-six-year-old attorney Rodolfo Nodal. Nodal had become the 2nd Battalion's communications officer and came from a distinguished family: his father had once been Cuba's Defense Minister.

For Nodal, as well as the other men of the Brigade, the nuances of a covert operation left the question of who was in charge—the US or the Cuban exiles—a bit fuzzy. Nodal and his friends set out to clarify the issue, not by challenging orders from the US officers, but by questioning *who should have the right* to issue orders in the first place.

To the Cubans of Armandito's 2nd Battalion, only the Miami-based Frente and its general staff had the authority to appoint the Brigade commanders—not the US camp commander, "Colonel Frank," and his 38 advisers. Urged on by Nodal, the 2nd Battalion drew a red line in the Guatemalan highlands.

Pepe San Román, the American-appointed Brigade commander, was in Nodal's cross hairs. San Román was a professional soldier, a graduate of Cuba's military academy and a US Army-trained officer who knew how to follow orders. But, as Peter Wyden explains in his book on the Bay of Pigs, "To Nodal and the other dissidents, Pepe symbolized total submission to the Americans, not only for the present but for the future in Cuba when Castro would be deposed."

At Camp Trax debates heated up. Cliques formed, strategy meetings assembled, conspired, broke up and re-formed and fist fights erupted. Training all but stopped. When two officers from the Miami general staff were sent home by "Colonel Frank" for "playing politics," tensions reached a crisis point. The Americans ordered all trainees to turn in their weapons.

"Nodal and his friends," Wyden says, "hid eight .45-caliber pistols to 'shoot it out, if necessary.'"

"Instead, there was a mutiny," continues Wyden. Some 230 men "resigned," including all of Armandito's 2nd battalion, the entire 3rd battalion—*and* Pepe San Román. However, Pepe, wise beyond his 30 years and having been imprisoned by both the Batista and Castro regimes, was fixated on success. He immediately turned around and signed up as an ordinary soldier, saying that the Brigade belonged to no one but "to Cuba, our beloved country."

The American training officer would have none of these shenanigans. He retorted that, "I am boss here, and the commander of the Brigade is still Pepe San Román," and ordered San Román to resume command.

But the astute San Román took the high road. He "asked that those men willing to fight with him and to 'forget about political things' step to the right," according to Wyden. After a bit more dickering, all but 20 of the men joined San Roman. The Cuban grunts had chosen their leader.

When asked about being an extension of the US military, Dr. Mario Abril, a Brigade 2506 veteran and professor of Music at the University of Tennessee at Chattanooga responded, "No, we thought of ourselves as independent."

* * *

After New Year's 1961, nearly 900 more men swelled the Brigade. But these weren't students, who would, in the end (at about 20%) constitute the largest proportion of Brigade members. Most of the new recruits were older men (the oldest was 61), who had careers and families; or farmers, peasants, and unskilled laborers, who'd had their modest landholdings or businesses confiscated, or whose Catholic faith was strong. Ex-soldiers rounded out the final tally at nearly 17% of Brigade members. By the time of the invasion in April, 2,681 men had joined. Their average age was 23.

Whatever their history, few were crucially motivated by recovery of their stolen property, a concern Cachorro dismisses contemptuously. Instead, strong and deep philosophical, moral, religious and ideological ideals drove them. Mario Abril, a student volunteer in Armandito's cohort who felt alienated by socialist rhetoric, explained his motivation this way:

"In those days, 1950s and at that age, 23-24, young men...vented their hormonal excesses, social excesses not in the way folks do up here (United States). We didn't get drunk, we didn't do drugs, what we did was...attempted to become activists in politics. There is a long tradition of Latin American youth who took charge and participated in momentous events in the political lives of their countries. Cuba was no exception..."

Racially—a non-contentious category in Cuba—but one which Castro tried to use along with class warfare to recruit support, the Brigade was pretty mixed but predominantly lighter than darker. Only about 4% would be called 'black' in the Cuban sense, with the rest mulatto, *café au lait*, swarthy or white.

Erneido Oliva, the Brigade's second in command and Armandito's commanding officer in the Battle of the Rotonda, was a strikingly handsome black Cuban with a huge forehead who had served first under Batista and then later under Castro. An honors graduate of the Cuban Military Academy and an instructor for the US Army's Caribbean School, Oliva was a professional through and through. When Oliva was captured, Fidel Castro interrogated him separately. He berated Oliva for betraying the Revolution, which, Castro said, "had been fought for black people." Castro reminded Oliva of the Varadero and Havana beach resorts that excluded blacks (an exclusion that was instituted by hotels that catered to American tourists of the 1940s and '50s, but which was otherwise unknown in Cuba). Oliva retorted that, "he hadn't come to Cuba to swim."

But perhaps that story is apocryphal (in that version). Both *El Chino* and Cachorro, who was sitting two seats away from Cruz, attribute it to Tomás Cruz, Cachorro's company commander and also black. But in this other version, the interrogation took place on Cuban national TV while Fidel was trying to milk the capture of the invaders for all the propaganda it was worth.

How did race virtually disappear as a contentious issue in Cuba, but persist until modern times in the United States, especially considering that the former eliminated slavery 22 years after the latter?

Slavery under Spanish colonial rule was nothing like what it had become in the United States on the eve of the Civil War. In the American south, negritude—to any degree, i.e., the notorious "one drop rule" enacted in several states—equated skin color with a deprivation of rights. In Cuba, slaves could marry, own personal property, testify in court and run businesses. One eighteenth-century observer noted that many had become skilled craftsmen, "not only in the lowest [trades] such as shoemakers, tailors, masons and carpenters, but also in those which require more ability and genius, such as silversmith's craft, sculpture, painting and carving."

Additionally, Spain's liberal manumission policy "resulted in almost 40% of African-Cubans being free in 1792," reports Andro Linklater in his book on the evolution of private property, *Owning the Earth*. The diverging legal and social attitudes toward race in Cuba and in the US presaged future developments in each country. The paradoxical contrasts are striking. Whereas Reconstruction in the US institutionalized policies that had grown more nakedly racist since Independence—equating skin color with the presence or absence of rights and talents—the opposite was true in Cuba. Under the influence of the Catholic Church, the fundamental humanity of Africans was uncontroversially established early on—slavery and skin color where philosophically separated. By the time of Cuba's Wars of Independence, Antonio Maceo, an Afro-Cuban, had become second-in-command of the rebel armies.

Cuba has always had an amorphous racial climate, one mostly misunderstood or puzzling to Americans. Racism, in the sense of hating or fearing a person for his skin color, is unknown. Skin color was never an impediment to respect. Skin tone snobbery, however, rarely surpassing trivial tut-tutting or even semi-serious priggishness was not uncommon. Color gradations, like degrees of body mass index ranging from the skeletal to the morbidly obese, extended into categories of people Americans would consider "white," with the too-pale also looked at askance, as if they were anemic and rickety.

Batista, while president, was denied membership in the Havana Yacht Club: he was considered too swarthy; although his gay son, Jorge Luis, was admitted. That he didn't take the rejection personally and, as a dictator, did not take reprisals, is inconceivable to an American. Instead, the president donated a marina to the Havana Biltmore Yacht & Country Club, as swanky a venue if not more and, voila, he and his family became members.

* * *

January of 1961 upped the ante and sealed the deal. On the 2nd of the month, Cuba charged at the UN Security Council that the US was preparing an invasion of the island. In a show of defiance, Castro paraded his newly-acquired Soviet arsenal, consisting of 50 heavy artillery pieces, 125 heavy tanks, 920 anti-aircraft guns, 170 anti-tank batteries and many rocket launchers down the streets of Havana (along with the promise of MIG fighters yet to come). The Soviet contribution to Castro's defenses also included 7,250 machine guns and 167,000 rifles and hand guns. The post-invasion Soviet military analysis of the conflict concluded that without those contributions, the invasion at the Bay of Pigs would have succeeded.

But arms and ammo were not enough to defend the island; Castro's men required additional training. Within days of JFK's swearing in as President, the Cuban Armed Forces High Command realized that there were no paramedics either for the army or the newly-created People's Militia, and that if the ever-present threat of invasion ever materialized, the casualties would be extremely high: most likely every man shot in combat would be dead in a matter of hours since no medical treatment would be available on the battlefield.

The Armed Forces General Headquarters rushed to establish the first Paramedics School in Cuba and began a nation-wide dragnet for suitable recruits with advanced studies. Arnaldo Remigio, a student who dreamed of becoming a doctor, enthusiastically joined. Remigio became a Cuban Army (*Fuerzas Armadas Revolucionarias,* or FAR) Paramedic and participated—at a distance—in some of the Bay of Pigs battles. He wrote an unpublished account of that conflict from the Cuban forces' perspective. As a 'grunt' on Castro's side, his insights are invaluable and I will periodically refer to them.

The day following Fidel's parade, January 3rd, the US cut diplomatic relations with Cuba. By the end of the month, just a few days after his inauguration, President John F. Kennedy authorized the CIA to proceed with Eisenhower's Cuba plan, now officially upgraded to consist of 1,200 men with a planned landing at Trinidad on Cuba's south coast.

By March, Kennedy was still grappling with transition issues, concentrating on getting his domestic programs and agenda rolling, and dealing with the Laotian crisis and the soon-to-be Berlin crisis. The Cuba project just wasn't a priority. In fact, not only wasn't he familiar with its details—such as they were—he hadn't given much thought to its implementation and its potential consequences, either domestically or in foreign policy. It was a sideshow without a date, something simmering on a back burner for possible use in the vague future—and something the previous Republican administration had dreamed up, which he figured had a life of its own and its planners and tenders would manage.

But one crucial piece of intelligence forced minds to focus. The MIG fighters the Soviets had promised Castro were due to arrive in Cuba sometime in April. Cuban pilots were already training in Czechoslovakia to fly them. This addition to the Cuban air force, whose combat readiness at the time consisted only of 6 jet and 6 prop fighters—easily destroyed on the tarmac by a surprise attack—would doom the Cuba project to failure. If the Cuban exile invasion was to succeed, it had to be scheduled before the arrival of the MIGs.

Kennedy was irritated by the sudden haste, but gave the go-ahead order to proceed with final preparations and the setting of a date. Still, he retained the option of cancelling the whole project at the last minute, a detail he adamantly insisted on but which, for a president, usually goes without saying. The insecurity in his vocal insistence to retaining a standard prerogative revealed his inexperience and insecurity.

Though military training in the Guatemala camps was proceeding apace, the political umbrella under which the military campaign would be fought was still mired in negotiations amongst the multiple Cuban exile factions. Without a Cuban government-in-exile that would lend credence to the operation and that would take charge once a successful beachhead occupation was established, the entire project ran the risk of failure and its covert status stood the chance of being blown.

It's not that the exile leaders hadn't given their imprimatur to the military operation; it's that their tendency to cavil over minutiae and stand on finely parsed principle prevented any sort of consensus. So the CIA invited the exile leaders to the Skyways Motel near the Miami International Airport for a meeting to impress on them the urgency of unity that the new situation required.

On Saturday, March 18, twenty-two Cubans representing the main anti-Castro organizations met with James Noel, former Havana CIA station chief, in the Skyways' banquet room. As Jim Rasenberger, author of *The Brilliant Disaster*, recounts:

> *"The meeting began with a scolding from Noel. There would be no more sweet talk, he told them; while they were squabbling over petty differences in Miami, they were losing Cuba. 'If you don't come out of this meeting with a committee, you just forget the whole fuckin' business, because we're through.'"*

> *"The threat worked."*

> *By Monday morning, left, right, center, and fringes united under one umbrella organization with a blueprint for economic and social policies, and a timetable for elections in a free Cuba. Thus was the successor to the Frente formed, now renamed the Consejo Revolucionario Cubano with José Miró Cardona as president of the "Revolutionary Council."*

Miró Cardona's legitimacy rested on the fact that he had been the last prime minister of Cuba after Fidel Castro's victory but before Castro personally took over the post. Prior to that, he'd been a law professor at the University of Havana when he was chosen for the office of Prime Minister immediately after the success of the Revolution, by Manuel Urrutia, Castro's first, hand-picked President (who also later resigned). Miró Cardona quit the position in disgust at the Communist influence in the new government after only five weeks in office.

* * *

How President Eisenhower's "covert action plan against Castro" became the Bay of Pigs is a diagram that resembles options on a wildly branching logic tree planted in an overlooked policy corner almost as an afterthought, but then fed growth hormones by several separate ambitious committees; pruned by a myopic Edward Scissorhands, and given more hormones by more self-important committees, none of which was aware of what the other committees were up to; and finally trimmed beyond saving by a neurotic gardener with a chain saw who couldn't see the tree for the branches. At different times, the plan ranged from a Fidel Castro-style, just-a-few-men guerrilla infiltration near the Escambray Mountains to a WWII Normandy-type invasion. In the end it was neither. The operation became an unwieldy mix of the two approaches, lacking any of either strategy's strengths.

1) THE PLAN: Originally, the plan was to be a guerrilla infiltration of a few hundred men near the city of Trinidad at the base of the Escambray Mountains. Those mountains already harbored anti-Castro guerrillas and the city wasn't known for its love of Fidel.

As the recruits multiplied and the Pentagon, the CIA, and other expert advisors offered their opinions, the infiltration was upgraded to an invasion in November, 1960. But the invasion, next to a big city, scared Secretary of State Dean Rusk and newly-elected President Kennedy—it seemed too high-profile for a covert action. So the landing location was shifted 100 miles west to the Bay of Pigs, a lightly inhabited swamp completely unsuited to guerrilla activity. The infiltration-turned-invasion then became a much bigger invasion supported by US air and sea power whose rules of engagement precluded any combat—unless first fired upon.

Along with the main invasion, two smaller ones were planned. One-hundred-and-sixty-eight men were scheduled to land near Baracoa, in Oriente province at the far eastern end of Cuba, not far from where Fidel Castro had first landed in 1956. Like the original plans for the main force, these men were to hie to the mountains and ensconce themselves as guerrillas. But they had an additional purpose: as a diversionary tactic that would give Castro the impression that the invasion was island-wide.

Ditto for an "invasion" in Pinar Del Rio province, at the far western end of Cuba. Dreamed up by the CIA, and executed so flawlessly that Fidel interrupted his command at the Bay of Pigs to rush to Pinar del Rio, this invasion was a complete ruse carried out with smoke and mirrors, loudspeakers, pyrotechnics, projectors, offshore hubbub, and not one single invader. While *this* invasion succeeded, the one in Oriente failed when the invaders discovered that a substantial force of Castro militia was awaiting them. They played it safe, tried landing again, but called it quits after a second attempt.

But back to the planning stage. Once the "action plan" had been upgraded to an invasion, the exile force required a "navy" for transport. Enter Eduardo García and his five sons, owners of the García Line, a Havana-based Cuban bulk shipping company with offices in New York. García, a Jabba-the-Hut look-alike, wasn't interested in profit, just getting rid of Castro. He donated 6 old and slow but serviceable ships at cost. But he didn't want to lose them. After being reassured that the exile "air force" (see below) would annihilate Castro's air force, and that a US Navy escort (used only as a deterrent, but authorized to return fire if fired upon) would accompany his ships to the 3-mile territorial waters limit, García agreed. As an added defense, the ships were retrofitted with .50 caliber, deck-mounted machine guns. For the actual landing, 36 eighteen-and-a-half foot aluminum boats were purchased to supplement the three LCUs (landing craft utility) and four LCVPs (landing craft vehicle and personnel) already available.

The Cuban exile air force consisted of 16 Douglas B-26 Invaders kitted up for offensive operations with rockets and bombs (out of 32 B-26s available), and a half-dozen C-46 and C-54 transport aircraft, but no fighters. The B-26s were to destroy Castro's air force on the tarmac in a surprise attack in conjunction with the seaborne landings.

Castro's air force consisted of only 20 planes—six Lockheed T-33 jet fighters, six ex-RAF prop-driven Hawker Sea Fury fighters, six Douglas B-26 Invaders, a C-47 transport, and a PBY Catalina flying boat.

Four days before the scheduled invasion and air attack, the 16 B-26s were halved to eight by a nervous President Kennedy, worried that the attack was too high profile. The decision doomed the operation to failure—not all of Castro's air force was destroyed. Those that were left sunk exile supply ships and killed many men in the attacking force. After the entire fiasco was over, JFK averred that he didn't realize how important the original air strike plan was, and that he hadn't been adequately briefed.

2) **POPULAR UPRISINGS:** Intelligence reports estimated that discontent in the Cuban population was widespread, and that internal resistance groups were present and well organized in every province, often with the help of exile infiltrators assisted by the CIA. By February of 1961, CIA-trained infiltration teams doubled their efforts in preparation for the coming "covert action plan," so as to be able to coordinate with the invaders, carrying out widespread sabotage and recruitment. The Brigade battalions, companies and squads were purposely undersized, expecting locals to join the effort and bring them up to full force. Armandito's 2nd battalion, for example, only had 183 men.

The invasion force was labeled a brigade because, in military parlance, a force of 1,400 to 4,000 men is termed a brigade. This is subdivided and organized into battalions of 300-1,300 men, companies of 80-250 men, platoons of 15-30 men, and squads of 8-12 troopers. For the invasion, the Brigade numbered 1,447 men.

The popular uprisings never materialized. Some sources attribute this to popular support for the Revolution. However, the truth is more revealing. Fidel Castro, as early as the summer of 1960, knew about the coming invasion—all of Cuba talked about it; he just didn't know when it would come. In early January of 1961 the *New York Times* disclosed the location of the training camps in Guatemala.

But he took pre-emptive action. The Escambray Mountains, a perennial refuge of anti-government guerrillas, needed to be cleared out—once and for all. On January 1st of 1961 he dispatched 70,000 troops in 80 battalions to clear the mountains of the no more than the 600 men and a few women who constituted the guerrillas.

His first move was to relocate—by force—the 10,000-20,000 peasants that lived in the area. On January 11, Castro visited the area to take stock of the situation. He sent Osvaldo Ramírez, Captain of the Escambray rebels, an ultimatum: "I know that you're an idealist. I propose that you come down and talk with me so I can convince you that this isn't Communism; and I guarantee that if I don't convince you, I'll give you plenty of guarantees that you can return up to your mountains."

Ramírez instantly replied, "Tell Fidel that I accept the discussion with him, but with one variant: THAT *HE* COME UP TO THE ESCAMBRAY AND THAT *I* GUARANTEE THAT IF HE DOESN'T CONVINCE US, WE'LL GUARANTEE *HIS* RETURN."

Castro launched the attack.

The fighting was fierce. By February 10, only 100 guerrillas remained alive. Still, it took until mid-March for Castro to declare that the Escambray was rid of vermin. Only a handful remained to carry on the resistance.

After he'd gotten rid of the vanguard of the resistance, Castro went after anyone and everyone whom his Committees for the Defense of the Revolution (neighborhood busy-bodies) fingered as discontents. According to Grayston Lynch, author of *Decision for Disaster: Betrayal at the Bay of Pigs*—as quoted in the *Cuban Information Archives*—he states that prior to the invasion there were 50,000 political prisoners in Cuba. Another 250,000 (or about 4% of Cuba's population) were arrested by the day of the landing, some summarily executed (with 200,000 in Havana alone). Of those ¼ million, 100,000 were arrested due to a US SNAFU.

Originally, the Bay of Pigs plan had called for Brigade air strikes against Castro's air force at dawn on the day of the invasion. At the last minute, someone moved the air strikes up two days, giving Castro advance notice of the invasion. The element of surprise was lost. Those 100,000 people were arrested during those two days.

The ¼ million detainees were herded into sport stadia, movie theaters, and any large place that could accommodate them, none with adequate sanitation, shelter or food. In a speech on April 24, five days after the defeat of the invasion, Castro explained his reasoning in terms reminiscent of Josef Stalin's apocryphal omelet remark:

> *"In conjunction with the actions of our military forces, the Committees for the Defense of the Revolution acted. It became necessary to arrest all suspicious people, it became necessary to arrest all those persons that for some reason might become active in or help the counterrevolution. In this type of operation, naturally, some injustices will always be committed, but it is inevitable."*

> *"I repeat that there might have been cases of injustice...(but) no one can be so egotistical as to waste any time on such unimportant questions that it detracts from today's and future generations' jubilation."*

"Fatherland or death!"

Fidel Castro made even better use of those two days between the air raids and the invasion. Besides incarcerating 100,000 Cubans, he drafted 200,000 into active military service and reinforced garrisons in the most remote parts of the island—no small feat for so small a country with limited transportation capacity. Many of those men and women would pay with their lives in combat for which they lacked training.

Cuba's population in 1961 was about 7 million. Nearly 1 million Cubans had exiled themselves to the US, Spain, Italy, Mexico and other countries. Counting prisoners and exiles, that's nearly 17% of Cubans actively opposed to Fidel Castro. For perspective consider Somalia in 2016, a failed state riven by war, famine and al-Shabab: fully one-sixth of its population now lives abroad. In Cuba only one man, Fidel Castro, managed the same trick.

In spite of all the regime's precautions, a few quite notable uprisings still occurred. On April 14, 3 days prior to the invasion, a spectacular act of sabotage totally destroyed *El Encanto*, Cuba's largest and most popular department store, which had been nationalized the previous year. The destruction was caused by introducing white phosphorous into the air conditioning vents—and then lighting it. The damage totaled 6 million dollars. On the same day in Santiago de Cuba, at the other end of the island, *El Ancla* and *La Comercial*, two big nationalized department stores, were firebombed with the loss of their entire inventory. Additionally, on April 16, 14 armed counter-revolutionaries led an uprising in Las Villas Province.

And, during the invasion itself, 50 to 60 civilians joined the invasion, helping to carry supplies, caring for the wounded, providing food and water and even taking up arms to fight Castro, with an equal number of Castro's militia switching sides and volunteering to fight with the Brigade.

3) PROPAGANDA: Radio Swan, located on a tiny, rocky islet claimed by Nicaragua, had a threefold purpose. Modeled on a propaganda radio station run by David Atlee Phillips during the CIA-aided Jacobo Arbenz overthrow in 1954 in Guatemala, it was meant to provide unbiased news reports into a country with state-controlled, heavily-censored media. Crucially, it also spun news toward its own ends and even disseminated plenty of disinformation— whatever aided the "covert action plan." Finally, it was meant to incite the Cuban population into open revolt, both with an artillery barrage of disaffection before the invasion and an outright call to arms during the attack augmented by the dropping of propaganda leaflets over Havana at the moment of truth.

Unfortunately, its cryptic broadcasts—with nonsense non-sequitur phrases such as "The fish is red; Chico is in the house; Visit him;"—especially during the unexpected failures of the original plan when scripts were lacking, caused it to loose relevance and reliability.

4) ASSASSINATION: Probably the best-known and publicized part of the "covert action plan against Cuba" was the CIA's Rube Goldberg machinations to assassinate Fidel Castro. Again, it wasn't quite that simple.

For one, the CIA had no experience with assassination. The idea originally came from Rafael Trujillo, the Dominican Republic's long-serving dictator who had a long-running feud with Castro. In Trujillo's attempt to overthrow the Cuban dictator (in retribution for Castro's attempt to overthrow Trujillo in June of 1959), he teamed up with the Mafia. Castro had rescinded the Santo Traficante, Meyer Lansky, and Momo Giancana casino franchises in Cuba. It's not safe to fool with mother Mafia. She wanted revenge. In August of 1959, Trujillo attempted an invasion of Cuba coupled with a Mafia-planned execution of the Cuban dictator. It failed; but as far as the Mafia was concerned, it was unfinished business.

Enter the CIA with Eisenhower's plan.

It wasn't the first time the Mafia and the US government had teamed up. Based on their highly successful and profitable initial collaboration—particularly in saved lives—the idea had merit. In 1943 Europe was an impregnable Axis fortress. Where to sneak in and get a toehold for the proposed Allied invasion of Europe? With Allied armies controlling North Africa and Mussolini's Italy beginning to fall apart, Sicily—only 96 miles from Tunisia—was the logical choice. But Sicily was the cradle and home of the Mafia—in spite of *Il Duce's* many attempts to eradicate it. John Julius Norwich in his book, *Sicily*, tells the story:

> *"American intelligence officers…understood that for the projected invasion to be successful it was vitally important to have the Mafia firmly on the Allied side. They therefore made careful approaches to the dominant boss of gangland crime in the United States, a Sicilian named Salvatore ('Lucky') Luciano. He had in fact been in prison since 1936 on compulsory prostitution charges, but was still very much in command. In late 1942, after long discussions, the two sides struck a deal. Luciano would have his sentence commuted; in return, he made two promises. The first was that his friend Albert Anastasia, who ran the notorious*

Murder Inc. and who also controlled the American docks, would protect the waterfront and prevent dockworker strikes for the duration of hostilities. The second was that he, Luciano, would contact other friends in Sicily, who would in turn ensure that the invasion would run as smoothly as possible."

Many ideas—eight according to the Congressional Church Committee; 638 according to Castro's chief of counterintelligence—were launched, including the infamous exploding cigar scenario. Only a few floated. None succeeded. One of the earliest plans was conceived by Félix Rodriguez, #2718 in Brigade 2506. On New Year's 1961, Rodriguez volunteered to assassinate Castro; the Americans took him up on it and flew him out of Guatemala to Miami.

He was given a German bolt-action rifle with a powerful telescopic sight. The plan was to secretly drop Rodriguez near Varadero beach from a yacht. From there he would be picked up by underground operatives and taken to a safe house in Havana, from where he would be able to shoot Fidel along an area he frequented. Three times he tried, but he never made it to Cuba. Two of the missions were scrubbed while crossing the Florida Straits; one for security reasons and the other due to mechanical failure. After the Bay of Pigs affair, Rodriguez joined the CIA. He was the last officer to interrogate *Che* Guevara and, as a Captain in the Bolivian army, conveyed the order to execute the guerrilla. The last picture of *Che* alive is with Félix Rodriguez.

Ultimately, the entire scheme was subbed out to the Mafia, with no CIA oversight or professional input (other than the poison-laced-cold cream type of ideas), other than money. At that time, anyway you looked at it, no amount of money could persuade anyone to commit suicide to kill a foreign head of state: they surely would be caught (with no virgins awaiting in the afterlife). The rationale for the attempt was that cutting off the head of the serpent, even if you yourself couldn't wield the sword, would atrophy the body. It all came to naught.

5) TIMING: At first, with the guerrilla infiltration plan, a few score men, relatively simple logistics and little urgency, the operation was roughly scheduled for September, 1960. As the operation grew larger and more complicated, delays became inevitable and they began pressing up against the presidential election season between November's balloting and January's inauguration—an extremely awkward time for an invasion of choice. So it was decided to postpone the invasion until the new president was in office. However, that delay caused more delays: the new Democrat president had to get up to speed on a military action bequeathed him by a Republican administration for which he'd be held responsible.

But then other factors impinged, counseling haste. Czechoslovakia was training fifty Cuban pilots to fly Soviet MIG 21s and the Soviet Union was about to supply Castro with high-speed Komar patrol boats to guard the coast. In the meantime, the Eastern Block was pumping arms into Cuba at an ever greater rate. New by president JFK wasn't briefed about Ike's "covert action plan against Cuba" until January 28, 1961.

Between JFK making up his mind as to the depth of commitment he was willing to give Ike's "covert action plan," its organic morphing into something bigger and more ungainly, and the delivery of brand-new Soviet MIGs scheduled for April—that would turn Castro's "air force" into a *real* air force—organizational plans continued going forward, while a final thumbs up or thumbs down decision was put off to the last possible minute.

As D-day approached, the President temporized after considering the last-minute counsel from the members of his administration that were skeptical of the whole operation: Arthur M. Schlesinger, Jr., Secretary of State Dean Rusk, Senator William Fulbright, and UN Ambassador Adlai Stevenson, who all thought that the operation was "too spectacular." So Kennedy ordered the CIA to, "reduce the noise level of this thing." In essence, he wanted to marry opposing and essentially incompatible goals— an immaculate invasion: invading Cuba without actually invading it. So, rather than invading next to a big city, the invasion was switched from Trinidad to a more remote locale, the Bay of Pigs.

JFK did not approve the invasion until a half-day past the deadline he'd been presented. That deadline was based on the invasion force's navigation time and the air strikes' flight time, with the elephant in the room being what to do with a disgruntled invasion force that might be told to stand down on the eve of attack. At one point while considering this conundrum, JFK was heard to muse about the last concern with, "If we have to get rid of these 800 [sic] men, it is much better to dump them in Cuba than in the United States, especially if that is where they want to go."

* * *

But was the Brigade ready? Armandito was raring to go; Cachorro, not so much. Though his commitment and dedication to the cause were one-hundred percent, and he instantly volunteered for what was described as a suicide mission, he was more reflective. Filled with a sense of honorable duty and the resigned conclusion that this project was a culmination of his life's trajectory to that moment, he took to heart the words of the Cuban national anthem, "that to die for the fatherland is to live." Nagging at him in the back of his head was his one and only training jump. Could he perform effectively? Would he? He was scared.

To assess the combat readiness of the Brigade, the Joint Chiefs of Staff sent three colonels to Guatemala as observers. They concluded that the Brigade was "ready, willing, and able to fight in Cuba." From weapons handling to leadership to morale, the evaluators gave the soldiers marks of "good," "excellent," or "superior." The Air Force colonel noted that the Cuban pilots were well-trained and even had more hours than the average USAF pilot had before going into combat in WWII.

The newly pervasive sense of urgency that now permeated the operation; President Kennedy's diffidence; the lack of a central operational command all contributed to disorganized, ad hoc, seat-of-the-pants decisions. On April 4, less than 2 weeks before the invasion, the landing site switch was made official: from Trinidad to the Bahía de Cochinos, a swampy indentation on the south coast of Cuba nearly 100 miles west of Trinidad.

David Atlee Phillips, the propaganda chief (and Pop's old Havana tenant), immediately noticed problems with the change. The new landing site was now too far away from the Escambray Mountains for any invaders to plausibly escape in case of defeat. Additionally, Bahía de Cochinos translated to Bay of Pigs. "How can we have a victorious landing force wading ashore at a place with that name?" No amount of skillful propaganda could spin rooting pigs into soaring eagles.

* * *

The boys, of course, knew none of this, other than what the rumor mill—a never-ending source of entertainment, some of it sometimes true—cranked out. They had no idea where in Cuba they were going, not even on Tuesday, April 11 when the first orders to mobilize were received at Armandito's 2nd Battalion. Eli César was on watch at Base Trax that night when he heard a convoy of trucks cranking up the narrow, abyss-bordered mountain road to the training camp at midnight. He knew something was up because supplies were never delivered that late.

He was right. The following morning his 3rd Battalion received orders to be ready to move out at 17:00 hours, an order that was further confirmed at noon on the 12th, the day after Armandito's 2nd Battalion had already decamped. The men felt well trained and confident. An incredible atmosphere of spiritual exuberance electrified the camp. The men of Cachorro's 1st Battalion of Paratroops, the last to move out, went round the barracks exchanging *abrazos*, hand squeezes and encouragement. Overcome with emotion, the men started dancing to a conga rhythm. Someone sang out, an adaptation of an old chorus:

Si tú pasas por mi casa
Y tú vez a mi mujer
Tú le dices que hoy no esperes
Me voy con la Brigada
Veinticinco, cero seis.
Mírala que linda viene
Mírala que linda va
La Brigada veinticinco
Cero seis, que ya se va.

If you're going by my house
And you see my lover, my lady
Tell her not to wait,
Not to hope for my return.
I'm leaving with the Brigade
Twenty five-o-six
Pretty woman here she comes,
Pretty woman there she goes
Oh my Brigade Twenty five-o-six
There she goes.

(Translated by A. R. Hatch-Miller)

Mobilization began with a 3-hour roller-coast ride, in overloaded personnel trucks, in the foggy night, down the single-lane Base Trax track to the Retalhuleu air strip. The white-knuckle ride focused minds. Though for the past 4-7 months the men's lives had been in play, unconditionally dedicated to liberating Cuba—and men had died in training—this was it, *this was finally it.* To César it seemed that the mountains stood in mute salute to them as they filed by, the silent echoes of the hundreds of thoughts that filled the trucks reverberating off the canyon walls until someone broke the tension with a bad joke and the rest followed with even worse jokes.

At Retalhuleu the men boarded C-46 and C-54 transports for the 2-hour flight—around neutral El Salvador and Honduras—to the Happy Valley air base where they would board railcars to take them to Puerto Cabezas on the Caribbean coast of Nicaragua, where the ships of the García Line awaited them. Throughout that long night of transport no one slept, except for deep, albeit short, cat naps induced by the rhythmic clack-clack of the train.

As the men shuttled through Happy Valley, Marine Colonel Jack Hawkins had come down for a final review of the troops—for the Pentagon, the CIA and the President. "These officers are young, vigorous, intelligent and motivated with a fanatical urge to begin battle for which most of them have been preparing in rugged conditions…for almost a year. Without exception, they have utmost confidence in their ability to win…I share their confidence," he wrote.

The last to leave Base Trax was Cachorro's 1st Battalion of Paratroopers with 171 men. No García Line for them; they were flying directly into Cuba out of Blue Fields, Nicaragua. Cachorro, in a letter to his son many years later, recalls that day:

"There on the runway the concept of the operation and what was expected from each group was briefly explained, along with the military code names for the locations of our jumps. One of my companions, a fisherman familiar with the area, told me in whispers, 'That's the Cienega de Zapata (Zapata Marshes) and we're going to jump near the Central Australia (Australia Sugar Refinery)'.

Right away, the Battalion chief, Alejandro del Valle, dismissed the group but requested 'the following personnel to remain in place.'

I heard my name.

Nineteen of us stood there facing del Valle. 'You've been chosen for a mission that is essential to the success of this operation. If this mission is not carried out, the entire operation is doomed to failure. I should point out that none of you will probably survive. Therefore, before briefing you on the details, if any of you do not wish to participate, you may retire without dishonor.'

It didn't surprise me that no one stepped away. I'd known Carlitos since first grade. Others had proven their valor in the Sierra Maestra fighting for and against the Revolution. We were all—black, white, young, old, poor, rich Cubans, so dissimilar yet united by our willingness to give our all, absolutely convinced that to die for the motherland is to live.

One of those nineteen was Carlos Manuel Varona, son of Antonio de Varona, Prime Minister of Cuba from 1948 to 1950 and later President of the Senate. The elder Varona was now part of the Revolutionary Council, the proposed interim government. His skin in the game was his 18-year-old son Carlitos, there of his own accord and full of piss and vinegar. When Varona *fils* heard he wasn't likely to survive the mission he declared, "What the fuck? This guy's crazy! He doesn't know what he's talking about."

10

Bahía de Cochinos

According to the Cuban Information Archives, the area known as "Bahía de Cochinos" does not properly translate into "Bay of Pigs," even though the word *cochino* means 'pig' or 'dirty'. The correct translation should read, "Bay of the Cochinos Fish," after the fish known as the "cochino," which lives in the bay. Alternatively, Peter Wyden, in *Bay of Pigs: The Untold Story*, says that the bay is named for the feral pigs that roam the area. These are descended from stock left behind by pirates to feed in the wild to provide meat during their sporadic visits to this remote part of Cuba.

But there's another, somewhat minor, controversy surrounding the name. Cuban exiles, Brigade members and US sources refer to the invasion by the name Bay of Pigs. In Cuba, the regime uses the term Playa Girón. Playa Girón is the small town where Brigade headquarters were set up, and it was the last redoubt of the Brigade's resistance. It was here where Castro declared final victory over the invaders. Playa Girón is not *in* the Bay of Pigs, but rather just east of it at its verge.

At the very head of the Bay of Pigs sits the even smaller enclave of Playa Larga. It was here, at the highway roundabout, that the Brigade won its biggest battle, the Battle of the Rotonda. And a spectacular victory/defeat it was.

There are only two land approaches to Playa Girón, one from the northeast and one from the northwest. The northwest approach, through Playa Larga, crosses the Zapata swamps on an elevated causeway. It is a narrow and singular access road. The northeastern approach, through San Blas, runs through thick vegetation and is much longer. Control of the two approaches would guarantee a safe beachhead for the Brigade headquarters. With its airstrip, Playa Girón would also be a dependable resupply base and a safe haven for establishing the Miró Cardona provisional government. It was at Girón where the majority of the troops and most of the big hardware of the Armored 4th Battalion were to land.

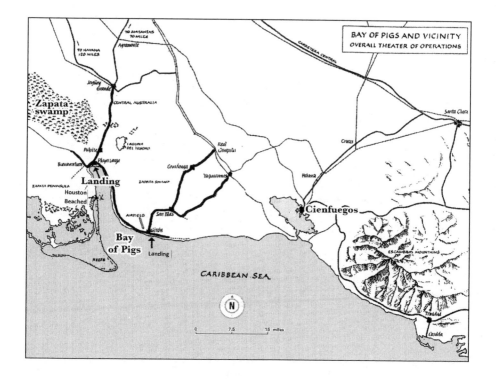

The plan for securing the approaches to Playa Girón depended on cutting Castro's access to the little town from both roads. This required the skillful deployment of paratroopers at choke points north of Playa Larga and San Blas before any seaborne landings took place.

Cachorro's 19-man suicide mission was to jump just south of Jagüey Grande, about 18 miles north of Playa Larga, and work their way south toward the Bay of Pigs blowing up bridges and culverts along the causeway, thereby preventing any advance from the Cuban army, which would be advancing south from bases in Matanzas. If possible, they were also to harry the troops, guerrilla-style, to further delay them. The *Central* Australia sugar refinery, on the southern outskirts of Jagüey Grande, dominated the area. This would become Fidel Castro's Bay of Pigs headquarters and the staging area for over 5,000 of his militia.

Australia Sugar Mill: Fidel Castro's command post during the Bay of Pigs invasion. Source: Estevan L. Bovo-Caras, Brigade 2506 Museum and Veterans' Association.

Facing the Cuban army at Playa Larga—those bits that managed to advance over the blown-up causeway—would be Armandito's 185-man 2nd Battalion and the 5th Battalion, about 400 men altogether. These would dig in at a strategic spot and seal the approach to Playa Girón.

Securing the approach from the San Blas area required a different approach, primarily because, unlike Playa Larga, San Blas was far from the coast. Here, most all of the combatants had to be parachuted in, with reinforcements advancing after a seaborne landing. The balance of the 1st Paratroop Battalion left over from Cachorro's 19-man "volunteers" at Playa Larga, part of the Armored 4th Battalion, and the 3rd Battalion, all had to hie to San Blas quick as a slurred Cuban insult. No bridges or culverts needed to be blown up. The men were to dig in and hold the line against any enemy advances.

The Playa Larga front would be under the command of Erneido Oliva; the Playa Girón/San Blas front, under Pepe San Román, military commander of the entire operation. The defensive positions at Playa Larga and San Blas had the potential for becoming "shooting galleries" for all who tried to pass. These were good plans—had Castro's air force been disabled.

* * *

The train deposited the troops from Base Trax next to one extremely long pier, lined by the freighters—serviceable, rusty tubs that did not inspire—of the Garcia Line. It had been an exhausting shuttle night. The men boarded the boats—the *Houston, Rio Escondido, Caribe,* and *Atlantico*—hungry and tired, and bivyed with their coats for pillows for the few hours left before daybreak. Armandito and the entire 2nd Battalion were assigned to the *Houston*. The following day, April 13, they awoke refreshed but still hungry. They were fed coffee, a Cuban essential, but no hot meals: the kitchens were not able to service larger complements than a standard crew.

It was a day filled with activity. Ships were loaded, heaved away, and others jockeyed for position for more loading. The men rested, practiced drills with the most recent recruits, cleaned their rifles, reminisced and discussed their prospects. Their lives, their family and friends, Cuba, perhaps even the world were on a tipping point. K-rations and canned goods were passed out. Canned pears were a big hit; K-rations not. Stoves for hot meals were prohibited due to the gasoline and ammunition on the boats. Smoking was also prohibited, but the Cubans lit up anyway. Sanitary facilities were dismal to non-existent. There were no showers, and the toilet consisted of a plank astern at the edge of the appropriately named poop deck, directly over the ship's propeller, upon which one squatted, bum to the briny. It was a very exposed and dangerous position necessitating a safety team (usually available as there was always a line) who were never short of gut-clenching comments.

At five o'clock in the afternoon on Friday, April 14, Nicaraguan President Luis Somoza appeared on the docks pomaded, powdered and surrounded by his security detail to wish the men a good voyage and success. "Bring me a couple of hairs from Castro's beard," he concluded, and the ships hauled anchor for Cuba.

* * *

The four freighters carried the majority of the 1,543 Brigade men. Two other ships, the *Blagar* and *Barbara J,* served as flagships, from which the commanders of the operation, including two US CIA operatives, would direct the action. The six ships took separate routes to Cuba, so as not to look like a flotilla. Each ship had a dedicated US naval escort. US Navy destroyers orbited a bit farther out. All the US ships kept their distance and were only sometimes barely detectable on the horizon—guardian angels with clipped wings, prohibited from engaging the enemy unless first fired upon. Even farther afield, almost like emanations and penumbras, hovered the *Essex* and *Boxer*, two US Navy aircraft carriers with only a stand-by remit. One night the men on the *Houston* even reported one American submarine circling the ship.

Nonetheless, ship owner Eduardo Garcia, his merchant crewmen and the Brigade leaders were concerned for their safety. They insisted that the old rust buckets be retrofitted with deck-mounted .50 caliber machine guns so they could defend themselves in case of attack. Running a bit behind schedule, the guns for the *Houston* had to be mounted en-route by Garcia's crew.

The men passed the time playing cards, talking and listening to Radio Swan, the CIA's propaganda station. When it announced the first air strike over Cuba, the men cheered, little realizing that the attack—truncated and rescheduled at the last minute by a nervous President Kennedy—warned Castro of the impending invasion, a warning that he used to hide his remaining planes and round up thousands of suspected dissidents.

The morning of April 16 dawned hot and still. The seas were boringly glassy. Few men had slept well. Aboard the *Atlantico* the men awoke depressed and disgusted. One of the hastily installed machine guns, during practice rounds, had broken its mount killing one Brigade member and injuring two. But morale improved as the day progressed. The chaplain celebrated mass; Radio Swan predicted a great victory; one last, hot meal (beef, mashed potatoes and beer), served in relays, was promised. Best of all, forty miles off the coast of Cuba, the six Brigade ships came together in a convoy. With the US support vessels on the horizon, they now felt like a real navy.

On board, squad leaders focused the ambient tensions by reviewing plans and procedures, and gravely emphasizing potential obstacles. Everyone was gripped by the 'big eye', that concentrated ball of determination in the gut of each man that indicated total psyching—a berserker with clarity. Still, they were nervous but philosophical: they would either win or die. New, camouflage uniforms were issued and donned. Packs, guns, and ammo were checked one last time. Pepe San Román, the military leader, and Manuel Artime, the civilian representative of the provisional government that would assume leadership of Cuba, led the men on the *Blagar* in a moving ceremony, raising the Cuban flag and closing with *La Bayamesa*, the Cuban national anthem. It was going to be a short night.

On the *Houston*, Erneido Oliva, second in command of the entire operation and commander of the Playa Larga front, led by example. The men spontaneously broke into *La Bayamesa* and raised the Cuban standard. Armandito, psyched but not one to worry, and always keyed up in a laid back sort of way, managed to sleep.

Garcia Line ship 'Houston', Armandito Lastra's 2nd Battalion's transport; hit inside the Bay of Pigs while unloading and scuttled on shoals. Source: Estevan L. Bovo-Caras, Brigade 2506 Museum and Veterans' Association.

* * *

Back at Blue Fields, Nicaragua, at 11 pm on the 16th, the separate contingents of the 177-man 1st Paratroop Battalion were boarding the planes that would take them to Cuba. It was a six-hour flight. Cachorro and the 19-man suicide demolition crew, under the command of Ruben *El Cojo* (lame) Vera, were to be dropped south of Jagüey Grande. Another, larger group, would be dropped at Palpite, 3 miles north of Playa Larga. The largest contingent of paratroopers, the vanguard for a battle-ready, defensive position, was headed north of San Blas to three separate locations.

Cachorro had entrusted himself to his fate, come what may. He was beyond scared; he'd reached a state of calm resignation and was concentrating on performing effectively—in spite of his one inadequate training jump. (He was in good company. General Maxwell D. Taylor, Chairman of the Joint Chiefs of Staff under President Kennedy, had made only one practice jump before the 101st Airborne Division's aerial assault on Normandy at D-Day.)

* * *

Shortly before midnight, the *Barbara J* and *Houston* veered northwest, away from the convoy, toward the Bay of Pigs, where they dropped anchor 5 miles shy of Playa Larga. The *Barbara J* dropped 4 frogmen to prepare the landing site for the 2nd and 5th Battalions. The other four ships headed directly for Playa Girón, with the *Rio Escondido* stopping 5 miles offshore. The *Blagar*, *Atlantico*, and *Caribe* continued to within 2,000 yards of the town, anchored, and dropped their contingent of frogmen to prepare the landing for the 4th and 6th Battalions, about 700 men, and most of the big hardware—the tanks, tractors, and trucks.

Just after midnight on the 17th, a Cuban military jeep at Girón shined its headlights on the *Blagar* frogmen's rubber raft, thinking they were fishermen in trouble. The raft squad leader wasted no time. He gave the first attack command of the invasion: "Fire!"

And so began the hostilities. The red and orange tracer bullets were visible on the *Houston* deep inside the Bay of Pigs 12 miles away.

The shots alerted Castro's militia, local residents conscripted but barely trained, to prepare for war, and a rag-tag crew rushed to the beach. The *Blagar* swung broadside to the shore and opened up with its .50 caliber machine guns. In ten minutes the beach was cleared. The frogmen signaled readiness at 1 am, and landings at Girón began, though heavy equipment was delayed until daylight due to surf and difficult-to-negotiate reefs.

By dawn the Playa Girón theatre had become a real war. The men on the *Atlantico*, amid heavy swell, were descending landing nets—port and starboard—into light, undersized fiberglass landing launches. As they neared land, the fully-loaded soldiers had to jump overboard 100 yards from the beach into 8 feet of water and wade in. Up in the sky, a C-46, en route to deliver the first contingent of 30 paratroopers of the 1st Battalion to San Blas tipped its wings in greeting. Nearing San Blas the pilot, Edward Ferrer, encountered militia (all of Castro's regular forces and reserves retained their Revolutionary name: militia) in jeeps, rifles pointed up at him, bullets tinging the plane. So he dropped his men just north of San Blas and wished them luck.

On turning around he noticed a Castro B-26, a survivor of the first Brigade air strike, out his window. Then the B-26's wing-mounted .50 caliber machine guns opened fire. Ferrer's cargo plane was unarmed, so he raced back to the beach and the protection of the Brigade ships. The Castro B-26, having approached from the north, now noticed the flotilla and landings for the first time. Distracted, the Castro pilot strafed the ships and landing boats, which, in turn, fired back, disabling one of its engines with a .50 caliber machine gun. Critically wounded, the Castro B-26 was expected to high-tail it home.

But the B-26 pilot wasn't through. Aiming his crippled plane kamikaze-style, he bull's eyed straight for the *Atlantico*. Every gun on the *Atlantico*—from .45 caliber hand guns, M-1 Garand rifles, Browning Automatic Rifles (BARs), to .30 and .50 caliber machine guns—opened fire. Every bullet must have hit. Miraculously, and only yards from the ship, the B-26 flipped over backwards and dropped tail first into the drink.

* * *

Meanwhile, up in the Bay of Pigs, the *Barbara J*'s frogmen were also shot at, this time near the end of their chore, from one of the nearby shacks. One of the frogmen, Andy Pruna, said, "We opened up almost automatically with our BARs (Browning Automatic Rifles) and we really gave them hell. We knocked out perhaps as many as twenty in a few minutes and the rest ran away..." But from their flank they spotted the lights of vehicles approaching. It was quarter-to-one in the morning. The frogmen gave the signal to unload and urged haste.

The *Houston* began unloading men and equipment onto its landing crafts at 1 am—in only slightly calmer waters than at Playa Girón. Right away, *la ley de Merfi* went into effect. The light fiberglass boats didn't prove up to the task and promptly capsized. Or their motors sputtered and choked due to the wrong mixture of oil and gasoline. Luis Morse, the relaxed skipper of the *Houston* dismissed them as "good for nothing." Soon only two of the nine were able to make the twenty-minute trip to the beach. As *Life* magazine characterized it, "The debarkation from *Houston* continued to be agonizingly slow." Even the rusty old winches that lowered them were barely serviceable, making an infernal racket that one Brigade member feared might be heard "maybe in Havana." Which they were at least in Playa Larga.

The order of debarkation was 2nd Battalion's G Company, followed by Armandito's E Company. F Company, the third to unload didn't get off until daybreak. As Hugo Sueiro, commander of 2nd Battalion, neared shore in the first landing craft shortly after 1 am, machine guns started firing at the *Houston*. It returned fire. The returning frogmen were caught in the crossfire, killing one—the first Brigade member to die at the Bay of Pigs.

The men hadn't expected combat right away. A peculiar terror dominated the landing crafts as they approached live fire in total darkness. Nervous jokes followed by the officers' "Shut up!" dominated the first group of small boats. The first soldier to land sank in over his head and had to be dragged back on board. Everyone bitched at the pilot. On shore, passwords were quickly whispered and shallow foxholes dug with calloused hands; in the rush to disembark many had forgotten their folding spades.

With everything going wrong, Erneido Oliva, overall commander of the Playa Larga operation, who wasn't supposed to land until the 2nd Battalion was ashore, decided it would be better for morale if he disembarked right away. But his staff was unprepared and nervous. Haynes Johnson describes the scene:

"In jumping from the ladder to the small boat below, one of the men struck the pilot and knocked him into the water. The boat drifted away. None of the seven men aboard knew how to operate the outboard motor and so they floated helplessly. At one point they were so close to the Houston's propeller they were certain they would be destroyed. Then for forty-five maddening minutes, while they heard the sound of battle on the shore, they drifted in the midst of the Bay of Pigs awaiting a launch from the Houston. Finally it came and at 2:30 am Oliva ingloriously reached the shore. By then only sporadic firing was heard."

Armandito and *Chino* clambered down the Jacobs ladders and landed on the beach sometime soon after Oliva, followed by the rest of the 2nd Battalion.

* * *

Which microwave radio station, the one at Playa Larga or the one at Playa Girón (both of which were missed by CIA intelligence), first notified Fidel Castro of the invasion is a moot point; but at 1:15 am (according to Peter Wyden) Castro knew of the landings at Girón. But he had no idea whether they were a diversion, commandos intent on sabotage, rogue Cuban exiles or a full-blown American invasion. He immediately called a meeting of his military command to brainstorm a strategy and formulate a response.

According to Arnaldo Remigio, the Cuban FAR paramedic, in an account given him by Comandante Dr. Figueredo—who was present—Castro arrived at 2:15 am carrying a 9mm Tommy gun. All the men at the table, in spite of holding the same rank of Major as Castro, carried no hand guns in their holsters, "since the early stages [of the Revolution] anyone approaching Castro for a meeting was carefully frisked and any hand gun removed."

Remigio continues with Figueredo's account:

"[Castro] *lit a long and thick Havana Cigar. After spitting the top part of the cigar, the spit with brownish saliva and the cigar slit fell on the armrest of a chair occupied by an army Major. The man jumped in the air like a wild horse trying to remove the rider and, after wiping away the spit from his uniform with a handkerchief he discarded it under the chair. 'What the fuck is going on with you? Castro yelled at the man. 'Some soldier you are! What about if that were a piece of gut of a dying man or better yet, what would you have done if that man vomited blood on you?'"*

"*The officer remained silent, his ashen white face was more than sufficient to express his sentiments toward the bearded bully in front of him, a man who was taking advantage of his higher rank and above all, of the healthy company of his twenty bodyguards, heavily armed, who filled the room in every angle.*"

After berating the men, fulminating about their incompetence and promising to demote them all, Castro decided on a proportionate response to the Bay of Pigs landings. He ordered the cadets of the Militia Leadership School, the 339th Battalion, aka the Cienfuegos Battalion—the crack troops of the Cuban militia—down to the Bay of Pigs on the double. The 900 men (Figueredo says 1,200) were stationed in Matanzas, about 80 miles north of Playa Larga. They had no idea where they were going. Additionally, this "crack" battalion had had only fifteen days of basic military training consisting of semi-automatic weapons handling and a cursory strategy lesson that came down to headlong attacks with all guns blazing. Only four semi-trained paramedics accompanied the battalion.

Their commander, Captain José Ramón *El Gallego* Fernández was in Havana, another 65 miles west of Matanzas. Cachorro's grandfather had been Fernández' teacher; Fernández was his favorite pupil. Cachorro and Fernández knew each other well. Cachorro describes Fernández as an honorable man—in spite of being a dedicated Communist. His honesty was a trait that would hurt him later when he testified at the Brigade's trial at El Príncipe prison in Havana.

Castro ordered Fernández to, "take a car and go to Matanzas at full speed," while he began preparations to head for the *Central* Australia, the sugar mill on the outskirts of Jagüey Grande where he planned to set up his headquarters, all the while repeatedly calling Captain Fernández demanding to know why he hadn't arrived yet. Shortly before 3:00 am Fernández left with five other men crammed into a jeep.

Haynes Johnson, in *The Bay of Pigs: The Leaders' Story of Brigade 2506*, reports that Castro wasn't informed of the invasion until 3:15 in the morning, and that, besides the Matanzas Leadership School militia contingent, he ordered a battalion of 900 men already stationed at the *Central* Australia, under the command of Osmani Cienfuegos (Camilo Cienfuegos' brother), to advance to Playa Larga. Additionally, he ordered Cienfuegos to mobilize several platoons of armed peasant militia to join the advance.

There are several, not always completely conflicting accounts, of exactly what happened and when on that fateful April 17 between midnight and 10 am. Even Peter Wyden in his book, seems to contradict (confuse?) himself. It doesn't surprise Cachorro. But one thing seems certain. Fidel Castro's focus was Playa Larga. It was 20 miles farther inland than Girón and provided a beeline to Havana. Even though Girón was the focus of the Brigade—as a relatively isolated redoubt in which to establish a safe base and a provisional government, and Castro, astute as always, was quite aware of the dangers a provisional government would bring—the best route to Girón was through Playa Larga.

At 4:00 am, Castro called Captain Enrique Carreras, his most seasoned pilot—though without any combat experience—and ordered him to sink the invasion ships while leaving the landing craft alone. Carreras had two hours before dawn—when he could see to fly—to pick a wing man and formulate a strategy.

Meanwhile, Captain Fernández, well ahead of the Matanzas cadet school militia, finally got to the *Central* Australia shortly after 8:00 am. The sugar mill manager reported—somewhat exaggeratedly ("Maybe five hundred of them!")—that the town was surrounded by enemy paratroopers (Cachorro's 1st Battalion, which had landed in the vicinity an hour or so before—see below).

At 3:44 am, Radio Swan, with less-than-convincing oratory and probably a bit prematurely, called on the Cuban armed forces to revolt. At Playa Larga, the local militia had tuned in to radio broadcasts, including Radio Swan, to find out what was happening. The voice there announced that they were being liberated from Communism and that Castro had been taken prisoner. The militiamen shook their heads in disbelief. David Atlee Phillips' propaganda had worked in Guatemala back in '54. This time nobody took it seriously—not even Phillips, who by now realized that the invasion was a catastrophe.

* * *

The 1st Paratroop Battalion transport plane, a C-46, arrived over Playa Larga at dawn carrying *El Cojo* Vera's 19-man demolition contingent, which included Cachorro, and the Palpite advance fighters. A second, heavy weapons and ammunition C-54 transport carrying both paratrooper groups' equipment followed closely. The C-46 was scheduled to drop the first contingent of paratroops at Palpite, 3 miles north of Playa Larga, and secure it. Outside Cachorro could see the invasion in progress and spared a thought for Armandito down below.

While both planes headed north, the pilots spotted 2 Castro planes in the distance and took evasive action. In the confusion, the pilots ended up dropping the men farther from the original drop zones. In the case of the Palpite drops, the men missed the dry roadbed entirely. The men landed in the swamp, under heavy fire, their equipment falling into the muck and sinking. One man was found dead, dangling from a tree in his chute. Nonetheless, they regrouped and tried to take Palpite but were driven back and forced to retreat.

After dropping the Palpite troops, the C-46 with the remaining paratroops, *El Cojo* Vera's contingent, continued north nearly to Jagüey Grande, where it encountered a Katyusha rocket launcher in the distance. The pilot immediately dropped altitude and gave the signal to jump. But it was almost too late.

Jumping out of a plane, during combat, after only one practice jump, is a terrifying ordeal. As the drop zone is approached, the men line up next to the door and clip their chute popper, a line that automatically pops open the parachute and immediately breaks after the jump. Each man checks the one in front to ensure that his line is not compromised in any way. Once the drop zone has been reached, a green light signals the paratroopers to begin jumping. They all know that the first man out is a juicy target. If that man knows his stuff, he'll kick out a gear bag before he jumps. A split second later, a one-word chant fills the cabin.

Arre! Arre! Arre!

Cachorro was first out the door. That, the low altitude, and his extra hundred pounds of ammunition, rushed him to the ground faster than any of the others, where he landed a bit farther south and separate from the rest. The little 17-year-old managed to successfully unload his hundred pounds of ammunition just before landing in chest-deep water only 200 yards from the causeway. His heart was pounding uncontrollably. He watched helplessly as two of his companions were shot in the air. It was at that moment that Cachorro realized his mission was doomed to failure, and that the entire operation would be a bust. Not only had the element of surprise evaporated, and the Castro forces mobilized, but much of the mission's equipment had been lost, sunk in the gumbo or disappeared in the nebulous distance. The nineteen-man demolition mission was late, lost, too lightly armed, and too scattered to be of any use. And it had lost *El Cojo* Vera, its leader. He'd landed on the opposite side of the causeway with no safe way to cross due to the constant militia traffic. No one ever saw him again.

Still, things were looking up. There were no crocodiles in sight. A pallet of K-rations had landed close to him, and he found dry land. He mused later that he could have survived right there for months. The helicopters that soon started crisscrossing the area didn't seem too interested in him. The northern extremity of the Zapata swamp consisted mostly of tall, razor-sharp grasses with islands of dry land and copses of overhead verdure. He was able to roughly get his bearings toward the area where the other men had landed, but he decided on caution. Cachorro sat alone, laying low, gathering his thoughts, for about three hours before deciding to look for the other men.

* * *

Meanwhile, back at the front…and Playa Larga was quickly becoming the main front; one that due to the disparities in final casualties and holding out of the Brigade forces would rival Thermopylae, events weren't unfolding as planned.

At dawn, on that fateful April 17th, as the two Brigade B-26s were heading towards Palpite and Jagüey Grande to drop Cachorro's paratroopers and the Palpite contingent, the two Castro planes that the Palpite-bound pilot had spotted that had caused him to take evasive action, actually consisted of 3 planes. One was a Sea Fury piloted by Captain Carreras, who'd finally gotten off the tarmac while it was still dark.

He'd chosen the prop plane not for its speed, but rather for its bomb-carrying capability. As wing man, he'd chosen another Sea Fury and a third plane, a B-26. Both accompanying pilots were so green that one, Del Pino, had never even fired from his plane in target practice. On his way to the Bay of Pigs Carreras was worried about colliding with his inexperienced pilots. Plus all three planes had serious defects: a funky gyroscope, an inaccurate bomb sight, automatic starters that didn't work, defective burners, and pirated parts from wrecks.

By dawn, the entire 2nd Battalion (except for one unit) from the *Houston* had landed. But the 5th Battalion was temporizing, to the point that the CIA operative overseeing the operation had to give them the 'courage talk.' It was understandable. The men of the 5th were the last to volunteer. Some had had only a few days of training before shipping out. Now they were thick in the maw. Sure they were terrified, all the men were; but without training, they lacked the confidence that well-trained men can use to tether their fear. But it was too late anyway.

When Carreras spotted the goings-on down at the head of the bay he exclaimed that it was "a Normandy invasion!" Acting fast, he dropped down low, got in very close—to compensate for his defective bomb sight—and dropped his bombs, immediately climbing again. Both were near misses. So he did a 180, began diving again, and released all eight of his rockets. It was 6:30 am.

Captain Morse on the *Houston*, about to pour a cup of coffee, felt a tremendous impact, but poured himself a cup anyway, "You never know when you can get another cup of coffee," he quipped. Carreras, gaining altitude, saw oil pouring out of the ship. Morse, leaning over the port side of the ship, "saw a gaping hole near the water line," and ordered the ship grounded before it sank. Miraculously, the rocket that hit the *Houston* did not explode, going right through its hull and out the bottom. Carreras, in response, zeroed in for a strafing run with his machine guns, raking the decks.

While Carreras was busy dispatching the *Houston*, his wing man, green Del Pino, scored his first kill. Ignoring Carreras' aerial combat instructions, to shoot only from "real close," when he could see the other pilot's helmet, Del Pino opened up on the tail of a Brigade B-26 at 200 yards and just kept firing until the enemy plane hit the water.

According to Jim Rasenberger in *The Brilliant Disaster*, Carreras first raked the *Blagar* with machine gun fire over at Girón before later turning on the *Houston* 20 miles away. Also, he says that machine guns on the *Barbara J* downed the B-26 that accompanied Carreras before Carreras sank the *Houston*. But once the *Houston* was disabled, the *Barbara J* exited the Bay of Pigs.

Either way, the loss of the *Houston* with its field hospital, heavy equipment and disabled 5th Battalion was a terrible loss. Captain Morse managed to run the vessel aground close to shore giving the 200 hundred men still on board a reasonable chance to escape; still, 20 men were killed by the raking and ten drowned (28 according to Johnson) during the emergency unloading. But the 5th Battalion was out of commission. Five or six miles from the Playa Larga front and facing a small contingent of militia, they hunkered down defensively.

Carreras' fuel was dwindling fast, but he was ecstatic, turning two belly rolls—the sign of victory—back at his base. Refueled, he headed back out for a second mission.

First he checked on the *Houston*. When he confirmed that the stern had sunk and it was out of commission, he headed for Girón, arriving shortly after 8 am (according to Wyden; Johnson says 7 am; Rasenberger, 9:30 am). Somewhere along the way two Brigade B-26s gave chase and shot at him, perforating his No. 1 cylinder. Carreras returned fire, hitting one plane; the other escaped, seeking refuge behind the friendly fire of the ships off shore—the *Blagar*, *Atlantico*, *Caribe*, and *Rio Escondido*. Nonetheless, Carreras didn't want to return to base with all his rockets still on the plane.

He set his sights on the *Rio Escondido*, and fired all four rockets. The ship exploded in what looked like a mushroom cloud that was seen and heard 16 miles away at Playa Larga. The *Rio Escondido* carried a ten-day supply of ammunition, food, gasoline and, critically, the central communications trailer for the entire enterprise. With the sinking of the *Rio Escondido*, the

Blagar, *Atlantico*, and *Caribe* retreated beyond Cuban territorial waters, promising to return after dark.

As Carreras climbed and banked away from his kill his engine started failing, trailing little flames. Back at his base, when he jumped to the ground, his legs were shaking badly.

* * *

What Armandito thought when he saw his ship, the *Houston*, bombed and sunk, he dismissed with a shrug. Though I said that all men are terrified when facing combat, it doesn't hold true for everyone. Armandito was fearless. He wasn't fearless due to bravado, or the 41 pound, .30 caliber Tommy gun he carried—which at one time during the fighting he lifted off its tripod, braced on his hip and let 'er rip—or even his strong Catholic faith: it was just the way he was. He was imperturbable. He created his own reality, even when reality imposed *its* reality on him. To those around him he was a rock, albeit a rough, unpredictable but lovable rock. By 9 am his Company, E, was facing a Battalion of *Responsible Milicias de Matanzas*.

11

La Rotonda

By 10 am on April 17 two of the three fronts were stable. The eastern front at San Blas was in the best shape. The paratroopers had landed successfully—if under air fire—with all of their equipment, meeting little resistance on the ground. A number of locals even joined the Brigade.

The central, Girón front, under Pepe San Román, though lacking much of its equipment due to the loss of the *Rio Escondido*, was stable, subject only to intermittent air attacks. The local militia had been defeated, 150 of them taken prisoner, with nearly 50 militiamen switching sides, volunteering to join the Brigade.

But the situation at Playa Larga, on the western front, seemed dire. Both paratroop contingents, Cachorro's and the Palpite group, were out of commission; the *Houston*, the front's home base, was sunk; and the 5th Battalion, which anyway was only meant to be a reserve unit, was out of action 10 miles distant.

There was one bright spot. Although Armandito's 2nd Battalion had been in constant combat since landing, they'd won every skirmish and managed to keep advancing inland. Playa Larga had been taken.

Erneido Oliva, the overall second-in-command and in charge of the Playa Larga front, was finally able to make radio contact with San Román and report on the situation. San Román told Oliva to prepare for the worst—the main body of Castro's army was headed for Playa Larga, a piece of intelligence he'd gathered from his prisoners. Oliva asked for a tank and a squad of infantry from the 4th Armored Battalion to beef up his forces for the onslaught. San Román responded that a tank was on its way and that the squad would soon follow.

Oliva prepared for the worst. He separated the 3 companies in the 2nd Battalion, sending F Company, the vanguard, under Máximo Leonardo *Ñato* Cruz González forward toward Palpite. Cruz had four squads, each with about 12 men, reinforced with one .50 caliber machine gun, and one each 75 mm and 57 mm recoilless rifles. They were desperately short of ammunition. Cruz, only twenty-three years old, was not an impressive man. He was short, dark, quiet and not well educated. He weighed only 120 pounds but had an impressively large nose whom recruits joked he would not be able to get out of the way of incoming bullets (his nickname *Ñato*, meaning pug- or flat-nosed, was a product of affectionate sarcasm).

Máximo Leonardo 'Ñato' Cruz, Commander of F Company at the Battle of the Rotonda. Source: Casa de la Brigada, thanks to Humberto 'El Chino' Díaz Argüelles, President of the Brigade 2506 Veterans' Association.

A second company, Company E, under Oscar Luis Acevedo—Armandito's company—Oliva deployed nearby to guard his western, or left, flank. Acevedo, thirty-one, was also short and dark, but best remembered for his constant talk and laughter. He too had four squads. Together, Cruz and Acevedo had about one hundred men. Acevedo however would later join Cruz during the Battle of the Lost Battalion. The third, G Company, he held in reserve back at Playa Larga, just in case Castro's navy came up the Bay to attack Oliva's rear.

While carefully advancing north, Cruz spotted a number of militia coming toward them out of the brush:

"I let them take a certain time to get together and I took advantage of the agrupación (massing). *They were very close and when they were together I fired*

at them with the 75 mm, with the .50 caliber machine gun, and with the 57 cannon. I destroyed them completely. The 57 made a direct hit on their truck with a grenade of fósforo vivo (white phosphorous). *I was looking when the grenade hit and the whole truck blew up and I saw the men jumping, dying and being burned by the fósforo vivo. The rest ran away and did not come back until 2 pm."*

For a brief respite all was quiet on the western front. It's as if both sides broke for lunch. Forty prisoners had been taken, some of them women militia members. A few volunteered to join the Brigade but Oliva had no weapons to spare, so he put them to work in other capacities. At noon Radio Swan reported that the Brigade was winning. Oliva murmured, "The radio of Castro was better."

Oliva used the lull to take stock of his situation. He suspected that the Palpite paratroopers, as well as Cachorro's team, had failed to secure the road. But he hadn't yet given up on the 5th Battalion, dispatching some trucks to pick them up; a venture he soon canceled when he discovered from the prisoners what was on its way. Cruz dug his men into secure, camouflaged defensive positions on both sides of the causeway, each side with an additional barrier of swamp and trees. It was a prudent move. "We were able to shoot well from this position," he later said.

At 2:30 pm two of Cruz' scouts, about 600 yards ahead, reported that the enemy was advancing, in tight formation, straight down the road. Looking through his binoculars, Cruz recalls: "There were not a hundred. Not two hundred. There were not five hundred. Probably over a thousand people with weapons were coming down the road, on each side of the road. And I said, 'Uh-oh.'"

The advancing troops were the poorly-trained, 900-man-strong cadets of the Militia Leadership School in Matanzas—the 339th Battalion—led by Captain Jose Ramón *El Gallego* Fernández whom Castro had awaked in the wee hours of the morning. They were advancing with more than 60 vehicles. Cruz was about to test the Thermopylae theory that a few men could hold off a much larger force at a strategic choke point.

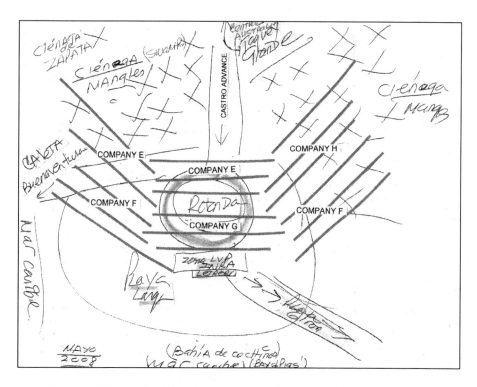

Labels visible in the hand-drawn map: Ciénaga Zapata, Ciénaga Mangles (swamp), Central Australia (Pueblo) Grande, Castro Advance, Ciénaga Mangles, Caleta Buenaventura, Company E, Company E, Company H, Mar Caribe, Company F, Rotonda, Company F, Company G, Zona Lira Letrero, Playa Larga, Playa Girón, Mayo 2008, (Bahía de cochinos) Mar Caribe (Bay of Pigs)

La Rotonda. This map, in all its primitive glory, was hand-drawn from memory in 2008 by Roberto Mancebo, one of the Rotonda battle combatants. The 1961 roundabout was later replaced by a Y intersection, so an accurate reconstruction was too difficult (if not impossible) to obtain. Countless inquiries to surviving Brigade members who participated in that battle failed to elicit any memory of the round-about intersection's measurements. Estimates varied from 25 to 100 meters for the traffic circle—a poignant indication of the intensity of the experience. One veteran compared the dimensions of the Playa Larga roundabout to the dimensions of the roundabout adjacent to the Palacio de los Deportes, along the Rancho Boyeros-Habana road, where the Brigade prisoners were first held. This roundabout measures about 100 meters in diameter. The superimposed red lines are approximations of the Brigade trenches, which Mancebo numbered between 15 and 25. Mangles=mangroves. North is at the top of the map

Cruz called Oliva. Instantly Oliva called Hugo Sueiro, 2nd Battalion commander, and both men headed for the front, ordering Acevedo's Company E to support Cruz. It was to be Armandito's first full-on engagement with an overwhelming force, yet the prospect didn't faze him. At the same time, the promised M-41 tank from Girón arrived with a squad from the 4th Battalion. The men kissed its side. "Maybe there will be a miracle and everything will turn out all right," one man said to Oliva.

"Don't be foolish," Oliva responded. "There are no miracles at a time like this."

Feeling a bit more confident, "We went to the front lines," recalls Oliva. Cruz takes up the narrative:

"When they were about five hundred yards from us they stopped, and they started putting up their mortars and getting their weapons prepared. They didn't send any forward observers to see where we were and they didn't know our positions. When I saw that they had all their weapons ready, I gave the order to open fire. I had to do it because they were getting organized there. When I gave the order to fire, you could see them flying up in the air. I threw everything at them with the three shells of the 75 I had left, with the 57, with the machine guns and all the weapons we had there. In ten or fifteen minutes there was a big mound of dead men all over the road."

One of the first explosive shells made a direct hit on a truck setting it on fire and blocking the road. And then a real miracle happened. Oliva was able to call for air support and, at 3:05 pm, two Brigade B-26s appeared and radioed for instructions. "Give it to them," Oliva said.

"The planes," Haynes Johnson reported, "made two or three passes, dropping rockets and NAPALM bombs." The carnage was horrible. The causeway was a solid wall of fire.

"It was awful," said Pedro Porraspita. "There were men screaming and running, and gasoline tanks blowing up. You could smell the burning flesh right away."

"No quedó ni el gato (not even the cat was left)," Cruz said. Out of 900 men only a handful survived. But then, at 3:30 pm, a Castro T-33 and a Sea Fury appeared. Both Brigade B-26s were out of ammunition. They were sitting ducks. Both were shot down.

*Jagüey Grande-Playa Larga causeway on Tuesday afternoon, April 18, 1961 after the
battle of the Rotonda.
Source: Estevan L. Bovo-Caras, Brigade 2506 Museum and Veterans' Association.*

As the battle wound down, a different sort of air support appeared.
Masses of *Auras tiñosas* (literally, "polluted airs," though *aura* is also the
species name), as the Cuban vulture is picturesquely called, circled and
swooped into the carnage, reminding the men how quickly life turns to rot.

* * *

At about that same time, early evening on the 17th, the first day of the
invasion, Cachorro decided to camp after wandering a short distance from
his drop spot. It was getting dark. Still, he could see, barely—his glasses lost
in the jump—and hear, any time he got near the road, hundreds of Castro
troops and tanks headed for Playa Larga and he shuddered at the thought of
the onslaught his buddies would soon be facing. He got as far from the road
as he could while it was still light enough.

Once he'd settled down, he heard a loud rustling in the grass. Prudently,
he audibly whispered the password, "*águila*." When he didn't hear the
counter-password, *negra*, he opened fire. Not a sound came back.

A thousand emotions rushed through him—it was his first combat, the first time he had ever killed another human being. He was just a kid. He never wanted to kill anyone.

The subject had been broached before, though in a context that was much closer to home. Civil wars, as the old saying goes, 'pit brother against brother; father against son.' One Brigade member knew his brother was in the Castro militia; under no conditions, did he want to shoot him. Although his companions reassured him that the chances of confronting his brother on the battlefield were nil, the soldier never stopped agonizing about the possibility. (And he was right. By the most improbable of coincidences, the two brothers faced off on the battlefield. When the Castro soldier saw his brother he threw down his gun and yelled, "I will not shoot my brother!" He was arrested and put in the stockade.)

Cachorro had steeled himself for this moment, but he was still terrified of approaching his victim. Slowly and cautiously, he advanced. There, hidden in the swale, cud still dangling from its lips lay a grey Zebu cow. It was a tale that, once told, he'd never live down.

* * *

The Battle of the Lost 339th Battalion, as the previous encounter came to be controversially called, netted many prisoners, which the Brigade was hard pressed to accommodate—on top of the 300 locals who had joined the Brigade effort—especially since they'd lost most of their support ships and were determined to treat them well. Oliva personally interrogated the prisoners. He learned that a great concentration of troops, including artillery and tanks, was gathering at the *Central* Australia also under the leadership of *El Gallego* Fernández (he whom Castro had awoken in the middle of the night to roust the Matanzas Leadership School cadets), and these were preparing for a major assault that night. Oliva had overheard Fernández talking on the radio and recognized him. Fernández had been Oliva's artillery instructor at the Pan-American School for Officers in Panama years before. Oliva immediately dispatched a messenger to San Román at Girón headquarters requesting reinforcements, ammunition and more tanks.

And then Oliva got a call from Cruz, reporting two ambulances coming down the road. "If they come to pick up their wounded, let them do it," responded Oliva.

As the ambulances approached, Cruz noticed a white truck with a Red Cross emblem following close behind. And behind that he saw other trucks filled with troops. It was a ruse, a fact later confirmed by Cuban FAR Paramedic Arnaldo Remigio, who wrote that medical personnel were so scarce and valuable that they were withheld from the front lines for service in rear-guard facilities. Oliva told Cruz "to start shooting." The bullet-riddled Red Cross vehicles would later become fodder for Castro's propaganda hopper.

The Red Cross vehicles engagement was the third and last combat at Playa Larga that afternoon—but not the last battle of the day. Oliva, anticipating what was coming, continued preparing for the worst. Cruz' company had borne the brunt of all three battles that day; they needed a rest—one they weren't about to get.

Oliva called for a retrenchment, three to four kilometers back, at the *rotonda*, or traffic round-about.

Oliva held nothing in reserve, ordering the third 2nd Battalion Company to prepare for battle. At 6:45 pm the reinforcements from Girón arrived: more men and armaments from the 4th Heavy Weapons Battalion, two more tanks, and ammunition. Some of the Castro militia prisoners asked for weapons to join the fight, but Oliva had none to spare. Even the 5th Battalion, last off the *Houston* and with only a couple of weeks of training, reported that they were marching towards Oliva's position to join the effort (they never made it). All told, Oliva's force numbered 370 men and three tanks, each with only twelve rounds apiece of antitank charges. Heading toward him were 2,100 Castro troops with 40 Stalin tanks and artillery.

Oliva knew they were coming, but he had no idea just how big the force was.

To prepare for the onslaught, Oliva decided to keep Cruz' company out in front, joined now with Acevedo's Company E; but he had them pull back to a more defensible position. Less than a mile from Playa Larga, a *rotonda*, or traffic round-about, funneled traffic coming down the causeway to Girón, Playa Larga, or west on a minor spur. Oliva established his lines at this choke point, with six mortars and two bazookas strategically placed on the sides to fire onto incoming attackers along the causeway. The men of Companies E, F, G and H were spread out about 100 feet on both sides of the round-about in fifteen to twenty 6-foot deep trenches.

* * *

At 7:45 pm what would come to be known as the Battle of the *Rotonda* began with an artillery barrage from four batteries of Soviet-made 122-mm howitzers. As Peter Wyden recounts, "They kept pounding, more than two-thousand shells in four hours. The concussions were terrible. Many men went into shock. They were too dazed to hear orders. But they did not break." One shell narrowly missed Oliva himself, hitting Juan Figueras, a mortar man. Though he lost his leg, Figueras kept on fighting.

Jim Rasenberger continues:

"Fortunately for the Brigade, Castro's artillerymen were still new to their equipment and not very accurate. Brigade radiomen, too, had managed to tap into enemy communications, so they knew where to expect the shells to land. They even managed to issue a few target readings of their own to fool Castro's artillery. 'Whenever we heard Fidel's mortar commander asking for the range and firing angle, we'd cut in and tell him, 'Compañero, up 15 and 10 to the right,'' a Brigade radioman later told Life. 'The barrage would miss us completely, and the fool would shout into his radio, 'You are nothing but a damned idiot, compañero!'''

At 11:55 pm the battlefield went silent: the artillery barrage was over. Oliva ordered the men to prepare for an attack. The air was thick and heavy with anxiety, fear, sweat, burnt explosives, mangled vegetation, cratered earth and mosquitos feasting on blood. Though the men could sense the approaching tanks and columns even before they could hear or see them, the first onslaught was more creepy than harmful. It consisted of millions of black and red land crabs, oblivious to the men and explosions, crawling through the swamps, over the men's legs and feet, driven by the spring mating season. "Don't fire until I give the word," Oliva ordered.

At midnight, Cruz spotted the first tank, at the head of a column of infantry, one-hundred yards up the narrow road. Twenty yards behind, another tank and another column; behind it, a third Stalin tank and column. When the first tank entered the rotonda, Oliva gave the order to fire and the Brigade's three M-41 tanks went into action.

It was tank against tank, firing point blank at twenty paces, accompanied by bazookas, machine guns and rifles sleeting into the infantry. The first tank was knocked out right away. The second one was knocked out by *El Barberito*, a tiny fighter, already blinded in one eye, who danced around it peppering it uselessly with his recoilless rifle, making not a dent in it. But the crew, overwhelmed by the relentless pounding, surrendered.

The third tank was rammed into submission by a Brigade tank that had already run out of ammunition. "Little Egg," Álvarez its driver, hurled his tank at it, backing up and crashing repeatedly into it, like "prehistoric monsters," according to one soldier. The Russian tank tried to position its gun against Little Egg to get in a close-range shot, but instead just got in the way of the ramming until its gun barrel split. When its caterpillar tread was hit, it limped away.

Oliva's forces were ill-prepared to fight tanks. Second Battalion forward observer Mario Martinez Malo said they had no anti-tank grenades, so they mostly resorted to climbing up on the advancing tanks, opening the hatch and dropping a regular grenade inside. He estimates that they took out seven to sixteen tanks this way. One *brigadista*, Graciliano Santamaría, who was out of grenades, jumped on a tank, opened its hatch and attacked its commander with his rifle.

In the trenches, Armandito's finger never left his .30 caliber machine gun except to reload. His strategy was to aim his fire eight inches above the ground, precluding the attackers' 'hitting the ground' for cover. Cuban Armed Forces Lieutenant Roger Lima, quoted in Cuban FAR Paramedic Arnaldo Remigio's memoir, said: "Close to me I saw two men falling to the ground alive and apparently unharmed. I could see no wounds on them, and with expressions of incredulity on their faces, I saw their legs but found no feet. They had their feet severed at the ankles by bullets."

Next to Armandito was a tracer (illuminated bullet) shooter and next to him was Felipe Rodón, a 57 mm canon operator, at 16 only one of two Brigade boys younger than Armandito and Cachorro. When the tracer shooter was ordered to pinpoint a target for Rodón, the tracer's location was inadvertently but immediately disclosed to the enemy. Instantly, return fire blew the tracer shooter's head clean off, blood spouting straight up like a geyser, splattering Rodón and Armandito. To Chino, Armandito seemed unfazed: the boy just kept firing continuously. Armandito wasn't one to be impressed by his own actions; he was just doing his duty. Hugo Sueiro, Armandito's 2nd Battalion commander, recalled that "We didn't know whether we were losing or winning; we just had to keep on fighting."

Off to Armandito's other side, just a couple of men over in the trench, one *brigadista* lit up a cigar. Roberto Mancebo, manning a .30 caliber machine gun, panicked, "*Coño, chico!* You want to get us all killed? Put out that cigar!"

The soldier, as crazed and unfazed as Armandito responded, "Mind your own fucking business! Just keep an eye out for whoever targets me and wipe them out!"

By 12:30 am the causeway was blocked with dead tanks. Infantry assaults came next. "Oliva said, 'Everybody out of positions and shoot,'" one soldier recalled, "and we shot everything we had. We couldn't see the enemy but we heard his screams." And then Oliva, to better direct the attack, stood up and began firing. "We just became killing machines," said Mario Martínez Malo. In the heat and confusion of battle, a bunch of Castro *milicianos* sought refuge in an abandoned Brigade trench. Martínez Malo continues, "There was no option but to blast them."

A bit later, a tank pulverized Martínez Malo's FO defensive wall of rocks. Pedrito González, in a nearby trench, yelled, "They've killed Martínez Malo!"

"I stood up and shouted that I was alive. My radio operator and I immediately realized we had to skeedaddle immediately from there. We decided to tear up the maps and destroy the radios so they wouldn't fall into the enemy's hands. They were too heavy anyway. We machine-gunned the equipment with our M3s. We just managed to save ourselves from another tank barrage."

Three dimly lit rooms in a small house in Playa Larga served as the 2nd Battalion's communications headquarters. One held prisoners; the radios crackled in another; the third, an infirmary, held a mortally wounded *brigadista*. "He was breathing out blood," a radio operator said. Afraid he'd fall into Castro's hands, the dying man asked for a gun. "I refused," said the operator. "Then he asked me to kill him. I had no right to take his life. So I went outside where the noises and flashes of the battle were like a giant hammer and chisel making sparks on the dark earth."

Few military commanders are both good tacticians and good foot warriors. Even fewer can perform both functions at the same time. To play a winning game of chess while going berserk takes a special temperament. It was at this moment that the 29-year-old Erneido Oliva crossed a certain line that transcended both roles and entered the realm of truly exceptional leaders. "He exhibited complete steadiness under fire and a quality of strength and decision that made men want to follow him," according to Haynes Johnson.

Up to now he'd held back his mortars, but at 1 am he ordered them to fire. At 3 am, after continuous battle, he had them loaded with incendiary white phosphorous. Oliva recalls, "The shouting of the enemy at that moment was just like hell. Everything was on fire. They were completely demoralized because that *fosforo blanco* really burns the skin. It was like a curtain, [everything was] completely covered with *fosforo blanco*."

In many ways white phosphorous is worse than napalm. Napalm is jellied gasoline, extremely flammable but susceptible to being extinguished. It burns the skin. Not so white phosphorous. Like a giant shotgun round, the incendiary pellets penetrate right down to and even through bone. Nothing extinguishes burning white phosphorous.

Hour after hour men fought and fell and died. More Russian T-34 tanks advanced, running over their own wounded but unable to get through because of the blocked road and surrounding swamps, sitting ducks for Oliva's remaining two tanks and limited artillery, followed by more militia. And they just kept coming and coming, running right into the 2nd Battalion's impregnable position. "But," as John Dille writing in a 1963 issue of *Life* magazine reported, "it mattered little as long as the enemy was so obligingly stupid in its method of attack."

"It was scary as shit," said one soldier, "…people moving in the shadows, shooting; you don't see shit, you just shoot and shoot and shoot, and every time you hear a noise, you shoot." Armandito, like a broken record, just kept firing…

At 3:45 am Oliva spotted one of his tanks retreating. He stopped it and asked what was going on. Torres Mena, the driver, responded that he was running out of ammunition and the shell-loading mechanism had broken. Oliva asked whether the spent shells could be unloaded by hand. Torres Mena said yes. Oliva told him to get back in position. But before Torres Mena could get back in, a soldier appeared out of the night, running and shouting that a tank was approaching. In the darkness, no one could tell if it was friend or foe.

And then it stopped. Out jumped the driver who ran towards Mena and Oliva waving his arms wildly. Suddenly, he stopped short and screamed, "It's the enemy!" and dashed back to his Russian T-34. "I was so surprised that I didn't shoot. None of us shot," Oliva said.

But Torres Mena reacted. He climbed back into his tank, loaded his shells by hand, and from twenty-five yards, shot his explosives. "There was a VOOM as the shell hit the Russian tank in the middle," Haynes Johnson writes, "For a second the tank turned a bright lobster red; then it was black; then there was a booming explosion and the turret erupted like a volcano as the ammunition began exploding." Torres Mena then returned to his position at the *rotonda*.

Oliva's third tank, driven by Daniel González Carmenate, suffered a crippling blow to its gun barrel adjusting mechanism. Oliva ordered rocks, logs, and anything available placed under its front treads to elevate the tank and save its firing capability.

At one point, Felipe Rodón, Armandito's 16-year-old trench mate—dubbed the Brigade's mascot—stood in the middle of the *rotonda* facing an enemy tank. From ten yards, Rodón fired his 57 mm cannon. The projectile pierced the tank and it exploded, but the shock knocked the boy to ground and, like a mortally wounded, but charging grizzly bear whose momentum is impossible to stop, the tank crushed him.

By 4 am the men were hallucinating and running out of ammunition. The fighting continued, but more slowly. By 5 am the two remaining M-41 tanks had run out of ammunition. Still, the enemy tanks kept coming, weaving their way through the wreckage. Two more entered the round-about in single file. The first was knocked out by a bazooka, but the second came in unseen until Commander *Ñato* Cruz fired tracers to outline its position. But it was too late.

"A shell exploded and Cruz fell. I was knocked down," recalls Adalberto Sánchez, his radio operator, "and remember feeling blood spurt from my back…and calling out to Cruz, 'Don't leave me,' but there was no reply."

Wounded severely in four places, Cruz was evacuated to Playa Larga. Sánchez was left for dead. Afterward, when the Brigade had retreated to Girón and the next onslaught of Castro militia advanced, Adalberto Sánchez, with vultures circling over him, was picked up and roughly thrown in the back of an open truck. He was probably Castro's first Brigade prisoner.

The situation at the *rotonda* was critical. Acevedo, Armandito's Company E commander, said, "Our men had no water, no food, nothing. It was a desperate situation. I couldn't support another attack…We could hear tanks coming. But suddenly, I cannot explain it, the enemy retired. So I had a chance to take my company out to Playa Larga." Now only Cruz's company and a few squads from the 4th Battalion remained at the round-about.

At 6 am another Stalin tank approached. It was too much for the dead tired men of Cruz's Battalion. After fighting valiantly day and night with extreme heroism, a group of men lost its nerve. Some began running. Haynes Johnson takes up the story:

"Oliva and Sueiro cursed and shouted for the men to return to their positions. Oliva grabbed a 57 mm cannon with the only shell he could find and ran to the middle of the road and knelt down and faced the tank. When the men saw him, they resumed their positions. Luckily for Oliva, the tank stopped and the driver got out and approached."

"Are you the commander of these men?" he asked Oliva."

"Yes."

"I congratulate you because these men are heroes. I would like to fight with you."

He was the first prisoner taken in what came to be known as the Battle of the *Rotonda*: 300 regular soldiers, 1,600 militia, 200 policemen, 40 Sherman and Stalin tanks against only about 170 Brigade men with 3 tanks. Roberto Mancebo, one of the Brigade combatants, reports that only two Brigade soldiers died.

For the three battles that took place that night, the Battle of the Lost 339th Battalion, the Battle of Rotonda proper and the Battle of the Red Cross vehicles—collectively (and somewhat confusingly) also referred to as the Battle of the Rotonda—Oliva's force suffered 10 to 20 dead and 40 to 50 wounded. Castro's forces never admitted their casualties. One estimate by a Castro doctor who later defected put the number at 500 dead and 1,000 wounded. Forward Observer Martínez Malo puts the number at about 3,000.

According to the April 22, 1996 issue of *U.S.News & World Report* (among other sources), the total number of casualties for the entire Bay of Pigs operation was 4,000 for Castro versus 67 Brigade members killed in combat. An additional 37 Brigade casualties were due to training accidents, execution by Castro, lack of care during imprisonment and a variety of other causes. (Jim Rasenberger puts the estimate of Castro deaths possibly as high as 5,000. The official Cuban figures put Castro's death toll at 176.) It was "the night of the heroes," as Oliva would later remember—none more so than he. Today, the Battle of the *Rotonda* is studied at West Point. When Roberto Mancebo described the action to a West Point class, the cadets were incredulous. "How were you able to withstand such an assault?" one asked.

"With tanks, bazookas and balls," answered Mancebo.

That the Brigade performed so well was due partly to the brilliant leadership of Oliva and Cruz. "After that battle, the men began calling Oliva 'Maceo,' after Antonio Maceo the great Cuban hero of the Wars of

Independence against Spain. Maceo, like Oliva, was a Negro," Johnson points out.

The Brigade's victorious performance was also due in part to the lack of leadership, morale and egregious errors of Castro's men; and, conversely, to the quality of the Brigade's training. But principally it was due to their nerve—a nerve forged by a keenly sensitive camaraderie and steeled in an idealistic conviction so intense that it precluded hating the enemy. Cachorro perceived Castro's soldiers as naïve, misguided, brainwashed, and forced to fight; that with a bit of straightening out and Cuban love, they'd see the light.

12

Golgotha

The captured tank commander told Oliva that more men were coming, and more behind them, and more beyond. At the sugar mill, from where he was now directing the operation, Castro had massed a Police Battalion, the 111th Battalion supported by a tank company, a special combat company, four howitzer batteries, a battery of 37 mm cannons, a company of bazookas, a battery of mortars and eight antiaircraft batteries.

But the 111th and the accompanying 123rd Battalions' race to the front was a disaster. In their haste to rout the invaders the Cuban High Command had commandeered forty bright white civilian buses to ferry the men and equipment—without separate accommodations for guns and ammo. Each bus carried forty men. After the men were seated, guns and ammo were piled high in the center aisle. The buses were outfitted with two sets of pneumatic doors on one side, with all the opening windows covered by steel security bars. In case of accident or attack, the men were trapped.

When the Brigade B-26s spotted the convoy, all hell broke loose. The thunderstorm of bullets and napalm destroyed thirty buses. Those that didn't explode became crematoria. Buses that were flipped on their side—their door side—became coffins. Men scrambled to break the rear windows with rifle butts. Only ten bus loads of troops took up the chase after Oliva's men, according to Arnaldo Remigio, the FAR Paramedic who treated the surviving burn victims that were miraculously evacuated to the rear.

Oliva knew his victory at the *rotonda* was bound to be short-lived. At 5 am on April 18 he sent a message to San Roman reporting that his situation was critical: He was out of ammunition and out of food; his men were exhausted, they'd been fighting without rest or food for nearly 30 hours; snipers had begun targeting his men; and he expected another major attack at dawn—he couldn't hold out. With buzzards flying overhead and the fires from the all-night battle still smoldering, the men of the Brigade were burying their dead around a lone tree. At 6:15 am San Román responded: "Resist until the last moment—the moment of death."

Oliva thought this was a useless gesture, disobeyed the order, and ordered a withdrawal to Girón twenty miles away. In a few minutes the Brigade forces were racing to board five trucks for the evacuation. But what to do with the 200 prisoners they'd acquired? Oliva had no "way to take them with us." So he told them that since the enemy was defeated, and they were advancing toward Havana, they were free to go.

On their retreat, a few miles out of Playa Larga, they met Harry Ruiz-Williams with 30 men from the 4th Armored Battalion and a truck full of mortars and ammunition. They'd been on their way to the *rotonda* front when their truck, swerving around a bomb crater, had overturned. "He told me with tears in his eyes that it was impossible for him to come and help when we needed him," said Oliva. Harry's men joined the retreat.

On their tail in pursuit were Castro's troops. Luckily the pursuit was slow: not only did the 111th and 123rd Battalions'—what was left of them— advance more cautiously due to rumors that the Brigade force was stronger than it actually was, but the Brigade would also intermittently stop to fight back. And then one of those not uncommon, tragic battlefield snafus materialized.

Communications between Castro's headquarters and the front at first depended on runners, not radio or phone lines. Every time Castro's 117th Communications Platoon (last-minute draftees from the Cuban Telephone Company) tried to restore phone lines to the front, the Brigade managed to cut them. In an effort to help the 111th and the 123rd, Commander José "Gallego" Fernández ordered an artillery barrage on the retreating Brigade. At the same time he ordered the 111th and 123rd to retreat three kilometers so they would not be in the line of fire. They never received the order. Fifty men died from friendly fire. At least by this time, the FAR had a few paramedics on the front lines.

Arnaldo Remigio, the FAR paramedic, wasn't one of them; he had been transferred from the Cienfuegos hospital to ambulance patient transport. In constant travel between the front and Matanzas city with wounded evacuees, he was able to piece together the details of the fight.

Oliva knew that Girón offered no respite. With Castro forces hot on his tail, he was effectively bringing the front to Girón. By 9 am the three leaders, San Román, Oliva and Artime, were in conference.

* * *

After one night alone in the swamps and a close call with a cow, the first fellow paratrooper Cachorro encountered was Bernardo, a childhood friend he'd known since first grade. They decided to continue their search to find the remaining 15 men after a night's respite. By the end of their second day out the two had become three when they encountered Manel, Cachorro's shooter (the .30 caliber gunner Cachorro was supposed to carry ammo for).

By that time they were going a bit crazy, tempers on tenterhooks. They'd been through so much so fast, and now, if caught—which was only a matter of time—they were dead. They'd even argued about uniform protocol. In an effort to dry his clothes, Cachorro had undressed one night. Manel admonished him to remain fully kitted-up in case they had to move suddenly. Cachorro, of course, didn't see things that way.

* * *

The San Blas, or eastern front of the Bay of Pigs invasion, was holding out well—so far—under difficult circumstances. Two parallel roads led into San Blas from the northeast. The main body of the paratroopers was to secure these two approaches. By 11 am on the first day of the invasion, Monday, April 17, the paratroopers had dug themselves in and were awaiting reinforcements by a contingent of the 4th Armored Battalion driving up from Playa Girón about 15 miles away.

At noon the now-united forces came under artillery fire followed by an attack from a Castro battalion. The Brigade counterattacked ferociously until the enemy retreated. By 6 pm, as the sun was setting, the two strong points on the San Blas front—defended by only thirty-eight men—were holding securely. Cachorro, in a radio interview many years later, was to muse the following about his fellow paratroopers during that battle at San Blas:

> *"I learned that I did not have a small fraction of the courage of Sergio Miyares, a schoolmate, who stood firing his 30 caliber machine gun in his arms in the middle of the road while hundreds of militiamen were coming closer shooting towards him. Or of my cousin Rolando Perez, with his bazooka yelling 'maricones (butt-fuckers) get closer, your shells don't even reach us' at the approaching tanks while he was hitting them with his rockets. Or of hundreds of similar examples that I could tell you."*

But Tuesday, April 18 dawned ominously. The enemy was attacking the San Blas front heavily with 20,000 troops. But then Castro's troops dithered. They'd captured two Brigade soldiers and questioned them. One lied, saying that there were more than a thousand Brigade troops holding that side of the San Blas front. However, the other one told the truth: He said that only 19 troopers had held that front. The Castro captain couldn't believe that only 19 men had driven back the previous day's attack, holding the front all through the night. He cursed the second man as a liar who was leading them into a trap, and decided to delay any advance.

While the Castro troops held off, both San Blas fronts retreated to San Blas proper, combining their forces. Meanwhile, 3rd Battalion, which hadn't yet been in combat, was ordered up to San Blas to help out. When they all met up, they consolidated a defensible position at San Blas town.

* * *

Meanwhile, Oliva and the victorious—but now retreating—Playa Larga contingent marched into Girón exhausted and out of ammunition. Oliva told them to rest, as they might have to fight in the afternoon. To cover the Playa Larga contingents' butts, Oliva and San Roman sent the 6th Battalion out on the Playa Larga-Girón road to protect the approach to Girón from the Castro forces in pursuit of Oliva's forces.

Second Battalion finally got a rest. The men lounged about on mattresses, in their underwear, eating canned fruit and drinking beer, and trying to ignore the sound of artillery coming closer. Johnson describes that, "Some men, too keyed up to sleep, too tired to talk, too tense to relax, nervously strolled along the shoreline." Armandito didn't walk—he slept, talked, tensed up *and* relaxed. It was who he was.

And then the aerial bombardment of Playa Girón began. San Román begged for US air support and cover, but the rules of engagement held. In frustration he called the US Task Force Commander "a son of a bitch." San Román added that without more ammunition, he couldn't hold out. Gray Lynch, the CIA coordinator between the American forces and the Brigade, promised help.

Then San Roman got a message from the Cuban Revolutionary Council—what was supposed to become the provisional government once Girón was secured—congratulating the Brigade on the victory at Playa

Larga. But San Román was in no mood. He continued his tirade, calling them all "sons of a whore" and said those troops were already in Girón having had to retreat. He said he didn't need their congratulations; he needed ammunition, medical supplies and support.

* * *

One narrative detour bears recounting here. Over on the Isle of Pines, Fidel Castro had expected a major landing, reasoning that as separate Cuban soil from the main bulk of Cuba, it would be a perfect foothold for the invaders to capture, declare a free Cuba and await reinforcements from the US government. Additionally, the 5,000 political prisoners in Modelo Prison—once liberated—would swell the invaders' ranks.

To preclude this scenario Castro sent 10,000 troops to defend the island and ordered Modelo Prison to be mined and blown up in case of attack. On April 18, the second day of the Bay of Pigs landing, one Brigade B-26 decided to fly over the Isle of Pines on its way back to Nicaragua. The pilot wanted to visually confirm the status of Modelo Prison and let the prisoners know that liberation was nigh.

But the defenders had other ideas. Though the B-26 didn't fire a shot, the men in the trenches unleashed a barrage of machine gun fire on the plane. So the pilot turned around, flew low over the trenches and opened up all of his .50 caliber guns on the defenders killing and wounding over 100 FAR soldiers. The prison escaped destruction only because detonation required final approval from Havana.

* * *

Castro's final advance on San Blas began about the same time as the aerial bombardment of Girón on the afternoon of April 18. The first sally was spectacularly repulsed by the untested 3rd Battalion. Eli César, in the trenches, proudly wrote that, "The enemy became aware that not only were we well-trained, but that our lives would only be surrendered at the highest price while we still had bullets."

But the assault resumed at dusk and continued throughout the night of the 18th into the dawn of Wednesday the 19th, by which time the 3rd, 4th and

1st Battalions had reached their limit. "That one didn't kill us," became their most common refrain after every close call. The men took to hearing each other's confessions and granting each other absolution in anticipation of death. Pepe San Román sent his brother Roberto to urge the men at San Blas to hold out a bit longer: ammunition and air cover were on their way. Confirming the promise, a squadron of US Navy fighters in battle formation flew overhead. The Cuban planes immediately dispersed and the ground forces paused.

But it was a cruel joke. The US planes were there only to flex their muscles, not deliver any punches. And the promised ammunition, which Gray Lynch—a special forces, John Wayne-type decorated hero—did everything in his power to deliver, never arrived.

When the Castro Cubans realized that the American planes were just for show, they resumed their attack, only to be turned back one more time. For naught; San Blas fell at 10 am in heavy combat. The *Brigadistas*, fighting all the way in strategic fallback were nearly out of ammo, and at 2 pm began to organize their retreat to Girón. They never made it. Blocked in front and behind, the men disappeared into the Zapata swamps.

* * *

Back at Girón the situation had turned desperate. Throughout the afternoon of the 18th Castro's planes ruled the air over Girón. By 6 pm, artillery fire and advance guards began to penetrate the little town's defenses. San Román, expecting an imminent attack from the west, sent Oliva with the 2nd Battalion back out on the road to Playa Larga to secure the approach. When the gravely wounded Maximo *Ñato* Cruz got wind that his men were headed out, he tried walking out of the infirmary. Manuel Artime, the political leader of the Brigade, ordered him to get back into bed. Cruz replied: "Please don't give me that order, because I don't want to be insubordinate to you, but my boys are being killed and I want to die with them." Then Cruz passed out.

But the attack didn't materialize, so 2nd Battalion withdrew to Girón's beaches for another creepy night without sleep, with the red and black crabs—the colors of Castro's 26th of July flag—swarming over them.

At dawn Oliva organized what the Brigade came to call "The Last Stand at Girón." He strategically massed seven bazookas and three tanks at a curve 6-8 miles outside Girón on the Playa Larga road, together with the 170 men of the 6th Battalion. He held Armandito's 2nd Battalion in reserve.

Peter Wyden describes what happened next:

"Shortly before 10 am one of [El Gallego] *Fernández' tanks lumbered around the curve. A bazooka stopped it. Then came an armored truck. Another bazooka hit took it. A second tank advanced and was blown up. A third met the same fate. Infantry assaults rolled against Oliva's men, one after another. One Brigade 81 mm mortar squad fired so fast that its weapons started to melt.*

At noon, Oliva sent *Chino* running the 6-8 miles to Girón to ask San Román for reinforcements and ammunition. San Román, desperate and with nothing to spare, ignored the request and dispatched *Chino*—running—back to Oliva.

Meanwhile, Oliva's strategically placed ambush yielded results. At 12:30 pm Fernández' column retreated after a "Dantesque" minuet of confusion when advancing militiamen were drawn forward by Brigade cajolery but, sensing a ruse, quickly backtracked; but then moved forward again to attack. Two militiamen who surrendered told Oliva that Fidel Castro was already in Playa Larga and was sending Osmani Cienfuegos (brother of the popular Comandante Camilo Cienfuegos who'd died under mysterious circumstances) with 3,000 men to Girón. So at 1:30 pm Oliva brought the 2nd Battalion into line.

Wyden continues:

"Around 2 pm one of Castro's tanks, firing from behind the three tanks that the Brigade had immobilized, knocked out the middle tank of the three that Oliva had stationed along the road. It was afire, threatening to blow up its two ammunition-heavy neighbors. Oliva shouted for someone to take the burning vehicle away. Little Egg Alvarez, wounded in the right ear and bleeding badly, got out of his tank, jumped into the burning one, and drove it up the road in a cloud of smoke and flames."

Little Egg parked it next to the mortar squad, precipitating yells from the men: "You damned nut, get that thing away from us before it blows us all up!" With the tank's fire extinguisher, he managed to put out the flames. Little Egg jumped out of the tank singed and bloodied, and ran back to his tank. Everyone thought he was sure to die. But before he could get into it, Oliva came up and promoted him to captain. "It was illogical but in a moment like that it was the only thing that I could tell a man who had done such a thing," reasoned Oliva.

Nearly overrun, with his men resorting to hand-to-hand combat, Oliva, in a desperate move, ordered G Company of 2nd Battalion to counterattack. Wyden continues, "The Company ran into murderous fire. Each side shot at everything that moved in the tangled vegetation." A buddy told Martínez Malo that he had 405 mortar grenades stashed away. With two other men they headed back to the stash, retrieved it and returned toward the enemy column. Setting themselves up, they discharged them all as fast as they could load them, buying enough time for Oliva to regroup. The suicidal counterattack brought a brief respite.

Out of ammunition, the mortars spent, Oliva ordered retreat to Girón and retrenchment.

* * *

When Tony Varona, ex-Prime Minister of Cuba and José Miró Cardona, last Prime Minister of Cuba, and the two top leaders of the Revolutionary Council—the latter provisional President of the proposed republic—were notified how the Brigade was faring, Cardona's eyes teared up. He insisted that the Council be flown at once to be with the Brigade. He wanted the chance to fight alongside his son and fellow exiles. "It is this which I beg," he implored the CIA men.

David Atlee Phillips, pop's Vedado tenant and now in charge of propaganda for the Bay of Pigs operation, was in the CIA War Room at Quarters Eye when defeat was imminent. The task force officers were in direct communication with San Román and Oliva on the beach. Phillips recounts: "The Brigade commander radioed that he was standing in the shallows. 'I have nothing left to fight with…Am headed for the swamp.' He cursed. The radio was dead. It was over." The time was 2:32 pm, Wednesday, April 19.

Many in the task force knew the Brigade commanders well. Some of the CIA officers turned "white with remorse and fatigue," others hid their faces, one "scratched his wrists viciously" staining his shirt cuff with blood. The suffocating agony overwhelmed one operative; he left the room to vomit.

Erneido Oliva was the last to know. At 4:30 pm, on foot, headed back to Girón during a lull in the shelling, somebody ran up to him and yelled that Playa Girón had fallen. "That's impossible," snapped Oliva. But when he got to headquarters, San Román and Artime were gone, already lost in the swamps, accompanied by their staff and forty-six men. Everything was chaos, with men running frantically about, abandoned tanks and vehicles everywhere, their carapaces punctuated by spent shells.

It was Castro who had called for that lull. He assumed from the number of casualties his men had incurred, that he was facing fierce opposition from 5-8,000 well-entrenched men. When it was reported to him that American destroyers were headed for Girón, he ordered a halt on all fronts. Assuming—again—that a landing of American forces was imminent, he dared not move ahead.

But those destroyers never arrived. It was another muscle-flexing show without a punch. At one point, according to Chino, a deeply frustrated Brigade member boarded a tank and fired at an offshore US Navy destroyer hoping to get a response against the enemy, and perhaps even to get the Americans to join the fight. "In the wake of that ship goes two hundred years of infamy," commented one soldier in rage as the ships reversed course.

Oliva blew up his tanks, disabled his trucks and destroyed what little heavy equipment remained and began leading his 300 men eastward in a column to the Escambray Mountains, according to the original plan and one still dear to his heart. But a few hundred yards into their march, two T-33s and a Sea Fury dived and strafed them. They disappeared into the swamps.

* * *

Cachorro, Bernardo and Manel had already spent three days in the swamps dodging helicopters that didn't seem interested in them and avoiding enemy contact. They were desperate for some experienced leadership and kept searching for their fellow paratroopers. Zig-zagging along a roughly parallel route to the causeway, they caught glimpses and heard rumbles of the forces heading for Playa Larga. They were not sanguine. After the Brigade had been defeated, the helicopters turned their attention on the stragglers and ground patrols were deployed to flush them out.

When the boys finally met up with some of the other troopers, it almost became a repeat of the zebu cow incident except with passwords and counter-passwords bandied about like an Abbott and Costello routine. Moralejo, the highest ranking trooper, took charge. Ruben *El Cojo* Vera, 1st

Battalion's second-in-command, never re-connected with them. Grayston Lynch, in *Decision for Disaster*, reports that he "fought a one-man battle against the militia until he ran out of ammunition."

The sixteen men wandered purposefully (though Cachorro couldn't figure out what purpose) through the swamp for 8 days, mostly at night, never all together, before they were captured. They remained in small groups, about 200 yards apart, so they couldn't be ambushed all at once and could provide cover for each other in case one group was attacked.

At one point, Moralejo ordered Cachorro and Carlitos Varona (the ex-Prime Minister's son) back to Cachorro's cache for food and ammunition. Along the way they encountered a baloney sandwich. Yes, a *baloney sandwich wrapped in cling wrap in the middle of the Zapata swamps!* They hadn't yet worked up an appetite, having taken a few of the K rations and figuring they could always go back for more. Nonetheless, they argued jokingly over whether it belonged to the finder, who the finder was, and whether it ought to be shared. Out came the .45s—jokingly again.

Looking back, Cachorro philosophizes that 17-year-olds under duress don't always think straight. Fortunately, sanity got the best of them before reality did. They holstered their guns and unwrapped the sandwich. The mayonnaise was a deep gray-green—not something to risk one's life on. The baloney and white bread, however, exhibited little deterioration.

They fought constant skirmishes with the militia sent to flush them out. At one point, on their seventh day out, they cornered Cachorro. The boy, out of ammunition and certain he was going to die, hid behind a palm tree hoping for the best. Ambivalent about religion, he didn't even have faith to comfort him. And then, like an improbable plot twist in a B-movie, his friend Rigoberto Varona, against all odds and wielding a weapon he'd never seen before, burst through, bullets flying all around them, grabbed Cachorro by the collar, and dragged him to safety.

Otherwise, with water and food, survival wasn't dire. But the thought of being captured and shot kept them going. After a certain time, their prospects began to seem hopeless, particularly so when someone proposed marching to the Escambray Mountains, impossibly far away.

But not to *El Cojo* Vera, who resolved on a daring plan, his lame foot never having held him back. After running out of ammo, he set off alone, discarding his camouflage uniform and acquiring peasant clothes. He hid during the day, walking at night and, once he was past Jagüey Grande, even hitchhiking and riding buses. He eventually reached Havana, where he took refuge in an embassy. In 1962 he escaped to Miami with the help of the embassy's staff.

Grayston Lynch takes up his story:

"A tremendous fighter, Vera returned to Cuba to fight again. In October 1962, Vera was on a sabotage mission in Pinar del Rio. The timing of this operation was unfortunate, for the missile crisis occurred while he was still inside. The place was crawling with troops, and he was captured by Castro's G-2. He escaped from a Cuban prison camp in 1965, but was recaptured three days later. He was badly beaten by the G-2 and returned to prison. He now [1998] resides in Miami, where he is very active in the 2506 Assault Brigade Association."

* * *

The Bay of Pigs was an unmitigated disaster—for the participants, for the CIA, for the Pentagon, for the State Department, for President Kennedy, for American foreign policy, and for the United States. David Atlee Phillips, our Havana tenant, who was Director of Propaganda for the Bay of Pigs operation, and later became Chief of the Western Hemisphere Division for the CIA, states in his memoir, *The Night Watch*, that he always agonized about the morality of any operation in which he was involved. A self-described supporter of Adlai Stevenson, JFK, Hubert Humphrey, and later, George McGovern, Phillips' conscience was thoroughly imbued by his idealism. Though the success or failure of a project was important to him—a common measure of virtue at the time—the rectitude of an operation was a more fundamental concern.

In his memoir, Phillips doesn't allude to much soul-searching concerning the Bay of Pigs. For him, it seems, the moral template for the Cuba project had already been established by Operation PBSuccess, the plan to depose Guatemalan President Jacobo Arbenz in 1954. When Tracy Barnes, a CIA senior officer in the Directorate of Plans tried to recruit Phillips as an adviser for the rebel radio propaganda team attempting to depose Arbenz, Phillips objected. "But Arbenz became President in a free election," he retorted. "What right do we have to help someone to topple his government and throw him out of office?"

Barnes replied that, "It's unacceptable to have a Commie running Guatemala," and added that the orders came directly from President Eisenhower.

"I'm still not sure that gives us the right to intervene," responded Phillips.

What Phillips finally came to understand was explicit in Barnes' choice of words: *Commie* instead of *Socialist*. It is that difference that justified the investigations of the House Un-American Activities Committee. Although Socialism and Communism share nearly identical economic philosophies, Communism, in addition, advocates the overthrow of non-Communist governments by *any means*.

Belonging to the Communist Party—far from merely being a free speech or freedom of conscience issue—was a treasonable offense. The right of free speech embedded in the Constitution's First Amendment excludes not only the "right" to falsely shout *fire* in a crowded theatre, it also does not include the right to advocate the violent overthrow of the US government. All Communist Parties pledged formal allegiance to the Soviet Union, and were, therefore, agents of a foreign power that were actively trying to overthrow recognized governments. Although the axiomatic allegiances of international Communist parties to the Soviet Union in, first, the Comintern (Communist International), and later the Cominform (Communist Information Bureau), were formally dissolved in 1956, strong ties of loyalty to the USSR remained throughout the 1960s.

President Dwight D. Eisenhower's authorization of both Operation PBSuccess and the Cuba Task Force was based on the fear of the Soviet Union establishing military bases in the Western Hemisphere that would destabilize and overthrow established governments in the area and pose a military threat to the United States. In both cases, CIA intelligence uncovered evidence of substantial armaments shipments from the USSR to both countries. For Ike, these were national security issues, and Phillips agreed.

At first, the US State Department did not agree. According to Peter Wyden in *Bay of Pigs: The Untold Story*, Dean Rusk, Kennedy's Secretary of State, opposed the operation but never said so outright. And Thomas C. Mann, the State Department's Latin America specialist (and soon to become America's ambassador to Mexico), thought the operation illegal, but later changed his mind and decided it was justifiable self-defense against Communist aggression. He mused, "When a sovereign state has chosen its policy, and if that policy threatens the security of the United States, at what point does the United States have the right to exercise its unilateral right of self-defense?"

So did Robert F. Kennedy, President Kennedy's Attorney General. Two days after the Bay of Pigs invasion, on April 19 when the Brigade was about to be annihilated, JFK—by now in a terrible funk—sought advice from his brother, who had not been intimately involved in the operation. RFK argued for more intervention, writing in a prescient memo "(I)n a year or two years the situation will be vastly worse. If we don't want Russia to set up missile bases in Cuba, we had better decide now what we are willing to do to stop it."

However, other countries might not see things our way—particularly the nuclear armed USSR and its minions, leading to dangerous confrontations. Hence, the concept of plausible deniability evolved. If pressed too blatantly, with concomitant loss of face, countries engaged in a never-ending cycle of confrontational tit-for-tat can escalate their aggressive responses into nuclear brinksmanship. Plausible deniability is an escape hatch from this inescapable cycle. To avoid such one-upmanship dilemmas, plausible deniability usually begins with a covert operation. Albert "Buck" C. Persons, in his book *Bay of Pigs: A Firsthand Account of the Mission by a U.S. Pilot in Support of the Cuban Invasion Force in 1961*, explains the concept clearly:

> *"When it was all over…we would deny that we had anything to do with it. No one would believe this. No one was expected to believe it. But it would be accepted. In other words…if we openly attacked Cuba with our own forces, and if, say, the Soviet Union had a mutual defense treaty with Cuba, then we would be forcing the Soviets to respond in accordance with the terms of that agreement. The Soviets don't want to be forced into an armed conflict with the United States any more than we want to force them. In a covert operation where we organize, supply and train a force of Cuban exiles, the Soviet Union may know exactly what we are doing, but as long as we continue to deny it, we avoid forcing the Soviet's hand."*

The distinction between an overt and a covert operation can be a slippery one, and one that can be endlessly debated. Just three days after the failed invasion, President Kennedy, declared that, henceforth, the US would fight fire with fire. In a speech before the American Society of Newspaper Editors and considered one of the most important presidential declarations ever made, he stated that US foreign policy had too long depended on traditional military approaches. In the future, in response to covert USSR interventions, the US would rely on *"forces of all kinds: power, discipline, and deception"* to fight Communist subversion—a direct reference to greater reliance on covert operations.

As one more justification for the Bay of Pigs invasion, JFK, in that same April 20 speech, invoked the Monroe Doctrine, stating that the US had a right to intervene if the USSR located military bases anywhere in the Americas (a red line he'd later have to uphold during the Cuban Missile Crisis).

But far more important and difficult to gauge is the attribution of responsibility to the agents involved in either overt or covert operations. Fidel Castro described the Bay of Pigs as a US invasion staffed by mercenaries. Cuban expatriates, on the other hand, prefer to describe it as a civil war in which one side was helped with money, expertise, and armaments by the USSR and Czechoslovakia, while the other was similarly helped by the US, Guatemala, and Nicaragua. And so did President Kennedy. At a press conference on April 12 he declared, "The basic issue in Cuba is not one between the United States and Cuba. It is between the Cubans themselves."

The question then becomes: How much aid from a benefactor turns a conflict into the helper's battle instead of the original principals' battle? It's a concern that has bedeviled many conflicts, particularly civil wars, from our own (where English aid to the Confederacy nearly precipitated war with Britain), to the Spanish Civil War (seen by many as a proxy war between the Axis Powers and the Soviet Union), to the Angolan Civil War (where helpers and allies on both sides included Cuba, the Soviet Union, South Africa, and the US) and, most recently, to the Syrian civil war.

For the Bay of Pigs operation, the US answer to that question was resolved by the following distinction: US aid to the Cuban expats would exclude American combatants, or bases and training on American real estate, in order to keep the operation Cuban and covert. Jim Rasenberger, in *The Brilliant Disaster*, summarizes the US role "as a very elaborate job of chaperoning." Arthur Schlesinger, then a low-ranking but close adviser to the President, spelled out these red line concerns to JFK about a week before the invasion. Kennedy took them to heart. At a press conference on April 4, the President flatly ruled out intervention by US forces. The policy was also made clear to the Cuban Revolutionary Council, headed by José Miró Cardona, and the administration made certain that it was understood and accepted. As Peter Wyden recounts:

> *"The exile Cuban leaders had to be convinced that 'in no foreseeable circumstances' would the US send troops and that American prestige 'will not be publicly committed to the success of the operation until we recognize a provisional government. We must tell the Revolutionary Council that it cannot expect immediate US recognition; that recognition will only come when they have a better*

than 50-50 chance of winning under their own steam; that this is a fight which Cubans will have…to win for themselves.'"

Additionally, both the plausible deniability and the 'who's in charge' concerns were further reinforced by the US government's rules of engagement: US forces were categorically forbidden, under any circumstances—even if the exile Cuban forces were being slaughtered—to fire upon Castro's Cuban forces unless first fired upon. Adequate plausible deniability was thus ensured (in spite of a few training sessions for frogmen in Puerto Rico and minimal other technical violations of domestic US law on the mainland, in Maryland, Florida, and Louisiana).

On the third and last day of the battle, these rules of combat were tested to, and beyond, their limit. With the last remnants of the Brigade dug in the sand some twenty feet from the water, Castro's Soviet tanks approaching— firing all the while—and the US Navy fleet standing idly by within range, Brigade 2506 Commander Pepe San Román pleaded for help—help the US forces had been forbidden to furnish.

But suddenly and unexpectedly, the tank barrage provided Captain Perkins on the *USS Eaton* his *casus belli*. Across his bridge whooshed a tank shell, landing in the water fifty yards too far. It was immediately followed by another shell landing fifty yards too short. Captain Perkins was certain the *Eaton* was being bracketed and the next round would be a bull's eye hit. He requested the Commander of the fleet, Commodore Crutchfield, for permission to return fire. Luckily, Crutchfield was on the bridge with Perkins vividly experiencing the tank shots. Had he not been there, Perkins would likely have returned fire without consulting Crutchfield. After all, he was being fired upon.

Crutchfield refused permission, though he did seriously consider returning fire. Had the shells landed "any closer," he would have. He reasoned that the shells were strays since they came from tanks and not artillery—much more accurate weapons, and ones not trained on the fleet. He didn't want to start World War III.

US Navy forces were agonizingly distressed at unfolding events. Admiral Clark, Crutchfield's superior in charge of the entire naval operation, had queried Washington three times, "Is there any change in the rules of combat?" Three times he had been turned down. Clark couldn't imagine withdrawal: "It's just too cold blooded and brutal to say, 'OK, fellows, this isn't working, goodbye now!'"

But that is just what the US Navy did. And Pepe San Román understood—grudgingly. But not the recruits. They felt betrayed; many were ready to turn their guns on the Americans. Thankfully, calmer heads prevailed.

Military operations are organized on a need-to-know basis. As any foot soldier will tell you, grunts know shit. Operational plans are held closely to prevent unwarranted leaks that might compromise the success of an operation. When a recruit joins the military, he accepts all orders on faith and follows them with unquestioned obedience. The Brigade recruits weren't aware of the US's rules of engagement, and assumed that the full force of the US military stood behind their operation. Cachorro, probably the only recruit in the Brigade to understand the subtleties and exigencies of this arrangement, was of course disappointed; but he never held a grudge against the US military, always thankful for the training, support, arms and money they received.

Fidel Castro's rules of engagement mirrored the US's. In spite of perceiving the Bay of Pigs affair as a "US invasion," he intuited that the US was only playing a supporting role in a counter-revolutionary civil war—and he wanted to keep it that way. He instructed his forces not to attack US ships or planes unless they attacked first. And his ally, the Soviet Union, followed suit. On April 19, the third day of the invasion, Grayston Lynch reports in *Decision for Disaster: Betrayal at the Bay of Pigs*, that US sonar picked up a Soviet sub entering the Bay of Pigs.

Rafael del Pino, Castro's youngest T-33 pilot, experienced both countries' rules of engagement in the heat of battle. When he spotted an American destroyer offshore, he thought it would fire at him. But, as instructed, he held his fire. Instead, spotting a number of small landing craft relaying reinforcements for the invaders ashore, he dove low and strafed them. At this point, he was certain the destroyer would fire at him. Instead, incredibly, it began moving away. Its presence escorting the landing craft was meant strictly as a deterrent, an impotent role its captain couldn't fully support, but accepted. (Del Pino flew 25 combat missions during the three-day battle, in which he shot down two Douglas B-26 Invaders and sunk several enemy vessels. As a result of his decisive role, Castro declared him a "Hero of Playa Girón" and promoted him to general. In 1987, with growing antagonism between the two men, he defected to the US.)

The rules of engagement were stretched and even, in at least one case, snapped. After a series of B-26 bombing and strafing sorties, the free Cuban pilots were exhausted, unable to continue without a respite. Yet the Brigade on the ground was desperate for cover. Back in Nicaragua, eight Alabama Air National Guard trainers volunteered to take over. Washington reluctantly gave its OK, but insisted that if they were captured, they were to confess that they were mercenaries fighting under their own volition, providing plausible deniability.

Two of the American-piloted B-26s were shot down by Castro. One B-26 was lost in the ocean; the other, with two Americans on-board, successfully crash-landed on Cuban soil. Reports of the men's fate conflict. One says they died in a shoot-out; the other that they were summarily executed on the spot by Revolutionary militia. One of their bodies was held by Castro for 17 years as proof that the US had, in fact, invaded Cuba.

Roberto Mancebo, both personally and in Patrick Symmes' book—*The Boys from Dolores*—reports that during the battle of the *Rotonda* four US Navy F-105 jets attacked advancing Castro troops with a rocket barrage killing many. Mancebo avers that the pilots were not authorized to attack, but that they performed this service out of frustration—of their own accord—because "they had the balls."

I was unable to verify this. *Cachorro*, Humberto *Chino* Díaz Argüelles and a group of Brigade veterans gathered for lunch at a Miami café did not recall any such incident. Though Brigade pilots flying B-26s did attack advancing Castro troops along the causeway leading to *La Rotonda*, according to this author's research, no attacking, US flown F-105s have otherwise been reported—except by the Castro government.

* * *

For the Cuban exiles, the 'who's in charge' question was answered more informally, even logically, by both the US and the exiles. At the top, José Miró Cardona was chosen—by both the US and the exiles—to become Cuban president of the new government that Brigade 2056 hoped to install after a successful landing in Cuba. His legitimacy rested on the fact that he had been the last prime minister of Cuba after Fidel Castro's victory but before Castro personally took over the post.

For the men of the Brigade (as stated previously), the nuances of a covert operation left the question of who was in operational charge—the US or the Cuban exiles—a bit fuzzy. So they set out to clarify the issue *mano-a-mano* through the aforementioned mutiny, where, through Pepe San

Román's deft handling of the situation, the US-appointed San Román was popularly chosen as leader by the Brigade members.

In truth, each ally was using the other for its own reasons. As Brian Campbell summarizes in his *Brigade 2506: Young, Idealistic, and anti-Castro* thesis, "The White House was using the soldiers to achieve the political objective of preventing the spread of communism (*sic*) in the Western Hemisphere. (In contrast,) the soldiers viewed the operation as a chance to return to Cuba and restore or create a democracy." As already quoted, Brigade 2506 veteran and professor of Music at the University of Tennessee at Chattanooga, Dr. Mario Abril, in no uncertain terms declared "We thought of ourselves as independent."

The notion that the Brigade soldiers were mercenaries lacks credibility. The Brigade soldiers were motivated by personal ideals and Cuban patriotism, not the interests of the United States or money. The $225 a month they received during training was a pittance, justified by the US as an investment in training for future potential US Army recruits. As Abril later stated, "You would have to pay me more than two-hundred dollars to be a mercenary."

* * *

The raw calculus of the moral and realpolitik mine field surrounding the Bay of Pigs affair wasn't lost on any of the participants. Four months after the disaster, in August of 1961 at the first Alliance for Progress conference in Montevideo, Uruguay, Cuba made a startling offer to the US.

Richard Goodwin, Deputy Assistant Secretary of State for Inter-American Affairs, represented the US. The Cubans sent *Che* Guevara. Guevara, in an uncharacteristically conciliatory frame of mind—no doubt primed by Castro—sent Goodwin, a cigar aficionado, a mahogany box of fine Havanas, and requested a private meeting. "What the hell," Goodwin later wrote, agreeing to the meeting, but warning Guevara that he had no authority to confer on behalf of the US government.

After some ice-breaking banter in which Guevara thanked Goodwin for the attempted invasion at Playa Girón—that it had done wonders for Castro and the Revolution—and in which Goodwin told *Che* he was welcome, and then suggested that the Cubans could repay the favor by attacking the

Guantanamo Naval Base, a proposal Guevara playfully declined, both men got down to business.

As Jim Rasenberger in *The Brilliant Disaster: JFK, Castro, and America's Doomed Invasion of Cuba's Bay of Pigs* recounts:

> *"Guevara told Goodwin that Cuba could not return American-owned properties expropriated during the revolution but was willing to provide compensation for them. Cuba could also agree not to forge any military or political alliances with the Eastern bloc and to refrain from fomenting revolution in other corners of Latin America, a long-standing concern of the US government. In return for these concessions, the United States would lift its trade embargo and pledge to stop trying to overthrow the regime."*

This was, in retrospect, not only a very reasonable deal, but one that exactly fit the US's fundamental concerns—though it did not address the Cuban exiles' aspirations. But it was not to be. Not only was Goodwin not authorized to negotiate at this level, at that venue, he never seriously pursued the offer with either the State Department or the President. In fact, by then, both RFK and JFK had dug in their heels and were dead set on overthrowing Castro and his Revolution.

* * *

The CIA has been criticized, rightfully so, for being an agency "out of control" and a "government unto itself," for its role in the Bay of Pigs fiasco. Yet, those words hide a more nuanced and richer underlying reality. Neither phrase is technically true; the CIA was acting under the direct orders of Presidents Eisenhower and Kennedy. It did what it thought best according to the remit it was handed—not for itself, but for the country and the President. Its personnel were motivated by patriotism and dedication to duty, not power.

The problem was that neither President was fully engaged in the operation. It didn't help that horses were changed in the middle of the stream (so to speak). Eisenhower turned on the ignition, and Kennedy went along for the ride. Neither assigned the CIA a necessary chaperone. In fact, the agency was subject to absolutely NO oversight, either from a bipartisan Congressional committee or a private Presidential oversight committee dealing with intelligence and special operations—someone who could provide an independent perspective and objective analysis. As Haynes

Johnson so succinctly put it, "No agency should be permitted to operate without some form of independent, critical outside examination."

As a military operation, neither the Pentagon nor the Joint Chiefs had control. As a foreign policy initiative, the State Department was left out of the loop. As a Presidential project, it fit no existing template other than the much smaller, miraculously successful—and singular—1954 Guatemala coup, upon which the Cuban operation was modeled. And it didn't fit the profile of a small, covert operation, one that the CIA alone could manage. The absurdity of the administrative supervision of the operation is best exemplified by the decisive meeting called to order by President Kennedy late in the evening on April 4, just a few days before the operation was due to launch.

JFK, disdainful of rigid protocol and formal channels, and surrounded by "the best and the brightest" (aka 'the arrogant and the all-knowing'), preferred more collegial, seminar-style brainstorming meetings where everyone—no matter what his position in the hierarchy or his expertise—could have his say; what Secretary of State Dean Rusk disdainfully but understatedly referred to as the new President's "very informal sense of administration." Everyone was there, about a dozen men crammed into a small room around a round conference table representing anyone with a finger in the pie: the President and his advisers, the CIA chief, State and Defense Secretaries and their advisers, military men, and even some who had no finger in the pie—Senator William Fulbright and Arthur Schlesinger Jr.

And that was the problem.

"Nobody in the tiny, drab meeting room knew what to expect. Within minutes, all were acutely uncomfortable—but, like the characters in *Rashomon*, all had differing perceptions of what was happening," according to Peter Wyden. Schlesinger was a "special assistant" to the President, with vague duties; just a grade above an intern, straight out of academia with no government experience. Fulbright had had nothing to do with the Bay of Pigs operation—he'd heard about the plan through the grapevine, felt uncomfortable about it, and sent the President a memo suggesting caution. JFK invited him to sit at his right side.

The structure of the meeting, with the President round-robbing around the table for an up-or-down vote on the operation, implied an equality among the participants that not only didn't exist, but one that inhibited everyone. As the senior member of the Cabinet, Secretary of State Dean Rusk felt he'd been herded together into a crowd of young people and had been reduced in status to become just one of the herd with each person holding one vote regardless of their position or expertise. Cabinet Secretaries believed their opinions should be heard separately and confidentially from underlings. Underlings were reluctant to contradict bosses; military men didn't want to opine on policy; and Schlesinger and Fulbright felt totally out of place.

Everyone (with a nod to peer pressure) except Fulbright voted to go ahead, with the exception of Rusk, who insisted on breasting his cards to retain his dignity. Kennedy's decision, after the two-and-a-quarter hour meeting, was to "sleep on it," putting off a final yay or nay until past the last minute.

It was no way to run a government.

After the debacle; after the Board of Inquiry reviews; after the Cuban Missile Crisis; after the repatriation of the Brigade prisoners; after all the post-mortems, the oversight lesson had been learned and corrective measures were put into effect. In the spring of 1963, a Standing Group (aka Special Group), composed of the Attorney General, the Director of the CIA, and the Joint Chiefs of Staff, along with the National Security Council, was designated to oversee and vet such operations. Additionally, a chastened President Kennedy decided to follow established protocol in order to facilitate candid communication.

13

The Round-Up

El Cojo Vera wasn't the only *Brigadista* to escape Castro's clutches by simply walking away. Over at the San Blas front another group of five paratroopers walked north, stealthily crossing enemy lines. They managed to get civilian clothes, food and shelter from sympathetic peasants. One of the boys called his grandmother in Havana for a ride. The old lady, taking advantage of the May Day celebrations in Havana, which this year were doubly festive—Yankee imperialism had just been defeated—drove down in an old jalopy to pick them up. Security on such a happy occasion would be lax.

On the way back to Havana, the car broke down. So they called a taxi. When the taxi got to them, the driver refused to go all the way to Havana. Nonetheless, he agreed to drive them partway. Along the road, a militia man at a security road block stopped the taxi. The soldier turned out to be anti-Castro. Sympathetic, he talked the taxi driver into taking the escapees all the way to the Argentine Embassy in Havana, which was already packed with hundreds of wanna-be exiles. After four months in the Embassy, the *brigadistas*, along with all the refugees, were evacuated to Brazil. Argentina had threatened to break off diplomatic relations with Cuba unless Castro allowed all the asylees safe passage out of the country. Castro relented.

For the May Day celebrations the government trucked in hundreds of rural folk into Havana. One *brigadista* took advantage of this free transportation, hitching a ride in an open truck full of *campesinos* all the way to Havana from just outside San Blas. From Havana's *Parque Central* he walked to the Venezuelan Embassy and sought asylum. The Miranda brothers, Luis and Alberto, also found asylum in the Venezuelan Embassy after dodging and fooling Castro's militia. They reached Miami on July 28th.

Nelio Lugo, with the help of some *campesinos*, reached Havana and sought asylum in the embassy of Panama. After thirty-five days, under the embassy's diplomatic protection, he managed to catch a flight to Miami.

And finally, at least one enterprising *brigadista* managed to get all the way to Guantanamo, nearly 700 miles away, to seek refuge in the US Naval Base.

* * *

In the chaos at the Playa Girón beach on the afternoon of the defeat, there were men from many battalions wandering about, disoriented, in a daze, trying to figure out their next move. Many of them were paratroopers of the 1st Battalion, led by Alejandro Del Valle, who'd landed at the San Blas front. Among them was Roberto San Román, Brigade leader Pepe San Román's brother. He'd been sent to the San Blas front at the last minute to encourage the men to hold out. Now he was back in Girón, more or less retreating—no one was sure.

Political leader Manuel Artime, Commander Pepe San Román, and overall 2nd in command Erneido Oliva were nowhere, having already disappeared into the Zapata swamps. Just offshore, at anchor, was a twenty-two-foot (some sources say 18') sailboat, the *Celia*. Twenty-two men, led by Del Valle and Roberto San Román commandeered it and made a beeline for the American destroyers due south. Only one man had any experience with a sailboat. The winds were in their favor. Night fell. They ran aground near Cayo Guano, a tiny island 12 miles due south of Girón manned by a lighthouse.

Some men wanted to overrun the lighthouse, kill the keepers and take the food. Del Valle and Roberto San Román decided against it. The men jumped out, freed the boat and sailed on. But by dawn the destroyers were nowhere to be seen. Some suggested heading west and landing in Pinar del Rio province, but R. San Román and Del Valle demurred, assuming Cuban coasts would now be heavily patrolled. Additionally, the winds were steady out of the north. They headed for British Grand Cayman Island.

On their second night out a big storm came in, tossing them about all night so badly they were certain it was the end. All twenty-two men bailed furiously with tin cans and GI cups. After the battering, the winds shifted to the northeast. With so little knowledge of sailing, all they could do was run with the wind. So they now headed for Yucatan.

At this point, the sun became the assailant, beating brutally and relentlessly every day. What little food and water was stockpiled in the *Celia* was soon gone. With twenty-two men in a twenty-two foot boat, they literally had to lie on top of each other, one man's head on another man's stomach. Vicious arguments broke out over trivial issues, the battle, and the hated, traitorous Americans.

Occasionally they'd spot ships and planes far in the distance, but not one saw the *Celia*. For four more days they sailed southwest. It was then that their thirst became so intense they began drinking their urine. The *Celia* had a fishhook which they deployed in conjunction with a flashlight as a lure. So far, they'd caught one fish, scrupulously divided into 22 pieces. And then, on their full fifth day out, they hooked a shark nearly as long as their boat. Haynes Johnson describes what happened next:

> *"For more than an hour, Del Valle and (a paratroop officer) fought to land him. Three or four times they succeeded in bringing the shark alongside, only to have it rush off with the line. At one point, Del Valle said he was going to jump overboard and kill the shark with a knife, and his men had to restrain him. When the shark was pulled close the last time, Del Valle hit it over the head with a paddle. The shark got loose, the paddle was broken and the flashlight was lost. For one long day that shark followed the boat."*

The loss of that shark and its subsequent determined stalking were not the worst things to happen that day. A sudden wind shift re-directed them north-west, away from Yucatan and toward Texas. It was going to be a very long voyage. Morale plummeted.

On the sixth day, things took an even worse turn. Inocente García, one of Del Valle's men—he had trained and led him—died. And then the wind too, died. For twenty-five hours they watched the sail hang slack, cursing and arguing with whoever took the verbal bait. Fish gathered underneath the boat, but they had no way to catch them. The fish attracted sharks, no doubt also attracted by García's body, which they'd finally agreed to bury at sea.

That night the wind picked up and they made some headway. But by the next day Raúl Menocal, scion of a family that had produced presidents, and two other men were found dead. The three bodies were thrown overboard. No one even mentioned what the castaways of the 19th century whaler *Essex* resorted to—cannibalism, though it might have saved more lives. Somehow, it seemed inconceivable to a Cuban.

By the eighth day without food or water, the men spent time cooling themselves off in the sea, holding on to a painter. Thoughts of suicide gripped some, with desultory attempts made. Johnson describes the scene:

> *"Some already had lost forty or fifty pounds. Their hair was long and matted, their skin was burned and cracked and their bodies were covered with blisters and*

boils. On each fingernail and toenail there was a distinct white mark, showing the place where the nails had stopped growing. They all had continual violent stomach cramps."

Some men had taken to raking in seaweed and eating it; they'd had nothing to eat for seven days. And then R. San Román caught a seagull with his hands. He took the chest and heart and divvied up the rest among the men.

On the tenth day Del Valle died. The death of García, the first man to die, had completely unsettled him. Fighting with the shark, like a bad ending to Hemingway's *The Old Man and the Sea*, fatally weakened him. As the leader, the loss of his other men utterly dispirited him. He'd lost the will to live. On the twelfth day, a sixth man died, with the now familiar green pus coming from his eyes.

On the thirteenth day they sailed in total silence. But then that night, it rained. Unable to catch enough water in their GI cups and tin cans, the taste of the raindrops was a mortifying tease. The next morning, another man died. On that day, a strange thing happened. A two- or three-masted sailboat spotted them and circled around them. They could see people on deck. But the boat did not come closer. Someone said, "We must be close to land. That's why they don't pick us up." The men continued sailing north.

R. San Román remembers, "I remember that morning. I was getting a little out of my mind. I don't know if I was crazy or not. It's like being dizzy. I caught some seaweed and said it had water in it and I ate it." In the afternoon he dove into the water trying to get cool. Then he began drinking salt water—gulps and gulps of it. Finally he pulled out his combat knife and said, "Kill me. I don't want to die as the others." No one took up the challenge.

At 5:30 pm on the fourteenth day, *The Atlantic Seaman*, an oil tanker bound for New Orleans from Venezuela, picked up the survivors, 178 miles short of the Mississippi River delta. But by then another man had died. Two more died on the rescue ship in spite of blood transfusions. Only twelve men survived the entire voyage.

* * *

Still others managed to escape Castro's clutches. President Kennedy had vaguely authorized a rescue mission for the stranded *brigadistas*. Every

American and Cuban on the destroyers and the García ships volunteered to go in and look for survivors.

On the morning of April 21st, fighting twelve-foot waves left over from the storm of the previous night—the one that had battered the *Celia*—a rescue team transferred to the destroyer *Eaton* while awaiting final confirmation and precise operational instructions for the rescue operation. With Castro's troops controlling Girón and the eastern shore of the Bay of Pigs, and slowly moving down the western shore, the danger for the rules of engagement to completely fall apart *after* hostilities had ceased was even more acute. There was no sure-fire method of assuring Castro's militia that the rescue operation was not a follow-up invasion; and, anyway, there was no way of knowing whether Castro would even allow rescue attempts.

At daybreak the next morning, the *Eaton* entered the Bay of Pigs proper, scanning the coast with binoculars, searching for survivors. The *Eaton* flew its largest American flag: it wanted to be clearly recognized by both survivors and Cuban troops.

On shore, though far from the mainland, and at the southernmost outcrop of reefs and islands outside the bay, it spotted what were remnants of the 5th Battalion. The men waved frantically as the destroyer continued into the bay, thinking they'd been missed. The *Eaton* reassured them with a signal but kept going, slowly passing the scuttled *Houston*, looking for more men before launching rescue boats. Peter Wyden describes an encounter:

"Two teams of frogmen, one of them led by Gray (Lynch), went ashore. One survivor had been drinking salt water and could not talk at all. Eventually they found twelve men. Some wore shorts. Most were naked. All looked like skeletons and bore deep cuts over their bodies. Gray could not understand the wounds until he went ashore and searched the woods. The thorns on the dry bush were so long and sharp that two complete sets of khakis were shredded off his body in three days and he too was covered with scratches."

Some survivors fared much better. One group of five had covered forty miles, traveling at night along the hard sand next to the water's edge, resting under the shade of trees during the day. They survived on shellfish and rainwater-filled stumps and rock hollows.

For several days, the six destroyers in charge of the rescue mission launched small motorboat crews, some with megaphones, to search for survivors. One day, a Castro helicopter was seen scouring the beaches, also looking for survivors. Each time it saw some, it swooped down almost to treetop level and opened fire on them.

Also looking for survivors was a single-seater, prop-driven, little Navy AD plane. It would fly along the shore, below the tree canopy, looking for survivors. When it spotted any, it would radio the rescue boats. One time it ran into the helicopter. The Americans were under orders not to shoot unless first fired upon.

Frustrated at the rules of engagement, the little AD slowed down to a hundred knots and started a "contact run," intending to knock the helicopter out of the air. But the helicopter was more maneuverable and would flip itself aside just before a collision. But at least it gave the whaleboat evacuating the Brigade members enough time to safely load and exit.

Castro did not care for this humanitarian effort. First, he assembled a flotilla of small craft, including PT boats, between the destroyers and the rescue crafts hoping for scraps. Since they couldn't shoot at the Americans, all they could do was wait and intimidate. Feeling at the top of his game (in his mind he'd just beaten the US), he sent two Sea Furies down from Havana to further harass the operation. Immediately, a considerable force of Navy jet fighters from the carrier *Essex* flew out to meet them. There were Skyhawks above, below, and on both sides of the Sea Furies. Still, they continued heading for the destroyers.

The destroyer crews were ordered to battle stations. The precise rules for attacking the Sea Furies, as Gray Lynch stated in *Decision for Disaster*, was "to take action only if they continued their forward progress, dropped below five thousand feet, and entered an area of five miles from the destroyers."

At five thousand feet and just before entering the five mile radius, the Sea Furies turned back.

For three days the US Navy controlled the west coast of Cochinos Bay. Fidel Castro never mentioned the incident, embarrassed that he was powerless to prevent it. The US Navy rescued about 30 men off the beaches.

* * *

"Little Egg" Alvarez, the tank hero upon whom Oliva had conferred a battlefield promotion, almost got away. Some of the men, in addition to the *Celia* sailors, took to fishing boats. "Little Egg," with a group of six, sailed east from the Bay of Pigs in a small boat victualed with rice and beer. After several days at sea, they landed on the Isle of Pines, site of Modelo Prison. All were captured.

April 25, eight days since the invasion and their jump, Cachorro and his fifteen not-all-together-but-not-all-apart companions had wandered north onto drier, more solid ground. Totally unaware of the rescue operations going on south of them or even that those operations had terminated that very day, they looked for water. Crossing an open field, in single, separated file, it was the first time Cachorro had seen the entire original group—what was left of them—all together.

They found a well. But Castro's militia, anticipating that they'd be looking for water, was waiting to ambush them. Suddenly, bullets were flying all around. The path to the well had been worn deep over many years, almost like a *sanja*, or watering trough. The paratroopers dropped to their bellies seeking what little protection the mini-ditch provided and prepared to defend themselves.

Cachorro struck his M-3 over his head and shot blindly. Next to him crouched a tall black trooper who just couldn't get enough cover in the shallow ditch. The big guy drew out a grenade, pulled the pin, counted to three, and accidentally dropped it between himself and Cachorro in the mud. They looked at each other, goodbyes in their eyes, saying nothing. Miraculously, the grenade didn't explode.

When they ran out of ammo, out came the .45 caliber side arms. Cachorro emptied his clip, saving one bullet for himself. He was convinced he'd be shot if captured and wanted to control his own fate. Moralejo, in charge of the group now that *El Cojo* Vera was gone, knew what Cachorro was up to and ordered him to "shoot it!," an order Cachorro reluctantly obeyed, blindly, over his head.

With the group now completely defenseless, someone attached a white handkerchief to an M-1 rifle, raised it up and waved it about, shouting, "Don't shoot!"

"*Cerco uno, alto fuego; cerco dos, alto fuego; cerco tres, alto fuego…*" and so on, in a complete circle, the militia commander ordered his men to cease fire. The Brigade boys were completely surrounded. Out they came, hands up in the air.

And then Castro's militia opened fire.

The paratroopers jumped back in the ditch. The militia broke out in laughter and their commander ordered Moralejo's men out again. Castro's men had shot over their heads just for sport. The militia were well prepared for this round-up operation and knew what to expect. A waiting Czech truck provided prisoner transport.

* * *

Wednesday evening on April 19, the final day of battle, a small group of paratroopers and members of the 3rd Battalion over at the eastern, San Blas front, decided to retire into the Zapata swamps (as many others on that front were already doing). They didn't know the war was over; they were simply out of ammunition, and hoped to reunite with reinforcements and resupply.

Behind a copse of trees the group came across a *bohío*, a typical rural clapboard dwelling with a thatched roof. They surrounded it and ordered all the inhabitants outside. Out stepped an older *campesino* pleading, "Don't shoot!" He said his 70-year-old blind mother was still inside. They ordered him to sit on the ground with his hands up and verified that he wasn't armed and that his mother really was blind.

After a thorough questioning the men asked the *campesino* to lead them into the swamps. Most of them, city boys, were terrified of the crocs, feral pigs and wild boars, iguanas, snakes and even the giant toads said to inhabit Zapata. The peasant demurred, worried about leaving his mother alone. But the *brigadistas* apologetically insisted. To reassure the couple, the soldiers shared some food with them and left crackers and cans of condensed milk with the old lady.

Two hours into the swamp with Padrón, the drafted guide, they found a dry, forested glade and decided to camp. Absolutely knackered they nonetheless reviewed their situation before sleeping. Was everything lost? Were they just isolated by chance? Had they inadvertently wondered behind enemy lines? They assumed the latter and decided—after a good night's rest—to try to escape. But what to do with their guide? After many suggestions, some pretty drastic, they decided to leave the decision until the morrow. Guard duty was assigned and the rest fell into fitful sleep due to exhaustion and tension.

Breakfast consisted of one mandarin orange each. Padrón picked up the discarded rinds: "They make good tea." In the distance they heard voices and motors. With bayonets cutting a narrow path they headed into the thick brush. For four hours they made little progress, finally deciding to make camp until dusk and travel at night when there was less chance of discovery. Padrón suggested dinner. He said that the center of the branch of a certain palm tree, boiled, was edible. It was utterly tasteless, but filling and the men appreciated the meal—and Padrón.

That afternoon they decided on a plan. They would separate into groups of three to five men each and each group would head out that night an hour apart from each other until all the men had dispersed. The first group would take Padrón and free him the following night. That way the guide wouldn't know where any group was. But before they could put the plan into action, they ran into a twenty foot constrictor. Padrón killed it and cooked it. They all agreed that it tasted like shellfish—delicious. Everyone got their fill.

Eli B. César, who wrote a memoir, *San Blas: Ultima Batalla en Bahía de Cochinos*, found himself in the third group. After walking for three hours they found themselves in mire, with water up to their knees. Luckily, they found a dry hummock and camped.

But not every night. César's group was out eleven days, sometimes so close to militia patrols that they slept mostly submerged, holding onto tree trunks, to better hide. The militia couldn't find them, but they were aware of *brigadistas* close by. They'd been eating roots and small freshwater fish they caught with their hands, but they were still ravenous. Castro's patrols would purposely cook fragrant food and yell out, "Come and get it, dinner is served!"

The evening of the tenth day they saw a deserted *bohío* and camped close by in the woods. The following day at noon they heard strange noises. A wild pig ran into the clearing in front of the dwelling. They tried to catch it by chasing it but, too exhausted, failed. They resorted to one rifle shot to take it down. Skinned and cleaned the pig was roasted on the *bohío's* brazier. It was an unimaginably sumptuous feast. The men slept soundly that night.

But the following morning, April 30, they were woken with bayonets at their throats. "We made a grave error: caught by our mouths like a fish," César philosophized.

* * *

Armandito and *Chino*, following Oliva's lead, headed into the Ciénega de Zapata's brine marshes in small groups, fighting until their ammunition gave out. Wandering aimlessly in the swamps, at first vaguely heading for the Escambray Mountains, either avoiding towns or heading for their outskirts, they changed objectives as hunger or thirst began calling the shots.

Armandito and his comrades were soon out of food and water. Totally dehydrated, they resorted to drinking their own piss.

Poor Cruz. Survival was toughest for the wounded men. Maximo *Ñato* Cruz, hero of the Brigade's stand at the *rotonda*, was hardly able to stand. Wounded in at least five places, he took to the swamps on crutches. But he was helpless. He soon collapsed and passed out. When he woke up, crabs were crawling all over him, chewing his wounded flesh where it had rotted.

Dehydration led to hallucinations. Time itself became a haze and night and day blurred into one timeless continuum. The more religious prayed constantly. Many remember suddenly losing their senses. Castro's men made no effort to go after the survivors; instead they tormented them with helicopters constantly firing aimlessly into the woods and artillery shells lobbed randomly, forcing them to head for the roads where militia patrols awaited them. Or even placing cans of Russian tinned meat as bait along the roads.

The strategy worked. When their thirst became so intolerable that even a firing squad meant nothing, the men surrendered. Haynes Johnson recounts:

"A Brigade soldier cried out, 'Shoot us, but in the name of humanity, give us water first!'

One of Castro's men replied, "There isn't going to be any shooting here,' and he handed over his canteen. Some militiamen threw them oranges, laughing and saying, 'You threw bullets and we throw oranges.'"

It was quite the change of pace. They were lucky to be alive. In the heat of the moment, Castro's troops weren't disposed to generosity in victory. The first few men caught had been summarily shot. It took the arrival of higher-ups, particularly *Che* Guevara, to put a stop to it. The invaders were worth more to Castro alive than dead, in both propaganda and monetary value. Additionally, Castro didn't want to give the US an excuse to invade if he carried out his promise of executing them all—a truly barbarous denouement.

Armandito and *Chino* were captured, like Cachorro, by an ambush at a well. In another unlikely coincidence, it was *Chino's* cousin, an ungrateful SOB according to *Chino*, who nabbed them. The two despised each other, from way back—family stuff. The cousin insisted on personally shooting *Chino* but was held back by his superiors.

He was lucky. FAR Paramedic Arnaldo Remigio recounts that:

"The three hundred survivors of the Police Brigade [111th Battalion] *were in a mood more than vindictive...and had not forgotten that terrible slaughter caused them by the Brigade. Our Police Brigade spread in platoon force and hunted and hunted the marshes and wild jungle and...found their prey in groups of two and three. Once the men had surrendered and had their arms in the air and weapons on the ground, a whole tempest of machine gun fire swept them and cut them to pieces...Some thirty-odd men of the Brigade died that way."*

All the rest of the men, 1,183 Brigade fighters, were captured (Wyden says 1,189, Johnson says 1,199, Leovigildo Ruiz says 1,207, Pablo Pérez-Cisneros says 1,204). They had faced a Communist, mostly conscript army of 60,000 men. Each man, each group of men, had his story. Castro militia members too, varied in their reactions to their captives. Some summarily shot Brigade members. Some tortured them. Others touched them, talked to them, and inspected them closely—they'd been told they were fighting Yankee mercenaries. Yet the men they'd captured were Cuban. When Cuban connections were made, some militia members showed kindness, even admiration. Most militia members simply followed orders. Many, oddly, asked for combs; though watches, wallets, wedding rings, and nearly everything else was confiscated.

Brigade 2506 prisoners at Playa Girón on April 19th.
Source: Estevan L. Bovo-Caras, Brigade 2506 Museum and Veterans' Association.

All prisoners were transported to, and processed at, Playa Girón. Haynes Johnson describes the scene:

"Girón was a scene of confusion: long lines of soldiers, jeeps and trucks and buses; nurses and officers; newspapermen, television cameramen and photographers; and Chinese, Czechs and Russians in civilian clothes—all moving about with a sense of importance. The center of attention, the objects of scorn and shouts, were the prisoners. Dirty, disheveled, gaunt, unshaven, most wearing only the T-shirts and pants their captors had left them, they came into town in long lines, bound together, poked by bayonets…silent and grim."

"They were approached by European and Asian newspapermen and women. A tall, blonde French girl asked a prisoner why he had come and he replied: 'To fight Communists.' After more questions, the girl remarked in disgust that he had been completely brainwashed by the imperialists. Stung, the prisoner spoke back: 'I'm glad I came in the invasion.' 'You're crazy,' the girl said and turned and walked away."

The prisoners were housed in locker rooms intended for the beach resort Castro had been planning for the town. Most were subjected to sham executions followed by interrogation.

Johnson adds that, "Of all prisoners, Negroes received the worst treatment." They didn't fit Castro's Revolutionary narrative and their presence on the invasion force infuriated him. Castro himself, coming down to Girón, interrogated them—just before their sham execution—accusing them of treason both to their country and their race. Osmani Cienfuegos, Camilo's brother, lined them up against a wall and told them: "We're going to shoot you now, niggers, then we're going to make soap out of you."

Pepe San Román's capture was unique. He accidentally walked into a lost militia patrol on April 25. He and his companions had found both food and water, though they'd had to dig for the latter and kill and consume raw the former. The soldiers who found him, to his great surprise, treated him kindly. "Oh, my brother, now you are in good hands. Don't be afraid! You will see how good we are." Though Rasenberger says that they also told him he'd be "executed by firing squad."

"They gave us sardines and beans and tuna fish and things like that and we ate as if we were dogs after a hunt," Pepe said.

Cachorro and his fellow paratroopers arrived on April 27 after a ride in the Czech truck. Soon after arrival they were caught totally off guard when Cachorro and one other trooper were lined up in front of a wall facing a firing squad. They'd been promised they wouldn't be summarily shot.

Instead of his entire life flashing before him, he was angry at Castro's troops for breaking their word. Commies just aren't trustworthy, even if they're compatriots, he concluded.

But more acute were his father's words—that he'd "never be able to live with himself" if he gave his seventeen-year-old son permission to join the Frente and he died or came back maimed. This was the defining thought that overwhelmed him. He'd steeled himself for death, but the distress of the image of his inconsolable parents was profound.

Afterward he was interrogated personally by *Che* Guevara who, he remembers, had half his face covered by a bandage. Guevara, the consummate ideologue, wasn't interested in particulars. Instead, he wanted to dig deep into the invaders' souls to find out what made them tick. Guevara couldn't understand the counter-Revolutionary mentality if it didn't include greed. He was so convinced of the justice of his own cause that he couldn't understand how someone could oppose it. After a fruitless give-and-take with Cachorro, Guevara asked him if he was a Catholic. Though Cachorro's faith at this stage in life was already faltering, he answered "yes," partly out of truth and partly out of defiance.

"How barbarous!" summed up Guevara, glibly dismissing an entire weltanschauung he couldn't understand. Many years later when Cachorro recounted this incident to me, I commented that Argentines could be pretty pretentious snobs. Cachorro retorted that, "*Che* thought himself particularly superior and that he held a very low opinion of blacks. But that his ultimate conceit was that he believed he could become a Cuban." The following day Cachorro's paratroopers were transported to Havana.

When Erneido Oliva was captured in the vicinity of San Blas and brought in, *Che* Guevara also questioned him. Why did he leave Cuba? Because they were Communists. Did he know the penalty for treason? Yes, the *paredón*. Wasn't he afraid of death? "Yes, I was also afraid of the dentist when he took out four teeth."

Eli César's San Blas group arrived in Girón on April 30. By this time the fake executions had been discontinued, but not the interrogations. On May 1 they too were transported to Havana.

* * *

Most of the prisoners were transported to Havana in trucks and buses, a three to four hour ride. Though, "In at least one case," Rasenberger writes, "this turned out to be the most harrowing experience of the entire invasion and its long aftermath."

One truck, an American-made, aluminum and plywood semi trailer with two mid-side panel doors, had been commandeered for prisoner transport. Like most semi trailers, it had no windows. Osmani Cienfuegos, in charge of the loading—Castro had left the previous day—taunted the men as they got in, calling them derogatory names. By the time one hundred men had been packed inside, the prisoners shouted "No more! No more! We can't breathe!" Cienfuegos ignored the pleas and ordered "forty more pigs" into the truck.

Cienfuegos' aide, concerned, protested, "Sir, we can't put any more in. They will die."

Armandito will never forget Cienfuegos' reply. "Let them die! It will save us from shooting them." Apparently, either he hadn't heard that Castro meant to keep the prisoners alive, or was ignoring his intent.

The last man loaded was the badly injured Máximo Ñato Cruz. "I hope you keep the door open," Cruz cautioned Cienfuegos, "Otherwise, we're going to die."

"You are going to be shot when you get to Havana, so what's the difference—dying now or dying tomorrow?" Turning to his men, Cienfuegos ordered, "Get the son of a bitch and throw him into the truck."

When there were 149 bodies in the trailer, the doors were closed and bolted. Armandito was not on that truck, but Mike Padrón the original owner of the truck—in another strange coincidence—found himself riding in it. Haynes Johnson describes the ride:

"It was one o'clock of a hot, sunny afternoon. In the total darkness inside there was panic: men shouting, packed solidly against each other, desperately struggling for air. 'It was the terrible heat,' one man said. 'Sweat ran like a river.'"

"Terrified, the men ripped off their clothes and beat on the walls with their fists and rocked the truck, vainly trying to turn it over—anything to stop it. From everywhere came shouts and screams: 'Oh, my god! I have no air! I have no air! I am going to die!' To one man, it was 'like Dante's inferno'; to another, 'it was an enemy you couldn't fight. I'd much rather be shot.' With belt buckles they scratched and clawed on the aluminum walls until they succeeded in making a few holes. They fought for the chance to reach these holes and the air. 'When you

are going to die,' one said, 'the first is a very deep sleep. If you sleep, you die.'
When a man began to pass out, he was grabbed and placed in front of one of the
holes until he revived and then another would take his place. On and on the truck
drove. From time to time, when the driver applied his brakes, the sloshing of
sweat on the floor could be heard. When the sun went down, moisture on the
walls and ceiling condensed and 'it began to rain for us.' Men began to die."

The men drank the "rain." Although sweating is the body's mechanism for cooling itself in hot conditions, sweat isn't cool. It's warm as blood. It is essentially blood. It comes from plasma. Sweat cools by evaporation. In extremely humid conditions, as in the semi truck, little to no cooling occurs. A human in extreme heat can sweat as much as four-and-a-half pounds an hour, over a few hours. In hot conditions, blood migrates to the skin to produce sweat to cool the body, leaving the brain with a blood and oxygen deficit. Heat syncope or fainting occurs. Lying down helps.

Heatstroke, however, can kill. With the blood migrating to the skin, it isn't just the brain that's deprived. The digestive organs are cut off from the things they need: oxygen, glucose, toxic waste pickup. The viscera start to fail and begin to leak bacteria into the blood. Mary Roach, in *Grunt: The Curious Science of Humans at War* summarizes: "A systemic inflammatory response sets in, and multi-organ damage ensues. Delirium, sometimes coma, even death may follow."

The journey, many thought, was purposely stretched to eight hours. By the time the truck reached Havana that evening, nine men were dead. Another died after he was unloaded, bringing the Brigade's death toll up to 114. Padrón, the truck's owner, survived the trip—as did Cruz, by this time little more than a bag of bones with an extraordinary nose.

14

The Sorting Out

Castro's prisons were full. He'd filled them prior to the invasion, prophylactically arresting the disgruntled, the malcontent and even the totally innocent. He didn't want to take any chances that a Fifth Column might sprout and join the invaders. Where to put the 1,200 *Brigadistas*? Just as he'd done initially with the suspected dissidents, Castro temporarily warehoused them in *El Palacio de los Deportes* (the Sports Palace) in the center of Havana. Here they were to be counted, processed, interrogated, catalogued by "social class" and paraded before the world as agents of US imperialism—"yellow worms". Trials and executions would come later.

Palacio de Deportes, Havana, Cuba, where Cuban dissidents were held just prior to the Bay of Pigs invasion, and afterward Brigade 2506 soldiers were incarcerated until prison quarters could be arranged. Credit: Ariel Pando. Date: 1959. Source: Pinterest.

Prisoners began arriving at the Sports Palace on April 24. Cachorro's group arrived at the Sports Palace on April 26, the same day the US Navy suspended its search for Brigade survivors. Their first meal was delicious: black beans and rice, *boniato* (Cuban sweet potato), and even *ropa vieja* (stewed brisket). They were so ravenous many men ate the paper plates upon which the meal had been served—so as to lap up all the juices.

Throughout their stay at the Sports Palace the prisoners ate moderately well. The cook had been the manager of the Vedado Tennis Club and knew some of the men. He made *pastelitos* for them and passed them out infrequently as an extra treat.

The regimen was rigid, very un-Cuban. The men were segregated by battalion, company and squad. Cachorro, a member of the 1st Paratroop Battalion, didn't get a chance to connect with Armandito or *Chino*, both 2nd Battalion members. They were forced to sit on hard wooden seats for twenty-one hours a day, forbidden to rise or even stretch. From three to six in the morning they were allowed to lie down, but with all lights on. Hygiene was impossible, bathing—non-existent, until two weeks after their arrival. With only one toilet per 120 men, toilet breaks were infrequent, grudgingly granted and required an escort. Dysentery was rampant; the stench overwhelming.

Cachorro remembers the medical treatment they received at the Sports Palace as adequate. All the men needing immediate care, including the hapless Maximo *Nato* Cruz, were treated in a hospital in Matanzas. Cachorro had an infected shoulder. Back in Guatemala he'd been bitten by a coffee fly. These can lay their eggs under a victim's skin causing complications later. Many weeks had passed since the bite and now the shoulder was very painful, discolored, misshapen and fetid. The medical staff opened up the shoulder—without anesthesia—and dug out the larvae with their fingers. The nurses recoiled in disgust. But probably not just at the worms. The poor boy was filthy and grew so much hair so fast that he looked like a cross between a museum rendition of Homo Erectus and a chimp—and smelled like both to boot.

Night and day loudspeakers blared out the names of each prisoner, calling them to account. The interrogations, including taped statements and signed "confessions" added to the fatigue and demoralization. Many felt betrayed by the United States. But there were bright spots. Cachorro was questioned by a sympathetic female interrogator. When she asked whether the boy had killed anyone, he suspected it was a loaded question.

Although he was certain of only one kill, the zebu cow, Cachorro answered that, yes, he had killed soldiers in action (in case he'd hit someone during the firefight at his capture). Whether his answer was a defiant, false bravado or a desire not to lie, the interrogator sensed a lack of certitude and a vague vulnerability. She temporized and wrote "no."

Cachorro noticed the answer and objected to the false report, thinking she might be—in some convoluted, counter-intuitive way—pulling a fast one. She quietly looked at him, paused, and said that he'd appreciate what she was doing later.

Next to Cachorro, on the wooden bench, sat Salvador, a fellow sky soldier whom he didn't know well. Salvador had somehow managed to get rid of his cammo pants and had acquired civilian pants, but he still had the yellow T-shirt that identified him as a prisoner. Salvador kept asking the guard who escorted him to the toilet—he went so often Cachorro thought he might have a touch of the dysentery that was going around—to get him a *guayabera*, a loose-fitting, traditional Cuban shirt. The request puzzled and irritated Cachorro. What did the man want with a *guayabera* anyway?

Finally, the guard got Salvador a *guayabera*—how or why remains a mystery. The next time he went to the toilet, he came out wearing it. While the guard was leading him back to the benches, Salvador gave him the slip.

By this time, Cuban reporters and sympathetic journalists from the international press had been allowed into the Sports Palace to interview the prisoners and report on the goings-on. Salvador had been a journalist before his stint in the Brigade and still retained his press pass. He had been a correspondent for a Mexican newspaper. After eluding the guard, he slipped off through the crowd, making a beeline for the exit, where he presented his press pass, walked through the gate, and disappeared for good. Had his press pass been for a Cuban paper, his deceit would never have worked. Years later Salvador ran into Cachorro in Miami, greeted him like a long-lost friend and recounted his daring escape.

The reporters were complemented by television crews. Castro wanted to milk the propaganda value of the defeat of US imperialism to the hilt while the story was still fresh. The interrogations were targeted at the weak and the pliant, the better to display them on camera for all the world to see. Haynes Johnson describes the show:

> *"For four nights, the parade of prisoners on television continued, until thirty-seven men had been interrogated at length. Despite the staging and selection, the propaganda show proved to be a mixed blessing for Castro. Some of the prisoners*

were abject, as the Communists expected, and some conceded their mistakes. 'I am completely sorry for what has happened,' Father Segundo de las Heras said, 'and I ask the Cuban nation to accept my sorrow. I am ready to do anything I can to make up for what happened.'"

But others, finding themselves on camera, found the courage of their initial convictions. Fidel Castro, capitalizing on his perfect sense of timing, had arrived on April 26—the last day of the spectacle—to personally interview a select few of the men whose propaganda value made the live, on-camera risk worthwhile. Carlos Varona, son of Tony Varona—the ex-prime minister of Cuba and member of the government-in-waiting— stepped up to the plate. During his questioning by Castro, he pointedly asked the dictator, "If you have so many people on your side, why don't you hold elections?"

And he wasn't the only one. Probably the most notable exchange was with Tomás Cruz (not to be confused with Maximo *Ñato* Cruz of the 2nd Battalion), a fellow paratrooper of the 1st Battalion sitting one man next to Cachorro. "You, *negro*, what are you doing here?" Castro asked, reminding Cruz that the Revolution had been fought for people like him, and of the swimming restrictions at some tourist resort hotels before the Revolution.

Cruz, with all the dignity he could muster, responded, "I don't have any complex about my color or my race. I have always been among the white people, and I have always been as a brother to them. And I did not come here to go swimming."

That night, Castro harangued the prisoners from 11:30 pm to 3 am, gloating over his victory and justifying his right to execute them all. However, near the end of his diatribe, he announced that the Revolution was going to be kind to them: Their lives would be spared—except for those who had committed war crimes under Batista.

* * *

When the leaders of the Brigade, Manuel Artime, Pepe San Román and Erneido Oliva were captured, they didn't join the other prisoners right away. San Román was questioned personally by Fidel Castro and Osvaldo Dorticós, the president of Cuba. San Román insisted on giving only his name, serial number and unit. Fidel was furious. "How in the hell can you come here attacking your own country, helped by our enemies? You are a traitor to your country. You have gone against all the rules and the laws of the world. And now you say you are not going to talk."

After ranting and raving for several minutes, Castro tried the "good cop" approach, "Let's talk like two people," he said. But Pepe wouldn't bite. So Castro lectured him. When he still got nowhere, Castro sent him off to a solitary cell. A few days later, *El Máximo Líder* returned with chairs and cigars to try the military officer-to-military officer approach, but Pepe wasn't much more forthcoming, demurring that he didn't want to argue and that he "didn't know how to speak very well."

Manuel Artime wasn't captured until May 2, after fourteen days in the swamp. As the political leader of the Brigade and official liaison with the US government, he was subjected to the most intense and savage interrogation of all. In a dark room lined with mattresses along the walls, Artime was shorn of his shirt and strapped by the legs, shoulders and waist to a chair with spotlights on his face. For three days—he thinks—the questioning went on. He was prevented from falling asleep—kept awake with coffee, cigarette burns and ice water dousings. He couldn't see who was torturing him. Again, the "good cop/bad cop" routine predominated, with lots more of the "bad cop" beatings and revolvers-in-the-mouth mock shootings. None of it worked; Artime revealed nothing.

Finally, he passed out. When he awoke, Osmani Cienfuegos drove him out to a small lake in the woods where political executions had taken place under Batista. He put a gun to Artime's temple, told him this was his "last chance to come through," and counted to three. When Artime remained silent, Cienfuegos put away the gun, drove him to the Sports Palace and stuck him in a cell. The interrogation was over.

Erneido Oliva was also kept in separate detention along with Brigade headquarters staff after his capture. On May 4 he was told he was going to be shot. Instead, he was taken to the Sports Palace. "It was very emotional when they took us there," Oliva said, "because all the people of the Brigade stood up and started applauding…"

Oliva was interrogated—though not mistreated—and then kept in solitary confinement down the hall from Artime. On May 14, when he was released for transfer, the Sports Palace was empty—not one member of the Brigade remained. They had been at the Sports Palace for twenty days.

One other interview bears mentioning. José Andréu, Deputy Commander of the Brigade and bearing the prestigious number 2501, came from a political family dedicated to public service. Before joining the Brigade he'd worked at the World Bank as a project manager. He was a lawyer and considered himself a socialist. Castro, in an attempt at finding common ground with him, interviewed him personally before granting him a television interview. Fidel suggested that since their political views were so similar, Andréu should just forget the past and join the Revolution. Andréu held firm. On TV he criticized the regime for its lack of democracy.

Afterward, Andréu was driven to La Cabaña fortress, the location of Havana's firing squad wall. Blindfolded and shackled he was placed in front of the *paredón*. He was shot with blanks and then returned to join the other prisoners.

* * *

The prisoners were transferred to the under-construction Naval Hospital on the other side of Havana. Conditions improved. Now there was one toilet per twenty men, and twenty men to a room—though the leaders were still kept separate. Showers were more frequent; towels, soap and toiletries available, and there were cots and mattresses for sleeping.

At the Naval Hospital the men were offered dental care. Cachorro—again—was incredulous. He was determined to take advantage of any perks offered, especially if they provided a chance for escape, a distinct possibility this time since the dentist was a bit of a ride away at the Police Hospital. He'd never been so happy looking forward to a visit to the dentist. Anyway, he did have a slight toothache...

Along the way to the dentist's office, for a few short minutes during a traffic jam, the four prisoners who'd taken up the offer were left alone, unguarded—or so Cachorro thought—while the *milicianos* checked out the cause of the delay. The boy immediately made a move to escape but was stopped by a soldier outside who warned him, "Don't even think of it." Anyway, how far could he get with cammo pants and a yellow prisoner's T-shirt?

It's a miracle that the Brigade prisoners didn't get lynched at the Police Hospital. The Police Battalion had suffered many casualties in the aftermath of the Battle of the *Rotonda* chasing down the Brigade's 2nd Battalion. The hospital was filled with their wounded.

On the way back from the Police Hospital, the soldiers transporting Cachorro and the few other prisoners that fit into their transport stopped at a café for a bite to eat. The militiamen ordered the prisoners to accompany them. In the café they bought the prisoners a meal. The men couldn't believe what was happening. Cachorro ordered a *medianoche*, known in English as a Cuban sandwich, and a *malta*, a very sweet, non-alcoholic version of a Guinness stout.

When Fidel found out about the Brigade's dentist's visit he was infuriated. The authorizing officer was dismissed from the army.

Other, more subtle changes ensued. With the prisoners divided into smaller groups and given a bit more latitude in their behavior, more guards were assigned; guards that inevitably ended up interacting with the Brigade members much more often, leading to some degree of fraternization. Cachorro and one of his guards began hanging out together, talking about their backgrounds and families. The guard was amazed to find out that Cachorro wasn't a *latifundista*, a capitalist exploiter or a *Batistiano*; that he was just a middle-class Cuban.

Cachorro found out that the guard lived only a few blocks from his aunt's house and walked past it every day after work. "If it's not too much trouble, and if it wouldn't get you into trouble, would you mind stopping by and letting her know where I am and that I'm all right?" he humbly requested.

The guard stopped by Cachorro's aunt's house that very day. The aunt invited the guard in and insisted that he stay for dinner. She invited the neighbor over. They all stayed up late talking.

Each side became aware of the other's humanity. Sometimes, a lone guard would flash a thumbs-up to a prisoner or group of prisoners. Small favors became more common. Rumors of release were rife. What was going on?

Four days after the Brigade's move from the Sports Palace, on May 17, Fidel Castro announced that he was holding the prisoners for compensation, ransom or indemnification—they were worth more alive than dead. One way or the other, Fidel said, the US "must compensate the Republic for the damage they have caused it." If not with money—he set the price at $25 million—at least with 500 tractors. "The tractors must be caterpillar type, not those with rubber wheels, no. They have to be good, so that they may be used to clear brush and jungle, to open roads, to make constructions by tractor," he added.

The following day Castro, surrounded by his guards, walked into Pepe San Román's room and announced that, "I have good news for you. Your brother is alive," adding that Roberto and the survivors of the *Celia* had been rescued by boat and were in the US.

"I have some more good news for you, San Román. You and all your men are going back to Miami," and he explained his proposal to exchange tractors for the prisoners.

The news was then conveyed to all the Brigade men along with instructions for each battalion to choose representatives—excluding the three top leaders—to go to the United States as a commission to present the plan. Hugo Sueiro, Armandito's 2nd Battalion commander was chosen as a member of the commission. They were under oath, their honor, and—doubtless—threats to the remainder, to return to Cuba once their negotiations were concluded. Castro instructed the ten members not to talk bad about him or, even, the US; to steer a middle course and to take care when talking to the press. The next day, May 20th, Cuban Independence Day, the commission flew to Miami. Castro granted them one week in which to conclude negotiations.

* * *

Cuban reaction to the Bay of Pigs victory was a bit schizophrenic. On May 1, International Workers' Day/May Day, a traditional Communist block holiday, Fidel Castro declared in a victory speech that Cuba was officially a Socialist Nation and had "no time for elections." FAR Paramedic Arnaldo Remigio takes up the rest of the story:

> *"It was late 1961 when we slowly started to realize that the Communists were really in charge of our country and that the stand of the Brigade 2506 was right all along…Thousands and thousands of the men who were part of the same infantry battalions fighting the Brigade 2506 presented resignations."*

The torrent of resignations made Castro realize that, at that rate, in two years time he wouldn't have an army. So he instituted military conscription for all Cuban males between 18 and 25. All others over that age were forced to join army reserve battalions.

* * *

United States reaction to the Bay of Pigs debacle was also a bit schizophrenic, as policy and public opinion in democracies tends to be. In spite of the careful rules of engagement adhered to, the plausible deniability built into its structure, and all the 'Chinese walls' erected to keep the entire affair a purely Cuban conflict, defeat and the victor's propaganda turned the Bay of Pigs into a US defeat. The Kennedy brothers took it personally, both to themselves and for their country. They were pissed off and vowed to eliminate Castro. On April 20, just one day after the Brigade's defeat, the President instructed the Department of Defense to develop a plan to overthrow Castro with overt US military force. On a more measured note, at a meeting of the US National Security Council on May 5, two weeks later, it was formally agreed that "US policy toward Cuba should aim at the downfall of Castro."

But when the President heard Castro's 'tractors for freedom' offer on May 17th, he decided to engage the dictator. The President and his brother felt a strong affinity for the Cuban patriots and a moral obligation to do everything possible to repatriate the Brigade. The President's actions throughout the entire Bay of Pigs affair had not been technically treacherous; however, he felt wretched for the grave mistakes he had made, and wanted to atone.

While it was simply a matter of fiat for a dictatorship to set policy by simply making declarations, a democracy's hands were, if not metaphorically tied with a rope, at least metaphorically crippled by arthritis; proper, and often convoluted, procedures had to be followed, and the concurrence of many factions had to be obtained. For one, the US government could not deal directly with Cuba because it had severed diplomatic relations with the island. Additionally, Castro was calling the proposed deal "indemnification," anathema legally and morally to the US because the concept admitted guilt to wrongdoing. And of course, ransom was also out of the question for the same reasons, though without the admission of guilt. What to do?

On May 19 President Kennedy called Eleanor Roosevelt, Milton S. Eisenhower—the ex-president's brother—and Walter Reuther, head of the United Auto Workers Union, and asked them to form a "Tractors for Freedom Committee" to negotiate with Castro. It was a bi-partisan group. All immediately agreed to serve.

Ostensibly, the committee would have no official standing; it was supposed to be a purely private initiative—never mind that it was the

President's idea; or that it was officially liaising with the President; or that it was being "sanctioned by the government," in Milton Eisenhower's words.

The 'private initiative' fig leaf didn't fly with the Republican opposition, which called it "illegal," "cooperation" with the Castro regime, and an "unforgivable sin." It was not an auspicious beginning for negotiations. Nonetheless, the Brigade commission and the Tractors for Freedom Committee met in good faith soon after the prisoners' arrival in Washington, DC.

The meeting focused on the types of tractors, their number and their value, while only addressing the nature of the deal almost as an afterthought. To Milton Eisenhower this displacement would present a serious problem, but he didn't push the issue.

The commission and the Committee reached a tentative agreement and concluded optimistically. "It was a nice interview," Hugo Sueiro said. "Everyone was in accordance with the idea that we would get the tractors."

Richard Goodwin, the President's liaison with the committee, stated that, "without the slightest doubt" they'd get the tractors. Even the State Department issued a statement declaring that "The United States would give its most attentive consideration to the issuance of appropriate permits for the export of bulldozers to Cuba, for the rescue of the prisoners." Even President Kennedy weighed in, publicly endorsing the committee and urging it to solicit funds from private sources for the prisoner exchange.

On May 27th the Brigade commission returned to Cuba as promised and conveyed the good news to the rest of the prisoners.

* * *

From this point on, the condition of the captives would be determined by the progress of the negotiations, with the threat of execution always in the background. For now, things were looking up. All of Cuba knew where the prisoners were being held. Family visits were announced. One morning the prisoners awoke to the noise of a great crowd outside the Naval Hospital. Haynes Johnson describes the scene:

"The [prisoners] *saw thousands of people—men, women and children— pushing, shouting and screaming. It was the first visit of relatives who had waited outside for hours. Women began singing the national anthem, guards tried*

to push them back and a near-riot occurred. The prisoners opened the windows and the throng roared a greeting. Women cried and waved handkerchiefs."

"It was one of the biggest emotions of my life," Pepe San Román said, "to see that building surrounded by thousands—thousands and thousands of people that wanted to see us."

The Naval Hospital was a medium, multi-story building. Cachorro remembers being on the second floor that day. Though the crowds had ostensibly gathered to visit their relatives in the Brigade, Cachorro's impression was that this was a demonstration—a demonstration that had the cover of legitimacy because it was using sanctioned visitation rights. And since the visits were open to all family members, which in Cuba (as reflected in this memoir) could mean fourth ex-cousins-in-law, the government had inadvertently permitted the largest quasi-antigovernment demonstration since Castro's triumph.

Cachorro spotted a cousin in the median and an uncle in a jacket nearby. He ran back and helped a wounded cousin, Pérez (the same Pérez who'd taunted Castro's tanks to "come closer, *maricones!*" at San Blas) in the Brigade over to the window—there were no crutches in the still-unfinished Naval Hospital—to see their relatives. Below the window, a mound of concrete aggregate had been piled high. Again, Cachorro got the urge to escape. Jump onto the top of the pile, slide down, put on his uncle's jacket and disappear into the crowd. But why bother? According to the news, they'd soon be free; and why endanger his uncle? Pérez talked him out of it, and Cachorro held back.

Tita, Armandito's mother, was there. Caring for her sick mother was her only reason for remaining in Cuba. She had no idea her son had been involved in the Bay of Pigs invasion. She didn't find out until the roster of captives' names came out in the newspaper. She was shocked, but it didn't surprise her; Armandito was capable of anything—nothing could stop him once his mind was made up. Now she had another reason to stay.

The confusion and size of the crowds hampered the first relatives' visits. Only a small fraction of the prisoners got to see their loved ones. Cachorro was one of the lucky few. His cousin, aunt and uncle managed to get in for a short, hectic reunion. But the following week, more visits were allowed, this time better organized, with alphabetical groupings on separate days. The visits took place in large rooms filled with relatives and prisoners. Pepe San Román saw Erneido Oliva for the first time since their defeat while he was being visited by his aunts and cousins. It was here, during a brief exchange with the second-in-command that San Román learned of the ten Brigade deaths in the semi transport under Osmani Cienfuegos. Any remaining bitterness he held for the US disappeared. It was redirected at Castro.

Tita Faget, Armandito's mother. Date 1981. Credit: R. H. Miller

* * *

For Castro the negotiations hadn't gone well. He was furious. The United States was interpreting the deal as an exchange instead of an indemnification. To Castro, the tractors were secondary to an admission of guilt and a public eating of crow by the US. He threatened to shoot the prisoners. On a different tack, he said that if the US insisted that this was an exchange, he was willing to swap the invaders for "an equal number of political prisoners from Puerto Rico, Nicaragua, Guatemala, North America..." and elsewhere. But he kept the negotiations open.

Castro wasn't the only one JFK managed to alienate. The Republicans—and not a few Democrats—piled on, calling the proposed deal a "ransom" and the bulldozers "war material" that would aid Castro's military machine, and urging people not to contribute.

On June 6, one day prior to the deadline he'd set for a conclusion of the talks, Castro invited the Tractors for Freedom Committee to come to Cuba to conclude the details of the deal. Eisenhower thought it pointless;

Roosevelt and Reuther declined to go. Instead, the Committee sent a delegation to represent them. "In Havana, Fidel prepared for them," Haynes Johnson recounts. "He replaced the militiamen guarding the Naval Hospital with a company of attractive militia women who marched and sang and chanted day and night in an exuberant display of the solidarity and happiness of the new Cuba."

The delegation arrived on June 13, briefly toured the hospital, saw some of the prisoners, and met with Castro. Instead of discussing the crux of the disagreement—indemnification vs exchange—the talks focused on the tractors, again: how many, what types, what ancillary agricultural equipment would accompany them, how much cash and/or credits in lieu of agricultural equipment or a mix of both might be satisfactory. Castro was quite flexible; he would accept any combination of tractors or money as long as the total amount equaled his original demands. But he wouldn't budge on indemnification. To him, the US was guilty of aggression and he wanted them to admit it by paying reparations, not simply a prisoner exchange.

Back in the US, the delegation reported the impasse to the Committee. The Tractors for Freedom Committee declined to accept Castro's wording and disbanded. The deal was dead—but not to Fidel. He thought he had a few cards left up his sleeve.

He summoned his Brigade commission. "Well, boys," Castro told them, "the Americans are not going to give you those tractors," offering them whiskey, brandy or Coca-Cola, ostensibly as a consolation; but more to indulge his sense of theatre and control because he then dramatically added that the deal was still on and that he was sending them back to the US to continue negotiating. He declined to mention that the Tractors for Freedom Committee had disbanded.

This time, however, the commission traveled by slow boat—a freighter carrying tobacco to Tampa. They were met at Key West on June 24 by the same immigration official who had welcomed them on their first visit. "He was different than the first time," Hugo Sueiro said. "We were told that we should go back to Cuba."

* * *

The bureaucratic battle that Hugo Sueiro, commander of the 2nd Battalion at the Battle of the *Rotonda*, and his fellow commissioners were about to engage would be nearly as overwhelming as the encounter at the *rotonda*. Though no one would die, the casualties would be serious, the battle would last much longer and, even though they again faced defeat, there would be few redeeming aspects.

The immigration official berated them as agents of Castro—but allowed them in. The press patronized them: Didn't they know the Committee had been disbanded? That the whole country was against Castro's blackmail scheme? That the tractors could be used for military purposes?

Though they'd argued their position with the immigration official, they politely but firmly declined to engage the press. They weren't going anywhere until their presence and mission was recognized. The next day, Nashville lawyer John Hooker Jr., who had been the executive secretary for the Tractors for Freedom Committee, arrived from Washington. He officially confirmed the news that the Committee *had* been disbanded.

The Cubans were persistent. They wanted the negotiations reopened. Could they at least take charge of the funds that the Committee had collected? Hooker promised to see what he could do. Haynes Johnson recounts what happened next:

"On June 30 Hooker told the prisoners it was his 'sad duty' to inform them that the negotiations were broken, irretrievably. He offered the prisoners two alternatives: (1) they could remain in exile in the United States; (2) they could go back to Cuba. He would not be able to give them the money from the Committee; seventy thousand envelopes that had accumulated in the Committee's Detroit postoffice box were going to be returned, unopened. However, if the prisoners wished, they would be given thirty days in which to raise the funds themselves and explain their mission to the American public. The prisoners accepted that proposal as the best possible one under the circumstances. They would be on their own until July 31 when they had to return to prison."

The Brigade commission hit the phones, with the better English speakers in the vanguard. They tried to contact Richard Goodwin, JFK's liaison to the Committee: not available. They tried Eleanor Roosevelt, whom Castro had called a "doddering old fool." No luck; she took the insult seriously. They tried Milton Eisenhower: he wouldn't answer the phone. They tried many other, lesser participants, all unreachable. No one would talk to the Brigade prisoners.

Rebuffed by the US government, they turned to the families of the men in the Brigade, a grass roots approach, and the only avenue left open to them. On July 5 they formed the *Cuban Families Committee for the Liberation of the Prisoners of War*, laying the foundation for the Sisyphean campaign to raise the now $28 million dollars Castro was asking for the release of the prisoners.

Alvaro Sánchez, Jr., a cattleman from Camagüey now living in exile in Miami, formally organized the Committee on July 10 and had it incorporated in Florida on July 24. His seventeen-year-old son, Eduardo, had left his freshman class at Georgia Tech to join the Brigade.

During the three weeks left them in the US, the ten commission members hit the fundraising circuit. The Miami Cuban colony gave generously. Women contributed their jewelry, even their wedding rings.

Richard Goodwin finally agreed to meet the prisoners' commission a few days before their departure. He made no commitments but promised to help the new Families Committee receive tax-exempt status from the government. In an attempt to convince Castro that their salvaging efforts had merit—Communists not usually being impressed with private initiatives—the prisoners' commission requested permission to bring representatives of the Families Committee to Havana. Castro agreed. Sánchez and Ernesto Freyre, second only to Sánchez in the Committee, volunteered to go.

Ernesto Freyre had been a partner in Gorrín, Manas, Macías & Alamilla, the largest and most prestigious law firm in Cuba before the Revolution, handling accounts for Bethlehem Steel, Chase Bank, RCA, US Rubber and others.

Unfortunately, at the very last minute, two members of the prisoners' commission refused to return to Cuba and sought asylum in the US. Haynes Johnson recounts the return of the now-eight member commission and the two Families Committee members to Havana:

> *"'They were the bravest men I've ever seen,' Sánchez said. 'Not even in ancient history is there any record of prisoners going back to jail voluntarily—and these men were going back for the second time knowing they had failed in their mission and there wasn't much hope. I remember on the plane how one of the boys kept asking me how many minutes before we got to Havana. But they never complained.'*
>
> *In Havana there was a tense moment when they landed.*
>
> *'There are only eight prisoners,' a Castro officer said sharply. 'Two are missing.'*
>
> *'No, you are mistaken,' Sánchez replied.*

'But there are only eight here. I counted them. I know.'

'No,' Sánchez said. 'Ten left and ten have returned.'

He counted the prisoners and then pointed to Freyre and himself and said, 'Nine and ten. Ten left and ten came back. Freyre and I will make up the difference.'"

15

El Príncipe

The progress of the negotiations continued to determine the prisoners' welfare. By July 1, the negotiations had all but died. When the remaining eight members of the Brigade commission got back to Cuba, they discovered that the prisoners had been transferred to *El Castillo del Príncipe*, a very irregular pentagon-shaped, moat-surrounded, Spanish colonial fortification with all the amenities of an 18th century prison.

El Príncipe castle and prison, Havana, Cuba. 1929.
Credit: Secretaria de Obras Públicas. Source: Wikipedia

El Príncipe is invisible. In spite of being over five stories high and located on the highest hill in Havana, it is centered on a broad summit and surrounded by forests and medium-rise buildings. Any line-of-sight view from below the hill passes over the castle's top.

The transfer of the prisoners too, was invisible. It was conducted in the middle of the night of July 17/18, busload after busload. Cachorro's bus traveled the empty streets of Havana between 3 and 4 am. He remembers that surreal ride—no one was out and about except for *El Loquillo* (the little crazy one). The man had acquired the nickname for his unpredictable behavior, though he wasn't really crazy. He and Cachorro had been friends and jai-alai players together. Their eyes met in passing and they waved to each other in silence. The moment passed as quickly as it had materialized. Years later, when the two ran into each other in Miami, both confirmed the eerie encounter. It vindicated Cachorro's sanity—by then he had relegated it to the Twilight Zone.

Outside the prison the captives were separated into groups of twelve and forced to run in at double time over the moat and down a long, helical ramp past a gauntlet of guards with bayonets, into empty cells. Once these were filled, the remaining 400 prisoners were stuffed into the *leoneras*, the lions' dens. Along the way, from the upper galleries, "mental" and common criminal prisoners shouted abuse.

Cachorro, Armandito and *Chino* ended up together in a *leonera*, named after the pits the Romans used to house the lions fed with Christians. Built before the advent of modern plumbing, the *leoneras* were akin to the hold of a sailing ship—the absolute lowest level, where ballast was held and every drop of detritus that the ship produced ended up. Water dripped from the ceiling; the dungeons were black and musty; the air foul, the surfaces fetid; rats and cockroaches roamed at will. Bright electric lights glowed around the clock. Only tiny windows high up on the walls let in any sunlight. The toilet was a hole in the floor.

There, Armandito endured his first and only beating. They'd been stripped naked and ordered to lie face down on the concrete while militiamen searched their clothes. Armandito carried 3 photographs and a letter, all of which were ripped up except for the photo of his girlfriend, which was dismissively tossed aside. When Armandito reflexively reached for it, the boots and fists landed on him. It was a valuable lesson that would serve him well throughout his incarceration: Morale was the most important survival tool; and morale didn't come from things like photographs, it came from within.

At first, the leaders—Artime, San Román and Oliva—were separated from everyone else. But later they were thrown into the *leoneras* with their men. It was the first time they'd seen and talked to each other in the three months since the invasion.

"That first day I lost my voice talking with all the boys," Artime said. "It was the biggest and happiest day that I had in all the time I was in prison."

Life in the *leoneras* was grim. The men had to sleep on the floor. Only a few *colchonetas*, small sleeping pads about the size and thickness of a yoga mat, were thrown into the pit. *El Chino*, a big muscular athlete, got one. "That's when his true character came through," remembers Cachorro. "He shared that mat with us on alternating nights so we'd get some passable rest."

Initially, the food was fine—*congrí* (black beans and rice), *picadillo* (hash), sweet potatoes and bananas—but scant. The men resorted to a voluntary *cooperativa*, Cachorro quipping that they were more Communist than the Communists. It was a system for pooling together food brought in by relatives with prisoners who weren't so lucky.

But it wasn't all sharing and reminiscing. This was the first time since their capture that such large groups of prisoners were able to congregate and interact with each other and their leaders with little oversight. Scores needed to be settled; old arguments resolved; hierarchies established; personal spaces delineated; battle memories reconciled; heroes and cowards recognized. Fist fights and petty peeves erupted, but also friendships rekindled and new ones created. Childish jokes and pranks helped to ease the tensions. Political differences elided and a new solidarity against the enemy evolved, catalyzed by *Pica Culo* (butt picker), the guard who took roll every day by poking each man with his bayonet. "We hated his guts the first moment we saw him," one prisoner said.

About the same day that the prisoners' commission returned to Cuba with the two representatives of the Families Committee, the prisoners were moved—at night—from their cells and the *leoneras* in the basement up to the rooftop. When they awoke the next morning, they couldn't believe their luck. *Pica Culo* announced that the Revolution was generous; though the men had been divided into three groups, they were free to move about the roof within the confines of their group and of their walls. Sunshine and breezes invigorated and lifted morale. Three-hundred-and-sixty degree views of Havana provided a much-needed illusion of liberty.

The roof top was a complex, multi-storied maze of outdoor and indoor space. The three groups were housed in three domino-shaped boxes, each with an open air patio. One was called the *galeras*, another the *bivac*, and the third the *sanatorio*. The *galeras* group was further separated into two halves. All had large cells that held about fifty prisoners each, outfitted with woven rope bunk beds. One of the small houses/air shafts in the patio of the *sanatorio* was the infirmary, where the very sick prisoners were housed. Another contained a barber's chair. There was also a water fountain at the *sanatorio* where the men could wash clothes or refresh themselves. The cells were numbered arbitrarily. Cachorro, Armandito and *Chino* ended up in *galera 15* with Artime, San Román and Oliva.

As soon as the prisoners were granted correspondence rights, Cachorro began writing his parents nearly every day. On one side he'd write his father "man to man;" on the back side he'd write his mom 'son to mother.' All together the letters constituted a diary of the Brigade's imprisonment at El Príncipe. Another prisoner, Júan Lambert, managed to obtain a miniature Japanese camera from a woman visitor. He kept it behind his testicles, under a red *Eleguá* handkerchief. No Cuban guard was going to inspect behind a Santeria *paño de santo* covering genitals. Before release he destroyed the camera. The exposed film came out with him hidden into the sliced heel of his shoe, a technique I once used to smuggle US currency out of Haile Mengistu Mariam's Communist Ethiopia. The photos were published in the January 4, 1963 issue of *Life* magazine.

* * *

Álvaro Sánchez and Ernesto Freyre watched as the eight remaining members of the prisoners' commission were marched into El Príncipe. Were they going to be marched in also? They had no official standing, no money, no liberty, perhaps no life—especially if they were accepted as replacements for the two men who had absconded and the entire Brigade was shot for treason. To top off their bad luck, Castro wouldn't talk to them.

Sánchez was optimistic. Neither man was imprisoned. "When we went there we had nothing," he said. "We never did get to talk to Castro that month but we did get to talk to his representatives." On August 16 he was allowed a visit with his son Eduardo.

But the next day Sánchez' hopes were dashed. Brigade prisoner Osvaldo Hernández Campos escaped. Either undergoing or faking diabetic shock, he was being transported to a hospital when he fled. Campos sought asylum in the Argentine Embassy. Haynes Johnson describes what happened:

"Castro was furious. It was the second time in two weeks that prisoners had escaped: first the two men on the commission of ten and now this one. Through his representatives he let Sánchez know that he could not trust the Brigade or its negotiators. Sánchez went to the Embassy and talked to Campos. He explained what it might mean to the cause of his comrades if he did not return; but Campos said he had been advised not to go back."

"In my opinion," Sánchez said, "that's what broke the negotiations." He remained in Havana until the end of August but was unable to see anyone or make any progress.

* * *

The bad news didn't dampen the prisoners' morale as much as the new digs, the reunion of the entire Brigade—though segregation into four groups still prevented complete reunification—and the presence of their leaders lifted it. The men were resigned to a long incarceration and decided to make the best of it. Though the threat of execution had not disappeared, it wasn't imminent. Military discipline was re-established—from the ground up. The men respected and loved their leaders and craved their own self-imposed discipline; it was a way of expressing control over their own lives. Cachorro, probably for his even temperament and sober personality, became *galera 15*'s assistant *jefe*, with Mancebo, a close friend, the *jefe*.

Covert contact among the men in the two *galeras*, the *bivac* and the *sanatorio* was established, further uniting the Brigade. The well-educated set up classes in philosophy, English, German, physics, geology, French and other subjects. Homemade chess sets and playing cards were devised. Organized prayers and rosary recitals capped the endless days. Starting in September, on the 17th of every month the men stood at attention and observed a minute of silence in memory of the invasion and those who had died.

Cachorro and Armandito, being some of the youngest, adapted well to captivity. Armandito and *Chino* resolved to "have fun" with imprisonment—screw the consequences (Cachorro was much more conservative). During an improvised game of baseball, the cobbled-together ball went over one of the walls separating two of the three groups of prisoners. *Chino* jumped down over the twelve-foot wall to retrieve it and couldn't get back up. He spent a two-week stint in solitary confinement for the infraction.

Perhaps it was just Armandito's wild unpredictability coupled with the uncertainty facing them, or even the strange dynamics of incarcerated men that pushed pranks and jokes into the almost unimaginable. or, as Huber Matos, Castro's first high rank purge casualty observed while in prison, "men fall into their own interior abyss." During one cornmeal mush dinner, Armandito approached Artime, San Román and Oliva with an outstretched arm and a cupped hand full of ejaculate, "Look what they're doing to us! There's something strange in my cum!" he declared indignantly—not that anyone wanted to look, or that anything could be seen. Cachorro speculates that he was possibly alerting the leaders that their food was laced with sterility-causing drugs.

The men looked at him like he was crazy, which they already knew, but which didn't matter—Armandito was brave, rock-solid, intelligent, strong and loyal, albeit oddly outlandish—and, anyway, they were all a bit crazy by then.

On September 6, fourteen Brigade prisoners were transported out of El Príncipe to Las Villas to face a military tribunal. The summary judgement found them all guilty of crimes committed under the Batista regime. Five were executed; the other nine were sentenced to thirty years imprisonment in the dreaded *Cárcel Modelo* on the Isle of Pines.

Two days later the prisoners in El Príncipe were served a sumptuous breakfast that included chocolate. By now they knew that such behavior presaged bad news. True to form, the guards announced the Las Villas' judges' decision. Just when they were getting used to a routine, they were reminded that every day was a gift from Fidel. "This hit us very emotionally," said Oliva, "because we had lost our first men, and also we thought that the rest of us would be put on trial."

Another day, when the guards unexpectedly brought in apple pies, the men became wary. Nonetheless, they carefully divided up the portions for the forty men in *galera 15*. After all, they were *apple pies!* Armandito looked on in disgust and let his defiance get the best of him: he stomped all over the pies. The men were furious, but didn't touch him; not only was he too big and strong, they all loved him and tolerated his eccentricities.

Soon after the prisoners' transferal to El Príncipe, word had gotten out in Havana that the men had been moved. Relatives immediately followed. At the prison, the *cola* (in Spanish, a queue is quite descriptively called a tail) of women queuing up in desperation to visit their men encircled the entire building. But it would be a month before *a* wife, *a* daughter, *a* mother, *a* grandmother or *a* sister—only women were allowed—was allowed to visit, and only on the fifteenth of each month. Visits took place *in* the castle's moat.

All visitors were strip searched. Militiawomen seemed titillated at making old women with radical mastectomies remove their bras and would comment crassly to one and all. Tita had the routine so well-choreographed that shame had no time to affect her. On the other hand, all manner of food, goodies, clothing and presents were welcome; however, little got to the prisoners. Tita would stop at one of the city's ubiquitous push-cart sandwich vendors and buy Armandito a *medianoche*: a piece of French bread with roasted pork, ham and Swiss cheese topped with anything else that strikes one's fancy. Armandito would cut it into bite-sized bits and share it with his comrades. Money, too, was welcome; but there was nothing to spend it on except tobacco and sugar. So all the prisoners bought and smoked the most expensive cigars they could get.

One of the first items relatives brought the prisoners was towels, an amenity they all treasured. When the towels got too dirty, the men would wash them and hang them out to dry. But Armandito didn't want to wash his towel, so instead he'd use the other men's clean towels—*but then throw them away*. It was incomprehensible behavior and the men were furious. Cachorro had a quiet word with Armandito and offered to wash his towel for him. But neither the offense, nor the proposed solution, registered with Armandito, whose expression resembled a dog's staring at a ceiling fan. From then on the men kept a close watch on their towels.

Armandito acquired the nickname *Plasta*, or shit patty; certainly for his obtuseness and unpredictable disposition, but mostly because it rhymed with his surname, Lastra. None but his closest friends dared use it to his face. The nickname didn't offend him, but no one wanted to take the chance since Armandito relished a good brawl.

Once when hard bread rolls had been distributed—so hard and heavy they resembled a hockey puck and had to be soaked in liquid before chewing—the teenagers indulged in a food fight with them. Since they were so dense—and actually dangerous—an older inmate stepped in and ordered the free-for-all stopped. Cachorro, refusing to turn the bread in, hid his roll under his pillow. When the older prisoner saw this, he demanded Cachorro's roll. The boy wouldn't give it up.

Exercising his authority, the older man sucker-punched Cachorro to distract him and grab the bread roll. In his reflex reaction Cachorro hit his head and passed out. Immediately, Armandito attacked the older man—no one was going to hurt his best friend. Other prisoners jumped in against

Armandito to help the faux officer. When Cachorro came to, Armandito was fighting 7 men and holding his ground. Like his personality and temper, his heart had no boundaries.

But his brain sometimes had a mind of its own. Perhaps he was sleepwalking, or perhaps he was acting out the continuation of a dream he'd just had. Or perhaps it was just his or the prison's craziness. But one early morning Armandito rose from his cot and headed for the still-sleeping Cachorro. The big guy started pummeling his little friend. Cachorro had no idea what was going on and, begging his best friend for mercy, asked him to stop. But Armandito wasn't all there right then. Finally, something in Armandito snapped. He caught hold of himself, started crying and asked Cachorro's forgiveness.

* * *

Poor Álvaro Sánchez. "I never felt worse in my life," he said, "because when we arrived in Miami there were thousands of families at the airport cheering us and shouting and we were completely defeated. They thought we had accomplished something."

Not one to stew in discouragement, Sánchez got down to work. His immediate aim was to officially replace the disbanded Tractors for Freedom Committee by seeking President Kennedy's recognition of and support for the Cuban Families Committee for the Liberation of the Prisoners of War.

The President never responded directly, but Robert Hurwitch, a special assistant to the Assistant Secretary of State for Inter-American Affairs politely acknowledged Sánchez' letter. The camel's nose was finally inside the tent.

Sánchez went to Washington and sought an appointment with Hurwitch. The assistant to the Assistant kept putting the Cuban off; but for two long weeks Sánchez persisted, finally playing the guilt card, "asking for the United States to come in and meet what we felt were its obligations." Hurwitch finally told him that it was impossible to pay Castro any ransom. Congress would never agree.

So Sánchez tempered his request. He asked for permission to start a fund-raising drive backed by a public relations campaign with the moral support of the White House and the State Department. At the end of September the government informally approved the request. Wasting no time, the Cuban Families Committee for the Liberation of the Prisoners of War moved its headquarters to New York and opened up a Madison Avenue office on October 1 and began the formal campaign to raise the ransom. But it wouldn't be until December that the Internal Revenue Service finally granted tax-exempt status to the Cuban Families Committee.

* * *

Meanwhile, the administration's policy towards Cuba took another, more militant turn. The CIA infiltration and intelligence gathering operations inside Cuba had more or less gone into recess during the Bay of Pigs operation. But by the summer of 1961, in fits and starts, they resumed. In September the first reports of probable missile launching sites under construction in Oriente Province reached the CIA—thirteen months before the Cuban Missile Crisis of October, 1962.

In response, on November 30, JFK authorized Operation Mongoose, an initiative to eliminate Fidel Castro and his Revolution, composed of an inter-agency team that included the CIA, the State Department, the Department of Defense, the Joint Chiefs of Staff and Robert Kennedy.

On the face of it, Operation Mongoose sounded just like President Eisenhower's Covert Action Plan Against Cuba, which later became the Bay of Pigs operation. And it even had a similar structure with nearly the same players. Hadn't the administration learned anything? What was the difference between the two programs?

For one, the Bay of Pigs operation was basically a free Cuban initiative that used US assistance; while Operation Mongoose was a US initiative that used Cubans to help carry it out. Cubans called the shots during the Bay of Pigs operation; the US government called the shots throughout Operation Mongoose.

Operation Mongoose was the beginning of the post-Bay of Pigs CIA Cuba infiltration program, which was to last until 1964 when President Lyndon Johnson officially terminated it. Though referred to as an 'infiltration' program, it consisted of much more than intelligence gathering, dissident evacuation and the promotion of democratic values. Sabotage, the initiation of agent provocateur incidents, the covert use of US Special Forces, psychological warfare and assassination attempts were all part of its remit to help overthrow the Castro regime.

Grayston Lynch, US Army officer and CIA operative who provided organizational help during the Bay of Pigs operation and participated in Operation Mongoose, says that Operation Mongoose "was the beginning of a secret war against Cuba, which, until it ended with the closing of the Miami station in 1967, saw over 2,126 operations run by JM WAVE [an Operation Mongoose special CIA task force] against Castro and his regime. A total of 113 of those operations was conducted by my commando groups." At one time JM WAVE was the largest CIA station in the world outside of its Langley, Virginia headquarters. JM WAVE employed 300 to 400 professional operatives, mostly in Miami and possibly including about 100 in Cuba, as well as an estimated 15,000 anti-Castro Cuban exiles both in offices and in the field.

Operation Mongoose should not be confused with the many free Cuban infiltration initiatives that proliferated out of the exile community after the Bay of Pigs fiasco and worked in parallel with Operation Mongoose— sometimes in concert with it, and sometimes in defiance of it. Those unauthorized resistance initiatives continued way beyond 1964.

* * *

After the failed invasion, it wasn't healthy to be related to a Bay of Pigs prisoner. So Cuca, Tita's sister and Armandito's aunt, left Cuba in August of 1961. Her husband Pillo was due to leave in November but had to delay his departure when his elderly parents took a health turn for the worse. But Tita stayed. The Revolution couldn't dampen her resilience. She stayed to care for her parents, my grandmother, and countless other poor or elderly relatives, shirt-tail relatives, ex-employees and friends. But most of all, she stayed to care for her son, Armadito, in any way she could—with food, clothing, money, moral support and love.

Cachorro and Armandito celebrated their September and October eighteenth birthdays without any hoopla. The prisoners' big hopes for a celebration rested with Christmas. Sánchez' Families Committee had begun a "Give Them Freedom for Christmas" campaign. With the IRS tax-deductible ruling, hopes were high for a holiday release. Haynes Johnson describes the goings-on:

"To pass their time the prisoners began making Christmas ornaments from paper, cigar boxes and red ink. Already some...had made small planes and boxes and a sled. On Christmas Eve, while some of the prisoners pulled the sled and others

sang *"Jingle Bells,"* Santa Claus, cotton beard and all, made a brief appearance—until the sled collapsed and the beard fell off. Late that night priests celebrated the Christmas mass and on the next day the prisoners put on a show, produced, written and directed by themselves. Guards, reminding the men how generous the revolution was, brought a special meal—small chickens from Bulgaria."

New Year's Eve was depressing. Álvaro Sánchez' fundraising efforts were falling on deaf ears. No news was bad news. Some prisoners tried drinking hair tonic with lemon juice at a futile attempt at conviviality. One Brigade prisoner attempted suicide with a can lid. Sánchez, up in New York was so despondent, the New Year's celebrations just made him more depressed. The Revolution's New Year's celebrations, with tanks and MIGs parading down the streets of Havana in full view of the prisoners, only reinforced the Castro regime's increased strength.

Nineteen-sixty-two would not be a good year—the food got worse and the treatment more severe. Emblematic of the declining conditions was a hepatitis outbreak in January. Cachorro blames the water. The prisoners' water came from two roof-top water tanks. Open on top, bugs, rats, bats and anything that hit the surface and was caught soon sank to the bottom. "The water had been there for centuries," he said. "It had been ladled out of the top. And then, for some reason, they started giving us water from the bottom. It came out black."

Eleven men became seriously infected; many prisoners turned a deathly yellow. Medicine sent from the US was available but withheld. *Chino* begged the pharmacist for it, who finally relented when José Borrás was found dead on his cot. But without syringes it was useless. After another round of pleading, *galera 15* got one syringe, but no one knew how to deliver a safe or even effective injection. So they experimented on each other.

At the end of January the recriminations and retributions began. The twenty-two men who had most courageously stood their ground during the television interrogations at the Sports Palace and had embarrassed the regime and Fidel personally were singled out, stripped and searched. Afterward they were taken to *galera 7* in the *vivac*. Artime, San Román, Oliva and three priests were put in isolation. The other sixteen were crammed into a cell designed for four men.

The rest of the men were then subjected to indoctrination. First, they were separated into "social classes"—rich versus poor. The poor were transferred to the *sanatorio*, the best digs in the castle. Their food and treatment improved and they were promised special visiting privileges and television if they cooperated with the Revolution. A commissar named Martínez conducted indoctrination classes.

Those didn't go over very well. One morning when Martínez arrived for class, "the men deliberately turned their backs on him and walked away," according to Johnson.

Cachorro ended up in *galera 21* in the *vivac*, along with Armandito and *Chino*. Again, he was selected assistant *jefe*. The *jefe* was Freddy, a no-nonsense, muscular six-foot-three black truck driver who had been a lieutenant in Castro's army. Freddy and Cachorro had left for the Guatemala training camps together. At the airport, Cachorro's dad, a slight bespectacled man who by then was very proud of his son's participation in the operation—in spite of not condoning his enlistment—grabbed the giant Freddy by his lapels, looked him in the eyes, and with an anxious solemnity told him, "*Mulato*, you're now in charge of my son. Make sure he comes back alive." Freddy took the admonition to heart.

Cachorro devised a rotating roster so each man would take a turn at sweeping and mopping the floor. One pretentious prisoner, Alonso Pujol, who was the scion of a well-connected political family, considered himself too important for such a task and refused to participate. Cachorro, too small to enforce the rule, called in his *jefe*, Freddy, to enforce it. Freddy picked the snob up by his armpits and, pointing to his name on the roster, asked whether that was in fact his name. The prig conceded; but then groused that, "this *escobaso* (sweeping) would cost the republic" after victory was achieved. Pujol would later become the only Brigade member to recant his participation in the invasion and offer his services to Castro.

* * *

Conditions in Cuba were deteriorating. In March the government began a food rationing program with coupon books that continues to this day. Things didn't improve for the Bay of Pigs relatives either. Tita's sister, Cuca, who had left Cuba the previous August, had left her husband Pillo behind to care for his elderly parents. Out of the blue, Pillo was arrested in February of 1962. No reason for the arrest was given either to him, Tita or Cuca. He remained imprisoned for 8 months. Without a charge, prescribed length of incarceration or access to a lawyer, he became dispirited, lonely, nearly broken and fell into despair. Then, without notice, he was suddenly released in early October, again without any evident reason, days before the Cuban

Missile Crisis hit the fan on the 14th of that month. He made it to the US just before all commercial flights were grounded in anticipation of war.

16

The Trial

Don't pity those who fought and died;
Pity those who never tried.

Fidel Castro had lost patience with the US's lack of engagement with the Cuban Families Committee's efforts to negotiate the release of the prisoners. On March 20 he announced that time had run out for the exchange of the prisoners for tractors. Two days later he announced that the "mercenaries" would be tried as "war criminals" on March 29. The news was conveyed to the Brigade by a graffito scrawled on the wall by a common prisoner.

What to do?

The leaders in *galera* 7 conferred and "decided to take the same position that Christ took in front of the Jews—to ignore them and not to say anything," Artime said.

Back in New York, on the other hand, Álvaro Sánchez cabled Castro offering himself up as a hostage in order to keep the negotiations going. Castro declined, saying, "This matter is now in the hands of the Revolutionary tribunals."

But not before time. Castro was determined to stack the odds in his favor before the trial started. He singled out those men who had shown the greatest weakness and malleability before the television panel in the Sports Palace and threatened them with violence if they didn't cooperate now.

With Pepe San Román he tried a different approach. The prison commissar told Pepe he was free to go; to forget the whole Bay of Pigs had ever happened. Pepe, surprised and confused, refused.

The men of the Brigade had their own ideas. The threats and enticements drew the men together "into almost perfect unity," in the words of Haynes Johnson.

Death was hanging over their heads. Communist mass trials never ended happily, especially military courts martial. The formal charges against the men of the Brigade included treason (Cause 111), a crime punishable by capital punishment. The men resigned themselves to their fate, a resignation that quickly turned to joyful defiance—a better choice than wallowing in fear and despair. The men celebrated life. They celebrated love. They celebrated Cuba. They celebrated their victory. Yes, their victory, their Thermopylae—a victory so spectacular, so morally correct that it overshadowed the loss of the war. In one *galera* the men continuously sang *La Bayamesa*, Cuba's national anthem; in another there was dancing and singing. Songs and poems—some without regard to propriety or the Brigade's legacy—were composed for the occasion. Cachorro remembers that the most remarkable turn-around—one he'd never had to face—was the men's attitude towards the United States.

Most had expected active battlefield participation from their ally and felt betrayed when the US declined to engage Castro's forces. Cachorro always understood that this was a *Cuban fight*, and that the US—if it attacked Cuba—would not only be crossing a dangerous geopolitical line, it would be initiating aggression against a tiny country that had not attacked it. It was not a price—morally or practically—worth paying by the US. One soldier, quoted in Johnson's book, explained the turn-around this way: "The only ally that we have in fighting Communism is the United States. And how are we going to go against the only ally we have? And besides, I have a wife and kid, and I want my name kept as it is, straight, vertical."

The defiant exuberance burst out of the cells on Thursday morning at 8 am, March 29, 1962 when the men were led into the prison's courtyard laughing and joking for their trial. Atop the perimeter walls cables and television cameras stood ready to record and broadcast the proceedings. The sun was scorching, the wooden seats hard, but the insolence of the Brigade was making a mockery of Castro's tribunal. The proceedings were never broadcast on radio or TV. When Artime, San Román and Oliva were escorted in, the men spontaneously stood at attention and sang *La Bayamesa*; then they mobbed the leaders cheering and shouting *vivas*. Johnson takes up the narrative:

"A Negro named Carrillo embraced Artime, and Martínez (the prison commissar) shouted for Artime to stop acting like a politician with a Negro. But Carrillo said, 'You are wrong; this is my brother.'"

"The noise rose and in the confusion a militia guard struck another Negro. Torres Mena, of the tank company, instantly leaped forward and hit the militiaman in

the face with his fist. When Martínez tried to halt the fight, a prisoner hit him. The Brigade was almost out of control. Sporadic fights began, two prisoners were bayoneted, some were hit with rifle butts. A bloody riot seemed inevitable."

"Captain Pedro Luis Rodríguez rushed to Pepe and Oliva and begged them to control the men. Pepe bellowed out a command and the entire Brigade, even those who had been wounded, as well as the Castro guards, snapped to attention. There was complete silence."

"Oliva stepped forward to a microphone and said, 'If we are going to die, we are going to die with dignity. When they shoot us we will sing the national hymn. This is not the time.'"

Pepe ordered the men to be seated and maintain their discipline 'before the enemy.' The men sat down. Then the trial began."

Brigade 2506 trial in Castillo del Principe. Tribunal in background. Source: Estevan L. Bovo-Caras, Brigade 2506 Museum and Veterans' Association.

The tribunal was composed of five judges—sitting under an awning in the shade—a prosecutor and a defense attorney who referred to his clients as cowards and traitors. Augusto Martínez Sánchez, presiding judge of the tribunal, began the proceedings by calling out: "José Pérez San Román. Do you have something to declare?"

Pepe rose, came to attention and marched briskly to the judges' dais. Coming to a stop with an exaggerated heel click he declared proudly, "I abstain." Artime and Oliva, when their turn came, followed suit. When Martínez Sánchez asked if anyone in the Brigade wished to make a statement, an impressive silence descended—you could hear the flies buzzing.

Martínez Sánchez, impatient and irritated, pulled out a wild card. "Is there anyone here who is not a member of the Brigade? If so, stand up, you are free." No one stood up to take the offer, in spite of the fact that several of the men had been García Line merchant mariners who had come ashore when their ships were sunk and had been captured in the general round-up of prisoners.

Finally, Martínez Sánchez, testing the limit of what by now seemed a conspiratorial silence, began calling on each Brigade member individually. Each man answered, as previously ordered by their leaders: "I do not recognize this tribunal. I have nothing to say."

After a couple of hundred identical responses, Martínez Sánchez, decided to question the men row by row, "First row. Anyone who has a declaration to make, stand up." Again, no one stood—in any row. Until one tall black soldier, Luis González Lalonry, in one of the last rows, raised his hand.

"Yes, stand up," Martínez Sánchez said, pointing at Lalonry. "What do you have to say?"

"*Me estoy cagando* (I'm shitting myself). I need to go to the bathroom," the prisoner replied. The Brigade burst into laughter. The tension was broken, but no one saw fit to add anything else.

It was now the prosecution's turn. Captain Pedro Luis Rodríguez, one of the militiamen who had tortured and interrogated Artime and questioned Oliva, walked up to the microphone and faced the tribunal. He began his testimony by berating the Brigade, accusing them of cowardice and fecklessness. After nearly an endless irrelevant harangue, Rodríguez finally presented some evidence.

He began reading from a document attacking the US which, he claimed, San Román had written to Castro. Once finished, the tribunal summoned Pepe forward. Ever the soldier, Pepe snapped to attention, marched up to the microphone, stood at attention and then switched to parade rest—actions that infuriated the Communists because they didn't recognize the Brigade as a proper military entity. They ordered him sharply not to assume military bearing, but Pepe remained at parade rest.

"All right, San Román, what have you got to say? You don't have to talk. You have defense counsel." Martínez Sánchez motioned to his court-appointed attorney.

"In the name of all the Brigade," Pepe said, "I refuse to accept the defense counsel who has been imposed on us by the government. We don't want anyone to defend us. We don't need any defense."

Captain Rodríguez, witness for the prosecution but now acting as prosecutor, waved the letter angrily at San Román and demanded, "What have you got to say about the letter? Look at it, San Román, look at your handwriting."

"I did not write that letter," Pepe said. "I recognize that it is a very good falsification. But it is not mine!" Johnson then reports that Pepe was ordered to move forward and write his name on a piece of paper. He did so, and afterwards resumed his military stance before the microphone. The signatures were compared, and Pepe admitted that they looked similar, but denied that the original was his.

Captain Rodríguez then read from another letter attributed to Pepe to his family in Miami, which had mildly critical remarks about the US. Pepe again denied it was his. Rodríguez, now fuming, pulled out another letter, this time from a woman Pepe once knew in Oriente Province, *to* Pepe.

"Pepe broke in to say that he did not have to speak about women before them. Pepe's trial was finished," Johnson writes.

* * *

And so it was for everyone—for that day. At 3 pm the tribunal recessed. "That's enough for today," declared Martínez Sánchez, the presiding judge.

It wasn't so much that the Brigade members, voluntarily assuming rigid military bearing under the glaring sun, without food or water all day, needed a break, so much as San Román's defiant performance that called for a pause. With Artime and Oliva scheduled to be questioned next, the tribunal didn't want to risk further embarrassment, and wanted to provide the prison authorities a chance to give the leaders some much-needed additional incentive to cooperate.

The three men were taken to separate cells. The chief of Cuba's G-2, accompanied by Captain Rodríguez, presented Artime with a statement admitting that he had been a puppet of the United States and that now he repented. He was given twenty-four hours to sign. To prod him along— literally—two guards with bayonets spent the night with him making sure he didn't doze off. Pepe and Oliva, though not asked to sign anything, were likewise deprived of sleep.

Post-first-day trial newspaper and radio reports announced that the prisoners had "confessed their crime and announced they wished to make no further statement." Several hundred female Brigade relatives knelt and prayed outside El Príncipe.

Friday morning began tensely. The prisoners had no idea what had happened to their leaders overnight. By 8 am, when the prisoners were herded back into the courtyard courtroom, the sun was already scorching. Security had been beefed up. After the Brigade's defiant attitude on the first day, many more armed militias surrounded the courtyard. A little after eight, from behind, came the order, "Atten-tion!" It was Oliva's 'command voice.' All the men rose and stood at attention. He, Artime and San Román marched to their seats in front under escort. Their presence, command and bearing reassured the men.

It was Artime's turn before Captain Rodríguez. Rodríguez read the document he'd demanded Artime sign the previous evening and asked him to acknowledge it as his own.

"This is a complete lie," Artime replied. Rodríguez, ignoring courtroom protocol, cursed in frustration. The Brigade, taking their cue from the captain to cut loose, broke into catcalls and laughter.

Unable to make any headway with Artime on the official charges, the tribunal resorted to irrelevant charges and character assassination. Back in 1959, while still working for the INRA, the National Institute for Agrarian Reform, Artime had organized the *Movimiento de Recuperación Revolucionario*, or MRR (Movement to Recover the Revolution)—the first and largest anti-Castro organization, and the precursor to the Frente and the Revolutionary Council, the united exile Cuban Front behind the Bay of Pigs—after hearing Castro give a speech on his plans to Communize Cuba. An officer from the INRA was called forward to testify. He accused Artime of stealing money from peasants, and added as an afterthought, that Artime was a man without dignity who "would sell his own mother."

Artime did not deign to reply.

Oliva was next. With the hero of the Battle of the *Rotonda* the tribunal pushed Communist logic to nearly its breaking point. They didn't even call Oliva to the microphone. Instead, they accused him of dereliction of duty to *the Brigade* by retreating from Playa Larga without putting up a tough fight against Castro! Oliva and Pepe just laughed at the absurdity of the accusation. It was a charge that perhaps only the Revolutionary Council, or Provisional Government in Exile in Miami might have had jurisdiction over—if there were the merest vestige of truth to it—but certainly not Castro's Revolutionary tribunal. Perhaps they thought that impugning Oliva's character might stir up something useful.

The remainder of the day focused on the lesser officers and the grunts of the Brigade. The tribunal wanted something to show for its efforts. They targeted the low hanging fruit—those men who had groused about US support or who had expressed any doubts about their involvement in the caper back at the Sports Palace. One by one these men were called to the microphone, their statements read out loud, or their own tape-recorded words played back over the loudspeakers. They were asked to acknowledge them.

Only two men confirmed both their written and oral statements. All the rest denied everything, even their own recorded words. One man, Areces Gutiérrez, a fellow grunt in Armandito's 2nd Battalion, after listening to his recorded voice, said, "That is my voice, but that was in a moment when many things had happened. Now I deny what I said then. Now I want you to treat me as your enemy."

One of the two men who acquiesced, out of the now 1,180, told a tortured tale. Ulises Carbó had been the spokesman for the ten members of the Brigade Commission authorized by Castro and the prisoners to negotiate the prisoner-tractor exchange. Carbó and Cachorro were close. Their families had been best friends for three generations. Carbó had received a late night visit the previous day: "I was pressed a lot the night before and told that if I didn't testify they would shoot San Román, Artime, Oliva and others. And I testified, because they told me that was the only way to save them. And the chief of the Brigade thanked me for saving their lives," he told Johnson when interviewed for Johnson's book.

Carbó's testimony was nuanced. He stated the obvious: that the Tractors for Freedom Committee had let them down; that the US had let them down; that the US had trained them in Guatemala and escorted their landing at the Bay of Pigs. But he added that he would never support Communism and that he was an enemy of the regime. Still, the courtyard filled with *coños*, boos and catcalls, the main complaint being that Carbó defied orders by even speaking. Once Carbó's testimony was parsed and the leaders confirmed his story, Carbó returned to the Brigade's good graces.

The other man, Alonso Pujol—the prisoner who had refused to sweep the *galera* as scheduled by Cachorro—turned coat. He blamed the US for everything and offered to help the Castro government. Pujol's father, at one time vice president of the country and—according to Cachorro—one of the most corrupt politicians in a country famous for skimming pols, had talked to Castro before the trial. Shortly after the trial, Pujol was set free. Haynes Johnson writes that Pujol's freedom was "bought" (his quotes) by his father. Cachorro intimates that the currency might have been information instead of money. Only the Pujols and Castro know what deal was negotiated. In the interim the rest of the *brigadistas* pretended Pujol didn't exist.

* * *

The trial's second day had unfolded as badly as the first for the regime. It, too, was not broadcast. The tribunal called for a weekend recess, with the trial to resume on Monday morning. Back in the *galeras* the Brigade composed a new song of exultation, declaring they were ready to fight again. The leaders, still in isolation, could hear it throughout the prison.

Miami erupted.

Over the weekend, one thousand women, expecting the prisoners to be shot, knelt in Bayfront Park in solidarity, prayer and vigil. Miami Cubans were ready to riot. Roberto San Román, Pepe's brother and a survivor of the *Celia* sailboat escape, raised $500 (about $5,000 in 2016 dollars) from the exile community and headed for Washington with two other Brigade survivors to get some action.

The next morning the three men headed for Robert Hurwitch's office at the State Department. Hurwitch had been Álvaro Sánchez' (of the Families Committee) last official US government contact. Back then, Hurwitch, after two weeks of putting Sánchez off, had—as the Cubans might characterize— offered only a cumin seed's worth of help, by granting the Families Committee official recognition so they could pursue tax-exempt status.

He was even less helpful this time, other than seeing the men right away without an appointment. Hurwitch made it very clear that there was nothing the State Department could do for the Brigade; and he did it in such a manner that the three Cubans became totally riled. They threatened to return to Cuba and share the fate of their comrades. But Hurwitch was only slightly moved. He apologized and promised to see what he could do.

Pissed off and oblivious to DC's Friday afternoon TGIF mentality, the Cubans hailed a taxicab and headed for the Justice Department to see the Attorney General himself. "We were real hot," Roberto said, "and we told the receptionist who we were and that we wanted to see Mr. Robert Kennedy." Within five minutes Roberto was in the Attorney General's office.

Johnson quotes Roberto San Román's account:

"This man was completely different. This was like talking to a Brigade man. He was very worried about the Brigade and he wanted to know everything that I knew—if there was any possibility that they would be shot, and how the people of Miami felt about it. We talked about the families and everything. Told him that for sure some of them would get shot, maybe not all of them, but some of them, probably at least the staff, and that Miami was boiling, waiting for some kind of action from the United States. That everybody was waiting. And if these men got shot the United States was going to have a rough problem in Miami. And, believe me, this was really the situation!"

The Attorney General listened intently, asked several questions and then said, "All right, Roberto, we are going to do everything we can. I give you my word we will do everything possible to keep them from being shot." Kennedy gave San Román unlimited access and added, "Call me ten times a day if you have to."

He was as good as his word, taking San Román's calls day and night at his office, the White House and at his home—and always acting on Roberto's information when opportunities presented themselves. Robert Kennedy finally brought the full diplomatic weight and measure of the United States behind the cause of freeing the Bay of Pigs prisoners.

During the trial's recess that very weekend—at Washington's urging—Brazil's President forwarded an emergency appeal to Castro to spare the lives of the prisoners, warning Castro that if the men were executed it would ignite such a storm of protest that the US would be forced to take some action against Cuba. Other Latin American embassies were urged to send notes of protest to Castro about the trial.

* * *

The third day of the trial began on Monday at 9 am. No more Brigade members were called before the microphone. Instead, witnesses for the prosecution, mostly FAR (*Fuerzas Armadas Revolucionarias*) officers and militia, testified. The first up was Captain José Ramon *El Gallego* Fernández, now promoted to Major for his performance at Playa Larga commanding the cadets from the Matanzas Leadership School. Fernández was the first officer Castro had called to counter the invasion. As a young man, he'd had Cachorro's grandfather for a teacher at Cuba's War College and he had become his favorite pupil. He and Cachorro knew each other well.

Fernández testified truthfully and went so far as to say that the Brigade behaved and fought honorably. Cachorro recalls that Fernández' testimony did not do the newly-minted Major any favors.

The next two witnesses' testimony was meant to reverse the impression Fernández had left. The first lied; the second impugned the honor of the Brigade, in particular by accusing Erneido Oliva of desertion based on a misunderstanding that hadn't been fully explained by Pepe to the *brigadistas* until after imprisonment.

This allegation brought Pepe to his feet, shouting, "That's a lie! You are a liar!" San Román was called to order. Ignoring the admonition, Pepe faced the Brigade and defended Oliva until the presiding judge ordered him removed.

For the men, the trial was all a charade with a predetermined outcome. They just wanted to return to their cells.

The last witness was the most hated of the Castro officials: Osmani Cienfuegos, the man who had ordered the men put on the overstuffed truck to die slow deaths. Cienfuegos ranted for more than an hour, abusing the men in the vilest of terms without presenting any relevant evidence. The Brigade had to restrain themselves from physically attacking Cienfuegos. The tribunal adjourned proceedings at 2 pm.

* * *

The last day of the trial, Tuesday, April 3, convened at 3 pm in the afternoon. No witnesses were called; instead, the prosecution and defense presented their summation. Prosecutor José Santiago Cuba Fernández, Cuba's Attorney General and, before the Revolution, a shoemaker, prefaced his summation by characterizing the Brigade as wealthy and cowardly individuals, pawns of the US; while the leaders were ungrateful traitors to their country.

In his formal summation, Cuba Fernández surprisingly called the Brigade "direct authors" of the invasion instead of attributing the entire project to the United States as Castro had kept insisting. Therefore, they were all guilty of crimes "against the integrity and stability of the nation" and they were "traitors to their country." In conclusion, he asked the court to impose "the most severe punishment our laws permit."

Antonio Cejas, the defense counsel—though taking longer—echoed the prosecution. But first he apologized, admitting that it was difficult for him to represent the men because he was a Revolutionary and the "participation of the defendants in the events they have been accused of has been amply proven." Then he called his clients mercenaries, traitors and cowards, offering no mitigating context or exculpating point of view. Finally, he asked the court to render a "just and generous sentence."

The tribunal retired to deliberate their verdict. The trial was over.

* * *

The prisoners were certain they would all be shot. Never mind that no verdict had been announced—and wouldn't be until April 7. Cachorro remembers those days as a never-ending darkness. Pepe prepared his political testament, "When you know you are going to die you feel different. You start to prepare yourself for the moment. The only thing that I was sorry about was that I could not leave a son."

The certainty of death brought about a certain release, followed by acceptance; an acceptance that turned to exultation. One soldier said, "The trial brought a very great spirit of unity. Nobody can feel what spirit we had unless he was there. When you're in prison with one foot in the grave, you know that it cannot be worse. But the ideals make you feel strong enough to defeat anything."

And so it was. The Brigade had defeated their enemies at the trial. It gave them an invincible sense of pride. As Pepe summed up, "A spirit had been born. We felt very happy for destroying the show that Castro had prepared. We beat them in the trial, and they were mad."

And they showed it. Haynes Johnson describes the regime's reaction: "Life in the prison became increasingly worse. Food rations were cut and the guards became even more insulting."

During the trial, over 2,000 mothers, wives, girlfriends and sympathizers of the prisoners had kept vigil outside the prison providing moral support to their men. Johnson continues:

"Outside, on the first day after the trial, a mob of three hundred men and women carrying pro-Castro placards and shrieking 'Fidel, Fidel,' attacked the small crowd of relatives still waiting outside the prison gates on Carlos Tercero Avenue. The relatives were beaten and forced to disperse. Cars were overturned, their windows broken and tires slashed. All contact with the prison now was broken and the relatives waited at home, listening to the radio for news of the verdict."

Armandito's mom, Tita, was there. But being a savvy sort quickly walked away and avoided any harm. Her previous visit would be the last time she saw her son in prison. Berta Barreto de los Heros, the Havana representative of the Cuban Families Committee, was also there leading the group.

BERTA BARRETO WALKING THRU THE HAVANA AIRPORT DURING HER NEGOTIATIONS TO FREE THE BRIGADE PRISONERS

Berta Barreto walking through Havana airport during the negotiations to free the Brigade prisoners. Source: Estevan L. Bovo-Caras, Brigade 2506 Museum and Veterans' Association.

The day before the verdict was announced, Barreto couldn't stand the tension any longer and went rogue. Barreto called her contact with the regime, declared that she had a firm pledge from the committee for the ransom money, and said it was imperative she talk to Fidel.

Berta Barreto benefited from a certain forbearance from Castro. Way back in 1948, before his assault on the Moncada Army Barracks, Fidel Castro had been involved in riots in Bogota, Colombia that ended in the assassination of a presidential candidate. He sought asylum in the Cuban Embassy. Barreto's then-husband, a diplomat, flew the young revolutionary out of the country back to Cuba. Fidel never forgot. Now her son Alberto was a war prisoner.

The next morning Barreto received a call from Celia Sánchez, Fidel Castro's personal secretary and closest confidante from the earliest days of the Revolution. She cautioned Barreto to make sure she was correct about the offer, and then suggested she call the US to further confirm the pledge.

Barreto immediately called Ernesto Freyre of the Cuban Families Committee, whom Roberto San Román had introduced to Robert Kennedy. Johnson's account, complete with innuendo, follows:

"She told him what she had done and said she had promised the $28 million. Freyre told her to call him back in an hour; he wanted 'someone' else to hear what she said. She called back and once more repeated her story, certain that someone was listening on another line. There was a pause while Freyre left the phone. When he came back, he said she was authorized to say the committee had pledges totaling from $26 to $28 million and was prepared to resume negotiations with Castro. Elated, Barreto called Celia Sánchez and told her the good news. Celia made no commitments or promises, but her tone was reassuring."

At 6 pm on Saturday, April 7, Álvaro Sánchez sent a cablegram to Castro confirming the offer and requesting a re-opening of negotiations to free the prisoners. Sánchez had been assured by Robert Hurwitch in the State Department that $28 million in foodstuffs was forthcoming. Barreto's bluff had seemingly paid off.

That night, between midnight and 3 am on Sunday, April 8, Fidel Castro went to the prison to personally announce the verdict to the prisoners before it was made public. But he played it for all it was worth. First, he visited Pepe San Román, waking him up, taking him completely by surprise and throwing him off his equilibrium. Sleepy naked men are very vulnerable. Since the news was basically good—no one was going to be shot Castro opened on a negative note: with rage, violence and profanity, the better to manipulate Pepe's emotions.

Then he became conciliatory admitting that many men in the Brigade had been valiant. San Román, finally awake and dressed, asked why that wasn't brought out at the trial and Fidel flew off again. So Pepe, egging him on, got sarcastic: "We are not brave. The only one who is brave is you. You and your men...Cienfuegos, he was so brave that he put my men on that trailer truck and killed ten of them. That was assassination!"

Castro denied it, saying "It was an accident." The argument escalated until Castro finally shouted, "San Román, you don't deserve to live."

Pepe yelled back that that was the only thing the two of them agreed on. Castro was so incensed he left without telling Pepe why he had come.

With Artime, Fidel had regained his composure, greeting him, "How are you, Artime?"

But Artime also resorted to sarcasm, "Very well, though not as well as you are. You're heavier than you were in *La Sierra*."

Castro smiled and asked Artime what he was expecting. "Death," Artime responded.

Castro toyed with him some more, praising the Revolution and bemoaning the fact that Artime was not a Communist. Then, still in good humor, Castro said, "Artime, you are wrong as always. To prove to you that we are truly generous, we are not going to kill you."

It was the same with Oliva. Castro delighted in asking them what they expected, drawing out the conversation and finally, magnanimously, announcing the terms of the verdict. He did the same with the Brigade soldiers, with a few theatrical variants and dramatic pauses:

> *"The Spanish made this castle uncomfortable—so uncomfortable that we're going to take you out of here. In four months you'll all be gone. I'm putting a price on your heads...$62 million."*

When it was made public, the verdict read:

FOR TREASON TO THE FATHERLAND:

1. Loss of Cuban citizenship.

2. Payment of an indemnification (varying individually from $500,000, $100,000, $50,000 and $25,000 for each prisoner of war), or 30 years at forced labor.

Each of the three leaders' ransom was set at half a million. As to the other prisoners, 230 of them had their ransom set at $100,000; 597 at $50,000; and 371 at $25,000 for a total of $62 million.

It was a phenomenal sum in 1962 dollars, worth about half a billion dollars today. When the full measure of the amount sank in, and the improbability of ever collecting it, the men's joy at not being shot evaporated.

How the prices were set was a study in playing market values and socialist dialectics to the hilt. For the three leaders, according to Johnson, Castro believed "they were so valuable to the Yankees" that he put a price of half a million dollars on each. Armandito and Cachorro were in the next division down; placed in the $100,000 category. For Armandito, it made sense. He'd been a human machine gun at the Battle of the *Rotonda*. But Cachorro...At first, he couldn't understand his high ransom. He hadn't killed anyone—as attested to by his interrogator at the Sports Palace—and he was the fourth youngest of the entire Brigade.

It was the calculus used to price the prisoners, "social class," that determined his price. Those in a "higher social class" were priced accordingly. Cachorro attributed his price to the fact that his grandmother had owned land. But he found out later that it was something else. His father was an "industrialist." He had owned a plastics factory that had the exclusive contract for producing Colgate toothpaste tube caps. But that wasn't all. He also had a contract for manufacturing those plastic, unrefillable liquor bottle top inserts that allow air in but keep the liquor from pouring out too fast—inserts still used in Havana Club rum.

* * *

After notifying the prisoners, Castro announced the verdict to the world. Later the same day he responded to Alvaro Sánchez' cablegram authorizing him to come to Havana to re-open negotiations for the prisoners' release. Two days later, on the morning of April 12, Sánchez, Freyre and two other representatives of the Families Committee landed in Havana and headed for Berta Barreto's home. Castro arrived 15 minutes later eager to negotiate.

He was in high spirits, reporting that, according to US newspapers, his offer to negotiate had been well-received by the American public (an entirely Pollyannaish view, as most editorials condemned the idea of paying ransom).

Castro set the stage by recounting the history of the negotiations so far and empathizing with the difficulties the Families Committee had encountered. He finished by confirming his confidence in their probity.

Freyre responded by repeating the terms the Committee had been authorized to offer: $26 million in foodstuffs. Castro responded that the situation had changed; that the prisoners had been tried, and that the court's verdict was sacrosanct and he couldn't change that; that the price was now $62 million, and that it had to be in cash; that he couldn't accept foodstuffs because, now that Cuba was rationing food and concentrating on building up its industry, the acceptance of food would give the impression that he was weak and needed "help to save his position in Cuba."

The Committee members threw up their hands; they replied that it would be impossible for them to raise $62 million. But Castro wanted a deal. He said, "I am going to make you this proposition," and he made them an offer they couldn't refuse.

Castro told them they could take the most seriously wounded prisoners, numbering about 40, back to the US with them—on credit. The Committee could pay those men's indemnities whenever they were able to collect the funds and deposit them in the Royal Bank of Canada. Once those men were paid for, further funds for the repatriation of the remaining prisoners were to be deposited in the same bank and, when the full amount had been reached, the remaining men would be freed.

Either buying time, bluffing, upping the ante or speaking from conviction, Freyre responded that the Committee was opposed to the liberation of the men piecemeal; that all should be liberated together.

Castro then declared that the Committee had the wrong attitude and that *he* knew the value of propaganda; that some success, by releasing the injured first, would generate excitement, build momentum and bring in contributions; that further releasing the men in tranches, say the married, the older (or the younger), the fathers, etc. could keep that enthusiasm going and keep the remaining prisoners in the public's consciousness. Finally, Castro reiterated the offer that if any family wished to pay their son's ransom, he would immediately free the prisoner.

In a reversal of ideology, the Committee said they were opposed to any such policy of liberating a particular individual whose parent happened to be wealthy. Castro again disagreed, saying that the more men who were freed individually, the fewer funds the Committee would have to collect.

All of this threw the Committee into a quandary. They didn't feel they had the authority to negotiate the new proposals, but they did not want to break off the negotiations. They told Castro that they needed time to study the proposals, *and* they needed to discuss the proposals with the defunct prisoners' commission.

Castro reluctantly agreed. But he was in a hurry. The meeting had lasted three hours. He sped to El Príncipe and ordered the sons and husband of Sánchez, Freyre and the rest of the Committee transported to Barreto's home for a visit at 5 pm; to be followed by the prisoners' commission—and Erneido Oliva—at 7 pm for a "nice dinner" (Oliva's words) of filet mignon and chicken for all provided by Fidel.

Before leaving the prison, the men who had been selected for the visit and the negotiations informed the other prisoners of the outing and obtained their approval before indulging in such a privilege. As they rode down the streets of Havana they were acclaimed repeatedly with shouts and cheers from the people on the streets wherever they stopped at traffic lights.

Barreto's home was a large, well-disposed villa centrally located in Havana. Nonetheless, it must have been crowded at Barreto's home. After visiting for a while, the sons and husbands were sent upstairs so that the Committee and the commission—along with Oliva—could discuss Castro's offer. The Cubans being Cuban first brought up the concern that accepting any part of the offer would validate the Revolutionary court's verdict and the concept of indemnification, and it would divide the men. But the prospect of freeing the forty sick men, whether their ransom was raised or not, proved too tempting. They unanimously agreed to accept Castro's offer. However, they drew up a number of points they would insist upon with *el máximo líder.*

Castro had proved himself a master of propaganda—again. He even allowed the sons and husband to remain at Barreto's house for the rest of the delegation's stay in Havana. When the prisoners' commission was returned to El Príncipe at ten o'clock that night, they were full of "lots of hopes because Alvarito Sánchez told us that the negotiations could become true."

On Wednesday, April 11, Freyre told Castro that the Committee had decided to accept his offer, but that there was little chance the ransom would ever be paid. Castro replied that they could take as long as they wanted to collect the money, and that they should have faith in the generosity of the American people, and that if they met with any serious obstacles to return to Cuba and discuss their problems with him. Fidel presented them with a list of 54 sick men to be released. Then he sweetened the deal even more, saying that about $26 million of the $62 million could be paid in food, medicines, surgical equipment, etc.; but that this was a secret protocol between himself and the Committee that could be invoked only as a last resort.

The Committee then raised the 'number of points' they wanted to bring up with Castro. All dealt with prison conditions and addressed items such as solitary confinement, visitation, overcrowding, commissary use and so forth. Castro granted all the demands but did not implement them all. He then scheduled the release of the wounded and sick for the very next day, Thursday.

Freyre balked. That was too soon for the Committee. He said that the Committee needed time to arrange transportation, proper protocols, notifications to US Immigration authorities, prepping of the prisoners, etc. So Thursday was instead spent notifying the prisoners of the release, inspecting the sick, prepping the men for freedom, warning them about proper press protocol and examining other prisoners that might qualify as sick in order to increase the number of those released. The examining physicians managed to increase the release roster to sixty.

* * *

Saturday morning, April 14, the 60 chosen wounded prisoners were taken into El Príncipe's courtyard. The prison windows were crowded with those remaining, watching the men preparing to leave. One prisoner who had lost an arm remarked, "It was like a cloud of yellow at the windows. It was very emotional because we were leaving our brothers. It was happiness and sadness all mixed together." It was exactly one year after the Brigade had sailed from Puerto Cabezas, Nicaragua to invade Cuba.

The men loaded onto buses and headed for Rancho Boyeros (now José Martí) airport where the Cuban Families Committee members were waiting on a loaned Pan American Airlines plane that would take them all to Miami. Sánchez and Harry Ruiz-Williams, a wounded prisoner who became spokesman for the returnees, pledged to return to prison if the negotiations failed. Harry considered himself a prisoner until every last member of the Brigade was freed.

At Miami International Airport, more than 20,000 Cubans had gathered to await the prisoners. Haynes Johnson describes the scene:

"A roar went up as the big plane taxied into view and a sea of white handkerchiefs fluttered over the heads of the crowd. As the door opened and the first prisoner appeared, a stillness fell over the airport. Twice the crowd attempted to sing the Cuban national anthem. Voices faltered and broke…the prisoners saw a color guard composed of men of the Brigade who had escaped and been rescued. They were carrying the Brigade flag, the Cuban flag and the United States flag. One by one the prisoners stepped through the door of the plane— bandaged, on crutches, legs, eyes and arms missing—and saluted the Cuban flag. The band played 'The Colonel Bogey March,'…and the men hobbled down the ramp. One of the prisoners knelt and kissed the ground. The crowd broke and rushed forward. Their tears and screams were seen and heard by millions of Americans watching on television."

"A lot of women were crying," Harry Williams recalls, "and when I came out of the door the first person I saw was Roberto San Román. So I gave him a big *abrazo* and told him, 'How are you, boss?' and he cried on my shoulder. Then I kept walking and I saw my boy who was crying and my wife, and I tried to get with them, but I had to go in an ambulance and they took me to Mercy Hospital."

Fidel Castro released one additional prisoner at that time. His father had paid the $100,000 ransom. Alonso Pujol, the recalcitrant sweeper and son of one of Cuba's past vice presidents left for Panamá on April 18. In late July, five other prisoners were released after their families paid their ransoms. That left 1,112 Brigade members in El Príncipe prison (depending on whose source figures are used).

* * *

The $100,000 price on Armandito's head even had repercussions for my immediate family. My grandmother's health had seriously deteriorated. Carmen, her mother, daughter and niece; Hilda Navarro, Pop's AIU/C.V. Starr secretary; and Tita were all caring for her. She could no longer leave the house; and so, due to the complex oversight and controls the regime exercised over money and bank accounts, she could no longer make the in-person bank withdrawals for necessities to maintain the household.

In a letter dated April 14, 1962 to Pop, Hilda tried to address the problem by suggesting that the account be put in Carmen's name, not just for ease of use, but also so that "Carmen should have something to fall back on." Addressing the letter to "Gustavo," Pop's alias, she wrote:

"First of all, let me tell you that the balance (of the account) would be about 2 grand. As to putting it into an account in her name (which I don't believe is too much, considering everything she has done), I don't believe there would be any major problem involved.

"What I fail to see is the advisability of opening up another current account in my name and Carmen's, as it might seem odd to the bank that we are draining Abuela's account and opening up another one with also two signatories. They might start inquiring as to whether Abuela is planning on leaving here and then, bingo! No more money. Also since Abuela pays the hipoteca [a mortgage/rent imposed by the regime] and this is very important, as it is really the only money that is being paid to the government and they are very particular about this—they may start to inquire why if she still owes some $8 or 9,000 (can't remember now)—her account is being drained and with what will she pay further hipotecas (very important that point). Remember, for people at the bank, this is her account.

"Another point, which I fail to see is the advisability of opening up another account in the name of Tita y [sic] myself. All her family's business, properties, etc. have been intervened. Also, as I suppose you are aware, is her son [Armandito]. He is among those that came over and is being held prisoner in the one hundred grand bracket. No dice there. And I would not like to be linked there. Present conditions here are very ticklish. I would probably start getting investigated."

Hilda goes on to say that the enlarged household "is quite convenient, according to new food regulations to be a family of five gets you a quart of milk a day, more food, etc."

I surmise that Pop approved of Hilda's proposal. Both he and Mina wanted Carmen well taken care of. However, whether the plan was carried out or not, I don't know because Abuela died a scant four months later.

17

High-Stakes Poker

It was a time of hope; it was a time of despair. With the trial over, their lives secure, negotiations for their release back on track and the liberation of their wounded, the prisoners had many reasons to be optimistic. But instead, a vague funk settled over El Príncipe, oddly competing with the sense of possibility brought about by recent events.

The men had been imprisoned for over a year; raising the ransom seemed an insurmountable hurdle; the summer heat drove tempers to breaking point and the men to sleep outside in the courtyards under jerry-rigged shade blankets—until the summer rains forced them back into the hot *galeras*. Conditions for those in the *vivac*—the high ransom internees—deteriorated.

The vat of cornmeal mush, macaroni or soup that was their main nourishment now usually included a Cracker Jack-type surprise, usually some sexual organs, live cockroaches, scorpions or even a rat. To the older men, this was an almost unbearable indignity; to Armandito, it was a celebration of fresh protein. Armandito's upbeat attitude didn't go over well with the militiamen. He was rewarded with a spell in solitary confinement (though *Chino* and Cachorro swear it was for a fight he got into). To Armandito, his week-and-a-half stint was no big deal, but his voice breaks when he relates that some men spent three months curled up in the holes.

Not that solitary at El Príncipe involved "holes." Armandito was referring—in a later interview—to solitary confinement at the Cárcel Modelo on the Isle of Pines, the dreaded prison to which he and Cachorro would soon, unbeknownst to him, be transferred. It was a prospect that hung over everyone's head. In Cuba, penal authorities had taken a truly novel and creative approach to the concept, vividly depicted in the movie *Before Night Falls*. The isolation cells were tiny concrete holes below the general concrete floor, roofed by storm drains through which all sorts of indignities could be poured. They were not large enough for a person to fully stretch out in. The hinged bars provided ingress and egress. On the plus side, air, light and the general prison hubbub—right above your head—made the experience more bearable.

On May 28 the $100,000 ransomees—plus the $500,000 leaders—were told that their ransoms had been paid. They were going to Miami. At one o'clock that night the 214 high-dollar prisoners began boarding twenty buses and headed south toward an airfield next to the Camp Columbia military base outside Havana. The men were loaded into four large planes with Artime, San Román and Oliva placed in a separate, small plane. Guards with mounted machine guns aimed directly toward the prisoners were stationed between the cockpit and the seats.

In the cruelest joke of all, the planes took off and headed north, but then banked and turned south while the militiamen laughed. Cachorro remembers that laugh as a stab into their very sanity. A prisoner who had his bearings called out, "It's the Isle of Pines."

The Isle of Pines, now renamed the Isle of Youth, is the large, comma-shaped island off the southwest coast of Cuba. On it stands the Cárcel Modelo, built in part by my grandfather, John Maurice, who was also Armandito's grand-uncle, in the 1920s during the Machado regime. At the time, it was a state-of-the-art humane, yet inexpensive, design based on the ideas of 18th century English Utilitarian philosopher Jeremy Bentham. But now it housed Castro's political prisoners and its reputation for humane treatment had evaporated; it had become Cuba's Dachau.

Pomponio, the chief of the Modelo Prison guards, greeted the prisoners at the provincial air strip. "So these are the dangerous ones, eh? Well, we'll see who's dangerous here. On the trucks, and watch out! Hold on, if one of you falls we'll shoot you right there." Then he sneered and warned that they were about to see a *real* prison. Cachorro, turning around to see where Armandito was, received a rifle butt in the spine that today, fifty-six years later, still requires twice-yearly epidural shots.

At the prison they received a warmer welcome from the seven thousand political prisoners in the *circulares*. "As the trucks drew closer, they heard shouts and screams and saw shirts and blankets waving from the windows… sheets were lowered with large printed letters: WELCOME THE MEN OF 2506 BRIGADE. Pomponio aimed his carbine and fired several shots below the windows. The sheets were withdrawn," Haynes Johnson reports.

Modelo Prison, Isla de la Juventud (Isle of Pines). Built between 1926 and 1928 under President Machado with John Maurice Fitzgerald, the author's grandfather, as a contributing contractor. Fidel and Raúl Castro were imprisoned here after their failed Moncada army barracks attack in 1953. During the Cuban Missile Crisis of 1962, the Brigade 2506 high-dollar ransomees, including the author's cousins, Armandito and Cachorro, were also imprisoned here, in the square buildings on the edges of the photograph. Source: www.isladelajuventud-cuba.com, Jose Alfonso Fernández Pestana.

Inside the men were stripped, spread-eagled against the wall, searched and poked with bayonets if they moved. The three leaders were separated from the group, along with a priest and one of the strongest and darkest of the Negroes, the latter two chosen for extra abuse: a version of the old Western B-movies' 'let's-see-you-dance' routine played with bayonets instead of bullets.

The men were given some clothes and fed. To their surprise, the meal—bread and goulash—was good, better than what they'd been fed the last few weeks in the *vivac* at El Príncipe since their trial. But their cell resembled the Black Hole of Calcutta.

The men were not installed in the *circulares*, the cells arranged in a circle around a central guard kiosk—these were reserved for the politicals. Instead, all 211 were stuffed into one squat U-shaped room, with 20-foot-high ceilings and windows 15 feet up, not designed for habitation. The cell accommodated the prisoners only if they slept in the fetal position curled up with those around them, head to toe. Each man had three square feet to himself. There were no mattresses; the men slept on the bare concrete. There was no sunlight. They never saw the sun or the sky, but the lights remained on all the time. To this day, Cachorro sleeps with a mask. He spooned with Armandito, a situation that resulted in the big guy's elbows and knees waking and bruising little Cachorro (though he insisted that this memoir record that he was *behind* Armandito).

The leaders each got their own isolated cells. It was the last time they'd see their men. Still, military discipline was somehow conserved, a routine that infuriated the administration.

Each of the leaders' cells alternated with an empty cell, to minimize contact between them. Nonetheless, Artime, San Román and Oliva devised elaborate distractions to maintain morale and sanity. Mornings began with calisthenics, keeping count in unison, followed by individual pursuits such as drawing and composing poems. After lunch, a nap, followed by classes. Pepe taught English; Oliva, military science. Artime taught Communism, anatomy, religion, and geography. After dinner they conducted what Artime called "the evening radio show," with all three leaders singing in turn. Oliva sang Mexican songs; Pepe, romantic songs; and Artime, congas and *guarachas*. In between, they would compose satirical commercials for socialist products and concepts, commercials that would irritate the guards. But, added Artime, "Sometimes they would laugh."

Afterward the men described an imaginary travelogue across Cuba, each from his own perspective, heatedly arguing about the details. Finally, they prayed together and said good-night.

Life in the pavilion, on the other hand, was "an endless hell of starvation and degradation"—in Johnson's words—for the 211 other men. There was no soap, washcloths, razors, toothbrushes or toilet paper—and only one toilet. Queues could get long and dysentery was common. According to one prisoner, "Everywhere was high fevers, the violent cramps, men falling down unconscious. We were all lined up for nights for the toilet, doubled over in pain. I figured out that each man had the toilet for 4½ minutes each day, and when we were sick we couldn't make it to the toilet."

Just as at El Príncipe, each man had to serve on a cleaning team about once every twenty days. "The night before it was your turn to serve was like the night before going to the *paredón*," one man remembered. "We used coffee sacks for mops and with the diarrhea and the vomit and the condition of the toilet, the things we had to do were indescribable." Returning to "bed" at night after a visit to the loo, Cachorro's feet were thick with excrement.

One time, the prisoners suspected that the drinking water had been contaminated on purpose. Mario Martínez Malo remembers getting intestinal cramps in the middle of the night. He headed for the toilet, spastically stepping over the other men. When he got there, the line was long and he couldn't wait: he dropped trow right there and let loose. He wasn't the only one. After that incident the Nueva Gerona fire department had to be called in to flush the fecal fouling off the floor.

The men had to eat with their hands. The food was atrocious and very limited. For breakfast, each man received a little coffee and bread. Cachorro never drank the coffee. It came in one container. By the time the container reached him, it was nothing but saliva backwash. For dinner, soup with beans, green potatoes, pumpkin or noodles. The two meals were never served at the same time. Sometimes dinner came in the middle of the night. All the men lost weight on the restricted diet, so much so that they began fainting from hunger. To keep them from dying, medics administered intravenous glucose injections.

There were no visits, no mail and no news, other than what little they could glean from the political prisoners using an elaborate system of sign language and code at a distance. The books and magazines they'd brought over from El Príncipe were soon gone, consumed as toilet paper.

Tempers flared and fights broke out, some artificially instigated just to break the tension and boredom. Cachorro remembers one man calling out, "*Maricón*, leave me alone!" when no homosexual pass had actually occurred. It was just to get a good rumble going.

Yet, the Brigade men managed to maintain their discipline. In fact, the hardships drew them even closer. A prisoner recalled that, "When one man was sick another cared for him, he washed him. If he shat himself a friend carried him away and cleaned him. It was something to see."

And the vermin! Huber Matos, Castro's third-in-command who'd been sentenced to 20 years imprisonment, spent part of his sentence at the Isle of Pines during the same time that the Brigade men were confined there, though neither knew of the existence of the other. He relates the following story:

The spiders were our friends. When the guards ordered us to clear their webs, we declined. The high ceilings, perhaps twelve to fifteen feet high, were solid with spider webs. Walking down the prison corridors, guards and prisoners alike gathered spider silk on their heads and shoulders if they didn't wave their hands as if conducting an orchestra.

The prisoners at the Cárcel Modelo on the Isle of Pines were on strike—mostly a hunger but also a work strike. All family visits had been suspended. No reason was given. The suspension and strike didn't affect the Brigade 2506 men—they'd never been allowed visitors in this lock-up. In fact, they weren't even aware of the strike, different groups of prisoners being kept separate for the regime's nefarious reasons. Along with the political prisoners in the *circulares*, the Huber Matos men, counter-revolutionaries of various stripes, the Bay of Pigs invaders, common criminals and other assorted inmates, the Isle of Pines held many thousands of prisoners in 1962.

To counter the strike the authorities conducted a search-and-destroy mission: they confiscated every inmate's possessions (except for the Brigade men who had no "possessions")—spare clothing, papers, books and hoarded food, both from daily rations (the portions of which varied unpredictably) and family visits. The items were piled in an immense heap at the end of a gallery that provided access to a large number of cells.

The Caribbean summer is hot and muggy. Before long the mountain of filthy clothes, rags, rotting food and old newsprint reached critical mass and came alive. The flies emanating from the giant, putrid incubator, every day, in ever increasing hordes became intolerable. And the stench! It permeated everything. The men had become resigned to the mosquitoes, flies, *jejenes* (gnats), bed and body vermin, cockroaches and rats that were their ever-present cell mates. Some even befriended particular rodents, making pets out of them, cuddling with them at night. But this new blitz, this onslaught of insect zombies was too much—even for the guards. Huber Matos describes the clouds of flies as "nauseating and filthy, straight out of a horror movie." Only the spiders, like partisan allies, joined the resistance, snaring a few flies here and there.

Family visits were reinstated, but only once every three months. The prisoners begged their families for the most effective insecticides available. Day after day they spread the stuff on the floors and walls. In minutes, piles of dead flies began accumulating, "fountains of future infections and an overpowering fetor," writes Matos. Over the course of days the dead fly piles reached "prodigious volumes." What to do with the mountains of dead flies?

The prisoners had access to an adjacent concrete patio for a few hours a day. The jailers had broken a meter-square hole through the six-inch slab to repair a drain pipe underneath, but had put off replacing the concrete. Into this shallow bit of exposed dirt the men piled the dead flies and set them on fire. To their surprise, the tiny, mushy cadavers turned out to be first-class combustibles. They repeated the process until all the dead flies had been cleared out of the cell galleries.

Matos thought that the ashes, mixed with the scant sterile, clay surrounding the exposed drain pipe, might be a suitable medium to plant something. But what? Matos had saved a few melon seeds from his last visit. He planted them.

Faster than he imagined, a melon plant fifteen to twenty times the size of a normal melon plant, with a solid, fibrous trunk shot up. Four huge melons appeared. Matos and his buddy shared one, giving another to the other prisoners to share and leaving two on the vine.

The guards didn't object to the gardening project. But when the prison authorities found out, they confiscated the melons, uprooted the plant and forbade all further gardening. "It irks them that a prisoner engages in any activity that resembles normal life," Matos drily concludes.

Tita tried to visit Armandito in the Isle of Pines, tried to send food and letters but was unsuccessful. In addition to taking care of her own parents, she was now looking after Pillo's parents after he'd been thrown in jail in February without charges. She stayed until 1965 when she finally came to the US, settled in Puerto Rico and took charge of the US Peace Corps' Spanish language immersion program.

* * *

For the 900 Brigade members left at El Príncipe, conditions deteriorated. After Castro's performance as generous cop with the Families Commission and the prisoners' committee, he switched to sadistic cop. No strategy was off limits to properly incentivize the Americans to repatriate the men—even breaking his promises. Visits, mail and food deliveries were cancelled. Three hundred men were thrown back down into the *leoneras*. Tobacco was forbidden and the periods of outdoor exercise ended. Still, discipline remained firm among the men, buttressing morale.

José Dearing González, Johnny López de la Cruz and Luis Haget Guzmán had had enough. During the month of May they devised a meticulously planned escape and began their preparations. Stealing the jute sacks (no doubt manufactured at my uncle John's now-nationalized jute factory) in which the daily bread came from the kitchen, they began cutting thcm into strips and interweaving them with the yellow, prisoner-issue T-shirts, which they died a dark color with ink, into two ropes—one to lower down an inner compound wall, the other for ascending the outer wall. Somehow, they forged a metal grappling hook and attached it to one end of the short rope. The most difficult obstacle to the plan was the unannounced, mid-night searches that were now common. But somehow they managed to keep their ropes and hook securely hidden.

One rainy night on July 14, using a homemade lock-pick, they unlocked their cell door and stealthily made their way over to the first wall. Using the longer, 90-foot rope, they descended to a patio from which they could gain access to the outer wall of El Príncipe. José Dearing went first. The rope, however, proved to be some 20 feet too short. Dropping the unexpected distance onto the cobbled surface in the soggy darkness, Dearing then ran the 100 feet separating his landing spot from the exterior wall of the castle with the shorter, now sopping wet, rope with the grappling hook. The other two men immediately followed.

Try as he might, Dearing couldn't throw the hook high enough to get it to grab; it was just too heavy now that the rope was soaked. Anyway, this rope also proved too short.

Luckily, about ten feet up the wall, there ran an old drainage pipe. With great difficulty, Dearing managed to climb the rock wall and reach the pipe. Once there, he managed to get to the top of the wall. There he anchored the hook and dropped the rope to Johnny López who, with the help of Luis Haget, also reached the top of the wall.

Luis Haget, heavier than López and Dearing and suffering from a sprained ankle from the 20-foot drop off the first rope, couldn't get a decent grip on the slippery, wet rope. After many failed attempts, he told his partners he'd find a place to hide to give them time to escape without detection.

López and Dearing pulled up the rope and dropped it down the outside of the wall, anchoring the hook securely on top. Hand over hand they descended the stone wall and crossed the dry moat, reaching the nearest street. From there they headed for the Havana suburb of Marianao, a few kilometers away to a "safe house" they'd been told about.

Unfortunately, the safe house had been busted a few days earlier, and when they arrived there, they were immediately arrested. The militiamen took the two fugitives to a G-2 interrogation center where they were aggressively questioned until they confessed to being escapees from El

Príncipe. Two days later López and Dearing were returned to the prison and rewarded with several weeks in solitary confinement.

Ricky Sánchez and *Chino* also decided they'd had enough. *El Chino*, being a low-value ransomee, had not been moved to the Isle of Pines with his buddies Armandito and Cachorro. But he and Ricky had been put in charge of the hepatitis patients in the prison's clinic. They devised a complex communication system composed of flash cards to contact a sympathetic woman who lived across the street from the prison. She organized getaway cars and safe houses for the would-be escapees. Using clinic sheets and dyed T-shirts woven together into two ropes, they planned an escape for themselves and the fitter hepatitis patients.

However, just before setting off, they received word that the Families Committee was on the verge of negotiating a repatriation deal and that an escape attempt would bring repressions and just might sour the negotiations. *Chino* and Ricky canceled their caper.

It's a wonder the negotiations were still alive. Between January and August of 1962, 5,780 counterrevolutionary infiltration actions were reportedly carried out in Cuba; 716 involving sabotage of important economic objectives.

* * *

By mid-June, however, the Cuban Families Committee was in a bit of a doldrums. They'd appeared at hundreds of luncheons, held many conferences with industry leaders, religious organizations, public office holders and celebrities, and appeared on radio, TV and newspaper and magazine articles. They'd gathered $239,000 in funds and had pledges of about $150,000 from various sources including Bacardi, plus many in-kind contributions such as an appearance on the Ed Sullivan Show, free rent for offices, and other such benefits. Still, it was a far cry from the $2.9 million they owed on the already released men, much less the $59.1 million necessary for the remaining prisoners.

Discouraged at their progress, the Committee sent Harry Williams, one of the released wounded prisoners, to see Robert Kennedy, whose door was always open to them. The Attorney General listened sympathetically and told Williams, "You need someone who can represent you. I think I know a lawyer who might help." Kennedy recommended James B. Donovan, a savvy negotiator imperturbable in the gray territory of secret operations. During World War II he'd worked for the agency that developed radar and the atomic bomb, and been chief legal counsel for the OSS, the wartime predecessor to the CIA. Afterward, he'd been an assistant prosecutor at the Nuremberg trials.

Six months earlier, in January of 1962, Donovan had negotiated the exchange of Gary Powers, an American U-2 pilot shot down over the Soviet Union in 1960 while spying, and Frederic Pryor, a Yale student accused of spying by the Soviets, for Rudolph Abel, the chief of Soviet espionage in the US. *Bridge of Spies*, a 2015 Hollywood movie starring Tom Hanks as Donovan, well depicts the complex negotiations and exchange of men at the Glienicke Bridge in Berlin. Now, he was about to run as New York's Democratic candidate for the US Senate against the popular incumbent, Jacob Javits (a race he lost due to his efforts to free the Brigade prisoners).

Donovan was a complex man. Five-foot-eight, stocky, with a great, balding dome of a forehead topped by sparse white hair, public life hadn't completely eliminated his Bronx street smarts—or humor. At forty-six years of age, he was slow spoken, with a deliberate manner and laser eyes that could penetrate the depths of the most obtuse soul. He had the Irish gift of gab. He could spin a tale or make an argument that, if it didn't convince right away, usually later led to a resolution of the controversy at hand. One part crass, two parts raconteur, three parts academic and four parts Einstein-at-the-poker-table, he could convince St. Peter that Satan should at least get a visitor's pass through the Pearly Gates—all this in an insurance lawyer whose sideline was dealing with genocidal regimes. Sent to Cuba to negotiate the release of the 1,113 remaining Brigade prisoners, he additionally—on his own initiative—secured the release of 9,703 detained Cubans with little or no affiliation to the failed invasion.

Donovan agreed to meet members of the Families Committee on June 20, the very next day after Williams' meeting with the Attorney General. Donovan listened intently to their plight and agreed to represent them *pro bono*—with one condition: the US government's imprimatur. Donovan wanted to ensure that his efforts did not conflict with US policy toward Cuba, specifically, that he wouldn't be in violation of the Logan Act, which prohibits private citizens from negotiating with foreign governments over matters in dispute with the United States.

So on July 2 Donovan met with Bobby Kennedy, who warned him that he was headed for failure but reassured him that the president was in favor of the endeavor, and that the administration would perceive it as "a private humanitarian effort" with which the US government sympathized. That was good enough for Donovan.

Donovan had already begun his research. First, he required the Families Committee to provide him with all their doings. In conjunction, he studied Fidel Castro—his ideology, his speeches, his personality, his biases, his quirks, his tastes, his sexual history. After digesting everything, he wrote a letter to Berta Barreto summarizing his assessment of Fidel Castro, the Cuban leader's approach to negotiations and an outline of how he, Donovan, would pursue negotiations. The letter had an underlying objective: Donovan phrased it in such a way that it would be obvious to Barreto that it ought to be forwarded to Castro as a 'laying on the table' of Donovan's cards, something Castro might interpret as naïve and revelatory, something that would make Castro think that he, Castro, was a step ahead of the negotiations.

It was high stakes poker, with each side bluffing and posturing to the max. Barreto, in the interest of seemingly open and transparent negotiations with Castro, proved herself Donovan's equal.

Two days later Celia Sánchez, Castro's personal secretary, met with Barreto at Barreto's villa. Barreto wanted to update Castro on the Committee's progress. The signs were reassuring. Besides meeting Barreto on her turf and on short notice, Celia Sánchez focused on Donovan's "candid" letter, which was indeed candid, albeit spinned for all it was worth. She also looked closely at the list of the Committee's sponsors, which now included many prominent figures in business and government. Barreto pleaded for the prisoners, aware that their condition had deteriorated. Celia Sánchez promised Barreto Castro's reaction right away.

Ten days later, Barreto was permitted to visit El Príncipe and update the prisoners on the status of the negotiations. Her son handed her a note from another prisoner:

"Inform Berta that we are starving to death…that they should hurry up because we cannot stand it any more and we either will go on a hunger strike or provoke a mutiny or whatever is necessary. Some of us have sicknesses in the lungs…most of us are going demented. And in the vivac either. Forgive me but we are out of our minds."

The letter went on to explain that when Barreto had been allowed to visit the prison much was kept from her—by the prisoners and the guards—out of concern for her heart condition.

Two weeks later, three hundred prisoners clashed with the guards. Four men were wounded.

* * *

Toward the end of August, Donovan asked Castro for permission to come to Cuba to negotiate the release of the prisoners. In spite of Castro's desire to rid himself of the men and cash in on their release, he perceived any dealings with the United States as a prelude to an invasion. He was wary. Just a few days before, twenty-three students from the Miami-based Students Revolutionary Directorate had shelled a Havana hotel from an offshore ship. They'd been aiming for the Blanquita Theatre where Castro was addressing a group of visiting Russians. This was only the latest attack. Small exile groups had been shelling Havana's shores for some time. In spite of the 5,780 counterrevolutionary actions carried out between January and August of 1962, Castro responded positively.

Donovan flew to Havana on August 30 with Álvaro Sánchez, head of the Families Committee as his interpreter. They stayed at Berta Barreto's house. Donovan, hungry for a flavor of the Cuban weltanschauung, turned on a TV news program. "Almost the first thing he saw on the screen was his own face. The commentator described him as a '*decoy that has come to cover another Kennedy invasion,*'" according to his son, John B. Donovan in his book *After the Bay of Pigs: Lives and Liberty on the Line*, with Pablo Pérez-Cisneros (Berta Barreto's son) and Jeff Koenreich.

Donovan and the Families Committee agreed to strictly leave all the negotiating to Donovan. That afternoon Donovan met with Cuba Fernández, the ex-shoemaker-turned-Cuban Attorney General. Donovan treated him "*exactly as though he were Chief Justice Charles Evans Hughes,*" according to his recollection. Donovan played his opening gambit: he conceded that the transaction would be an indemnification. It was a shrewd concession. The following afternoon Donovan, Sánchez, Freyre and Barreto were due to meet with Castro at the Presidential Palace.

Meanwhile, however, US invasion threats were heating up. Congressional Republicans were calling for an invasion and Castro was responding that one was inevitable. The very day that Donovan and Cuba Fernández were meeting, two Cuban gunships fired on a US Navy patrol aircraft over international waters near Cuba. Pérez-Cisneros, Donovan and Koenreich take up the story:

"These navy patrols had markedly increased since the Soviet Union had begun sending shipments of supplies to Cuba and the U.S. military attempted to determine their contents. Following this incident, the White House promptly announced that American planes would now be authorized to return fire if provoked."

Nonetheless, Fidel Castro kept the appointment. Castro was seated at a long table, alone. Both men took a measure of the other. The fastidiously groomed Castro, as Donovan was later to report, seemed every bit the head of state he was and not the ranting buffoon so commonly portrayed in political cartoons. Still, Donovan had no patience for Castro's tendency to pontificate and be hypnotized at the sound of his own voice. Donovan's lack of Spanish served him well in this instance: whenever the *máximo líder* wandered into pontifical territory, Donovan would interrupt asking for the clarification of some small point thereby tripping up Castro's gathering orotundity.

For his part, Castro warmed up to Donovan, responding to the Irishman's anecdotes and humor with generosity and respect. It probably helped that Donovan focused on pleasantries and preliminaries as an integral part of the bargaining framework he intended to establish instead of getting right to the point, courtroom-style. Donovan emphasized that he did not come as a representative of the American government, but as *"a private citizen on a private mission"* representing the American people. After a few meetings Castro told the lawyer, "I thought you might be just another shrewd American politician. But I've come to see you in an entirely different light."

Having softened Castro with his indemnification move, Donovan asked for forbearance: He told Fidel that he was not in a position to offer cash; the ransom would have to be paid in some other form. Over four hours of explanation from every possible angle as to why cash was impossible (best not to sell humans, politically a non-starter; etc.), small talk, blandishments and questions-and answers, Castro agreed to give "some thought" to the proposal.

The following day Castro tentatively agreed to accept food and goods in lieu of $62 million in cash, except for the already agreed upon $2.9 million in cash for the 60 injured prisoners. It was a great step forward. Alvaro Sánchez was convinced that Jim Donovan was a miracle worker: "He's the greatest poker player in the world. He began negotiating with nothing and kept it up face to face with Castro for hours…with nothing. Nothing!"

Donovan suggested that Castro draw up a wish list of goodies he'd like, and the next day, September 2, returned to the United States. Meanwhile, Sánchez and Freyre remained in Havana at Barreto's house.

Over the course of three weeks, a series of lists of food and hard goods—with crates of samples of the goods included in the lists—were sent to Donovan. Castro being a canny negotiator, sent samples of cloth and shoe leather to avoid getting poor quality goods. Plus he insisted on pricing the goods at world fair market value.

During Nikita Khrushchev's Premiership of the Soviet Union—at about this time—the central planners of the USSR's centrally planned economy had no idea how to price consumer goods. They had ramped up consumer goods production after their dearth during the war and the Stalin era. Marxist theory was wedded to the "labor theory of value," whereby goods were priced according to their labor input without regard to the scarcity of the underlying materials or the capital investment necessary to produce them. Consequently, supply became severed from demand. The Soviet planners had no idea how to price goods, so they sent price spies to the West to note the prices of goods so they could set prices in the USSR. And now Fidel Castro was stipulating "market prices" for the goodies he was craving.

Wholesale prices were even more mysterious *and* questionable. In socialist ideology, middlemen are considered speculators, adding little to nothing of value to a commodity. After conferring with his associates, Castro upped the ante to price the requested goods at wholesale prices—a near 60% reduction from market value in some cases.

"When Donovan studied the possibilities of meeting the demand, he found it would fill 68 ships. Not only did this pose an enormous logistical problem, it bulked too large to be acceptable to the American public," according to Warren Young in a January 4, 1963 article in *Life* magazine. Additionally, a new US embargo on shipping to Cuba had just been instituted. Donovan decided to go back to Cuba on October 3 and explore a different option.

The following day Donovan offered Castro—through an intermediary—medicine instead of the potpourri of goods he'd requested. But he wrapped them up in an attractive package. He presented a commitment from Pfizer and Merck (then Merck, Sharp & Dohme), two large pharmaceutical companies, to fly large quantities of medical products to Cuba. He added that Pan American Airlines and the Red Cross were holding seven planes in New York and Miami ready for the airlift. Finally, he presented two letters of credit with the Royal Bank of Canada, one to cover the debt of the sixty wounded prisoners, and another for $53 million in cash to guarantee the delivery of the medical supplies.

Twenty-four hours later, Donovan was invited to discuss the new proposal with Castro in person. But *el máximo líder* was at his villa in Varadero, the now-famous beach resort 80 miles from Havana. Castro sent Captain José Abrahantes, Under-Secretary to the Minister of the Interior, to drive Donovan to Varadero. Donovan had dealt with Abrahantes before. He was a pudgy, hard-core Communist ideologue with an anti-American streak exacerbated by his macho self-importance. Abrahantes greeted Donovan with the traditional "How are you?"

When Donovan responded with "Not too well," Abrahantes "*got this crooked smile on his face*" recalled Donovan.

"Would you like to take a little ride with me?" asked the captain.

James Donovan suffered from bursitis, a painful and often disfiguring inflammation of the joints. The previous night it had flared up so acutely that he was riven by nausea. He'd hardly slept. His arm was in a sling.

Donovan was driven, at speeds of up to one-hundred miles an hour, careening around and playing chicken with traffic, and accelerating entering corners. Abrahantes, obviously enjoying himself, never uttered a word to Donovan. It was one of the most frightening experiences of his life.

Donovan did not comment to Castro about the ride. He and Castro had developed a friendly rapport, complete with banter, small talk, jokes and little favors and solicitudes. He didn't want to spoil the mood. This time, Fidel had his personal physician present for the discussions, someone knowledgeable about medical supplies. Castro agreed to the new proposal, with one change: he wanted these products also at wholesale prices, thereby increasing the quantity for the same amount of money. Castro and Donovan agreed to meet again on October 10 to iron out the details.

The ride back was even worse than the ride from Havana, because it was now dark. Abrahantes was passing cars on the right, on curves, on hills and on bridges at full speed.

In the meantime, Donovan took a quick turn-around trip to Miami to receive a bursitis treatment. Afterward he drew up a memorandum summarizing the points agreed to in the last meeting. When Abrahantes came to Barreto's house to pick up the document he waxed lyrical about the good treatment the prisoners were receiving.

This was too much for Donovan who, throwing all pretense at diplomacy aside, unleashed his Irish wrath. Barreto's son describes what ensued:

> *"'How do you figure that? You know, you're foolish in holding these prisoners of war under inhumane conditions. Instead of bargaining, you ought to be practical. We are the only market for these boys. Where else are you going to sell them? Perhaps you're thinking of reverting to something Hitler found very profitable. He found that the prisoners in the concentration camps were very good for soap. If that is what you have in mind, maybe you can arrange to be put in charge. You would qualify, I think.'*
>
> *Captain Abrahantes flew into a rage, and expressed astonishment that Donovan would say such a thing. Recovering some self-control, he said—'We don't think that way about things.'"*

Donovan, still in high dudgeon, then addressed the specifics of the bargain:

> *"You keep talking about the $62 million. You would think this were some amount ordained in heaven. But in reality it is a figure Castro just pulled out of an opium dream."*

When Abrahantes replied coldly that the $62 million was established by the military tribunals, Donovan thundered:

> *"Military tribunals? Who are these military tribunals? No one ever heard of them. If Castro told the tribunals to get on their hands and walk around the house right now, they'd start walking. Military tribunals! This is a joke. I don't mind playing charades once in a while, but let's be realistic once in a while too."*

The exchange didn't continue long. Abrahantes left the house in a foul mood with the typed memorandum. His report was damning.

Abrahantes tried to convince Castro that Donovan was out to trick him. The captain was pushing for holding back the Brigade leaders from any deal. He recruited Osmani Cienfuegos, the officer responsible for the death of ten prisoners in the overcrowded semi, to his point of view. Rumors indicated that he was also trying to enlist Raúl Castro and Che Guevara.

Adding to the uncertainty presaging the upcoming meeting, Ernesto Freyre casually alluded to Donovan that Russian missiles were being openly unloaded from Russian ships in Havana harbor. "They were what appeared to be Nike missiles!" he said.

Donovan was stunned but skeptical. Then he remembered that Barreto's husband had told him about restricted areas in Pinar del Rio where huge quantities of concrete and steel beams were being delivered in convoys of trucks. He made a mental note to report to the American government.

The October 10 meeting did not go well. Castro, surrounded by hardline ministers and specialists, presented a hostile atmosphere. Donovan described the Minister of Public Health as "a typical product of a nice family, who went to a good school, never earned a buck in his life and who is on cloud sixty-nine somewhere over Cuba. He is an idealist. A weak guy along for the ride." As to the Minister of Foreign Trade, Donovan pegged him as someone who "goes in for very dark black horn-rim glasses which I'm sure he thinks accentuate his brilliance and deep perception. The sort of character who gives $125 to the Executive Club, so he can have a gold key to the executive toilet, while he sits around calculating the best methods for generating six-tailed pigs or the like. He is quite sure of himself and can explain anything to you."

After the requisite pleasantries, Castro, audibly irritated, brought up the discussion Donovan had had with Captain Abrahantes about making soap out of the prisoners and Donovan's ridiculing of the military tribunal. Castro admonished Donovan that if he wanted to discuss political matters he should do it with Castro himself, and that he would rue the day the discussion ever began. He summed up by accusing Donovan of discourtesy when all courtesy had been extended to him.

This was Donovan's cue. He told Castro about Abrahantes' driving, and his lack of lunch and refreshment on the day of the Varadero visit. Castro acted astonished and edged toward an apology. But Donovan, having changed the subject, turned the topic toward the negotiations.

The Cubans wanted further price discounts on the medical supplies, the shipping costs and the insurance premiums covering the shipments, plus an increase in the Royal Bank of Canada's performance bond. A long and fruitless discussion on how prices are set ensued. Finally, they were going to prepare a *new* list of products.

Donovan would have none of it. "We are doing you a favor. We are discharging you of a liability. Do you want [the deal] or don't you? If you have changed your mind about the essentials we agreed upon—there is not much point in my staying here. If this is the way you want it, perhaps we should stop the discussion now and take it up when you think we should."

An uncomfortable pall descended over the meeting. Castro, seemingly in a corner, backtracked a bit: "Well, while I am pessimistic in this matter, I don't think we should in any way abandon it. It should be pursued to the end, but I think every detail should be explored."

Berta Barreto, edging toward despair, impetuously stood up and spoke directly to Castro in Spanish, "As a mother of a son in prison, I beg you to keep negotiating. Don't let it end this way!" And she began to cry.

Then Ernesto Freyre jumped in, engaging Castro in rapid Spanish on details necessary to reach agreement. Donovan had insisted on one incontestable detail from the Families Committee for the negotiations: only he could negotiate, and Álvaro Sánchez, his translator, was required to translate word for word—without any flourishes—Donovan's and Castro's utterances.

Donovan, furious at Freyre's interference, at being ignored and at the emotional turn of events, stood up and declared, "That's it!" and walked out. The negotiations were broken and Donovan prepared to return to the US. That night Cuban television reported that Donovan was a CIA agent.

18

Liberation

Those first two weeks in October of 1962, when the negotiations broke down and the world approached the threshold of nuclear catastrophe, contained other, less pressing, events.

Cachorro turned nineteen. He well remembers his birthday on the Isle of Pines. "Somehow my friends got me a piece of bread, just for me, and we sang. Of course I shared it with the twelve. I invented (I'm sure many starving people have done it) a technique of halfway swallowing what I'd chewed and regurgitating it, over and over again to fool the brain."

Cachorro's future father-in-law, Pillo Casanueva, was released from his 8-month imprisonment for never-revealed, unspecific charges. He managed to catch one of the last flights to Miami before all commercial flights to the US were cancelled due to the Missile Crisis. But when he reached the US, Mariano Faget imprisoned him in the OpaLocka detention center.

Mariano Faget—if you'll recall—had been in charge of the Foreign Counter-espionage Activities Department in the Batista administration and had escaped the island with Batista on the same plane. He was Armandito's great-uncle and knew Pillo, his nephew-in-law, well. MariCris, Pillo's daughter (and my close cousin) takes up the story:

> "My father supported the Revolution before the Marxismo-Leninismo of it became evident. It was philosophical support—not the bomb or guns type—and for that the illustrious Mariano Faget, my great-uncle, stuck him in the detention center when he arrived in Miami. The fact that he had just been released from El Morro after nearly a year of imprisonment for crimes against the Revolution didn't change that.
>
> My grandfather died at Jackson Memorial Hospital without seeing his son again because of that detention. My very proud mother, Cuca, went to Mariano, her uncle, to beg for Pillo's release from detention so he could see his father. Mariano refused on the grounds that my father was a Communist. So she never spoke to Mariano again, and neither did any of us Casanuevas. Hell, I don't even want

to speak to Marianito; and he's just an idiot with nary a wisp of his father's ruthlessness or cruelty."

(Marianito Faget, Mariano's son, became an INS [Immigration and Naturalization Service] official. After 34 years of service, in the year 2000, he was convicted of violating the Espionage Act, including disclosure of government secrets to a boyhood friend, a member of the Castro regime who wanted to do business in Cuba. He was released a few years ago.)

* * *

On October 14, a US U-2 spy plane flying over Cuba photographed at least two medium-range ballistic missiles along with launch pads and missile trailers for more to come. Thus began two weeks during which the United States and the Soviet Union came to the brink of nuclear war. President Kennedy demanded that the missiles be removed. The crisis consisted of the threat that failure to remove them would precipitate armed attack. In anticipation, the US mobilized the navy to blockade the island.

On October 26 Castro informed Khrushchev that "the Soviet Union ought never to permit circumstances in which the imperialists could launch a first nuclear strike...and that if they invade Cuba that would be the moment to eliminate forever such a danger—no matter how hard and terrible that solution may seem..."

Fidel Castro had a streak of brinksmanship, an uncontrollable desire to "play chicken" come what may. José Rasco, a classmate of fifteen years, recounts the young Fidel making a bet with another classmate that "he (Castro) was capable of crashing head first, on a bicycle at full speed, against a concrete wall in full view of the entire school. And he did it, at the cost of cracking his head and ending up unconscious in the infirmary."

When Castro first requested nuclear missiles from the USSR, Khrushchev jumped at the opportunity. But he didn't fully trust Fidel (whose name ironically is from the Latin root *fides*, meaning faith), so he complied only on condition that the Soviet Union retain absolute control over them. Though Castro agreed, it infuriated him. That fury was further aggravated when he was left out of the Kennedy-Khrushchev negotiations and subsequent missile removal that defused the 1962 Cuban Missile Crisis.

On October 30th Khrushchev responded to Castro: "In your cable...you proposed that we be the first to launch a nuclear strike against the enemy.

You do understand the consequences of this. This wouldn't be a single strike, instead…the start of a thermonuclear world war…Evidently, in such a case the US would suffer great losses, but the USSR and the entire socialist camp would also suffer much. As to Cuba and the Cuban people…At the start of the war Cuba would burn…"

The next day Castro confirmed to Khrushchev that he well understood the consequences: "…I knew…do not presume that I ignored…that (the Cubans) would be exterminated…in case of a thermonuclear war…"

Thankfully no one was paying attention to him: he had made it quite clear that he would not have backed down whatever the consequences. Perceiving the entire event as an unpardonable breach of Cuba's sovereignty, he soured on Khrushchev. Relations with the USSR worsened. China and Mao Tse-tung's more uncompromising brand of Communism became his new best friends.

* * *

Castro feared a US invasion more than he feared apocalyptic annihilation. The first to feel his fear were the Brigade prisoners on the Isle of Pines. The men wondered about all the livestock suddenly and incongruously surrounding the prison. The guards appeared wearing helmets, loaded with weapons and ammunition belts. Extra locks were added to the leaders' cells. All the lights were turned off for the duration of the crisis. The prison commander announced: "Well boys, your suffering is about to end. It looks like the Americans are about to invade. We're not going to torture you or mistreat you. But you can count on this: if they come, you are going to be the first to go." Castro had both the Modelo Prison and El Príncipe mined. The prisoners were warned, under pain of being instantly shot, not to look out any windows (where that was a possibility).

For two to three weeks during the missile crisis, seventy-three prisoners—including Cachorro and Armandito—were removed from the communal cell all 211 prisoners were sharing. They were installed in a separate room, the very same cell where Fidel Castro and five other revolutionaries had done time in 1953. Back then, Castro had been allowed conjugal visits, correspondence rights, reading material, and commissary privileges. He wrote home, "I take two baths a day due to the heat…later in the small restaurant available, I dine on calamari and pasta, Italian bonbons, fresh drip coffee and an H. Upman #4 cigar."

Modelo Prison, Isla de la Juventud (Isle of Pines), cell where Fidel Castro had been imprisoned in 1953; and cell where in 1962 seventy-three Brigade prisoners, including Cachorro and Armandito had been incarcerated during the Cuban Missile Crisis. Beds were absent in 1962. It is now maintained as a museum of the Revolution. Source: www.isladelajuventud-cuba.com, Jose Alfonso Fernández Pestana.

Now they all could stretch out a bit more—with difficulty. Their bodies, especially their butts, were covered with calloused and suppurating skin from lying and sitting on concrete constantly. Getting up was always a fainting opportunity.

The new room was adjacent to the punishment cells used on the politicals. Cachorro was kept awake all night by the going-ons there. Prisoners were first hosed down with ice water and then beaten with the hoses. But they never screamed in pain or for mercy. Instead, it was *"Viva Cristo Rey!"* and taunts to the guards such as, "You missed a spot there" and "You're losing your strength." An even worse torture—for Cachorro—was that Castro's cell was next door to the prison bakery. Every morning the aroma of freshly baked bread drove the starving inmates into paroxysms of olfactory insanity.

At El Príncipe the guards whispered to the prisoners, "The gringo is coming." At Modelo, *Negro Feo*, as one guard was known, inveigled himself with the prisoners by providing daily newspaper accounts of the crisis and telling them that he had never been an avid Castro supporter. *Negro Feo* declared that he loved the Americans. He explained that the cattle were a live warehousing of food "just in case," and that he'd share. The prisoners began calling him *Negro Lindo*. When the crisis was over, he reverted to his old, hypocritical *Negro Feo* self, reminding the prisoners that he'd always been a supporter of the Revolution.

* * *

While Donovan was packing up to return to the US after severing negotiations, Alvaro Sánchez had a quiet word with him, saying that the prisoners "are not responsible. They will die if we end it now." Donovan agreed to keep trying, but Ernesto Freyre was barred from face-to-face negotiations.

The next day, just before boarding the plane to Miami, Donovan wrote a long message to Castro addressing all the points brought up in the previous meeting and asking for Castro's new drugs list. He concluded by saying that he was ready to resume bargaining.

The re-opened bargaining continued right through the Missile Crisis with detail and counter-detail going back and forth. In Haynes Johnson's words, "That it did not destroy the mission is a matter of history. Perhaps the most astonishing aspect of the Cuban crisis is that the negotiations for the Bay of Pigs prisoners remained open all those searing hours." Castro, still intent on making a deal, had spent most of his time in an underground bunker prepared to see his country blown to smithereens.

Attorney General Robert Kennedy insisted, "Keep it open. Keep it going."

Alvaro Sánchez, still in Havana at Barreto's house since August 30, was permitted to see a few prisoners at El Príncipe and visited the Isle of Pines on November 16. He was appalled at the condition of the men at both places. On November 19, he and Barreto flew to New York to report on the situation.

On November 24 at the Waldorf-Astoria Hotel they met with Robert Kennedy. "I'm a cattleman, Mr. Attorney General, and these men look like animals who are going to die. If you are going to rescue these men, this is the time because if you wait you will be liberating corpses. Bring them home to their families by Christmas," pleaded Sánchez.

The Kennedys were riding high after settling the Missile Crisis. Christmas was a month away, hardly enough time to conclude a deal. RFK ran a serious risk in making a promise he couldn't keep, plus the US government couldn't contribute to the ransom. Nonetheless, Kennedy responded, "You are right. I think this is the moment. *We will.*" From that moment on, the US government threw its power and prestige into raising the ransom. In Jim Rasenberger's words, "It was as if, overnight, Donovan's horse and buggy had been traded for a race car, complete with crack pit crew and sponsorship."

Just what did that mean? Overcoming a thousand hurdles such as getting Republican support for the effort; getting tax deductions for contributions from the pharmaceutical companies at retail prices without having to disclose costs or markup data; getting assurances that if the drug companies worked together on the contributions they would be exempt from anti-trust charges; finessing the minor legal obstacles *pro bono* from willing law firms; easing bank and insurance concerns; securing donated transportation services by air, rail, truck and ship *and* making them tax deductible; helping the Red Cross with logistics; expediting hundreds of permits and cutting miles of red tape; twisting hundreds of arms and bending twice as many ears; preparing Immigration and Naturalization officials and Department of Health, Education and Welfare for the arrival and processing of the prisoners and much, much more—everything with the assurance that there were no rewards from the administration for participation and no retributions for abstaining.

The lack of government involvement had become a fiction. But, notably, the Families Committee later reimbursed the government's expenses.

* * *

November and December brought a glimmer of hope to El Príncipe prison in spite of enduring misery. Word of the continuing negotiations hinted that "prison cannot endure forever," in the words of *brigadista* José Eugenio Sosa. His prison diary reveals conditions at the time:

"The food is still deficient... macaroni and red beans with 80% of it sauce... noodle soup and rice... once a week Russian meat... half an ounce for each of us... am trying hard to eat, but until now I can't... a month and five days... without sun... dreamt of my little son... a little American... and María Luisa, the little girl that I haven't seen yet."

The last obstacle to consummating the deal was an iron-clad guarantee of funds behind the letter of credit from the Royal Bank of Canada. It insisted on formal guarantees from American banks for the $53 million backed by a surety bond from a reputable insurance company.

On Monday, December 17, two $26.5 million letters of credit were obtained from the Bank of America and the Morgan Guarantee Trust Co. of New York, backed by the Continental Insurance Group of New York. For Jim Donovan, this secured the deal, and he made the announcement.

Louis E. Oberdorfer, assistant Attorney General in charge of the Department of Justice's Tax Division, gave the order for the first shipment of drugs to be transported to Florida and loaded on planes at Opa-Locka airport and on the *S.S. African Pilot* at Port Everglades.

On Tuesday morning, the 18th, Donovan, Sánchez, Barreto and Mrs. Virginia Betancourt, who had a husband in the Brigade and was a member of the Families Committee, left Miami on a plane for Havana. They were to midwife the operation, putting out fires as they flared up.

They met with Castro for four hours. Questions about the substitute drugs and their values flared up, as did Castro's distrust of the Americans. On Wednesday, Donovan flew back to the US, contacted Dr. Leonard A. Scheele, former Surgeon General of the US, and returned to Havana with him on Thursday to clarify Castro's questions. Castro was still suspicious. So Donovan suggested that Castro send Cuban technicians to the US to verify the suitability of the goods being loaded onto the *African Pilot*. Castro did so.

On Friday, December 21, the Cuban government received the vital letter of credit from the Royal Bank of Canada. It was immediately confirmed by the Cuban government. Castro gave his OK to the deal and sent three doctors on a special flight at 1 am Saturday morning to check the supplies being loaded in Miami.

The three approached their task with alacrity. They objected to the presence of certain goods such as Listerine, Alka Seltzer, ExLax, Aspirin and Midol, believing them to be useless. Arguments ensued. Demands made. Firm diplomacy threatened. When the Cuban technicians announced they would stay until Christmas Day if need be, killing the "Home by Christmas" objective, John Nolan, a volunteer lawyer threatened bad publicity—*very* bad publicity. He suggested they confirm their plans with Havana.

The Cubans conferred and called Havana. They were told to come home.

Saturday night, December 22, Fidel Castro showed up at Berta Barreto's villa with cigars and champagne. He, Donovan, Sánchez, Barreto and his driver held an impromptu celebration talking at length about democracy, Communism and religion.

* * *

When the release of the prisoners was announced at the Isle of Pines and El Príncipe, reaction was muted—another cruel joke. They'd been let down too often. But when the meals dramatically improved, including bags of raw sugar to fatten them up, and they were allowed out in the sun for a little color and vitamin D, hopes soared, "It was so big it was just driving us mad," said one prisoner.

On December 22 guards brought sacks of food donated by their families for Christmas. The prisoners feasted and gorged themselves on pork, ham, turkey, chicken, fruit and cheese. They were delirious with excitement. Everyone got violently sick, except for Cachorro, a model of moderation. Actually, he'd dreamed of food so much, the reality was a bit anticlimactic. One piece of Bazooka bubble gum that he couldn't resist drove him mad with pain. After months of not chewing, his gums couldn't take it. No doubt a touch of scurvy might have affected him.

Artime, San Román and Oliva were shaved and given haircuts, shoes and fresh uniforms. Major Gálvez, the Modelo prison director, told them, "Tomorrow you are leaving."

Artime asked sarcastically, "May I ask which *bartolina* we are going to now?"

Major Gálvez answered, "Miami."

"We couldn't feel the happiness," Oliva said. "We couldn't realize it was true."

Sunday morning December 23, at 7:30 am, Artime, Pepe and Oliva were taken from their cells. With elaborate solemnity, they bid farewell to Lenin, whose poster had graced the wall in front of their cell.

When it came to releasing the other prisoners, Cachorro refused to leave, saying he wanted no part of a medicine and food bonanza that would benefit the Castro regime. Hugo Sueiro, 2nd Battalion commander, ordered him to comply, "You are ordered. We need you in freedom." Cachorro was deeply relieved. As they marched to waiting buses to take them to the Nueva Gerona airport, the politicals in the *circulares* cheered and yelled coded messages saying to "come back and free us!"

Conditions in Cuba had deteriorated so much that the guards at El Príncipe begged the prisoners to leave their old boots, telling them that they could get new ones in the US. Some prisoners walked out to the buses barefooted.

The Isle of Pines prisoners arrived at the San Antonio de los Baños airfield outside of Havana at 10:30 am. Haynes Johnson describes the scene:

"The airport was alive with activity. Castro militiamen were everywhere, all carrying loaded weapons. Berta Barreto and her committee of ladies, some twenty in all, were seated at tables with their list of prisoners. Farther down the line the Castro government officials arranged their final check point, and at the very end were the U.S. Immigration officials. In back of them were the planes. The day was clear, the sun was shining and there was a steady breeze across the field."

The men were herded into a large hangar, outfitted with new beds and mattresses, sheets, pillows and blankets all made in China—things quite scarce in the new Cuba, but a final propaganda coup for the regime. Cachorro slept on the floor—it was what he was used to, *and* he wanted no favors from Castro. New clothing and shoes followed, military or civilian.

At noon lunch was served. Cachorro picked duck with rice and red beans. Choices included beef, chicken and beer. One US Immigration official commented, "Things in Cuba aren't so bad. They really have a lot of food."

One of Barreto's ladies overheard him and said, "You know something? This is the first time I've eaten meat in ten days. Where I live there is no meat."

At 2 pm the *African Pilot* docked in Havana harbor delivering the 20% of the shipment promised in order to begin the prisoner release. An hour later the buses carrying the El Príncipe prisoners began arriving at the airport.

It was then that Berta Barreto got another rogue idea. She suggested to Donovan that he speak to Fidel about permitting a group of relatives of the prisoners, including Oliva's wife and child, to go back on the empty ship. Haynes Johnson takes up the story:

"Donovan told Fidel it seemed senseless to send empty ships back to the U.S. when Fidel could use them to rid himself of liabilities. Fidel thought a moment and asked: 'How many of these worms can we get on that empty ship?' A

thousand, Donovan answered. 'Get a thousand and let them go out. We don't want these worms here. All they do is give us trouble and eat our food. Every mother, father or relative who wants to go out, let them go.' Speaking to Mrs. Barreto, Castro said, 'Berta, make up a list and get them ready. This will be my Christmas present.'"

When she heard this, Berta Barreto went into overdrive. Addressing the members of the Families Committee present, she said, "Go into the hangar and ask the prisoners to make a list of the names of anyone that they want to leave the island." Donovan then asked the Swiss Ambassador to contact Washington to take advantage of Castro's offer by including names of people the US wanted to get out of Cuba, including the parents of the children flown out of Cuba during Operation Peter Pan.

While Donovan, Castro and the other functionaries were standing on the airstrip, four Mig fighters coming in low over the horizon, undetectable until the last second, buzzed the airfield startling everyone. Everyone ducked. Some shouted, "What is it?"

Without skipping a beat Donovan yelled, "It's the invasion!" Castro, who had doubtlessly ordered the display of power but who had also worried for months that the US was about to invade, burst out laughing. Seeing the normally humorless Castro laugh, the other Cubans started laughing also.

Castro had said he'd begin releasing prisoners at 5 pm if the ship were unloaded. Ship, planes and men were ready. Castro and Donovan each were waiting for the other to make the first move.

Donovan gave the go-ahead to unload, followed by Castro's order for the prisoners to begin boarding the first plane. One of Castro's militia guards winked broadly at them. In about a half hour the first 108 prisoners lifted off Cuban soil.

Castro, never one to miss a good propaganda opportunity, left for Havana harbor. He showed up on the deck of the *African Pilot*, had his picture taken with the captain, and exhorted the dock workers to hurry up.

At 6:06 pm the first plane landed at Homestead Air Force Base. A Cuban woman clutched her throat and screamed, "My God, they're really here!" and fainted. Again, Haynes Johnson:

"An air force lieutenant colonel announced that the second plane was already on its way. A cheer went up from the large crowd of newsmen and television technicians and Red Cross and Immigration officials. It was dark by the time the

plane stopped and the engines were cut off. Spotlights played about the field. One by one the men came out."

When the door opened, Carlos *Cachorro* Manuel León Acosta and Armandito Raúl Lastra Faget were the first prisoners to step out. Armandito was fit to jump out of his skin with excitement. Cachorro was still dazed or, as Huber Matos, Castro's first high rank purge casualty observed of some men while in prison, "[he'd] fallen into his own interior abyss." The *Miami Herald* described him as having eyes "bathed in emotion." He'd imagined this scene so often in prison that the reality became surreal. His mother walked right past him, unable to recognize the boy who now weighed 113 pounds. Armandito's mom, Tita, wasn't there; she was still in Cuba. Every December 23rd, Cachorro celebrates a birthday—it was the day he was born again.

The first plane carrying the freed Bay of Pigs prisoners landed at Homestead Air Force Base in Florida on December 23, 1962 at 6:07 pm. The first two prisoners off the plane, descending the stairs near the bottom are the author's cousins, Carlos 'Cachorro' Manuel León Acosta and Armandito Raúl Lastra Faget. Working back up the stairs, L to R: José Ibarra Calero, Rolando Cabezas, José Andreu, Amado Gayol, Jorge Gutiérrez. Credit: Eduardo Hernández 'Guayo' Toledo. Source: Miami Herald.

Armandito Raúl Lastra Faget escorted by Miami Mayor Robert King High (in black suit) right after descending to the tarmac upon arrival at Homestead Air Force Base in Florida. Behind the mayor on the left is Carlos 'Cachorro' Manuel León Acosta. Date: December 23, 1962. Credit: Eduardo Hernández 'Guayo' Toledo. Source: Miami Herald.

Three more flights followed. The fourth flight landed at Homestead at 9 pm. Four-hundred-and-twenty-six prisoners had been freed. No more flights were due in that night. The men were fed—roast beef, mashed potatoes and ice cream—examined by doctors, offered new clothes and handed $100 each to start their new lives. Finally, one more bus ride: to the Dinner Key Auditorium, where their families awaited them.

Cachorro's family reunion at Noche Buena, December 24, 1962, the day after his arrival in the US. Cachorro is in the center, fourth from left. Next to him on the left is Orlando Bebo Acosta, the uncle that forged the parental permission for both Cachorro and Armandito to join the Bay of Pigs operation when they'd just turned 17. Cachorro's mom, Sylvia costa, is on the far left. Credit: Manuel León. Source: Carlos León collection.

Harry Ruiz-Williams and a few of the earlier returned wounded prisoners were on hand to orient the men on each flight for the transition from prison to plenty that was overwhelming them. Of primary concern was the press. Harry reminded them not only that not all the prisoners were out yet, but that Cubans in Cuba weren't free yet. Therefore they must not do or say anything that might impede either objective, especially not to make any bitter statements that would hurt the precarious relations between Cuba and the US.

The men kept a discreet silence. Almost nothing of consequence was reported about the Bay of Pigs invasion or subsequent imprisonment. They were all quite wary of talking. Cachorro told me that, even amongst themselves, the men didn't talk about the Bay of Pigs, in spite of forging intimate and unbreakable bonds actively pursued throughout 55 years of exile. For many, exile became "a long catalogue of bitter encounters with journalists, officials, rivals, and accusers and the distrust of outsiders…" according to Patrick Symmes.

Radio interview with (L to R) José Andreu and Cachorro after their return to freedom in December, 1962. Source: Carlos León collection.

* * *

Late in the evening of December 23, Fidel Castro put the brakes on the operation. He reminded Donovan that he, as yet, hadn't been paid the $2.9 million in cash for the 60 wounded prisoners he'd already released on credit. Castro wanted his money. Another 623 prisoners remained in Cuba. Castro threatened to halt the release if he didn't receive the money within twelve hours.

Donovan went into overdrive. That night at 2 am he sent John Nolan to confer with the Attorney General. At 5 am, after discussing the problem with Deputy Attorney General Nicholas Katzenbach, Nolan called Kennedy.

They—and Katzenbach—conferred for 45 minutes. Finally, after explaining all the details of the conundrum, Kennedy asked, "John, what are you going to do now?"

"Well, I'm going to go back (to Cuba)," he answered.

"Don't you think you ought to wait until you can see whether we can get the money or not?"

"No, I think I'll rely on you to do that…I'll just assume that you're going to get it. And I think, really, that's the only way to play it."

"Okay," replied Kennedy.

Back in Havana, Donovan asked Nolan, "How did it go?"

"Well, I think it's going to be okay," he replied. Donovan didn't pry assuming everything would work out fine.

Bobby Kennedy hit the phones. Right away Richard Cardinal Cushing of Boston and a sponsor of the Families Committee anted up $1 million. The rest was gathered within hours. But it was Christmas Eve and the banks closed early. Getting Castro a check for $2.9 million by 3 pm would be a challenge.

In spite of his ultimatum, Castro allowed two more prisoner flights out in the morning. That brought the number of men liberated up to 643. But at noon, he shut the operation down again. Prisoners, families, reporters and the hundreds of people involved in the operation had no idea what was going on. Some, including Families Committee chairman Álvaro Sánchez, panicked.

But the Royal Bank of Canada came through. The check for $2.9 million was in Castro's hand by 3 pm.

* * *

Late in the afternoon the last three planes received the signal to depart. San Román, Artime and Oliva were the last to board. Donovan turned to Castro to bid his goodbyes and sign a receipt for the men. Haynes Johnson captures the scene:

> *"Said Donovan, in a loud voice: 'You know, Premier, I have been thinking of all the good I have been doing for the people of Cuba these past weeks. I have relieved you of almost 1,200 liabilities and also I have been helping the children, the sick, the poor and the elderly among the Cuban people. I think that when the next election is held I'm coming back and run against you. I think I can win.' Castro, with a long look and a long puff on his cigar, replied: 'You know, doctor, I think you may be right. So there will be no elections.' The two men shook hands, and Donovan [along with Berta Barreto] boarded the plane."*

The plane landed at Miami International Airport at 9:45 pm. When Roberto San Román saw his brother, he broke into tears. Minutes later, Robert Kennedy called and congratulated each of the three leaders and said, "I'm looking forward to seeing you soon, and I think the President would like to speak to you also." Pepe San Román describes his arrival:

"We were taken in a bus to a place where our families were waiting for us. It was the Dinner Key Auditorium. There we found lots of people, members of the Brigade that had escaped, and others that had been left behind in Base Trax and they tried to take us on their shoulders. Then I saw my mother and then I saw my wife, and I ran to them but the crowd wouldn't let me get to them. The same thing happened to Erneido (Oliva) and Manolo (Artime). Finally I got to them and I almost killed my mother and my wife and my kids with the embrace I gave them. It was a very great moment because I never thought I would see them again. And then they came and took us, Erneido and Manolo and myself, to the microphones, and Manolo spoke for us and I don't remember what he said because I was just crazy with happiness. And when he finished we were taken on the shoulders of our men and they walked around with us until I had a chance to get down and I went back to my family."

* * *

One-thousand-one-hundred-and-thirteen prisoners had been rescued. All told, James Donovan was able to negotiate the release of an additional 7,857 individuals related to the Bay of Pigs affair, including the prisoners' families' on the *African Pilot*, some American prisoners, and other vaguely related individuals to the operation between December 27, 1962 and July 4, 1963.

When bidding Donovan farewell on the tarmac at the airport, Fidel Castro invited the lawyer to return and spend some time with him in Varadero. Donovan took him up on it. Whether it was to aid in pursuing the further negotiations for the release of the additional 7,857 people or the two men had developed some sort of friendship, only they knew. Both men were canny operators. Two incidents shed some light on their subsequent relationship.

On one of his last trips, in April of 1963, Donovan decided to take his 18-year-old son, John, with him. He was well aware that some risk was involved. The idea did not go over well with Mary Donovan, his wife. He wanted the trip to be an education, but he warned John that Castro had bought into the personality cult that had built around him. Castro too had a son and Donovan thought he'd appreciate the gesture. The UK *Daily Mail.com* reported:

> *"Before the trip, the CIA provided Donovan with a diving suit to give to Castro as a gift. After Donovan's death, it came out that some in the CIA had tried to poison it. If Donovan had given a poisoned suit to Castro, it could have made 'my father an unwitting accomplice to Castro's assassination,' John said. 'It might have been just as serious as the Missile Crisis, conceivably. But my father might have suspected something, because he just went out in New York and bought his own diving suit. My father just gave it to him and Castro put it on, and went snorkeling in it, right there, in the Bay of Pigs.'"*

19

The Return

On the tarmac at Homestead Air Force Base Cachorro was asked how it felt to be free again. The boy was in a daze. He responded that he was only here temporarily—until he could regain his strength and return to Cuba to continue the fight. At home he slept on the floor, sat on the floor and expressed little interest in food. Offered a steak, he responded that all he wanted to do was take a long warm shower by himself.

The day he'd left for Guatemala, a close aunt of his had died. She'd left a 3-year-old daughter behind. After the shower he'd wanted so bad, the now 5-year-old cousin asked him, "Is my mother coming home now?" Cachorro broke into tears.

Armandito, on the other hand, wasn't given to quiet moments of intimate reflection. His appetites exploded the minute he hit freedom. Eating, brawling, getting laid and continuing the fight against Castro were his priorities, all of which he pursued as if he'd shotgunned a cocktail of stem cells and cocaine.

With his mother, Tita, still in Cuba and only extended family to harbor him, Armandito rented an apartment with the $175 monthly stipend the CIA continued to pay the Brigade members until spring of 1963. Armandito shared the apartment with a few buddies and awaited orders to resume the fight.

Both boys had joined the Brigade as members of the *Movimiento de Recuperación Revolucionario*, or MRR. They were still members—and the MRR was still fighting Castro. It was only a matter of time before they jumped back in the fray.

* * *

President Kennedy was spending Christmas with his family in Palm Beach, Florida, only minutes away from the returning prisoners. Three days after their arrival, on the 27th of December, he invited the three Brigade leaders, Pepe San Román, Manuel Artime and Erneido Oliva; the head of the Families Committee, Álvaro Sánchez, Jr.; and Harry Ruiz-Williams up to see him.

He wanted to apologize.

Kennedy tried to explain, to give context to his apology. He mentioned the many Cold War problems the US faced at the time of the invasion and the inadequate briefings he'd received. He asked, "Did you really expect US air support?" Pepe San Román replied that at the military briefings prior to the invasion, they were *not* told they would have air support. However, their CIA trainers in Guatemala had said that "the skies will be ours."

It was a very fine distinction, one subject to multiple interpretations— too many for the stakes involved. But the men, honorable military officers all, accepted the apology and explanation in stride.

Erneido Oliva later remarked to Haynes Johnson, "It was very easy to see that Kennedy felt responsible for what had happened to us and for our long time in prison." Oliva's equanimity was only exceeded by his magnanimity. The day before, out for a walk with Harry Ruiz-Williams, Harry had suggested they get breakfast at a diner. Johnson describes what happened:

> *"Oliva said they would have to be careful because some places in the United States would not serve Negroes and he didn't want to create a problem. At the first restaurant the waitress refused to serve them. 'No, sir, I can't,' she said…'I was looking at this man who had come out of prison and I felt so sad to see how he looked,' Harry said. 'He was very quiet but I knew it hurt him deeply. So I said, 'Come on, we'd better go.' And we left"*

The President concluded the meeting by asking the men if, together, they could hold an event in Miami to celebrate their release. All agreed, though many in the Brigade had mixed feelings, including Cachorro.

Though he knew Kennedy was responsible for the cancelled air strikes, he didn't hold a grudge against him for the lack of US air support. He intuitively understood that US fighter jet support was out of the question. That would have made the invasion a US operation with global repercussions the US was unwilling to entertain. Had it been a US operation, it would have made no sense to exclude US ground troops or navy ships, leaving the free-Cuban contingent a merely token presence.

Cachorro, however, was in no mood for a public, political spectacle—especially since the Brigade had failed and the job was far from over. Some of the Brigade members refused to attend, believing that the event would be hypocrisy, since they blamed Kennedy for the cancellation of the air strikes, but most attended, including Cachorro in his near zombic state.

The event was held at the Miami Orange Bowl. Forty-thousand people packed the bleachers. The men of the Brigade stood on the lawn, in front of a raised platform with microphones on the 50-yard line. When JFK and First Lady Jacqueline drove in, the crowd erupted in a deafening roar. After the military band played the US and Cuban national anthems, Kennedy strode across the grass and into the lines of the khaki-clad Brigade men, greeting them and shaking hands with unrestrained enthusiasm. Tomás Cruz, the black company commander who'd told Castro he hadn't gone to Cuba to go swimming, impulsively stepped forward and embraced the President.

When the formal ceremonies began, Kennedy was flanked by San Román, Artime, Oliva and José Miró Cardona, the Cuban civilian exile leader. Pepe San Román spoke first. He vowed to finish the job, "Whenever, however, wherever, in whatever honorable form it may come, we will do what we can to be better prepared to meet and complete our mission." Then he turned toward Kennedy. "Mr. President, the men of the 2506 Brigade give you their banner—we temporarily deposit it with you for safekeeping."

Erneido Oliva quietly handed the gold-and-blue flag to the President. "It was the great moment of my life," Oliva said later. The colors had flown over the command post at Playa Girón for three days. Before Castro's troops entered the village, a soldier had taken down the flag and squirreled it away until he succeeded in reaching asylum in an embassy in Havana. It was then taken to the US.

Kennedy acknowledged the honor and responsibility the flag represented, asked the Brigade to sit down on the grass, and pledged to return it to the Brigade in a free Havana. The stadium thundered with applause.

At the conclusion of the President's address, Jacqueline Kennedy stepped to the microphone and, in Spanish, said:

"It is an honor for me to be today with a group of the bravest men in the world, and to share in the joy that is felt by their families who, for so long, lived hoping, praying and waiting. I feel proud that my son has met the officers. He is still too young to realize what has happened here, but I will make it my business to tell

him the story of your courage as he grows up. It is my wish and my hope that someday he may be a man at least half as brave as the members of Brigade 2506. Good luck."

It was the only part of the event that Cachorro remembered.

* * *

The previous September, just before the Missile Crisis, a Joint Resolution of the Armed Forces and Foreign Relations Committee of the US Senate had declared that the United States was determined:

"1. To prevent by whatever means necessary, including the use of arms, the Marxist-Leninist regime in Cuba from extending by force or threat of force its aggressive or subversive activities to any part of this hemisphere;

2. To prevent in Cuba the creation or use of an externally supported military capability endangering the security of the United States;

3. To work with the Organization of American States and with freedom-loving Cubans to support the aspirations of the Cuban people for self-determination."

That Resolution was based on a more-to-the-point directive from the Chief of Operation Mongoose, which stated: To discredit and isolate the regime; to harass the economy; to assist exile groups and Latin American governments to take actions; and to be prepared to exploit a revolt.

Those directives, the missile crisis and the Kennedy's hate for Castro gave birth to Operation Mongoose in November. Operation Mongoose, Kennedy's answer to the failed Bay of Pigs invasion (and introduced in chapter 13) was a continuation of the infiltration and intelligence-gathering CIA operations originally initiated by President Eisenhower. Though they waxed and waned during and after the invasion, they were independent of it. In fact, a number of operatives in Cuba had been caught, so to speak, with their pants down when the Brigade landed at Playa Girón. They hadn't been notified of the invasion and had to quickly make themselves scarce when they heard about it.

So began a multiple years' long CIA anti-Castro operation informally and collectively known—along with the private exile initiatives—as the 'infiltration program.' This included the promotion of democratic values, intelligence gathering, dissident evacuation, sabotage, the initiation of agent provocateur incidents, the covert use of US Special Forces, psychological warfare and assassination attempts to help overthrow the Castro regime.

The infiltration program had begun before the Bay of Pigs invasion as part of an earlier de-stabilization program. Prior to the Bay of Pigs invasion, infiltration activities were easier and more informal, often depending on sympathetic locals that had no connection with underground activities to provide impromptu aid. After the Bay of Pigs, Castro tightened the screws. Félix Rodriguez, already mentioned as #2718 in Brigade 2506 and the man who volunteered to assassinate Castro, was infiltrated into Cuba just before the Bay of Pigs invasion in an operation that, as far as he knew, was unrelated to the invasion. In fact, he didn't know about the invasion, even though his infiltration was related to it. On that fateful April 17, he was caught unawares in Havana as part of a group of thirty-five men that went into Cuba to distract Castro's forces. Only fifteen survived through the invasion and its aftermath.

Castro's tactic after the Bay of Pigs and the execution of the twenty infiltrators was to send communist provocateurs into areas where infiltrators had received backing. They would say to some farmer, "Hey, we just arrived from Miami and we need your help." If the farmer helped, he was arrested and publicly executed for anti-revolutionary activities, according to Rodriguez. The technique was very effective and made post-Bay of Pigs infiltration operations much more difficult.

The first two intelligence reports from the infiltration operations after the Bay of Pigs came in September and November. Operatives inside Cuba were the first to report on the installation of Russian missile bases. Throughout the fall, during the ups and downs of Donovan's negotiations, already-freed and escaped Brigade members were being trained in Florida for missions to Cuba. One of the men participating was Roberto San Román, Pepe's brother, the man who had sailed the fishing sloop *Celia* to New Orleans with twenty-two men.

Roberto's first mission, in November, was to sail into Cárdenas Bay and blow up a bridge and a key railroad yard. But when they got inside the bay, five ships began following them, so they aborted the mission.

The second mission, bigger in scope, was to blow up the Matahambre copper-silver mines, Cuba's largest, in Pinar del Rio. After excellent training including scale models of the shafts, "they put us in a ship that was good for nothing," bitched San Román. After one engine, the battery and the radio went dead, the ship began taking on water. San Román and his 6-man crew abandoned ship and headed for Miami in the small catamaran they had brought along for the landing.

"So again I was in the ocean without food or water," he told Haynes Johnson. They were picked up by a freighter and taken to Texas. "That is a typical mission. The idea is good, and then it breaks to pieces," was San Román's assessment.

Manuel Artime and Erneido Oliva also joined the CIA effort, staging commando raids on Cuban shore installations from bases in Costa Rica and Nicaragua. But probably the most high profile—and most improbable—individual to join the CIA's infiltration program was Juanita Castro, Fidel Castro's younger sister. Juanita's collaboration journey began only ten days after Castro's triumph. It wasn't ideological; it was humanitarian—she'd strongly supported the Revolution.

Cover of Juanita Castro's book, Fidel y Raúl, Mis Hermanos: La Historia Secreta. Left to right: Raúl, Juanita & Fidel Castro. Source: Book cover, © 2009, Santillana USA Publishing Company, Inc., Doral, FL.

On January 10, 1959, a high school friend whose brother had been detained due to his ties with the previous government sought her help. His life was in danger. Would Juanita, as 'sister of Fidel' resolve the matter? Juanita knew the young man to be a decent sort and got him out. From that moment on, she writes in her memoir *Fidel y Raúl Mis Hermanos: La Historia Secreta*, her full time job became saving people who'd been incarcerated without due process or who were liable to summary execution simply for having associated with the previous regime.

She made it a point to nurture contacts at all the prisons but hit a brick wall at La Cabaña where *Che* Guevara ran a Cheka-style execution assembly line. Guevara not only made her wait, but when he finally saw her he told her not to come around pleading for anyone's life.

Finally, Juanita complained to her brother about the injustices. Fidel told her to be patient, the Revolution was in transition and mistakes were inevitable but reassured her that all would soon improve. Like everyone else, she believed him. So she got into the spirit of things and applied her entrepreneurial bent to building a free rural hospital in Oriente with donations. But even there, the arrests and confiscations around her (not to mention Fidel's recommendation that Guevara inaugurate the clinic) soured her. In spite of being named a Ministry of Health Delegate, her public interests waned. She bought a small radio station in Havana, the CMK, though as part of the media, it too was soon confiscated. Meanwhile, she continued her rescue activities.

One afternoon in 1960 she got a desperate call from her older sister Angelita. She'd been arrested. Juanita immediately rang the Minister of Justice, Augusto Martínez Sánchez (and later to be presiding judge at the Brigade's trial). Sánchez responded sarcastically that Angelita wasn't under arrest, just detained because she was "attempting to liberate a counter-revolutionary of his problems". She hung up on him, drove to the prison and insisted on her sister's release. The warden, Abelardo Ibarra, reluctantly complied, but later complained to Fidel who, in turn, gave Juanita a dressing down in front of their mother accusing her of acting as if she were "above the Revolution". All she could think was, "If this happens to the Castro family, what must it be like for other Cubans?"

By April of 1960, when my immediate family left Cuba, leaving Cuba had become no simple matter. Restrictions on travel, bank accounts, foreign exchange and the transfer of property clamped down from above. Juanita's efforts took a turn from saving the summarily condemned from death and prison, to helping dissidents, the threatened and the persecuted to escape abroad with a nest egg. For this she required a cover and a safe house, so she bought a boarding house in Vedado, a Havana suburb. The arrangement soon turned into a dangerous cat-and-mouse game with the G2, Cuba's KGB; but also with the various members of her family. When her mother, on a visit, found out, she pretended not to notice what was going on. There were many close calls, but her cover survived—barely.

At dawn on April 17 of 1961, the day of the Bay of Pigs invasion, Juanita went into overdrive. She received a call from a G2 double agent saying that a big round up was under way—the prisons were filling and the overflow were being warehoused at the National Palace of Sports, the Cerro Baseball Stadium and the giant Blanquita Theatre. Her best friend and collaborator, Ely Esteva was missing. Juanita rescued as many as she could by brazenly walking in, rounding up those detainees she knew, and brazenly walking out with them using the magic of her surname.

Shortly afterward, she was approached by her friend, Virginia Leitao da Cunha, the Brazilian ambassador's wife for a special, secret meeting with a new 'friend' who had a proposition. The meeting took place in Mexico. So began Juanita's involvement with the CIA. Juanita demanded only two things: no salary (she didn't want to be in the 'pay of the CIA') and she wanted no part with attempts on her brothers' lives.

She was naïve. But it underscored the purity of her motives—she wanted to aid what she believed were the Revolution's true ideals. Ignorant of the CIA's numerous attempts to assassinate her brother, she became CIA operative "Donna", an unwitting albeit distant abettor in that effort, but now with greater resources and contacts for saving lives. The arrangement later became part of the CIA's Operation Mongoose; messages were conveyed via a secret short wave radio installed for the purpose at her boarding house.

Did she experience any remorse betraying her brother? "No, for a very simple reason: I did not betray him. He's the one who betrayed me…along with the thousands who suffered and fought for the (promises of) the Revolution."

It's incredible that for nearly three years, until her departure in June of 1964, she avoided detection, especially considering that the world's third and fourth best intelligence services, the G2 *and* the KGB, had their eyes, ears and fingers in every pie in Cuba. But perhaps she didn't.

Carlos Alberto Montaner, a writer and journalist who contributed the prologue to Juanita Castro's book, elaborates:

"In 1964 the Cuban secret services had punctually informed Raúl Castro about…his sister's activities…Raúl was Minister of Defense. He went to see her and, in a tone that alternated between menace and affection, he explained that such behavior had to cease immediately. Juanita understood that she had to leave the country…She was about to be incarcerated. That she wasn't, and that she was allowed to leave for Mexico, was only because he loved her, because his fraternal affection tempered his responsibilities as military chief of the country… Fidel would have acted differently. Fidel certainly didn't know everything Raúl knew."

No one knows for certain what Raúl knew. He at least knew something about the smuggling of people and assets out of the country. By not putting an immediate stop to it, he—in effect—aided her efforts, something his brother would never have tolerated. Juanita avers that, "In hundreds of cases in which my mother and I saved people, it was thanks to his intervention— direct or indirect." If he knew about the CIA contact and chose to ignore it, he became a tacit CIA collaborator. For all her initial naiveté, Juanita Castro certainly came to understand exactly what was going on.

* * *

But Operation Mongoose was only the government's operation. According to Cachorro, there were 65 or so independent Cuban exile infiltration groups working in parallel with Operation Mongoose, sometimes in concert with it, and sometimes in defiance of it—the relationships were very fluid. Many of the independent operatives were college students who moonlighted as cloak-and-dagger agents on weekends. One group was sponsored by Frank Sinatra. The US Coast Guard turned a blind eye to these boats, their crew and their cargo.

After a month or two of recuperation Cachorro was ready to get back into action. His first assignment was simple: deliver gasoline to a secluded cove on a key the MRR used as a base of operations. He and Armandito were provided with a VW microbus whose rear seats had all been removed and replaced with empty five-gallon canisters. So as not to draw suspicion, the boys were instructed to fill the canisters at different gas stations, a task that would take all day.

Everything seemed to be going according to plan until Armandito lit up a cigarette. Gasoline fumes filled the VW's cab, overflow puddled on the floor and a thin patina of fuel drips collared the containers. They drove with all the windows open. A chain smoker, aggressive driver and fearless hulk unencumbered by consequences, Armandito was oblivious to any danger. Cachorro, however, was, by now, teetering from one butt cheek to the other with anxiety. "Armando, you shouldn't be smoking," he tendered.

"Ay, coño! Que pendejada!..." and off he went with torrents of indignant protests in colorful Cuban as if he'd been admonished by a nagging wife to sit up straight or wipe the dribble off his chin. Armandito kept smoking.

They reached the cove, unloaded the canisters and filled the outboard's tank, warehousing the rest of the fuel for other uses. Armandito then headed to sea on his first mission. Cachorro drove the VW home alone.

Cachorro's first offshore mission was an embarrassment to him. Again, he was the lowest man on the totem pole. They were headed for Cuba. Cachorro had no idea what the objective of the mission was. No one had clued him in on details. When they landed on a small, uninhabited cay, Cachorro jumped out, got on his knees and kissed the ground. The team leader remarked, "I didn't know you loved Great Britain so much." They'd landed on a Bahamian island for a break before getting to Cuba.

* * *

Operation Mongoose (aka the Special Group—CIA Cuba projects had many, many names; be thankful I don't overwhelm you with all of them), being a clandestine CIA program, its operatives were sworn to secrecy. Chuchu, one cousin-in-law who was too young for the Bay of Pigs operation, joined the Special Group after that disaster. At sixteen, he became a radio/telegraph operator. He declined to be interviewed for this book citing his CIA secrecy vow and extant contacts still in Cuba whose lives would be endangered by the slightest revelations—though he did disclose one close call.

Once, while biding his time in a safe house in Oriente Province, he was talked into visiting a nearby bar by his hosts. "The danger was minimal!" they enthused. After a couple of beers, a group of *milicianos* walked in. Chuchu shook like a Chihuahua in Saskatchewan but managed to retain his composure. His was an unfamiliar face in the crowd, one that would inevitably draw attention and raise questions. But the militiamen did not notice. After a prudent interval, Chuchu and his hosts left. It had been a close call.

Another operative, Rolando Martínez, is a close friend—and hero to—Cachorro. Like his uncle Bebo, Martínez was a 'professional' revolutionary. He'd fought Batista and now he was fighting Castro as part of the CIA Special Group. Martínez, in the space of a few years, made over 300 infiltrations into Cuba, though he never discussed these with Cachorro, again, due to secrecy concerns. Rolando Martínez developed useful clandestine connections which he used when it suited him. After the infiltration program he became one of the Cuban plumbers that burgled the Democratic National Committee headquarters at the Watergate Hotel—the scandal that caused President Nixon's resignation.

But one Special Group operative, Captain Bradley Earl Ayers, wasn't sworn to secrecy because he never joined the CIA. In 1976 he wrote *The War that Never Was: An Insider's Account of CIA Covert Operations Against Cuba.* Bradley was the executive officer of the Army Ranger Training Camp at Eglin Air Force Base in Florida where selected officers were trained in the techniques of clandestine jungle and swamp operations, patrolling, guerrilla warfare, demolitions and amphibious operations for small units.

In the spring of 1963 Bradley was summoned to the Pentagon and offered a job training Cuban exiles for covert operations. Briefed that the CIA had been conducting covert paramilitary and espionage activities against the regime of Fidel Castro for some time, but had not been achieving the success they hoped for, he was informed that with professional training they hoped for better results. Additionally, he was told that many of the raids were being conducted independently by ill-equipped, poorly organized exile groups. The hope was that an improved CIA cadre might coopt or at least set an example for the independents.

Bradley accepted the job. He went on army leave, kept his rank and salary, but did not join "the Company." The assignment was kept secret from his family. At CIA headquarters he was briefed on details and given a cover identity. All Cuban operations had code names which began with the letters AM: AMTRAK, AMARK, AMTHUMB, etc. Each separate group worked independently, but all reported to Miami CIA headquarters—JMWAVE.

Under cover as a real estate broker and developer, he began his search for a training area on Key Largo, Linderman Key and the Flamingo-Cape Sable region at the edge of Everglades National Park, concentrating on the most desolate, swampy, bug-infested areas he could find, the better to avoid detection. Concurrently, he researched what was going on in Cuba. Bradley writes:

"During late May and early June 1963, there was a pronounced increase in exile raids and bombings, refugee escapes, and other indications of internal unrest. One of our groups conducted a successful commando raid in Camagüey Province, and someone else blew up a ship in Havana Harbor. The newspapers said it had been done by secret exile frogmen, and Castro blamed the CIA. Naturally, we all rejoiced when anything like this happened, but at no time did we acknowledge, even in private, that our people had been involved. Customarily, either by prearrangement...or because of their own wish to capitalize on the political impact of such incidents, one of the...independent exile groups, such as Alpha 66, would publicly take credit for the raids."

There were always two or three operations taking place simultaneously, so Bradley requested permission to accompany one. He wanted to see firsthand how the missions were run and get the measure of the men involved. In two weeks he was on a V-20 speedboat zipping through the night to intercept a mother ship some seven miles off Tea Table Key in the Florida Keys. Bradley, however, as an American, would have to remain on the mother ship. He wasn't allowed to enter Cuban territorial waters. The mother ship, an old minesweeper, was of Costa Rican registry and its entire crew was Cuban or Central American. Its cover was that it was prospecting for oil.

The team of six for the mission was what was left of one of the very first units the CIA supported after the Bay of Pigs. The group had once numbered twenty to thirty men, but some had been killed, captured, quit or been rejected for security reasons. Bradley thought the six were flabby, soft and indolent—with the exception of the team leader. After one training exercise the team had returned completely exhausted.

The mission was relatively simple and theoretically untraceable. The mother ship was to drop the team at night in two rubber rafts with "silent" outboard engines three miles off the northwest coast of Cuba near Bahía Honda. They were to bury four cache containers at a designated spot in the mangroves, and then hide during the following day until nightfall when they would return to the mother ship. Later, agents inside Cuba would recover the cache.

Captain Luis of the mother ship had been briefed about the habits and locations of Castro's coastal defenses in great detail—the number and modus operandi of the Russian Komar-class patrol boats, including the names of their commanders and crew members, the searchlights and gun emplacements, the foot patrols with dogs and the local civilian informants.

Each of the team members carried a .45-caliber submachine gun with four clips of ammunition—except for the leader, who only had a .45-caliber pistol in a shoulder holster. Bradley, concerned that the men had loaded their weapons and kit haphazardly, asked the men to execute a few jumping jacks. The clank of metal against metal, the disheveled results, the dropped equipment and the flapping straps resulted in a consolidation of kit and a tightening of all straps and buckles.

Captain Luis had violated the three-mile limit and was within one mile of the shore when the team set off. Afterward, he headed out to sea to pass the day before returning to pick up the men, this time approaching about a thousand yards off shore.

Just after 2:30 am, an aluminum paddle scraped against the hull. Bradley rushed to the side of the old minesweeper. One raft, with three men aboard, was just visible in the water. After noisily climbing the cargo net, the men said that the other raft, with the team leader, was far behind. It carried a fourth passenger, a wounded Cuban who had escaped the militia that afternoon. He was being tracked by dogs when he stumbled upon the team.

Suddenly, gunfire erupted from shore raking the water nearby. Bradley and the crew hit the deck. Peering over the low gunwale, Bradley spotted moving lights onshore, heard barking dogs and more machine gun bursts. This time the slugs struck the minesweeper.

"There they are! There they are!" Bradley had spotted the other raft less than a hundred yards from the minesweeper. However, Captain Luis had just revved the engines and was about to make a run for it. "For Christ's sake, tell Captain Luis to hold on for a few more minutes," Bradley ordered. "They're almost here!"

The powerful coastal searchlights finally silhouetted the raft as the men paddled frantically toward the mother ship. Rifle shots bracketed the rubber boat. A crewman on the minesweeper uncovered a machine gun on the upper deck, grabbed a belt and slammed shut the receiver. But the gun jammed. Bradley takes up the story:

"The raft was now less than fifty yards away. There was another burst of machine-gun fire from the shore, followed by an agonized cry from the commando boat. It was sinking. It had been hit, probably many times. The crewman at the machine gun above me was working frantically with the stubborn weapon. In an instant he had it cleared and had opened fire in the direction of the shore lights. Two of the commandos from the sinking raft were in the water, struggling to swim toward the ship, but their heavy equipment made it impossible, and they

cried out for help. Marcus and Captain Luis opened one of the life rafts lashed behind the bridge and pushed it over the side. It crashed into the water directly below me, scattering paddles and life vests. The steady pow-pow-pow of the heavy machine gun sounded above me, and some of the lights on shore disappeared."

Bradley and a crew member climbed down the swaying cargo net and grabbed the two swimming commandos who had managed to reach the life raft still dangling next to the big ship. They were crying hysterically. Bradley called for crew members to help them aboard while he and another man jumped in the life raft and headed for the sinking commando raft. "Amigo, amigo, here!" led them to the rapidly sinking raft.

The commando team leader clung to the rope handholds with one hand. His other arm held the unconscious wounded Cuban they'd helped to escape. "We pulled the men into the life raft and I paddled frantically," Bradley wrote. When they reached the minesweeper, two crewmen pulled the leader and his rescue aboard. While Bradley and his assistant climbed the cargo net Captain Luis poured full power to the idling diesel engines and headed for safer waters.

A big storm enveloped them, minimizing the possibility of pursuit—but also the possibility of airlifting the wounded man to a hospital. Who he was and what he'd done remained a mystery, but his wounds were caused by a severe beating with a heavy instrument. The man died before reaching Florida. It was little consolation that they'd risked their life to save him. As to the cache the commando's delivered...?

* * *

Armandito and Cachorro were invited to join Operation Mongoose under Manuel Artime's tutelage. The founder of the MRR and political leader of Brigade 2506 had joined the CIA after his return to the US. But the two boys were torn. Artime and Cachorro's uncle Bebo, the professional revolutionary who'd forged a letter of permission that got them into the Brigade, had some differences of opinion over methods and operational independence. The boys stuck with the uncle and the independent MRR.

Still, there was much fluid overlap between the independent groups and between the independents and the various CIA operations, with boats, equipment and men slipping seamlessly from one operation to another. Most of Armandito's and Cachorro's missions used the *Francisco*, a borrowed boat.

A crew of Cuban freedom fighters, part of Cachorro's infiltration team. Left to right: Miguel 'Miguelón' Olmo; Ricardo Luís Casanueva (MariCris Casanueva's cousin); in the center, Orlando 'Bebo' Acosta, Cachorro's uncle 'Bebo', the 'professional' revolutionary who forged parental permissions for both Cachorro and Armandito to get into Brigade 2506; Ricardo 'Rico' García, Manolo 'Croqueta' Rodriguez-Aragón. Only Ricardo is still alive (2016). Date: Circa 1963. Source: Carlos León Acosta.

As weekend warriors, they'd get little sleep over the two days they operated. During middle-of-the-night and dawn return drives, Armandito usually drove while Cachorro nodded off. But that arrangement, with the unpredictable Armandito at the wheel, was a double-edged sword. Once, at 3 am, asleep on the front seat, Cachorro woke up to find himself in the middle of a brawl. Who had started it and why he never found out, but he got up and pulled his weight backing Armandito. Another time, while stopped at a traffic light, a group of gringo thugs taunted them, "Hey spics, what are you up to?"

At two more stop lights the gringos continued their taunts. Finally, at the last stop light, Armandito got out of the car and ordered the thugs out of theirs. The four gringos just laughed at him. So Armandito pulled out his gun and ordered them out again. When they got out, he ordered them to turn around and not look at Cachorro's license plate or he'd shoot them all. The gringos complied.

Armandito then got into the gringos' car and drove off with Cachorro following him, leaving the gringos stranded at the intersection in the middle of the night. Cachorro doesn't remember what became of the car.

No one in their crew exceeded Armandito's zeal. He'd always volunteer for the worst jobs. Prior to particularly dangerous operations, the team leader resorted to drawing straws. If Armandito didn't draw the short straw he'd offer to exchange his straw for the short one, sometimes putting on a full-court press to be allowed to go. The big boy was captured twice—by the Bahamian navy. The first time, he was released but tailed back to the US. The second time, the Bahamians incarcerated him.

Over the two-and-a-half years Cachorro operated, Cuba's *Seguridad del Estado* has a record that he participated in nine trips to Cuba, landing only a handful of times (and we're sticking by that story). Most of his missions consisted of delivering letters, documents, intelligence, and such; though he'd once had to deliver a load of explosives. Another time he was tasked with extracting someone out of Cuba. Often, he manned the .30-caliber deck-mounted machine gun on the *Francisco*.

That all his missions, even the nearly botched ones, never culminated in his capture—and there were some that came awfully close—made Cachorro suspect that he had a secret protector, a double or even triple agent, likely from the CIA. Cachorro is nearly certain of this but refrains from elaborating or even thinking about who it might have been for fear of disenchantment or, even worse, that his ability to read people was totally undependable.

* * *

After his reconnaissance run on the minesweeper, Bradley Ayers had a much better idea of how to improve operations training. He decided on the

Flamingo area outside Everglades National Park for small boat training, an already established base that was working adequately. Ditto for basic weapons training, land navigation and other miscellaneous subjects being taught at a location in the South Miami area. For survival and small-unit training he chose upper Key Largo, and he settled on a complex of three houses on stilts on Plantation Key as safe-houses.

But Bradley's primary focus would be on physical conditioning and morale, training the he himself would direct. Each planned mission required ad hoc training targeted to its objectives. "Often a mission would have to be scrubbed just as a team had completed training. This was sometimes due to events in the target area and sometimes to a policy decision," he wrote. With another assignment scheduled who-knows-when, maintaining the fitness and morale of the idle teams became another concern.

Meanwhile, Castro's Russian arsenal was growing, with more sophisticated weapons and equipment, more Russian advisers and reports of a Russian antiballistic missile submarine base along the southern coast of the island. More Cubans were being imprisoned, tortured and killed and more were attempting to escape, so Castro beefed up his coastal surveillance.

To counter these trends, the CIA wanted improved commando training and the addition of parachute and underwater demolition training (UDT); more infiltration and intelligence-gathering operations; and increased assistance to the guerrilla bands and counterrevolutionaries inside Cuba.

Now the CIA wanted Bradley to personally supervise the small boat training in addition to his other duties. With his adrenaline still in high octane mode after his first commando mission, Bradley requested to go on a V-20 operation to better assess their performance and needs. He'd barely begun his reorganization of the program and suspected he'd be turned down.

But at the last minute, authorization came through. The mission would leave from Tampa Bay in a large fishing trawler—their cover—towing four V-20s and carrying six commandos. Their orders were to blow up a railroad bridge, along with the adjacent phone, electricity and telegraph lines, on the Sagua la Grande-Isabela railroad, a key supply line in the central part of the island. The trawler would release the V-20s just outside Cuban territorial waters, and wait for their return. Three of the speedboats carried two commandos each; the fourth, carrying Bradley and the mission organizer, a Mr. Martínez, would remain outside the 3-mile limit as a backup and observation boat.

The seas were rough. Suddenly, at the point where Bradley and Martínez were supposed to turn back, a coastal patrol boat's searchlight highlighted all four V-20s. The three commando boats gunned their engines heading for the coastal maze of islets, cays and mangrove swamps. Martínez and Bradley followed, figuring that the open water escape route would be blocked by the patrol boat in pursuit.

Then they heard an agonizing engine whine followed by a loud crackling. At full speed one of the V-20s hit a coral reef and hurtled into the air and then crashed down, spilling its occupants into the water. The boat was lost. Then Bradley's boat struck the reef. For a moment they were airborne, plopped down and hit again bouncing back into the air like a skipping stone. On the first impact Bradley was thrown forward striking his face and mouth on the top edge of the windshield. On the second impact his head hit something and he was out cold.

Bradley came-to to the staccato sound of machine-gun fire and the sight of phosphorous tracer rounds across the night sky. The beam of a searchlight swept the mangroves in front of them. The Cuban patrol boats had temporarily lost them when they'd turned into the island maze. With two boats down and the patrol boats less than half-a-mile away, Martínez and Bradley were sure it would be only minutes before their game was up. The other two V-20s were nowhere to be seen or heard.

Bradley was bleeding from the head and had lost two teeth; Martínez was lying in the stern moaning, an ugly cut on his forehead and clutching his left arm, now dangling uselessly at his side. Across the shallow water they could see the other V-20. The commandos were struggling to free it from the coral outcrop. In a trice they set it free and waded it over to Bradley's boat. Martínez composed himself, turned the ignition switch to the "on" position and, to everyone's surprise, both engines sputtered to life. Then one of the other boat's engines also sprang to life. But Bradley's boat wouldn't move. The two commandos and Bradley rocked and pushed the heavy craft until it came free.

More machine-gun fire, but this time it was farther away. Apparently, the patrol boats had taken a wrong turn. The commandos awaited Martínez' instructions. Should they continue or turn back? Their boat carried one-third of the explosives to blow up the bridge, and their team was vital to the success of the mission. In an instant, Martinez said: "Take our boat. It still has two good engines."

Bradley helped the men transfer the heavy satchel charges and equipment into the backup craft and he and Martínez painfully boarded the badly damaged—it had a boat-length gash just above the waterline—one-engine V-20 to make their getaway.

Heading north they exited the channel only to find a large Soviet patrol boat only 200 yards away, lying in wait with its spotlight aimed right at them. Martínez gunned the engine. Bradley maned the pedestal-mounted .30-caliber and fired at the spotlight. He kept firing until he extinguished it.

Alone in the black night and heavy seas, they cut the power to preserve the engine and took turns bailing and steering. Martínez lost consciousness just before dawn, but Bradley managed to locate their trawler soon thereafter and the two men were rescued.

A day later, on their way back to the US they spotted an odd-looking square rigger with no lights or flags. It was listing badly and there was no sign of life aboard. However, as they drew closer a man climbed atop the low cabin and began waving frantically. When they were close enough to communicate, everyone joined excitedly in conversation. They were Cuban refugees…escaping from the Communist island…adrift and in need of help. There were fifteen refugees, some too old or sick to stand; two infants and a young boy; the rest of all ages. One old couple was close to death. They'd lost their small engine on the second day; their food on the third day; their water the night before. They'd been adrift for a week. They were badly sunburned, with dry, cracked skin and open sores swollen with infection.

The trawler captain loaded the refugees on his boat, set the square-rigger adrift and headed for Key West, immigration and medical help.

Only one commando V-20 from the operation made it back to the US. And only after a harrowing escape from Cuba. A second one limped up on remote Cay Sal were the men shipwrecked. They were later rescued by the Coast Guard. The third boat, with four commandos, ran aground, and was captured by the militia. Since they'd succeeded in partially blowing up the railway bridge and had done extensive damage to the telephone lines, they probably faced a firing squad.

* * *

By early October of 1963, all the training programs Bradley Ayers had been charged with were actively engaged or ready to begin. The man was a perfect combination of field experience coupled with administrative know-how. That fall, at a remote barbecue location, Bobby Kennedy and a group of CIA operatives met with Bradley for a confidence-building session. Bradley was being tasked with a major operation that included UDT and, in the future, parachute training. But the big news was that he was to train a special commando force to hit the Regla oil refineries, the largest on the island, on the east side of Havana Harbor.

The raids were having an effect. That fall, at a reception in the Brazilian embassy in Havana, Castro said: "Kennedy is the Batista of our time, and the most opportunistic President of all time...The United States are fighting a battle against us which they cannot win."

And then, in late November, Bradley received a roll of toilet paper with the following message:

NOVEMBER 22, 1963

PRESIDENT KENNEDY

HAS BEEN SHOT

BY AN ASSASSIN.

SUSPEND ALL ACTIVITY.

KEEP MEN ON ISLAND.

COME ASHORE WITHOUT DELAY.

The FBI and Secret Service, striking out wildly for any clues to the assassination, descended on the JMWAVE complex to review security dossiers and files on exile organizations. The inactivity and policy vacuum stretched into months.

Bradley Ayers had grown very fond of Cubans (and of one in particular, in spite of being married) and had adopted their cause as his own. He believed the new administration's focus on Vietnam was misplaced when the Communist danger in Cuba was so close to home. He was particularly concerned about the lack of maintenance of the training equipment, which represented an investment of thousands of CIA dollars during the policy hiatus. Though administrative duties resumed and missions remained on the books, few operations were approved except for intelligence-gathering missions. Dissipating resolve and growing disillusionment permeated all personnel. Bradley tried to keep his commandos' spirits high by visiting often and engaging them in long bull sessions on strategy and tactics, but these increasingly turned to speculation about the new Johnson administration's Castro policy.

The CIA's mission activity vacuum was being filled by the independent exile infiltration forces. Not only were they increasing their operations, new and more militant exile groups were popping up. These served only to alarm the American officials responsible for carrying out Johnson's policy toward Cuba, such as it was. The Coast Guard, Border Patrol and Immigration authorities tightened their surveillance of Florida waters. No longer were they to turn a blind eye. Stiff penalties were imposed on raiding parties attempting to slip through the restrictive cordon.

Finally, in late 1964, Bradley's CIA superior told him that major foreign policy changes had been made: the paramilitary programs developed by the previous administration were being phased out. The commando group for which he was responsible would be given a security debriefing and be terminated with one month's pay in advance. All equipment was to be removed and the safe-houses thoroughly "swept."

Only one spark of hope remained. Manuel Artime, with CIA authorization and funding, planned to move paramilitary operations off-shore to Nicaragua. There he planned to establish a free Cuban government-in-exile and continue the struggle. He met with Bradley Ayers over the course of a few days intending to recruit him to come to Nicaragua and organize and train the commandos. Bradley was very impressed with Artime's energy and competence and immediately agreed to his proposal. But for some unknown reason, Artime's CIA funding evaporated and nothing came of the project. Still, during the two-and-a-half years Artime's program operated, they staged fourteen missions, of which four achieved their objectives.

* * *

Sometime in 1965 Cachorro came home at 3 am exhausted, bruised and bloodied and covered in mud. He'd just returned from a mission that, luckily, had only involved battling mangroves. Going into the bathroom to clean up he was startled to see his father completely naked sitting on the toilet. He'd never seen his *Papi* naked before.

Yet, the elder León displayed no embarrassment or even awkwardness. "You know, *hijo*, you're killing your mother."

Few words were exchanged. Cachorro hugged his naked father—again without the slightest trace of awkwardness and, then and there, retired from his infiltration activities. The following day he enrolled in the MBA program at the University of Florida.

Not long after that, Armandito called and asked to borrow Cachorro's '52 Ford. Armandito's car wasn't functioning and he had to get to work. Cachorro knew Armandito—he told him to take good care of it, not drive it over 60 mph and check the oil. It wasn't in the best shape and Cachorro wanted it to last. Armandito said he'd return it the next day.

It was the last time Cachorro saw his car—and Armandito, who seemed to have vanished.

Three years later the phone rang. It was Armandito. He was calling from Puerto Rico. His mother, Tita, had finally left Cuba in 1965. She was running the Peace Corps Spanish immersion course for trainees in Ponce. Armandito had moved there to be with her. Cachorro was overjoyed to hear from him. Finally, he asked Armandito about the car. Armandito, dismissively and complainingly, answered that the car wouldn't get him to work, that it had blown up and that he'd abandoned it on the side of the road—that it was *mierda*. So Cachorro asked him why he hadn't called. Armandito responded, "It didn't occur to me…"

* * *

In 1972 Armandito married Lauristela Ortíz, a stunning Puerto Rican redhead. On one of their many airline trips between San Juan and Miami, they were startled when the man seated in front of them stood up, pulled out a gallon jug of gasoline and poured it all over his seat. He then threatened to light it on fire unless the pilot diverted the flight to Havana. They were being hijacked.

It was 1984, not a propitiously numbered year. Armandito, the man unencumbered by fear, was rattled to the core, eyes bugging out, breaking into a stinky sweat—the sweat of the damned. Lauristela tried to comfort him. They then both remembered that they weren't carrying passports since a San Juan-Miami flight was a domestic milk run. Armandito would be unidentifiable to the Cuban authorities. He wouldn't be taken away in handcuffs.

Upon landing at José Martí airport, Armandito fell to his knees and kissed the Cuban tarmac. The passengers were escorted into the airport and waited until arrangements could be made to send them home. During the many hours of waiting the couple bought nearly the entire stock of Cuba T-shirts and souvenirs.

Armando 'Armandito' Lastra Faget and his wife Lauristela Ortíz. Date: Circa 2005. Source: Lauristela Ortíz collection.

Armandito and Lauristela opened and ran "El Antiguo Malecón" café in San Juan, Puerto Rico. If you're ever there, stop by, say hi and eat some great Cuban/Puerto Rican food.

Today, Armandito's mom, Tita, and Cachorro's mother-in-law, Cuca, live in Little Havana, Miami, close to their large extended family—those who had immigrated to the United States, anyway. Back in Cuba, brothers Julio and Gustavo Díaz Horta, not-too-distant cousins who'd remained close to the extended family circle, soldiered on under the Castro regime until 1980. Their lively correspondence kept us informed of deteriorating conditions on the island well into their nineties. But of our/their great uncle Fidel Otazo, only his name is remembered.

* * *

Arnaldo Remigio, the paramedic who participated in the Bay of Pigs affair in Castro's army, was an Army Reserve Battalion paramedic in

January of 1966 when he applied for an exit visa. He was forced to resign from his job. "In order to support me and my family I worked as a truck driver for heavy loads, English teacher, selling cakes door to door—cakes made by my friends who gave them to me on a consignment basis—and I smuggled them out of my apartment along with everything I could sell, even my shoes and clothing," he wrote.

He was finally allowed out of Cuba in February of 1968. Three days later, in New York City, he obtained his Social Security number and landed a job at Merrill Lynch, Pierce, Fenner and Smith. By the time he died at the age of 77 in 2015, Remigio had become Vice President of International Banking for Credit Lyonnaise Bank in NYC.

* * *

In the summer of 1963, only two-and-a-half years after it was built, Haynes Johnson and one of the leaders of Brigade 2506 returned to the Sierra Madre Mountains of Guatemala in search of Base Trax. Johnson tells what happened:

"High above the Helvetia plantation, in sight of the volcano, with the sound of River Nil far below, we reached a place where the road should have been. It had vanished. Eventually, from fearful Indian peasants in those mountains and later from Cubans who were the last to leave the camp, the story came out. Two weeks after the invasion all of the records at the camp were placed into a freshly dug hole and a bulldozer covered the hole with earth. Soon after that, Guatemalan soldiers and laborers came. They broke up the camp and carried away every last vestige—including the cement foundations for the barracks. Then the road itself was bulldozed and covered. Now the jungle has taken over and all that one might find to link that territory with the Bay of Pigs is a stray shell or perhaps a rusting can."

Operation Mongoose was, in one form, terminated in 1962; but it continued under different appellations until 1975. Noam Chomsky, no fan of the CIA or the Cuban exile efforts, has said that "it is possible that the operation [was] still ongoing [in 1989], but it certainly lasted throughout all the 70s."

PART III
INNOCENTS ABROAD

20

La Habana

The 2 am wake up call jarred in spite of already having been awake for five minutes. Years of alpine starts had finely tuned my internal alarm. The Miami-Havana charter flight left at 7:30 am, but CTS Charters required a 3 am check-in time for the 33 minute flight to Havana. God—or maybe also Castro—knows why.

All flights between the US and Cuba are special, authorized "charter flights," somehow complying with the Logan and Helms-Burton Acts. Only authorized visitors to Cuba can acquire a ticket. Becoming 'authorized,' for at least the past fifty years, required written permission from the US Treasury Department after submitting a lengthy, time-sensitive application that fit one of their, again, authorized travel categories.

President Barack Obama upended that procedure in December of 2014 by making compliance with the authorized categories "on the honor system." In other words, prior submission of an application for vetting by the US government was no longer necessary. If someone believed they fit one of the authorized categories, they could obtain a charter ticket and travel to Cuba from Miami—no questions asked. However, during the trip, they had to keep a log of all activities and expenditures, and, after their return, were subject to "the questions being asked" bit—having to justify their trip to US Customs and Immigration.

I had all my paperwork in order, in duplicate. The Cuban authorities also wanted to know what we were up to. I'd heard that the least restrictive travel categories—from the Cuban government's paranoid perspective—were the educational and religious categories. Our group of five was traveling under the Education category. We were looking at the possibility of running bicycle-based adventure education programs on the island. Though I'd qualify also as a journalist or independent researcher, these categories would have triggered the necessity for Cuban government permission with, if approved, a Cuban government minder to accompany me—and I would have to pay his expenses and salary. Since we planned to bike across the island, I'd probably also have to pay for his vehicle expenses since it would be highly unlikely that the minder would be up to biking 1,200 kilometers.

It was my impression that 'illegal' US travelers—those coming from Canada or Mexico and not obtain US government permission—were the most welcome, in the sense that dunning fees and procedures didn't apply to them. I could understand the Castro regime's thinking: to welcome US scofflaws and penalize those who complied with the laws of the imperialists. As a courtesy, Cuban immigration officials refrained from stamping US passports with Cuban visas.

* * *

At 3 am, Miami International was all but deserted. We couldn't find the CTS Charters kiosk. Tina and I were the first to show up at the spot where the kiosk was supposed to be. Roy and Brenda Smith, to save a few bucks, had opted to overnight in the airport. Up they came, dragging their duffels and bike boxes behind them.

Roy and Brenda Smith were essential to this project. Roy, a Lancashire mountaineer and adventurer with the first ascent of Alpamayo in the Andes under his belt, and many years running adventure education programs for American colleges, had introduced me to serious adventure. We'd climbed Mt. McKinley and Mt. Kenya together, kayaked the coast of Baja California and led a group down the remote Omo River in Ethiopia while it was under the regime of Mengistu Haile Mariam. We'd been friends for over 45 years. He knew the nuisance value of everything and the price of nothing. Roy's wife, Brenda, a retired schoolteacher and trekking leader kept Roy on a budget, tempered his flights of fancy and served as his *aide de memoire*. Roy had trained as a surveyor and taught survival to the British armed forces during the Mau Mau rebellion in Kenya. As a sideline, he'd smuggled explosives into Somalia for walking-around money.

Tina Cobos, my lover, a biker, climber, kayaker, river guide and real estate agent watched my back and never failed to bring a smile to the sourest grump—which Roy and I could turn into at times. She had a degree in electronics; I had a Master's in Anthropology.

George Yen, the fifth biker of our group, was Taiwanese and had recently retired as president of Toastmaster's International, but still ran his industrial pipe fittings factory and import/export businesses in Taipei. Flying straight from Taiwan, he'd meet us in Havana. He'd been my roommate in college and, a few years back, had hosted Tina and me when we biked the perimeter road of Taiwan. He was due to turn 70 while in Cuba. This trip was a celebration. His Master's degree was in Foreign Relations and he was more or less fluent in Mandarin, Hakka, English and Spanish.

Roy and Brenda, self-described "democratic" socialists, would make for lively companions and foils to Tina's and mine anarcho-capitalist libertarianism—grist for any writing projects any of us might contemplate. This trip, after all, wasn't just about biking in a living museum or plumbing the depths of my own fading memories; it was an empirical expedition into the 20th century's most transformative ideologies as experienced on the ground by competing perspectives. George, a *noblese oblige* industrialist, would temper our rhetorical excesses.

* * *

Pretty soon a uniformed guy muscled a podium across the terrazzo floor and placed it by a column next to us. It read CTS Charters. An old man came up to me and asked in Spanish if Tina, Roy, Brenda and myself constituted the *cola*, or line, for the check in.

Slowly, the *cola* grew with modestly dressed Cubans, all relatives of island residents, I surmised, lugging improbable goods to their kin: truck tires wrapped in cellophane, collapsed baby trams, window-mounted air conditioners, Costo-sized boxes of diapers and such.

Finally a white-shirted attendant showed up to man the podium and signaled us forward. She was having a bad morning and insisted on sharing it. After silently reviewing our paperwork she motioned us over to a free-standing scale to have our luggage weighed, after which our bike boxes and duffels disappeared. The weighing attendant signaled us over to a permanent kiosk along a wall whose neon signboard now lit up with "CTS Charters."

More waiting: computer problems. When the second kiosk opened for business, two shiny-suited, strongly-cologned men with gold rings, salamander grins, slicked-back hair and no luggage cut in front of us up to the dais. All smiles and good humor with the attendant, boarding passes quickly in hand, they exited left. It was our turn.

Now came the shakedown. CTS Charters (and for that matter, all the Miami-Havana charters) have complex, expensive, and low-weight baggage allotments—including carry-ons! Excess baggage charges run as high as $4 per pound. Together, including our bikes, Tina and I had 170 lbs. Our excess baggage bill came to $550. Argue as I did, it was useless: CTS configured the excess baggage formula so it skewed in their favor. I felt assaulted without foreplay. I wondered how much the guy with the truck tires had to pay. Roy bragged that his bill was lower—by $75; he'd packed their bikes in light cardboard boxes. More waiting.

At 7 am sharp, we began boarding. Our plane, the label "X-Tra Airlines" painted on its tail, was a single-aisled, four-seats-abreast, short-run affair. I kept my eyes glued to the window, wanting to examine closely the infamous 90 miles that separated our two countries; the 90 miles so many had risked their lives crossing on derelict fishing boats, cobbled wooden rafts and inner tubes for a better life; the 90 miles so many had lost their lives on due to too much sun, not enough water, an uncooperative Gulf Stream, piscine sharks and olive-clad sharks.

When the Cuban coast and countryside came into view my heart skipped a beat. It had been 56 years since I'd left. Rancho Boyeros airport—now José Martí airport—is a small affair. It was now painted orange. After a smooth landing, blue-clad workers wheeled stairs up to the plane's door. The passengers filed out.

On the steps' platform I took a deep breath of the Cuban air and gathered my bearings. When I reached the tarmac I didn't exactly kiss the Cuban ground, though my tears did.

But I couldn't indulge the moment. I was leading a group whose command of Spanish didn't extend much beyond *sí* and *no*; was possibly smuggling in a computer for Tondy and Tania, my very distant relatives and our hosts in Havana; and was about to face Passport Control and Customs in a police state.

Inside the large foyer fronting Passport Control, tiny aisles lined one side of the room in front of the Passport Control officers' glass booths. Short lines of RoadsScholar—previously Elderhostel (a fine outfit I'd previously worked for)—American tourists on group educational excursions crowded the aisles. All wore black scapulary name tags with the RoadsScholar logo. Our group was conspicuous for its lack of name tags, a detail immediately noticed by a khaki-clad, official-looking young man with a clipboard.

I wondered to where the Cuban-American passengers had been herded. The Castro government considers anyone born in Cuba, regardless of their present nationality, a Cuban, and one subject to special, onerous rules. They'd probably been herded into a different foyer.

While I was sussing out the situation, the man with the clipboard approached Roy and Brenda and, in highly accented English, asked what the purpose of their trip was. When Roy innocently blurted out, pointing at me, that he and I were writers, Tina ran to the rescue.

I'd warned all of us to stick to the Educational Prospectus I'd drawn up; that any other purpose—especially 'writer'—would open up a can of worms and possibly ruin the entire trip. I suspect that Roy didn't take the admonition seriously, was simply careless or just forgot. Tina blurted out that we were actually teachers and would later have to 'write up' our reports. By this time I'd reached the group.

The young man asked to see our itinerary and proposal. I swamped him with paperwork—multiple printed pages of both documents, along with letters of sponsorship from two colleges and a university, and lengthy personal resumés for all of us. In my best faux English-accented Spanish I summarized their contents. The man gave the documents a cursory look, made some notes, returned them to me and asked if we were carrying any electronic devices.

Roy pulled out his camera, his cell phone and his tablet. The young man made a note of them. Then Brenda did the same thing, followed by Tina. When the official got to me, I pulled out my camera and was about to pull out the Lenovo Chromebook I'd brought for Tondy when the man lost interest, stopped taking notes, said he was through with us and motioned us into Passport Control.

Whew!

When my turn came, the Passport Control officer fixed me with such a prolonged intimidating stare, that I steeled myself for the G2 to bust in and haul me off for questioning. After what seemed much longer than the five minutes the procedure took, he finally dismissed me. Out that door, we entered a large room with only two luggage carousels for Havana's international airport. It was crowded with many uniformed female militia and all the recent arrivals milling about awaiting their stuff. Two hours later, our bike boxes appeared—dead last, and only after Tina had slipped into the back and prodded someone with a smile and a kind word.

In contrast, Customs was European-style: If a passenger had nothing to declare, out he went on his honor! We couldn't believe it.

Currency exchange was next. Cuban banks and currency exchange kiosks accept Canadian dollars, Euros, Sterling and US dollars for exchange into Convertible Pesos (CUC), which are priced at par with US dollars. However, US dollars are burdened with a 10% commission—another way to exercise displeasure toward the imperialist monster up north. So we'd brought Euros to Cuba to exchange.

Confusingly, Cuba has a separate, "local" currency also labeled 'pesos.' Each of these *moneda nacional* pesos (CUP) is worth about four cents. This currency is used to pay wages and is accepted at stores that provide rationed goods, to which every Cuban is entitled with his ration booklet. The fiction is that local pesos at ration stores are on purchasing power parity with convertible pesos, a fiction that is now official—or being eliminated (your choice)—with the new, hopeful policy of combining the two currencies.

The problem is that subsidized, rationed goods are in scarce supply; those goods gravitate toward convertible peso stores where prices are more realistic. No matter how hard the government tries to control supply, demand exerts a strong force. And now that convertible peso stores are open to all who can afford them, the force of demand is getting even stronger. The cheaper ration stores always have long queues of expectant buyers and few items available. Distinguishing between CUCs and CUPs can be a challenge to the inexperienced tourist, particularly when one receives mixed notes for change after a purchase.

One American biking tourist who visited—illegally—in the 1990s, when shortages of household items were common, was afflicted with Montezuma's, er, Fidel's revenge. Unable to obtain toilet paper—or any suitable substitute—he accumulated the $3 peso *moneda nacional* graced with *Che* Guevara's face. He was no fan of the Argentine and experienced great satisfaction using those notes as a substitute.

Tondy, our B&B host—and very distant relative—and his brother had come to pick us up at the airport. They'd been waiting for four hours when we finally exited the terminal. I'd sent him a picture of Tina and me so he could identify us. He'd brought two vehicles, one legal, and the other one, a non-descript old Studebaker that was not authorized to transport tourists. It had a Toyota steering wheel; had to be pushed to start; and the doors had to be held closed while driving. The Studebaker was his brother's and it was parked two blocks away so as to avoid detection by the airport police.

Distribution blackboard at a ration store in Trinidad. The subsidized staples available here can only be bought with a ration coupon and moneda nacional (CUP pesos). The store is out of the following staples: beans, cigarettes, matches, baby food, toothpaste, eggs, and soap. Date: February, 2016. Credit: Roy Smith.

* * *

The legal taxi was an old Willy's Jeep, lovingly maintained with an added custom rear cab suitable for six passengers Black María-style or, in this case, four bike boxes. We loaded these up. I got in and off we rode with Tondy's brother to get his illegal taxi. We parked a block away from it and waited for a call from Tondy notifying us that the airport police were busy busting someone else, an almost continuous affair. This was the signal for Tondy's brother to hie in and pick up Tondy, Tina, Roy and Brenda.

The drive into central Havana was a feast of sights and smells: old cars with retrofitted diesel engines and diesel trucks and buses, the black smoke pouring out of their exhausts failing to ruin the ride; horse drawn carts and bikes everywhere, but all the traffic light. Impatient to test my rusty Cuban Spanish, I engaged my driver—politics and economics, of course; some degree of trust having already been established from the mere fact that Tondy had engaged him and he was complicit in Tondy's brother's illegal cab.

The driver raved about his new enterprise. He was his own boss and could work as much or as little as he wanted. He loved his Jeep. Expressing his pride in his new life (the self-employed reforms having only been passed in 2010) he bemoaned the lack of motivation in most of the government work force saying, "Workers don't love their work; only the self-employed love their work." Then he interrupted himself to point out Mazorra, the big Havana insane asylum.

As a kid, I'd pass by it on the way to or from the airport or my dad's VW plant, located in the neighborhood. Mazorra was a kind of trope for being crazy, used in any number of ways associated with a joking accusation of eccentricity or worse. I took pictures of it, one of the few buildings along the drive to be well maintained, and one that would envelop my sisters, aunts and cousins in nostalgia—the way it was doing so to me now.

I asked him if he thought the reforms and rapprochement with the US would last. "We can't go back," he said, "Fidel educated us and now we're onto him."

We passed the *Palacio de los Deportes*, the big stadium where the dissidents and suspected dissidents from the big prophylactic round-up just before the Bay of Pigs invasion had been held; and later, where Armandito, Cachorro and the rest of the Brigade 2506 prisoners had first been incarcerated. Banners announced an upcoming soccer tournament.

The driver noticed my rubbernecking at nearly everything, especially women. He told me, "Cuba is the land of beautiful butts." I agreed with him, noting that anthropologist Oscar Lewis' pioneering studies of sexuality in Puerto Rico and the Revolution in Cuba, rated Puerto Ricans as the most highly sexed people in the world, with Cubans coming in a close second.

* * *

Tania, Tondy's wife, welcomed me as if I were long lost family, which in a sense I was. Tondy's aunt was my cousin Alina's nanny until Alina left Cuba. Tondy's father is Alina's nanny's brother. Alina's nanny is still alive in Cuba and Alina keeps in contact with her. Alina told me, "You used to know her; obviously you can't remember her."

Tondy has 7 siblings, one of them is Dunia. When Dunia arrived in Miami, she made contact with Alina through her aunt, Alina's nanny. Dunia had no family here in the US, just her husband and son, who at that time was 5 years old. Alina took Dunia under her wing. Alina, and by extension the rest of our family, are her only family in the US. Dunia tells everyone Alina is their godmother. Alina takes up the story:

> *"When things began to get complicated with Tita's and Cuca's health, she started working for us as caregivers. Already 5 years have passed. She adores las viejas, and for that we are so thankful she crossed our path. Very special lady. The ironies of life: who could have predicted that the family who cared for me until adolescence would have later cared for my mother with the same love they cared for me."*

Tondy's and Tania's house was nearly completely encased by other structures. It shared walls with the adjoining houses on each side, had another dwelling atop and backed up to another building. It was long, deep and narrow, but the aisle that connected all the rooms was unroofed and open to the sky. The entire block, on both sides, were row houses except that not all were homes and not all were alike. The structures were anywhere from 50 to over 100 years old, and backed up to Havana's famous Malecón, the seawall bookended by Morro Castle. The home faced a narrow, very busy street redolent with the by-now sickening diesel fumes.

Tondy's family's big luxury was a flat-screen TV in front of which Tania's mother sat all day watching pirated cable channels from Miami. These are widely available for a $10 per month subscription fee. Even though they're illegal, the authorities turn a blind eye to them. Tania remarked that those in charge of enforcing the regulations were probably regular subscribers. She added that, "Here in Cuba we have nothing; but we have the latest."

Since their B&B had only opened for business the previous November, Tondy had kept his government job in the gastronomy department of the Tourism Ministry while Tania took charge of the B&B.

After settling in—Tondy and Tania having moved Tania's mom out of a bedroom to make room for all of us, in spite of government regulations restricting private B&Bs to only two guest rooms—we set about putting the bikes together. Diego, their three-year-old son insisted on helping, carrying on a dialogue that was more monologue, oblivious to most of our group's lack of Spanish, and inspecting every tool as if it were a Faberge egg. His interest in the Etch-a-Sketch and Slinky I'd brought him for his birthday didn't last long.

When he reached school age, Tania wanted to send him to a private school, the state schools, in her opinion, being useless and full of meaningless propaganda. But she was terrified of doing so. Private schools were illegal. The one in her neighborhood moved around constantly, meeting in different homes at different times, the teacher always evading detection and arrest. She was glad she didn't have to face that decision yet.

George Yen, the fifth member of our group, was due in the next day when we were scheduled to take the overnight bus at midnight to Baracoa on Cuba's far eastern end to begin our cross-island ride. But for now we headed out to test the bikes, register at the US and UK embassies and obtain an internet card for our tablets.

On the way out the door Tania admonished me to put on a helmet, like the rest of our group had donned. Prior to the trip we'd discussed whether to take biking helmets. Cuba's highways are nearly empty of traffic and there is no helmet law. Cuban bikers don't wear helmets unless they're part of a sports team. Brenda, a doctrinaire helmet advocate, was adamant about wearing hers and Roy wearing his. I suspected Tania was unfamiliar with biking helmets so I asked her why I ought to wear one. "To protect you from the sun," she said. "The Cuban sun is strong."

I told her I had a hat for the sun, but that for now we were only going for a short ride along a traffic-free street, and I explained the function of the helmets on the rest of our group's heads: to protect the head in case of an accident. She gave me a look that said, 'that's a new one on me,' and added a common Cuban saying when exposed to a novel idea: "*Mira que los blancos inventan!*" (Roughly, 'What will white people come up with next!')

The Malecón was closed to traffic. Northwesterlies were pouring breakers over the sea wall. Traffic cones and police enforced the closure. But pedestrians—joggers, tourists, fishermen, saxophone players, lovers and dreamers—still walked the sea wall promenade. We'd been told not to photograph or engage uniformed personnel. But I thought it appropriate to ask permission from one, "Could we ride our bikes down the untrafficked boulevard to the US Embassy?" The cop said—in quite the formal demeanor—yes, but admonished us to be careful.

On the way over we passed many landmarks: the Havana Hilton Hotel where Fidel had first set up headquarters after his victory in 1959 and the Hotel Nacional, which my grandfather helped build in the 1930s. In front stood the monument to the sailors killed on the USS Maine in 1898, an explosion that precipitated the Spanish-American War and led to Cuba's independence. Close by, a statue to Calixto García, a general in three of Cuba's indepence uprisings and once buried at Arlington National Cemetery, faced the Florida Straits. These monuments didn't mean much to my companions, but a Malecón-side, thoroughly restored bar did; and Tina and Brenda wanted to try a real mojito.

Hotel Nacional, built in 1930 under President Machado. Author's grandfather is reputed to have been a contractor in the project. In front and to the left is the Monument to the 'USS Maine', the sinking of which was the 'casus belli' for the Spanish American War, which led to Cuba's independence from Spain. Credit: R. H. Miller.

The buildings fronting the Malecón are all row-style, sharing adjoining walls. However, some are collapsing (according to *Moon Handbooks*, almost 100 important colonial houses collapse a year in Havana), some are in disrepair, some have been restored, and some are under restoration. Some of the ones that look completely decrepit from the outside nestle homes or businesses inside. One sign along the boulevard boasts that restoration of the Malecón, which began in 2002, is an ongoing project. Styles vary from colonial to catch-as-catch-can. One restored bit of row building boasts a Russian restaurant whose waiters walk the sidewalks with meal deal signs boasting the wonders of Russian cuisine (what? 'Turnips and mud'?).

More than 900 of old Havana's 3,157 structures are of historic significance. As *Moon Handbooks* reports, "Only 101 were built in the 20th century. Almost 500 are from the 19th; 200 are from the 18th; and 144 are from the 16th and 17th. Only one in six is in good condition. Most are crumbling into ruins around the people who occupy them."

A plan for the restoration of the old city was instituted in 1997. Through the efforts of Eusebio Leal Spengler, the official city historian and man in charge of reconstruction, Habana Vieja was designated a UNESCO World Heritage Site in 1982, attracting foreign donations. Leal, a powerful member of the Central Committee, triages the rescue effort. Museums and public buildings are his number one priority, followed by hotels, restaurants, and schools. Housing comes in dead last. Without proper property rights, even with the recent reforms, many residents of buildings slated for renovation end up being relocated against their will into modern but soulless slums far from their old neighborhoods.

One example of the latter is the multi-story building fronting the *capitolio*, Cuba's capitol building. All the residents have been told to move out. My informant, a realtor (more on that improbable occupation below), had no idea whether they'd receive compensation, new digs, or what. He didn't know what plans the government had for the building.

On the other hand, the *Gran Teatro* (my grandfather John Maurice's first construction commission) is an absolutely stunning example of the second category. Perfectly restored to its original condition complete with floating statuary, balconies and recesses, and pinpoint nighttime lighting, it resembles a giant, multi-storied baroque confection from the Belle Epoque. Always packed with foreign tourists, Roy, our Lancashire native, couldn't stay away.

And yes, that 'realtor.' On a walk along the Prado, Havana's pedestrian promenade connecting the *capitolio* with Morro Castle, Tina and I ran into him. His 'office' was an ad hoc-appropriated, built-in bench along the alameda; his desk a paper-laden clipboard; his offerings and sign displayed on a hand-held, one-sided clapboard. He'd been a university economics professor. Though we'd seen many 'For Sale' signs on many buildings, including the humblest of abodes, we saw no real estate offices. The bench he was occupying wasn't his; it was just an available spot among the licensed art and trinket vendors along the Prado. I excitedly elbowed my wife Tina, a realtor in Arizona, to engage her interest.

Bad move.

A middleman agent of finance—the epitome of freewheeling capitalism—just didn't fit into her perception of a socialist economy. Either the man was deluded or he was a scammer (an unlikely scenario: the police are ruthless with physical and financial crimes). I insisted on us engaging the man. Immediately she confronted him with, "How can you own property in Cuba when there are no property rights and the state can confiscate your property at any time for any reason?"

Havana real estate agent with sign on Prado promenade, 2016.
Credit: R. H. Miller.

The poor man, without a vestige of the ingeniousness of an American used-car-salesman, took on a pained and thoughtful look. He didn't know where to start, but he understood that Tina had zeroed in on the heart of the matter. Translating his response was an exercise in empathy. He told us of the building across the street from the *capitolio* whose residents had just been told by the government to move out: the government needed the space. He didn't know whether compensation, alternative housing or even a grace period had been granted. He was the first to admit that Cuba had no property rights and no judicial system to enforce them. Nonetheless, what was he to do? New laws, albeit extremely constricted, allowed for the buying and selling of cars and real property. No mortgages were available; only cash transactions. Interest is still illegal. But he was making four-times the salary he'd made at the university. He had nothing but hope and an optimistic outlook, "This time the people will not let the changes be reversed."

I reminded him of the roadside billboards that read, "The changes in progress are for MORE SOCIALISM"—a sure sign, he counterintuitively agreed, along with Obama's upcoming visit—that the changes now have a better chance of sticking than any previous promises.

"The changes in Cuba are for MORE SOCIALISM."
Credit: R. H. Miller.

* * *

When we returned to Tondy's, we packed our bike panniers for the trip and left for the bus station at 3 pm. Although the bus didn't leave until midnight, we didn't want to ride our bikes at night. The Viazul bus station was located in my old neighborhood. I planned to use the intervening time to visit my family's home and old haunts.

In the meantime, George hadn't arrived yet. His flight had been delayed. We left a message that we'd await him in Baracoa, where we were going to spend an extra day; or he could catch up somewhere along the way.

Our little bike convoy kept a tight file, passing by the US Embassy, the North Korean and Vietnamese Embassies, the Hotel Meliá Cohiba—Havana's plushest—and the Cementerio Colón where my grandmother was buried. I was leading the group, concentrating on traffic, street names and turns when suddenly, totally unexpectedly, there on the left, I saw the Cine Acapulco where I'd gone to the movies as a kid. I was taken totally by surprise. I skidded to a stop and nearly fell over trying to place a foot on the kerb.

Acapulco movie theatre. Unchanged since 1959. Credit: R. H. Miller.

It hadn't changed at all. I stood and stared. I took pictures. I had a surreal sense of displaced reality, as if awoken from a dream that had suddenly become real. I focused on the ticket window, where we'd waited in line so often, and the marquee, where we'd always glanced when driving by to find out what new movies were showing. Holographic memories from the past alternated in quick succession with the present view—like subliminal adverts. I knew we were close to home now.

I grabbed a hold of myself and attended to the traffic. A deep gulp, a quickening of heart and a dream-like perception clouding my empiricism didn't help. Familiar sights were popping up in quick succession—sights half-remembered and half-forgotten, and only half-altered by the passage of time. There, off to the right under an awning, was the café kiosk where I'd shared a coffee with Pop sixty years ago.

When we got to the zoo I turned in blindly, unthinkingly, looking for the peanut vendors that had hawked, "*Maní, manicero!*" at the entrance. I headed for the gate without consulting our group, simply telling them to wait outside. It was 4:30 pm. They'd just closed admission to new entrants. Those still inside would be herded out at 6 pm.

I just had to see the croc and cayman pool near the entry; to see how much my memory coincided with reality. I begged and cajoled, explaining that I'd grown up here, that my old home was up the hill, that I'd just returned after 56 years, and that our bus left at midnight. "Could I just look at the croc pool?"

One of the attendants (they were all dressed in military uniforms) whispered to come back in three minutes. I walked over to my group and explained, then walked back to the entry gate. The boss had just left and the man who'd told me to return in a trice invited me in. "I can't not welcome you. Welcome back." He said the pools were still well-stocked and escorted me around them. Crocs, alligators and caymans were each in separate enclosures. I told him about the old custom of throwing coins on the crocs' backs. None of the reptiles had any coins today. "People can't afford that any more," he responded.

Afterward, we headed up the hill, past the Viazul bus depot to look for my home. I was determined to find it on my own. The neighborhood, Alturas del Vedado, is the highest landform in Havana (except for El Príncipe castle) and bordered a side canyon of the Almendares River. So, hellbent for frenzy, I headed for the highest point, an exercise that, with fully-loaded bikes tested the patience of our group. The first uphill street dead-ended at a military base. The guard's glare unnerved me—after all, there was no reason for a foreign biker to be anywhere near the base. After a couple more hills that led nowhere I wanted to be, I decided to ask directions. Trouble was, the name Alturas del Vedado had changed and everyone I asked couldn't remember it. But it was still a well-treed neighborhood filled mostly with stand-alone, large single family homes.

I tried asking for the cross streets: 36th Street, corner of 43rd. One old lady vaguely pointed me in one direction. She wasn't sure; this area of Havana was definitely not on a grid system—too many hills. Going up 36th Street, I passed a building that looked vaguely familiar; it resembled the large home of a childhood friend. Now it looked like apartments. And then, before I recognized anything, there on the sidewalk was a ziggurat-shaped stele with 36 on one side and 43 on the other. I looked up and there was our house, behind a block wall with a sign that read *Ministerio de Capacitación e Investigaciones* under the seal of Cuba.

I was now really fast-forwarding in slow motion, the clutches of a thousand emotions and memories grabbing for my attention. A uniformed guard at the gate asked what we wanted. I told him I'd grown up in the house he was guarding. He was two years younger than me and had lived in the neighborhood since he was a kid. He immediately took to me and recounted neighborhood gossip—who'd lived where and when. The house was now an advanced training school for mid-level bureaucrats. He couldn't let me into the house, but he offered to take only me all the way around it, inside the block fence. I could look in the windows and take pictures, but I couldn't take a photo of him—he'd get in trouble.

Author's home in Havana, 2016. Cuban guard, author and Brenda Smith. Credit: Tina Cobos.

I shared my memories with him, including memories of the trees that had graced the yards—the mango I'd climbed and fallen out of, the breadfruit I'd tormented my sister with, the flamboyant that had created a shady canopy over the entire back yard. He knew exactly why and when they had either died or been cut down. It was a consolation that all three had died of old age or disease. However, no new trees had been planted. Instead, the house was aggressively being added on to, with construction extending onto the *solar*, or empty lot, adjacent, which used to be my favorite hang-out. The swimming pool was full of demolition debris.

Two months before my grandmother's death in 1962, the Cuban government had inventoried all the home's accouterments. Two months after her death—and just before the Cuban Missile Crisis—they returned and took all the furniture and air conditioners. They found $800 dollars in cash stashed inside the units. Carmen, our *tata*, and her family were kicked out while "some Russians" (according to my aunt Marta) moved in. Carmen was relocated to an apartment.

After reminiscing with the guard I walked the old neighborhood with my companions, pointing out our first house—the one Pop had rented to David Atlee Phillips, the CIA agent—and the other houses whose occupants I'd known, recounting their stories. It was apparent that people of importance lived along these streets; all the homes were immaculately maintained with fresh coats of paint and attractive landscaping.

By this time Roy had had his fill of Cuban nostalgia, so we headed for the bus station where I queued up at the ticket counter. The lobby was full of Canadian and European tourists; Cubans mostly travel by truck in cargo holds modified for passengers. When I got to the front of the line the attendant told me we'd missed the bus. It was scheduled for 12 noon, not 12 midnight—never mind that our tickets didn't specify am or pm—plus she wouldn't credit our old tickets for new ones. This was Thursday; the next bus to Baracoa with open seats didn't leave until Monday—at noon.

We swallowed our disappointment, mounted our bikes and rushed back to Tondy's before it became totally dark (or he'd unexpectedly rented out our rooms).

* * *

The delay wasn't completely unwelcome. George finally showed up, though his bike didn't. And it gave us more time to explore Havana, extend our visas and get an internet card, available from the state monopoly provider, Etecsa, or from authorized hawkers at wi-fi spots, usually located in designated parks. Though guidebooks report that visa extensions are easy to get, for a variety of hair-pulling details, Catch-22s, and extra, collateral expenses, they are not. Try as we might, after six visits to different immigration offices, we never succeeded.

So I set out to find my grandmother in the Colón Cemetery, 138 acres of tombs, chapels, vaults and mausoleums containing about a million deceased. It's laid out in a grid pattern that is 45 degrees off the surrounding street grid giving it the impression of great antiquity, though it was only laid out in 1871. I had no idea where she might be resting. She'd died and been buried about a year after we'd left.

Outside the necropolis' ornate gate, a street sweeper sat in the shade, taking a break, smoking a cigar. Garbage, like many things in Cuba, is full of contradictions. Cubans are a very clean people. One informant told me that trash collectors are particularly well-paid. In general, the streets are quite clean. But… Mounds of garbage dot cities, towns and the countryside every once in a while, almost as if they've been warehoused in discreet piles and then forgotten.

I struck up a conversation with him. He was pushing a two-binned push cart and sweeping with a hand-made broom. He had a very photogenic face with bright blue eyes and was chewing on the stoggie. Intermittently picking up trash—there wasn't much—and sitting in the shade, his proud demeanor and fit physique caught my eye. After some introductory remarks and typical Cuban give-and-take I asked if I could photograph him. He was proud to be so noticed and posed as if he were about to be on TV. Apropos of nothing, he declared, "We want capitalism back." I asked him to elaborate. He said things were much better before the Revolution; there was more opportunity, more dynamism and more wealth.

The offices of the cemetery consisted of a high-ceilinged room with three sets of tall double doors—all open—and about a dozen desks haphazardly occupied. Everyone was dressed casually: shorts, T-shirts, blouses and slacks. All were drinking beer. One man was holding forth bombastically, declaring that they were lucky, that even though they hadn't been paid in weeks, the grave diggers and gardeners hadn't been paid in months. No one said a word. I found out later that he was the manager.

I queued up in front of a desk where a woman was answering phones and talking to someone who'd come through the door. She asked what I wanted. I told her I was looking for my grandmother's grave and that, no, I didn't know where it was or even exactly when she died, other than 1962. She told me to take a seat and someone would soon help me. The manager offered me a beer. Not one for sitting, I paced.

Cuban street sweeper, 2016. Credit: R. H. Miller.

A half-hour later, Yulesy, a beautiful young *mulata*, said she could research my grandmother, but that it was a big undertaking and that a little gift—Cuban government wages being $1-2 per day—would be greatly appreciated. I readily agreed. After another half-hour wait she came back out and invited me in to the stacks in the back room. She told me to bring my bike.

All four walls of the 16-foot-ceilinged room were packed with folios and tomes, many brown, tattered and torn, holding the cemetery's records. Nothing was computerized or even on microfiche. A large oak conference table dominated the center of the room. There must have been other, similar rooms to hold the records of a million souls.

I steadied the ladder while Yulesy climbed up to reach a folio and hand it to me. Then two more—the records for 1962—and we began a page-by-page search for Ana María Díaz y Otazo. After a folio-and-a-half I spotted her name. For an instant, time stopped. I stared at the cursive writing on the tattered, yellowed page, the entry connecting me to a memory of her stern visage—now mostly remembered from old photographs—and her kind demeanor. Yulesy interrupted my reverie, saying that the entry in this folio led to another folio where her death certificate and burial details were recorded. I helped her get the next tome down.

Cementerio Colón (cemetery) archives, Havana, Cuba. Keny, the gravedigger on left; Yulesy on right, 2016. Credit: R. H. Miller.

There it was. Page #515, entry #2057 dated July 16, 1960. Nineteen-sixty!! The scribe had filled in the blank after *mil novecientos* with *sesenta* and had forgotten to add the *y dos*.

I pulled out my camera to photograph the pages. Yulesy motioned me not to; her boss had just entered the room and photos were not allowed—the records were confidential. Nonetheless, he kindly allowed me two photos, one from each tome. Yulesy wrote down the location of the grave for me. I told her it was meaningless. The cemetery was a maze; would she please lead me to it?

On the walk over, a gravedigger, Keny, joined us and complained about not getting paid. His salary was $10 a month, way less than the commonly reported rate. Yulesy, half jokingly, asked if I'd take her to the US with me, and told me about her 2-year-old son; that he was very cute and not as dark as her—lighter, like her colleague—and had blonde hair. The gravedigger said no, the kid was as black as her though he did have blonde hair, albeit nappy. I told them about my own African heritage. She asked that I take a picture of the boy back to the US with me to give to relatives. It had taken 20 minutes to find *abuela's* grave.

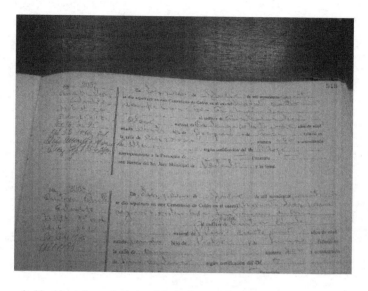

Archival burial record of Ana María Díaz y Otazo, author's grandmother, in Cementerio Colón. Credit: R. H. Miller.

Ana María Díaz y Otázo had been born before Cuban Independence: she'd been a Spanish citizen. She'd died without us, her family. I had no idea how her burial had been organized or who attended. If her death certificate had been filled out incorrectly, what else had gone wrong?

A letter dated July 18, 1962—two days after her death—from Carmen, our *tata*, who along with her family had moved in with my grandmother so she wouldn't lose the house, recounted *abuela's* final days. The four-page letter, written on onionskin paper, was nearly illegible, with tight, cursive, down-trending tiny penmanship; its stream of consciousness perfectly captured the atmosphere of a painful death. She'd been suffering from acute diverticulitis and was in agony, pain medication being already scarce. Carmen and the rump household staff took turns at her bedside holding her hand and comforting her. *Abuela* said she was ready for death. Eddy, my mother's Communist cousin, was a great solace, coming by often to visit. Carmen said that the doctor had refused payment; and added that 'things' were dire in Cuba.

Somehow, Tita had been involved, though she'd had her hands full with her son, Armandito, and her brother-in-law, Pillo, both in prison, and her parents sickly. Every Sunday she'd joined *abuela* for lunch, a ritual they both very much looked forward to. Tita managed to find half a grave for her aunt—my grandmother—who must have been buried in the fetal position. I couldn't image my portly, formal grandmother curled up like that. I tried to imagine those times, those difficulties. I lingered at the grave, taking pictures, letting the moment brand itself into my consciousness.

The author at his grandmother's grave in the Cementerio Colón, Havana, Cuba.
Credit: Tina Cobos.

I offered Yulesy $5. She said no, to wait; she needed to play politics with her boss and insisted I give it to her in front of him and give him a tip also. Terrified to do that, I argued with her. The last thing I wanted to do was bribe a government official, a serious offense in Cuba. I told her that her boss was "a loose canon," a term I had to explain to her. She laughed and explained that, *after* a favor, the offering was a thank-you gift. In contrast, bribes always preceded a favor. Back at the offices, the three of us went into the back room. The manager shut the door. I gave Yulesy $5 and offered him $1. He thanked me and shook my hand.

* * *

On the ride back to Tondy's, I met my first beggar. He was a wheelchair-bound amputee with only one leg. I asked him if he was a veteran of the Angola war. He said, no, it had been a car accident that took his leg. He gratuitously added that, "Cuban health care sucks. I spit on Fidel." Down the road, a young man, a male nurse it turned out, asked how much my bike cost. He said he'd traded in a similar quality bike for a laptop. He and his wife had applied to immigrate to Canada. I warned him that Canada's health care system was, in principle, no different than Cuba's. He said he knew that, but that going to Canada was only a step to reaching the US: it was much easier to get into Canada. They were awaiting a Canadian OK; they'd already received a Cuban exit visa which, as a consequence, had cost them their jobs.

My next project was to visit El Príncipe Castle, where the Bay of Pigs Brigade had been imprisoned. Guidebooks barely, if ever, mention it. Along the way I rode by the University of Havana, where Tita, her brother, and Fidel Castro had attended at the same time in the 1940s. The multiple cascading steps spoke volumes, recalling all the old photographs of past failed coups, including one of Castro's, which had sparked and fizzled right there.

I couldn't see El Príncipe. I rode my bike all the way around where it was supposed to be. Atop a tall but not too steep a hill, the castle was invisible behind the trees, buildings and slope. Riding up the one access road, I reached the gate. In my best fractured Spanish I asked the guard if El Príncipe, the famous 18th century Spanish fort, lay inside. The guard took one look at me and told me to go away, the area was restricted.

It was Sunday. Pope Francis and Russian Orthodox Patriarch Kirill had met in Havana on Friday. It was the first such meeting in 1,000 years since the schism that separated Christianity into Eastern and Western branches. Pope Francis was keen on reunification; Patriarch Kirill, not so much. Cuba was considered neutral ground for the convocation. The boulevard along the Malecón was closed, I surmised, for a popemobile parade. Police lined the sidewalks. I asked one if the pope had come by yet. He looked at me and replied flippantly, "*El papa y la malanga!*"

Papa means 'pope' or 'potato.' *Malanga* is a very starchy root vegetable that tastes like a potato on steroids. The cop's double entendre was a combination of his disdain for the pope and religion, and his sense of humor with the rich tradition of Cuban word play, with just a touch of assonance and rhyme.

Back at the B&B, George's bike had finally shown up. He'd had to visit the airport twice and entreat the man in charge to help him. It helped that George was Taiwanese and could get by in Spanish. With a little detective work he determined that the bike was stuck in Los Angeles, due to a confusion with airport code labels. After it was delivered, we all pitched in and helped put it together for our Baracoa departure the next day. Though he'd been on many organized bike tours, George was no hands-on adept.

That afternoon we all set out for a shakedown ride to the *capitolio*, Cuba's magnificent capitol building. Surrounded by scaffolding all the way up its cupola, it was as if my grandfather's work had never been completed. Originally intended for Cuba's Chamber of Representatives and Senate, today it stands empty and closed, a mute monument to Fidel Castro's disdain for democracy. Nominally the *capitolio* is the home of Cuba's Academy of Science. The reconstruction is meant to house Cuba's National Assembly sometime in the future. Try as we might, the guard in front wouldn't let us ascend the steps for a closer experience.

On the way back, George insisted on riding through Havana's Chinatown. Chinese immigrants first settled in Cuba at about the same time they went to the US to help build the railroads. Some California Chinese even later moved to Cuba after accumulating fortunes, fleeing increasing persecution in the US. At one time, Havana's *Barrio Chino* was the largest in Latin America. But the vast majority of the Chinese (and Jewish) communities left Cuba soon after the Revolution in 1960, wealth accumulation not being a revolutionary virtue.

Today only about 400 Chinese remain along with perhaps 2,000 descendants. Nonetheless, George was able to find one, speak a little Mandarin with him and treat himself to a dim sum.

21

El Oriente

Viazul buses are modern, comfortable Chinese exports. Viazul carries bicycles for a nominal fee. The driver, welcoming us, stated that we'd stop for meals, breaks, and scheduled stops, but, unfortunately, the toilets didn't work. If anyone needed a bathroom break, to please notify him and he'd pull over, adding, "We've asked the Chinese to come and fix the toilets, but they've forgotten us. I don't think the Chinese love us anymore."

The sixteen-hour, overnight bus ride was better than most cabin-class airplane rides. We arrived in Baracoa at 6 am dingy with sleepless disorientation and stiffness. A blazing orange sun rising out of the Caribbean next to El Yunque, Baracoa's iconic table-top peak, greeted us. The air was hot and muggy, the dense vegetation extending encroaching tendrils into the town. Manuel, our B&B host, was there to meet us. He led us along Baracoa's malecón to his home.

Baracoa is Cuba's oldest and most remote town. Located on the north coast of the eastern tip of Cuba, it is separated from the rest of the island by the eastern branch of the Sierra Maestra range. Though founded in 1511 by Diego Velázquez, it was only in 1964 that the Carretera Central finally reached Baracoa from the vicinity of Guantanamo, connecting the town to the rest of Cuba. That road connection had to be laboriously engineered and built over a 2,074 ft pass across the precipitous eastern Sierra Maestra. It is one of the few towns in Cuba with a natural potable water source, piped by gravity from reservoirs fed by mountain streams. An odd, legless, oversize pink statue of Christopher Columbus bearing a vaguely inscrutable smugness dominates the main park.

But there is also a defiant statue of Hatuey, the Taino chief considered Cuba's first "National Hero." Hatuey knew what the Spanish were capable of—his people had suffered at their hands in what is now Haiti. The year before Velázquez' expedition set sail, Hatuey led 400 of his people in canoes across the 50-mile-wide Windward Passage separating Haiti from Cuba to warn the aboriginal Cubans of Velázquez' coming invasion.

Christopher Columbus statue in Baracoa, Oriente, 2016. Credit: R. H. Miller.

Three-hundred prospective settlers accompanied Velázquez to settle on Cuba's far eastern shores. A year after Baracoa's founding, Hatuey laid siege to the little settlement keeping the Spaniards confined. But the Spanish captured and burned him at the stake in 1512—defiant to the end. When implored to convert so he could go to heaven, Hatuey asked, "Will there be Spaniards in Heaven?"

"Yes," answered the priest.

"Then I'd rather go to hell."

* * *

Manuel's house was a happening place. Its two masonry stories were topped by wooden scaffolding and forms: Manuel was adding a third story to expand his B&B. The ground floor was occupied by Baracoa's only "bike" shop, run by his dad. It didn't have a sign or sell bikes, its stock of parts was nearly non-existent and not on display; his parents lived in the back room. But every morning lines of bikes and pedi-cabs—any wheeled conveyance that rolled on anything resembling a bike tire—would come by for air, flat patching, tire replacements or repairs of any sort. Upstairs, Manuel's pet parrot had the run of the place, entertaining guests and residents and waking everyone up at 6 am.

Bike shop, 1st floor of Miguel's B&B, Baracoa, Oriente, 2016. Credit: R. H. Miller.

"Manuel's wife made a fabulous breakfast of hot chocolate (Baracoa is the cocoa capital of Cuba), bread, eggs, cheese, mango jam, guava paste and coffee—sooo delicious!" Brenda wrote in her journal.

Tina had accidentally sat on her glasses and broken their little arms during the long bus ride. We asked Manuel where she might be able to get them fixed. He directed us downtown to an unsigned office maned by a nurse at a desk. We sat and awaited our turn. Optometry, being part of Cuba's famed health care system, was not part of the new self-employment reforms. We were curious to see how the system worked.

Since we didn't need an eye exam, the nurse directed us to a dutch door in the back. Behind the door was a large room lined by a broad counter all around, topped by work stations filled with all sorts of glasses-related paraphernalia. A technician immediately served us. He examined Tina's glasses and bellied up to his station. We watched as he took the little arms apart, reached for what looked like a coat hanger, cut, bent, soldered, tapped and fashioned new arms from scratch; the entire process taking about half-an-hour. Then he put them on Tina's head and made final adjustments. The bill came to $7 CUPs (local pesos), or about .29 cents in CUCs (convertible pesos). I tried to tip him, a kindness he refused.

We couldn't believe it. Back at the B&B, Brenda extolled the benefits of free government health care. Tina replied, "Why bother to charge at all?"

The discussion broadened into US-Cuba relations and Manuel joined in: "The Cuban and American people are all fine; it's the governments that are the problem."

Roy piped in with one of his signature insights, "The people *are* the government!"

To which Manuel replied, "That's what Fidel says."

Brenda's journal records that evening's meal: Manuel's cook prepared a dinner "of marlin and shrimp in coconut milk, red beans, rice, 'potatoes on steroids' (as per Bob; aka *malanga*), green beans and fried sweet potatoes—Yummy!"

* * *

The following morning we assembled for a group picture before heading out of Baracoa. We were a motley crew. Tina, Roy and I rode mountain bikes with fat tires; George and Brenda rode touring bikes. All of us—except George—dressed in loose, long-sleeved, light-colored cotton clothing with bandanas draped from our hats or helmets to protect us from the hot sun. George, on the other hand, was a portrait of velo couture; he wore nylon-blend biking togs with custom arm and leg warmers—after all, Taiwan manufactures most of the world's bikes and nearly all its roads are lined with bike lanes.

For openers, we were facing a steep, brutal 2,000-foot climb. Tina opted out; not from lack of ability, but because she was still recovering from a broken back suffered in a rock climbing accident two years prior. She was afraid of taxing her back and imperiling the rest of her trip. Manuel hired a taxi to take her up to Alto de Cotilla, the road's summit.

Author's bike group in front of Miguel's B&B about to set out on their ride across Cuba.
L to R: Roy & Brenda Smith, Robert Miller, Tina Cobos, George Yen.
Credit: Miguel. Source: R. H. Miller collection.

Manuel also called ahead to arrange lodging for us in Guantánamo and Santiago de Cuba. There is no B&B directory for the island, so Cuba has a well-developed informal network of private business relationships. B&B owners all either know or know of each other. Referrals generate a 10% commission. We'd rely on one night's host to arrange our following night's lodging. Occasionally, in isolated areas where no B&B existed, we'd have to depend on rural government "motels" or *campismos*, workers' rural holiday camps. Such was the case for our first night's stay out of Baracoa.

Wally and Barbara Smith, authors of *Bicycling Cuba*, describe *campismos* thus:

> *"Guests stay in small cabañas, usually built of cement blocks. A typical campismo cabaña will have single beds or bunk beds for two to six people…and a tiny bathroom. In the better ones…the toilet will usually flush and the shower will have cold water…However, water failures are common and some bathrooms are bucket-powered. Campismos may have a cafeteria serving inexpensive meals. Sometimes the cafeteria will be closed, or the food may be gone."*

Manuel couldn't contact the Rio Yacabo *campismo*, our first day's destination over the sierra on the south coast of Oriente Province. We hoped for the best.

On the way out of town, a sign boasted the completion in 1964 of the connecting road between Baracoa and Cajobabo, the little town on the south coast, which completed the original scope of the Carretera Central: "Yesterday's capitalist fraud; today's Revolutionary reality." I decided not to take offense in the name of my grandfather.

A Cuban sport biker, Alexei, out for a training ride to the summit and back caught up to us and accompanied us. His bike had been a gift from some Finns. As we began the interminable climb, the heat and humidity wrung us out. Alexei pulled over at a *bohío*, a traditional Cuban thatched hut dwelling, and yelled a greeting to its inhabitants. He asked them to pull down some coconuts for us. With a long-poled contraption one of them harvested five coconuts and deftly sliced wafers off the top until he revealed the white meat inside, which he then punctured gently. He handed the coconuts all around. Each held about a liter of refreshing, delicious coconut water, which dribbled down our chins and shirts as we held the coconuts up to our mouths and craned our necks back to drink.

George Yen drinking fresh coconut water along the ride over the Sierra Maestra out of Baracoa, Oriente. Credit: R. H. Miller.

I asked how much we owed him. The man shuffled his feet and avoided our gaze. Alexei explained to me that what he'd done, if we remunerated him, was illegal; they didn't have a permit to sell coconuts. But since we were along a deserted road, a long ways from any settlement, with little chance of a policeman coming by, Alexei suggested we give him $1 CUP per coconut, or about .20 cents total in CUCs. I gave him one CUC; he gave me change in CUPs.

Small homestead with traditional 'bohíos' (palm frond dwellings) along the Carretera Central in the Sierra Maestra, Oriente, Cuba. Credit: R. H. Miller.

Just after the refreshing effects of the coco water had worn off, Alexei said there was a spring of *cold*, potable water pouring out of a bamboo pipe another kilometer or so ahead. It came just in time. It was the best tasting water in all of Cuba. We stood under the pipe, fully clothed, soaking ourselves and drinking our fill.

Cuba bottles distilled potable water for drinking. But for some reason I couldn't fathom, it tasted awful. As the trip progressed I tried squirting lime juice in it, freezing it, or mixing it with a little pop. Nothing improved its flavor. Whenever I could, I'd get coconut water or buy tinned orange juice, the only available sort imported from the UK—*SPAR* brand. When Roy saw that he just shook his head incredulously. Cuba is a citrus producing country; the UK is not. It didn't make sense to import British OJ.

The summit at the top of the pass was crowned by a viewing tower, a small café, and fruit and *cucuruchu* peddlers. We were all too nackered to climb the tower, and the café only sold beer, pop and *tilo*, a delicious hot local tea. Government owned, it accepted only CUPs, which, luckily, we'd now acquired some from the coconut change.

So we bought fruit and *cucuruchu* from the hawkers, who'd take either currency. *Cucuruchu* is a mix of coconut, sugar, honey, ground nuts and fruits such as mango or guava wrapped in a cone-shaped banana leaf. Extremely sweet, it is nonetheless a unique treat.

The hawkers were wary, keeping a lookout for cops. None were licensed and all faced a fine, if caught, of upwards to $1,500—or jail time—an impossible sum for impoverished *campesinos*—most of them black—for which, ostensibly, the Revolution had been fought. They pushed us to buy whole sheafs of bananas and kilos of oranges. Not able to carry large loads on our bikes, we instead offered them pens and toothbrushes, which we'd brought along as goodwill gifts, and even money. One young man, a fierce pride in his eyes, wouldn't take money or even a pen unless we bought his *cucurucho*. He was no beggar. Many had walked miles uphill to sell their wares. Alexei said that the only way to get rid of them was to announce that police were on their way.

Oriente Province, so close to Haiti, has a predominantly black population, the remnants of waves of economic migrants seeking better opportunities in Cuba. Fidel Castro, a native of Oriente, grew very fond of his rigid Haitian tutor when, at the age of four he'd been entrusted to her care.

After an invigorating down-hill run on the south side of the sierra, Tina and I hit the village of Cajobabo on the south coast. A big billboard announced that José Martí and Máximo Gómez had landed there in a rowboat on April 11, 1895 to join the latest uprising against Spanish rule. Martí was the intellectual statesman behind Cuba's independence movement; Gómez was a general and veteran of previous insurrections.

The Carretera Central now ran along the Caribbean on the south coast of Oriente. The vegetation changed from lush tropical forest to arid foothills, with spindly cacti dominating the limestone bluffs. The air temperature on my bike thermometer hit 100 degrees Fahrenheit. We got to the Campismo Yacabo Abajo at 5 pm, absolutely nackered and cramping. It was located in the middle of nowhere right on the beach, a few desultory palm frond cabanas fronting the water. The attendant was closing up her office, about to go home. I requested three rooms. She said sorry, they weren't prepared to accommodate foreign tourists and, anyway, there were no rooms available: they were expecting a bus-full of road workers.

Though not graced with the gift of gab, a total failure at negotiation, and pretty much lacking in useful social skills, I explained that we were traveling on bikes; our 75-year-old participant was close to cardiac arrest from pedaling over the sierra; there was no alternative lodging anywhere nearby and we were willing to settle for just about any shelter with a bed. She called her supervisor and told me to wait outside.

The supervisor saved the day. He apologized for the attendant's attitude and said he could accommodate us if we stayed only one night and would settle for one room with air conditioning and two without, at $12 and $6 CUCs per room respectively. I gratefully accepted. At that point, George rode in.

I pushed our luck asking if we could get a meal. The supervisor ordered a maid to spiff up the rooms and make the beds. He added that he'd talk to the cook.

Roy and Brenda showed up at 6 pm, Roy looking like a corpse, all white with zinc oxide, for protection from the Cuban sun. Not being much of an altruist, I picked the air conditioned room for Tina and myself. The supervisor said the cook would serve us a simple dinner at 7:30 pm for $5 CUCs each. Cold showers revived us.

Dinner consisted of large flank steaks, fries and a salad with beer. The kitchen, such as it was, inside a dry-stacked, cinder block veranda covered by corrugated tin, had a spindly 2-burner propane stove and a grill balanced on bricks and fueled by firewood.

We slept the sleep of the dead—except for Roy and Brenda. Without air conditioning, they'd had to keep the door and windows open all night. Mosquitoes and *jejenes*, Cuban no-see-ums, feasted on their flesh. Next door, a Cuban family played loud music on their boom-box until 1 am when Brenda, not as shy as Roy to interfere with local customs, finally asked them with hand signals to turn it off. The irony, I found out later, was that they were 'sharing' their music with the tourists. They would gladly have turned it off at 8 pm if only they'd known.

On to Guantánamo! Riding rolling hills along the shore. The 75 km day, with temperatures again hitting 100 degrees, nearly killed us, until a torrential rain thankfully soaked us. Later on, at a small village, what looked like an ice cream vendor was yelling, "*Guarapo, guarapo frío!*" I stopped the group and bought everyone an ice-cold, freshly-pressed sugar cane juice for $1 CUP each (4 cents).

Kitchen at the Campismo Yacabo Abajo, on the south coast of Oriente Province.
Credit: R. H. Miller.

Afterward we stopped at a roadside fruit stand. Family members came out from the back to engage us, asking where we were from, where were we going, what did we think of Cuba, and so on. Taking their idiomatic communication cue from me, they overwhelmed poor Roy, who couldn't speak a word of Spanish, peppering him with well-intentioned overtures in animated Cuban street talk with no conception of an Englishman's personal space. The too-close informal attention stiffened Roy's back. He turned defensive and walked away. Later, I urged him to memorize, *"No hablo español,"* as a useful tool.

Two Land Rovers full of uniformed personnel drove up. All poured out and judiciously ignored us. Laughing nervously among themselves, they fingered the mandarin oranges. The family members retreated to their house; we mounted our bikes and rode off. I wondered whether the officials didn't want to be friendly with foreigners or whether they didn't want to appear friendly with foreigners in front of co-workers.

Entering Guantánamo we passed a large military base with an obstacle training course that extended for miles next to the road. It was probably Castro's response to the US naval base in Guantánamo Bay.

Acquired in 1903, the US naval base was primarily established to protect the eastern approaches to the strategically important Panama Canal and, according to the Platt Amendment, to allow the US to protect the independence of Cuba. The base is leased for $4,085 per annum. Another clause in the Platt Amendment recognizes Cuba's sovereignty over the area. Castro has refused to cash all but one rent check, reportedly stashing them in the top drawer of his desk as a protest against what he considers an "illegal occupation."

The B&B Manuel arranged for us, Elsye Castillo, had a titillating atmosphere. Drop-dead gorgeous gals, lycra-legged with skin-tight tops welcomed us. One woman's T-shirt read, "Tits make the woman." Giant posters of a scantily-clad Jennifer López, Sofia Vergara and other hormone-stirring beauties lined the walls. Egyptian cat statues stood mutely along the edges of the hall. This was no mom-and-pop, grandma-and-kids private home renting out a spare bedroom. For once I was happy to be the translator and go-between.

That night we ate at our first state restaurant, the *Año 1870*. Outside the door, a young man said the restaurant was no good; he'd take us to a *paladar*, a private restaurant. These had been legalized at different times in the past but now seemed well established. Back in Havana we'd dined at *paladares* and found them to be quite good. The young man said the *paladar* was close, but after walking for three blocks, we turned back—we were just too tired.

Inside the *Año 1870* we were the only clients. There was only one waitress. She said to ignore the menu; they only had pan-sauteed chicked cutlets and rice. The food was passable and the service nearly so. There was no tipping; only an added service charge. To the *paladares* in Havana, there was no comparison.

Back at the B&B the front door was open: a hose ran from the building to a hole below the street. Inside, an overripe beauty whose clothes could barely contain her abundance told us she was the night attendant, "If you need anything, come see me." She did not sit behind a desk; instead, she lounged on a divan like Goya's Maja, explaining that she had to monitor the pump to fill the roof gravity tanks. Curious, I asked what that entailed.

She explained that, early in the evening, the city releases water into the mains. In a couple of hours the water level in the mains gets high enough to reach the house pipe feeds. At this point, home and business owners turn on an electric or gasoline pump to pump water from the mains into a home cistern. Another couple of hours later, around 11 pm, another pump pumps the water from the cistern up onto one or more rooftop tanks. Voila! Domestic water. Rural areas depend on trucked water and cisterned rain water. For all the trouble this takes, the state charges only a pittance for water.

We decided to take a rest day the following morning. The mountains, heat and distance had taken their toll. I flirted with the idea of taking a taxi to a nearby mountain where I could get a bird's-eye view of the US naval base. There's a McDonald's inside, the only one in Cuba, but visitors are not allowed into the naval base. Instead, I rested, read and caught up on my journal.

* * *

Big day to Santiago de Cuba: 90 km with hills. Started early. Three strangers asked us to take them to *Yuma*. Part of the ride was on an *autopista*, or freeway—a four-lane, divided highway with a green median and absolutely no traffic except for the occasional bus, truck, ox or horse cart. A large group of young teenage Cuban sport bikers caught up with us. We all stopped to wonder at each other and take pictures.

Santiago de Cuba, nicknamed "The City of Heroes," has been the birthplace of many independence revolts, including Fidel Castro's 1953 insurrection.

When Fidel Castro stepped onto the pages of history on July 26, 1953 with his attack on the Moncada army garrison in Santiago, he tripped. Never mind that Batista had been in power for only one year and that, in Marxist terms, a "revolutionary situation" just did not exist. This first attempt to overthrow President Fulgencio Batista proved suicidal for most of the participants. Not only did they meet stiff resistance (which Castro should have expected), but all his planning had been little more than careless wishful thinking coupled with impromptu expediency (some rebels even had to ride public buses to the assault). One participant remembers Castro running around screaming hysterically, shouting orders that made no sense. Pure luck saved him. Those who weren't killed in the strike were soon rounded up and brutally shot in cold blood by the soldiers. A few, such as Fidel and his brother, laid low for a few days and then turned themselves in after pleas for clemency from well-connected family members made surrender a possibility.

The survivors were tried in a civil tribunal. At the trial, Castro acted as his own lawyer and summed up his defense with what would later become his most famous speech, "History Will Absolve Me" (in which he has three references to Cachorro's great grandfather). A sympathetic judge, Manuel Urrutia Lleo, voted for leniency (Castro was grateful and later appointed Urrutia Provisional President after the triumph of the Revolution; he lasted only six months). The Castro brothers were sentenced to life imprisonment on the Isle of Pines.

The Moncada Army Barracks is a national treasure, the Castro Revolution's Concord and Lexington, where its first shot was fired. It covers an entire block and is painted a striking golden yellow with white highlights. Cuban and 26 of July flags fly from every façade. I tried to imagine the rebels' assault 63 years previously, while our group took pictures of the returning Cuban-American in front of Moncada.

Moncada Army Barracks, Santiago de Cuba, where Fidel Castro began his revolution in 1953. Now a museum. Credit: R. H. Miller.

Santiago is Cuba's second largest city and its first capital. Hernan Cortéz sailed from Santiago's harbor to conquer Mexico. Finding the B&B Manuel had engaged for us was a challenge. The proprietor, a Spanish literature and grammar professor at the university, had subbed out the lodging to another operator, to which she led us, who in turn had subbed out feeding us to another.

B&Bs, or *casas particulares*, operators have a tight network. Room reservations often mean nothing since they're not backed up by a deposit—credit card numbers not being operative in Cuba, and telephone promises as reliable as Castro's promises. So they often overbook, off-loading double bookings on nearby B&Bs. But bike bookings, especially from another B&B operator, carry a bit more weight. Still, it's a delicate juggle during high season.

Our new hostess asked if we wanted dinner. Indeed we did; a nighttime meal at a B&B being preferable to a state restaurant or a distant *paladar*—and dependably delicious. In this case our separate dinner hostess served us fried chicken, salad, *malanga* fritters and plantain chips. Proud of her presentation, she hovered over us for the entire meal noting with satisfaction every 'hmmm', gulp and swallow.

The dinner minuet became a fun ritual. At first, it tried my patience: everyone wanted to participate yet no one was familiar with Cuban cuisine or the vagaries of socialist market availabilities—plus, it fell to me to translate every gustatory whim, objection or detail back and forth between individual members of the group and our hosts. After a few of these negotiations, I took the task on solely.

The first decision was determining what meat the host had available. Initially I'd lean toward chicken out of respect for my "vegetarian" companions. Cubans don't do vegetarianism. Although Castro pushed salads—mostly cabbage—on them during the "Special Period" in the '90s and, at least for tourists, they remain a dependable staple composed mostly of cabbage, tomatoes, beets and cukes topped with canola oil and vinegar. Cubans much prefer meat, beans, rice and starchy veggies—yuca, malanga, and plantains—preferably fried.

Invariably, the chicken portions would consist of a giant thigh and leg with meat so white one could have mistaken it for a breast. We saw chickens everywhere, scrawny but free range. While riding in a taxi one day with Brenda, one of our erstwhile vegetarians, she wondered how the chickens we were served were so big when the ones we saw roaming about were so rickety. So I asked our driver. He said Cubans don't kill their chickens, they're for eggs. Eatin' chickens are stamped with *madinusa*. Not familiar with the term, I asked him what it meant. He looked wryly at me, sideways, and then I got it: Made in USA.

When I told Brenda she gulped and said, "You mean we've been eating Purdue chickens? From now on let's ask for pork, at least it's organic."

Sole proprietorship pork butcher in Las Tunas. Credit: Roy Smith.

Pork is *the* ubiquitous Cuban meat, nearly always available. Beef was the least available meat, even though we saw lots of cattle in the central provinces. Apparently it's reserved for the nomenclatura and tourists. Though not available in government ration stores, it can be obtained by anyone at convertible currency stores—if one has the money. Beef cattle are a government monopoly. One informant told me that, occasionally, a beef would suffer an "accident" or unexpectedly die of a "sickness." A sympathetic veterinarian would confirm the tragedy, and all concerned would share in the bounty.

Lechón asado. Credit: Tina Cobos.

During the Revolution's early years, when pretty much everything became the property of the state, every cow, pig and chicken became government property. Not a few *campesinos* paid the ultimate price for slaughtering their backyard animals for a meaty meal without permission.

At one B&B where the owner was tickled pink that I was a Cuban-American, it brought out her impish side. I requested *ropa vieja*, a traditional brisket or flank steak dish. She thought about it for a minute and said, "We can do that. And it'll be the best *ropa vieja* you've ever had."

I responded, "Remember, I had a Cuban mother."

Without skipping a beat she retorted, "It'll be the second-best *ropa vieja* you've ever had." We both laughed.

Fish is widely available but of varying quality. Whenever it was offered as fresh and a good species, especially *pargo*, Cuban Red Snapper (nothing like it!), I opted for it. Cuba hasn't overfished its stocks. But not for eco-ideological reasons; rather for "sugar cane-curtain" reasons: to limit small boat traffic along its shores, both to minimize escape and infiltration attempts. Additionally, small enterprise fishing businesses haven't been allowed: the state provides the fish. Lobster is often available. It is to die for—huge, cheap, and delicious.

Most guidebooks grouse that Cuba's ubiquitous side dish, *Moros y Cristianos*—day-old black beans and rice mixed together—is dry, boring and tiresome. I always asked for stewed beans, red or black, straight and fresh, richly spiced traditionally. Nearly all B&Bs were glad to comply. Even though we'd usually arrive at our lodging around 3 pm and request dinner at 6 pm, most had electric pressure cookers and could serve our gang on time.

Many visitors to Cuba express a desire to see the island before it's completely opened up to globalization and, as they snidely speculate, "McDonald's invades." Contrary to popular US perception, Cuba does have a fast-food restaurant chain—*El Rápido*, a state run enterprise. Guidebooks and trip accounts tout it as dependable, with food quality varying from passable to good, especially the chicken—again, a thigh and leg combo. We never ate at one—but not for lack of trying. The ones we stopped at were either out of meat, not serving food due to something malfunctioning (but still open with full staff just sitting around), or some other reason.

* * *

The Santiago to Bayamo run is 124 km with a very hilly first half, but afterward slipping through a break in the middle of the Sierra Maestra mountains. The only accommodation in between to which our guidebooks alluded was the state-run Motel Mirador Valle de Tayabe, about one-third of the way to Bayamo. With on other choice available, we decided to depend on our luck at the government motel.

Identical tower blocks of socialist housing lined the avenues along the Santiago exit, reminiscent of Kruschev-era East German apartments. While the latter stand in mute abandonment after German unification, memorials to a failed idealistic dream, Santiago's were draped with drying laundry.

Nearly all of us had to walk some of the hills exiting Santiago. At lunchtime, we passed the *Iglesia de la Caridad del Cobre*, Cuba's cathedral to it's patron saint. The church is in the little town of El Cobre at the bottom of a picturesque mountain valley. Hawkers peddled statues, scapularies and icons along the road. Three women blew provocative kisses at me as I rode by.

Stopping for lunch under a tree, the silence was broken by overhead engine noises. Two helicopters appeared in off-set formation. Cuban airspace is conspicuous for its lack of activity. A nearby memento entrepreneur pointed up and yelled, "That's Raúl Castro up there." He said that Raúl had been in Santiago strategizing with the FAR (*Fuerzas Armadas Revolucionarias*) on controlling the Zika virus. He was heading back to Havana now.

Socialist tower housing somewhere on the Carretera Central along Cuba's midriff, 2016. Credit: R. H. Miller.

Six kilometers from the government motel, the road rose steeply up. It wasn't named *Mirador Valle de Tayabe*, 'Tayabe Valley Look-out,' for nothing. We were already sprawled over our bikes like Salvador Dalí clocks from exhaustion when we rode in on the beautifully landscaped colonnade. I walked into the office and asked for rooms while the group melted on the lawn around a shady tree.

The uniformed attendant said they didn't rent to foreigners and added, for good measure, that anyway, they were full; all the rooms were occupied by the workers that were building additional rooms. So I asked for her supervisor. She said he was on vacation and unavailable. I said we'd take an unfinished room. I asked for an alternative suggestion. I asked if we could camp on the lawn. I even used the old 'cardiac arrest' line I'd used at the *campismo*. I even had her walk over to the window to look at our group, sprawled on the ground like survivors of the Baatan Death March. Nothing worked; the blasé woman couldn't be moved.

I gave the group the bad news. George seemed ready to pass out. It didn't help that he was diabetic. Roy, again looking like a drained corpse, gave us his courage talk, saying things could be worse—much worse. Then he recounted how Chris Bonnington, stuck on the North Face of the Eiger, overdue, cold and hungry, had to open a tin of bully beef with a piton. Brenda rolled her eyes.

Tina suggested I talk to the workmen. They'd been sympathetically listening in, some shaking their heads at the woman's coldness. One told us that back in Palma Soriano, at the base of the big hill, just after the bridge over the Cauto River, there was a B&B licensed for foreigners. I was very skeptical; no guidebook mentioned any lodgings in Palma Soriano.

We mounted up and coasted down the hill. Sure enough, a small pink house with the B&B insignia on the door lay 100 feet from the road. It looked newly-built and deserted; however, someone answered our knock. The lady, with financial help from her son who'd married a Puerto Rican, had just opened for business. It was an unlikely location—a small, insignificant town, within easy vehicle distance from anyplace more interesting. She didn't offer meals, but she had three $10 rooms with air conditioning—and she had a fridge full of cold beer and pop. She offered to call us a taxi for a ride into town to a *paladar* she suggested for dinner.

I'd introduced our crew to shandys, a mixture of half beer and half lemon-lime soda. The beer cut the pop's sugar, while the pop cut the beer's alcohol. Incredibly thirst-quenching and refreshing, it was the perfect substitute for Cuba's awful bottled water during or after a hot day on the saddle. We downed quite a few waiting for our horse-drawn taxi, Palma Soriano lacking any motorized ones.

The following morning Brenda and George opted to take the previous evening's taxi up the hill while Roy, Tina and I re-rode up that brutal incline. We laughed at the sight of two bikes and passengers loaded all askew on that surrey with the fringe on top. "Bad form," I scoffed.

The ride to Bayamo turned out to be easy but, again, hot. Baire, along the way and an otherwise nondescript town, welcomed us under giant flowering trees, pink and white with Japanese cherry blossoms. A large billboard reminded us that Cuba's War for Independence had begun here with the *Grito de Baire* (shout—uprising—of Baire) on February 24, 1895.

Perhaps.

Riding into Baire. Credit: Roy Smith.

Cubans had been rebelling unsuccessfully against Spain since 1826, but it wasn't until 1868 that the effort got serious. Known as the Ten Years' War (1868-1878), the uprising ultimately failed. During those years, José Martí, now considered the apostle of Cuban independence, was only a 16-year-old student. A school essay advocating Cuban independence got him convicted of treason. His mother, outraged at the sentence, wrote to every Spanish official she could contact. His sentence was finally commuted due to his status as a minor. He was exiled to Spain where he continued his studies.

Though he played no active part in the Ten Years' War, his writings on Cuban Independence, his poems (the song *Guantanamera* to the fore) and his scholarly essays became very influential throughout Latin America. Between 1880 and 1890, the peripatetic Martí spent much time in New York and traveling throughout Central America, the Caribbean and Mexico advocating liberal causes, acting as consul for Argentina, Paraguay and Uruguay, lecturing, writing, organizing political clubs, and raising money for Cuban independence.

Just as in the 1950s, and in 1960, the 1890s Cuban revolutionary groups were riven by factionalism, each advocating slightly different approaches to, and ideologies for, the revolution. Martí's genius was his ability to unite all the factions into one organization, the Cuban Revolutionary Party, and then draw up an overall plan for the insurrection that all were agreed on.

The revolution was to begin in Oriente with simultaneous uprisings in the main towns, followed by successive risings moving progressively eastward along the island and culminating in Havana. Martí left New York for the Dominican Republic in January of 1895 to join General Máximo Gómez for a landing near Baracoa. On February 24, 1895 the plan went into effect. Thirty-five coordinated revolts—*gritos*—took place at Santiago, Guantánamo, Bayamo, Manzanillo, Ibarra, Bayate, Baire, et al. Spanish authorities first became aware of the Baire uprising, and termed the revolt *Grito de Baire*. Ever since, Cubans have been trying to rename the event *Grito de Oriente*—to spread the credit—with little success.

Martí and Gómez, as stated before, landed at Cajobabo on April 11. Though the Oriente uprisings were mostly successful, those farther west were only partially so, with Havana's a total failure.

Martí, an academic intellectual, was no soldier, a shortcoming the military leaders never let him forget. To prove his dedication, Martí intemperately charged into the fray at the Battle of Dos Rios, just a few miles from Baire. Riding on a white horse and wearing a black coat, he made an easy target. He was shot dead on May 19, only a month after his landing at Cajobabo.

Martí's death galvanized the fence-sitting Cubans who were ambivalent about independence. Many now joined the revolt. By the time the United States declared war on Spain over the sinking of the *USS Maine* on April 25, 1898, a Spanish intelligence communiqué declared that the only territory the Spanish held was the ground its soldiers stood upon.

Historians are divided on whether the Cubans had pretty much succeeded in defeating Spain, or whether US intervention in the War of Independence was a necessary addition. To Castro, the US stole Cuba's independence.

* * *

At Santa Rita, the last town before Bayamo, we stopped at a café for refreshments. George and I made a beeline to a coconut vendor and treated ourselves to coconut water. The others sat under the shady veranda and drank shandies. One café client, a dark-toned black, engaged us, asking where we were from. When we said we came from the US, he responded that when he immigrates he'll head for Germany. The US was too racist.

Brenda piped up, "Hooray for Obama!" He agreed.

So I said, "Boo for Obama!" He gave me a thumbs down.

Then Tina added that Obama was just like Fidel, "Too many rules!"

Our new friend replied: "Fidel, white devil; Obama, black devil."

On the way out of town, a very thin old man, in front of a ration food store, begged us for something to eat. He said he was hungry. He looked it. Tina made him a sandwich.

Bayamo was thick with soldiers. Again, we were shunted from one B&B to another. Our host informed us that we'd have to wait outside for an hour-and-a-half; the army was going house-to-house fumigating against the Zika virus, and the fumes were too poisonous. We complied. Non-compliance was subject to a $500 CUC fine. Tina and I walked over to the nearby park where FAR soldiers were taking a break. I wanted to eavesdrop on them and get a feel for what sort of person becomes a Castro militiaman. The next morning the street gutters were full of dead cockroaches.

Bayamo is Cuba's second settlement, also founded by Diego Velázquez (Baracoa's founder) in 1513. The Ten Year's War began with a rising in Bayamo. Cuba's national anthem, *La Bayamesa*, or the hymn of Bayamo, commemorates a victory of Cuban forces over the Spanish at Bayamo at the beginning of the Ten Years' War in 1868. It was composed impromptu by Perucho Figueredo immediately after the battle while he was still on horseback. Figueredo was captured and executed by the Spanish two years later.

* * *

We lost Brenda on the run from Bayamo to Las Tunas, our next destination, a scenic but hot 82 km. The separation opened the door to a minor leadership crisis. As an adventure educator I know how to lead groups successfully; and, conversely, I can be a good follower. But for adventures with friends, I believe in the anarchy of consensus (or lack of it), where no one is forced to do anything they don't want to do. I am neither a leader nor a follower, believing that the strength of the group lies in the self-reliance of its individual members—an aphorism that drew a major eye roll from Roy since it clashed with his communitarian ideals.

In this case, he had a point. My knowledge of Spanish, Cuba and bike touring made everyone dependent on me. Nevertheless, I urged everyone to learn some Spanish and read up on Cuba; to carry their own set of maps and guidebooks; to bring a full kit of bicycle tools and spare parts *and* know how to use them. In that spirit, I insisted on every member carrying a copy of each day's lodging stats—address and phone number—as a safety margin.

Brenda and Tina were fans. George stuck by me like an altar boy to a priest, and Roy danced to his own tune. We found Brenda waiting for us at our Las Tunas B&B. She'd written down the address and, when she got lost, hailed a taxi, showed the driver the address and got a ride.

But then, just before entering Las Tunas, I lost Tina. Glancing in my rear-view mirror, she was nowhere in sight. So I waited. When she didn't appear, I retraced our path. When she finally showed up she was gasping for air, pedaling hard to catch up to me. She'd spotted a baby goat—Tina has never encountered a cute animal that didn't need rescuing—being chased by a distraught man. The goat had escaped its enclosure. Tina helped the man corner the goat, herding it like a cowgirl on a bike. In return, the man offered her a fresh coconut, all sliced and ready to drink.

Our hosts, Karen and Roger, spoke good English. Their home was a beautiful, new two-story house, which they shared with his mother, who also ran a licensed B&B, creating a profitable 6-rentable-room enterprise. Karen was a psychologist, still working for the state—psychology not being one of the allowable pursuits in the recent self-employed reforms. Roger had been an accountant, another strictly state employment career. With everyone employed by the state; no taxes, overhead, or profits, who needs accountants? Perhaps with the rise in self-employment it'll become a growth career. Roger had quit his job in order to manage their profitable B&B, and to pursue an advanced degree in economics.

"Can you study Milton Friedman and Friedrich Hayek?" I asked.

His eyes brightened up and he said, "Next year," adding that they were only for advanced students and that the state allowed their study since knowledge of 'the other side' was necessary.

I wondered how objective the presentation of 'the other side' might be and brought up the regime's Orwellian manipulation of language, especially with regard to the words *alquiler* and *renta*. *Alquiler*, meaning 'rent' is disappearing; it is being replaced by *renta*, originally meaning investment—interest or dividend—income. Since the latter concepts are illegal in practice and anathema morally in Communist economics, *renta* now means 'rent.' Its original meaning is now widely forgotten and *alquiler* is disappearing, replaced by *renta*.

We both agreed that improved US-Cuba relations were a positive step forward. Roger added, insightfully, that the US embargo was not unilateral—that Castro doesn't want it lifted in spite of his fulminations against it. For one, he uses it to rally Cubans in common cause against the US. Moreover, if the US were to unilaterally lift the embargo, Castro would balk, imposing tariffs, regulations and more capital controls. The last thing the Castros want is an invasion of American capitalism, which a lifting of the embargo would precipitate. The embargo is, anyway, a red herring. As one insightful wag rhetorically asked, "Why don't they get what they need from other countries?" But he added that there is no going back to an earlier regime; that the Cuban people would resist because there is too much support for open markets. However, he clarified that change must come incrementally and not precipitously—that would be too disruptive.

As to property settlements, a big stumbling block in the normalization of relations between the two countries, Roger said that the confiscations took place fifty years ago and his generation shouldn't be held responsible for compensation.

I responded that my family's house was now owned by the *Ministerio de Capacitación e Investigación*—a ministry the function of which neither of us could discern. He added that Castro had more ministries than soldiers. We both laughed. But then I pointed out that returning our house to my family would not affect him. He gave me a thoughtful look that spoke volumes. He had never thought of property compensation in individual terms, only as something between governments and corporations. He didn't respond; he seemed to need time to mull that over.

22

La Cadera

The following day we left at 8 am for Guáimaro, a small town only 45 km away on the Las Tunas-Camagüey provincial border, one of the few boundaries that the Revolutionary government kept nearly intact when it reconfigured Cuba's provinces after its victory (the other being Matanzas Province). The border roughly separates Cuba's big eastern 'foot' from it's midriff 'torso', and even more roughly divides the mountainous region of the far east from the the great central plains.

The island has been described as a long—746 miles—recumbent crocodile lazily lording over the Caribbean. Yet Cuba is not an island: it is an archipelago comprised of up to 4,000 islands, with the Isle of Pines (Isle of Youth)—the largest—as an accent gráve under the croc.

The six original provinces were created in 1879 by the Spanish colonial government. From east to west they were Oriente, Camagüey, Las Villas, Matanzas, La Habana and Pinar del Rio. In 1976 Castro redrew provincial boundaries, adding eight new provinces in order to rationalize provincial populations and areas. But with Havana's population growing so fast, the government modified boundaries once again in 2011. Exiled Cubans have resisted recognition of the new political boundaries, viewing anything that Castro does as treasonous, particularly having the gall to change the geography of the Pearl of the Antilles, something perceived as immutable. Now there are 15 provinces and one "Special Municipality," Isla de la Juventud (nee Isla de Pinos), once part of La Habana Province.

The historical Oriente Province, which we were about to exit, is now divided into Santiago de Cuba, Guantánamo, Granma, Holguín and Las Tunas provinces. The old Camagüey Province was divided into new Camagüey and Ciego de Avila provinces. Las Villas became Cienfuegos, Villa Clara and Sancti Spíritus provinces.

The original La Habana and Pinar del Rio provinces on the west of the island were subjected to radical surgery. These are now, from east to west, Mayabeque, La Habana, Artemisa, Pinar del Rio and Isla de la Juventud.

***

Camagüey Province is cattle country. Gray—and white—Zebus are the dominant breed. Cowboys are common. Rolling savannas predominate with vast fields of sugarcane interspersed. Tita's family, when they'd immigrated from Catalunya, had settled in Camagüey. Her father had managed a sugar refinery for an American company there. It was on the plains of Camagüey that Fidel Castro's two advancing fronts, one under Che Guevara, the other under Camilo Cienfuegos, came together for a united assault toward the capital.

On the way out of Las Tunas, one guy begged us to take him with us to *Yuma*. I told him we were only going to Guáimaro. He laughed. We covered the short distance by noon. It was along this stretch of Carretera Central where I was able to spot, underneath the edge of the eroded asphalt, the original concrete base underlying the road my grandfather had helped build in the 1920s. Roads with a concrete top or underlayment last four times longer than pure asphalt roads. Today, governments gravitate toward asphalt or chip-seal roads because they are much cheaper. It's a testament to the longevity of concrete and the Machado regime for using it (in spite of the graft associated with the building of it) that the Carretera Central has survived so well for so many years with minimal maintenance.

Roy and I had both caught some sort of debilitating respiratory flu that made cardiovascular exertion hell, so we were glad for the rest a short day afforded us.

Guáimaro would be just another unexceptional Cuban town if it wasn't for the Guáimaro Assembly of 1869, Cuba's first constitutional assembly. In preparation for future independence, the delegates elected a president and decreed the emancipation of slaves.

Norma's B&B was modest and partially under construction. She raised piglets in the back. A pet parrot squawked constantly until it got a cracker. Inside we were greeted by a retired Canadian postal worker wearing a *Che* Guevara T-shirt and pretentiously performing Tai-Chi while he talked with us. He was not a guest. I nicknamed him the Ugly Canadian.

The Ugly Canadian was a new-age bourgeois socialist investor. He'd invested Norma's niece with his child and was now building a B&B a block away to compete with his "aunt-in-law." But he wasn't married to Norma's niece, who was in the adjacent room sewing and intermittently coming out to make contact with him. He ignored her affectionate overtures, engrossed in telling us how wonderful Castro's revolution was and elaborating on how Castro took property from Americans who were exploiting Cubans.

Piglets at Norma's B&B in Guáimaro. Credit: R. H. Miller.

Without the least sense of irony he then bragged about how he was using his girlfriend to build his B&B and about how cheap labor was in Cuba. I wondered who was exploiting whom in this scenario. Cuba has inchoate property rights—if any at all. A hopeful first step in a foreigner's securing them is to marry a Cuban, a detail the Canadian was ignoring. Although Norma's niece seemed naïve, she was holding all the cards: she was getting a B&B built with foreign money; a primary claim to whatever property rights went with it; and a child fathered by a foreigner, a filip that upped her chances of immigrating.

Just before going to bed Norma announced big news: the TV had just reported that US President Barack Obama was due to visit Cuba on March 21 (2016). Raúl Castro had extended the invitation.

Until Castro's Revolution, Cuban-American relations, both formal and informal, had always been close. Cuban exiles from the wars of independence settled in Tampa and Miami. Refugees from Cuban Communism settled in Miami, New York, Los Angeles, even Phoenix. They're everywhere. Americans have always—even now—been welcomed by the people of Cuba. The Cuban government encourages illegal American tourism through third countries by not stamping passports, so the visitor can avoid detection when returning through US Customs. Intermarriage and investment (I know) was ubiquitous—and the latter can't wait to resume. Conversely, the US retains a policy of admitting all Cubans who reach our shores.

To Cubans, Obama's visit was an honor ranking right up there with the Pope's visit, and one not vouchsafed to the island since President Coolidge's visit in 1928. *El mulato*, as he's informally referred to by some in the Cuban fashion of conferring nicknames on everyone, and his historic visit, brought the promise of hope and change to the island more concretely than any pronouncement ever made by the Castros.

American flags were everywhere—in cars, taxis, horse- and pedal-drawn taxis, even clothing—even before the visit was announced. Warned by guidebooks and savants to minimize exchanges with uniformed personnel, and *never* to photograph any, I found the admonition accurate. They were all serious, unfriendly, incorruptible, suspicious and avoided any sign of curiosity. Once the visit was announced, my mischievous brain couldn't wait to test those premises—after all, the visit was empirical evidence that we were no longer enemies.

The ride to Camagüey city was a long, hard eight-hour slog, made worse by the day's weather report: a "cold front" that delivered neither cool temperatures nor rain—only a head wind that turned the gentle uphill route into a struggle. It didn't help that neither Roy nor I had shed our flus. Another passer-by shouted out, "Wait a sec! Take me with you!" more in greeting and fun than fully seriously.

Batista army tank captured during the Revolution on November 5, 1958. George Yen and Tina Cobos in front. Credit: R. H. Miller.

At one point we stopped for lunch at a de-treaded Batista tank on a low platform. The plaque by it read "Little tank belonging to the army of the tyranny neutralized in the action of November 5, 1958." A very handsome family—mom, dad, son and daughter—riding a buckboard spotted us and stopped to pass the time. The son, muscles bulging out of his tank top and gold tooth glowing, tried to talk me into taking his sister, a twenty-something-year-old beauty. I said I was already married and pointed to Tina. They all dismissed the objection saying the girl didn't mind—she wasn't jealous. We all laughed at that—even Tina after I'd translated.

Cuban family that tried to talk the author into taking their daughter to the US.
Credit: R. H. Miller.

But it was in passing soldiers, policemen and god-knows-what uniformed functionaries that the real fun started. I'd yell, "We're not enemies anymore!" and I'd add some typical Cuban sassy word-play non-sequitur as a true native would. I managed to get a few smiles and even some playful responses. One FAR (*Fuerzas Armadas Revolucionarias*) soldier returned a greeting; a policeman engaged in word-play. Unbelievable! Things *were* changing and there was hope.

One guy in Sibanicú who'd learned a bit of English from TV—he was quite serious in this pursuit—engaged Tina in conversation. He said that we were neighbors, so there was no point in being enemies. Tina agreed and told him to ask Fidel why we were enemies. He responded, "I can't do that," with a big grin.

Camagüey is Cuba's third largest city. It too was founded by the peripatetic Diego Velázquez in 1514. The city's historic center has been well maintained and periodically renovated. It is a UNESCO World Heritage site.

That night, at dinner, our leadership crisis hit the fan. Brenda, Tina and George had dubbed me the "indispensable facilitator," since I remained adamant against becoming "the leader." It wasn't just a semantic distinction: a leader calls the shots; a facilitator leads the group in achieving consensus. The achieving consensus bit had become lengthy and tiresome, mainly because only I had first-hand knowledge of all the factors involved in making itinerary decisions; factors that took time to explain and discuss, and which, inevitably, always led to a pre-ordained conclusion that I'd already come to.

It was obvious that we needed a rest day. The distance to Ciego de Avila, our next scheduled destination, was an impossible—in our state—120 kilometers. But it was also obvious that we were running out of time to reach Havana on schedule. Breaking up the distance to Ciego de Avila was no solution: it would eat up more days. What to do? Rather than open an endless discussion on the subject, I announced that I was ready to become the group's leader and take on the responsibility of making decisions and watching out for my charges. Serio-comically following faux formal parliamentary procedure, I asked, "Does someone want to nominate me?"

Tina and Brenda immediately did. George smiled and repeated some pithy, appropriate Chinese aphorism, the jist of which was something along the lines of 'it is better to accept fate than to try to run away from it.' Roy kept quiet. I asked for a vote. Tina, Brenda and George voted for me. Roy kept on keeping quiet. I said the vote had to be unanimous or I wouldn't accept. Brenda gave Roy that look wives of many years give recalcitrant husbands. Roy then voted for me.

Once I was in power, I announced my decision to solve the rest day/schedule conundrum: we would hire two taxis to transport us, our bikes and our gear from Camagüey to Ciego de Avila. We would rest *and* move forward at the same time. Everyone loved it—even Roy. I was surprised no one had thought of it.

Our hostess arranged two taxis for us, one an old 1957 Chevy Bel Air green *pisicorre*, or station wagon, with a roof rack; the other a late-model

Kia. Tina took over the loading, standing the bikes on the roof rack, canting them slightly inwards and dynamically tensioning them with opposing ties, all the while climbing and traipsing all over the *pisicorre*. The driver was impressed.

Tina and Brenda load bikes atop 1957 Chevy Bel Air for taxi ride to Ciego de Avila.
Credit: R. H. Miller.

Roy, Brenda and George rode in the vintage station wagon, while Tina and I chose the newer car. Before long, Brenda joined us. Most of Cuba's famous old cars have been retrofitted with Japanese diesel engines whose fumes are the bane of city dwellers, particularly during rush hours. But while the visible exteriors of the vintage cars have been bonded and painted, the floors are peppered with holes that funnel exhaust in. Roy and George rode with their heads hanging out the windows, their eyes all googly when we reached Ciego de Avila.

On the drive out of Camagüey I had one request. I'd read Denver, Colorado mayor Guillermo Vicente Vidal's memoir, *Boxing for Cuba: An Immigrant's Story*. A native of Camagüey, he'd included the address of his home in that city. It was right on the Carretera Central. A photo and five minutes of reflection was all I wanted. The building looked brand new. From the looks of it our driver surmised it now filled some sort of government function, though it posted no sign.

Camagüey Province is famous for its cheese. Unlicensed vendors selling one or two wheels balanced on a flat board dipped in and out of the bushes along the Carretera Central alternatively displaying their cheeses to passers-by and hiding from the authorities. Brenda and Tina couldn't resist buying one.

The purchase led to a discussion of Cuban food and prices. It was at this time that we found out about the *madinusa* chickens. Our driver also told us that Cuba grows no wheat, but exports rice. At the same time, Cuba imports rice from China and Brazil—go figure. He raved about the quality of Brazilian rice. Rice is a Cuban staple, eaten every day, like tortillas are eaten with every meal in Mexico.

Our driver's private taxi license cost him $14 CUCs and he paid an additional 10% tax on his receipts. Diesel in February, 2016 cost $2.77 CUCs per gallon (the comparable price in the US was $2.00). Asked how easy it was to fudge on his fare take, he responded that it was nearly impossible: the tax authorities used extremely invasive methods to double-check estimated receipts. At the end of the 2-3 hour ride, Roy gave the drivers a $20 CUC tip. I wondered how traceable or declarable that tip was...

Our Ciego de Avila B&B was right on the Carretera Central. The lovely, well-maintained, two-story pink house had a curious plaque in front: Villa Jabón Candado (Padlock Soap Villa). Some long nearly forgotten childhood memory stirred. Jabón Candado was the laundry soap we'd used at home when I was a kid. Before the Revolution it was the #1 selling laundry soap in Cuba.

Villa Jabón Candado, Ciego de Avila, Carretera Central in foreground. Notice the upside-down anchor logo indicating a B&B for foreigners above the house's sign. Credit: R. H. Miller.

Back in 1863, Juan and José Crusellas, two brothers from Catalonia, Spain, opened a factory in Havana to produce soap and candle—Crusellas & Company. In 1897, they introduced a laundry soap using the brand name "Candado".

In 1929 Crusellas & Co. entered into a joint venture with Colgate-Palmolive. Under the terms of the agreement, Crusellas & Co. would manufacture and market the American company's products on the island. While this new arrangement resulted in the proliferation in Cuba of the US brands, it didn't seem to affect the popularity of Candado soap. Crusellas & Co. was a pioneer in the use of radio and television advertising in Cuba. Its jingles were extremely catchy and popular. Many older Cubans still remember them.

I asked Marilin, our hostess, why she'd named her home after a long-gone soap brand. She said that over a period of 20 years prior to the Revolution, the Crusellas Company had held an annual promotional contest in which the winners received new houses. There were years when numerous houses were given away. The houses came with the "Villa Jabón Candado" logo on the façade. We saw another one the next day in Jatíbonico. But she just shrugged her shoulders when I asked her how she scored the house, implying that the benefits and detriments of the Revolution amounted to a crap shoot—rather like the Jabón Candado contest.

Crusellas & Company was nationalized by Castro's revolutionary government in October 1960. The Crusellas family was forced to go into exile. The company was re-founded with the same name in Miami in 1967 and continues to be a going concern.

Marilin was an MD; she taught microbiology at the local university. But it was the B&B that provided the real income for the family. Her mother prepared us a delicious dinner that evening. When Marilin got home I asked her about the CDRs, the Committees for the Defense of the Revolution, signs for which we'd been seeing all over the island.

The *Comités para la Defensa de la Revolución* are neighborhood committees designed to protect the Revolution from internal enemies. Organized in 1960, every block has one, with about 130,000 throughout the island and 15,000 in Havana alone. They are under the direction of the Ministry of the Interior, which handles most aspects of state security. Christopher Baker, in his *Havana* guidebook, explains their function:

> *"Anyone nay-saying the Revolution, mocking Castro, or dealing on the black market (economic crimes are political crimes, seen as a security threat to the state)*

is likely to be reported by the (CDR) block warden, a loyal revolutionary or self-serving sycophant who records what he or she hears from colleagues and neighbors."

Araceli Alonso in her anthropological study, *Out of Havana: Memoirs of Ordinary Life in Cuba*, reveals a bit more through her informant, Rosa:

"When I was president of the CDR, I was supposed to...report all kinds of irregularities, like people having dollars...Were they buying something not allowed...a TV or an electrical appliance only allowed to foreigners?...blue jeans?...Part of my responsibility was to report the names of those who acted different from the norm...those people who listened to the Beatles, women who complained about the quality of the rationed food, boys and young men who had long hair...All these things were antisocial, and they couldn't go unpunished."

CDR (Committees for the Defense of the Revolution) sign. Credit: R. H. Miller.

In 1991 during the Special Period when the USSR imploded, Rapid Response Detachments, ostensibly volunteers from local CDRs, were organized and deployed to deal with public expressions of dissent. "This they do through distasteful pogroms called *actos de repudios*, beating up dissidents, much as did Hitler's *Blockwarts*. Like Nazi street gangs, the brigades are said to be a spontaneous reaction by outraged Cubans," adds Baker.

The CDRs perform some useful services. They organize blood drives, take retirees on vacation, discourage school absenteeism, patrol neighborhoods to guard against delinquency, and generally run a tight *barrio* ship.

Marilin perceived the CDRs more as *barrio* busybodies than G2 operatives, their relevance having lessened somewhat after 2000, though they remain strong in the area of old Oriente Province, the Castros' home territory.

* * *

Our next destination was Sancti Spíritus, 76 km away, and the capital city of Sancti Spíritus Province. We were off at 7:30 am. Very cool morning.

On the ride out of Ciego de Avila we passed the local *Partido Comunista de Cuba* headquarters, the first one we'd seen. Brenda exclaimed, "See, Cuba is Communist!"

This rekindled a discussion we'd been having on and off for some time. Counterintuitively, I'd been arguing that Cuba wasn't Communist, only Socialist—a fine Marxist-Leninist distinction that came across as purely semantic to her. Castro never refers to Cuba as Communist, always as Socialist. That is because, in Marxist-Leninist ideology—as controversially modified by Josif Stalin—Communism is a utopian ideal that will only be achieved when every country is Socialist.

Previously, Friedrich Engels had always insisted that Socialism and Communism were equivalent and inseparable, and in economic terms, they are: the government owns and controls all economic activity or, as it's classically worded, the state "owns the means of production." To Engels, Communism/Socialism could only come about when the whole world adopted Marxist-Leninist ideology. Engels believed that socialist markets in some countries were incompatible with capitalist markets in other countries. The two just couldn't mix in a world economy.

However, Stalin won the argument. Right after World War I, the Russian Revolution and Civil War, when much of Europe was experiencing Socialist and Communist upheavals, Lenin and Stalin, believed that Marx's world revolution was at hand and the world was on the threshold of achieving Socialism/Communism. When the vision didn't come to pass, Stalin declared that the Soviet Union had achieved "Socialism in one country," a concept that was anathema to Trotsky, Zinoviev and Kamenev—so Stalin eliminated them and united all world Communist parties under his control. National Communist parties strive to entrench Socialism in their countries to bring about the Communist ideal.

It was Stalin's heretical declaration that forever severed Socialism from Communism—and it's a distinction that the Castros' adhere to.

I'm not sure Brenda was impressed; she has her own ideas about socialism.

We stopped for lunch under a few shade trees. Up came Eduardo, a weathered, 67-year-old *campesino*, garbed in traditional khaki topped with a straw hat. He said he'd worked the fields all his life and now was a cane field "guard," spending his days guarding the cane. It seemed as useful an endeavor as paying someone to watch over the wheat fields of Montana. I asked him what dangers the cane field faced. He just shrugged his shoulders. I suppose one can't be too safe.

Eduardo resignedly told us he makes $1 CUC per day, but added that Cubans had everything they needed except money. A friend of his pulled up in a cart pulled by two oxen with a following horse and came over to visit. He was delighted that George was from Taiwan because his brother was in China. We shared cheese, cookies and granola bars with them. They stared at the Costo granola bars trying to figure out what they might be. When I told them—I described them as dry, sugar-free *cucuruchu* bars—they decided to save them for later.

Sugar cane harvest along the Carretera Central. Credit: R. H. Miller.

Every two minutes the oxen would inch forward as if trying to escape in slow motion. It was comical. Eduardo's friend would shout a sharp "Jo!" the Cuban equivalent of 'whoa,' and the oxen stopped. After a suitable interval, off they'd go again.

Approaching Sancti Spíritus we got our first view of the Escambray Mountains, Cuba's other range, where so many other, unsung revolutions, both against Batista and Castro, had simmered.

Sancti Spíritus was founded in 1514 by, again, Diego Velázquez. The city is laid out in a modified grid pattern, so we didn't struggle to find our B&B, which happened to be located right next to the central square. The plaza is surrounded by elegant colonial buildings and arterial blocks of pedestrian malls

Most of our lodgings to date could not accommodate us in three rooms, the average home B&B having only one or two rooms to rent. Our hosts always arranged for George, the odd man out, to lodge somewhere near-by. "Los Richards" in Sancti Spíritus was different. Run by two brothers and their wives, they were able to combine their resources—like Roger and Karen and his mom in Las Tunas—into something fancier than the run-of-the-mill B&B. Our three rooms all fronted an inviting patio with bar.

I'd been requesting *picadillo*, a ground beef-based dish, for dinner at many B&Bs, but for some reason, hamburger was difficult to obtain. Los Richards were the first to offer it to us. Everyone loved it. We retired early.

"The night was raucous with loud noises and music from the street until very late," Brenda recalls. Rosie, one of the Richards' wives, apologized for the night's noise. She was no fan of rock & roll and added that she and Richard had also been kept awake. Not so Tina and I. We slept the sleep of the just. Rosie added that she ought to have called the police, but the look on her face indicated that that was a door that required serious consideration before opening.

I suggested that she might have called the neighborhood CDR. She made a dismissive gesture saying, "*Comités, shcomités!* No one cares about that anymore!" Of course, that opening segued into politics. Apropos of nothing she declared she hated Donald Trump. So I asked her about the Cuban succession.

She said that Raúl Castro is due to step down in 2018, but that his vice president is a non-entity. She thought that a Castro would succeed but she couldn't finger one, there are so many.

Fidel's family tree is messily complex. Fidel had 6 full brothers and sisters (in order): Angelita, Ramón, Fidel, Raúl, Juanita, Enma and Agustina; and two siblings from his father's first wife: Lidia and Pedro Emilio. Fidel's love life was even more Byzantine. In 1948 he married his teenage sweetheart, Mirta Díaz-Balart, a woman whose family were intimates of Fulgencio Batista and whose brother would soon become a minister in Batista's government. They had one son, Fidelito. But differences—in aspirations, in politics, in families and in fidelity (in spite of his name, Fidel was *el máximo* philanderer, being nicknamed *El Caballo*—The Stallion—by Benny Moré, the popular entertainer)—soon undermined the marriage. He didn't marry again until 1980; but the number of his affairs and assignations rivaled the length of his speeches.

In his Sierra Maestra redoubt he took up with Celia Sánchez, the woman who would later become what Juanita Castro described as "the right hand, left hand, both feet and beard of Fidel." After the triumph of the Revolution, Castro wallowed in female adoration. Yánez Pelletier, a confidante who'd once saved him in prison from poisoning, became his procurer. He was known as "minister of the bedroom", a nickname coined by Raúl. When Pelletier fell from grace, Celia Sánchez became his intimate executive secretary moving into Fidel's quarters with him. Though at that point severely circumscribed, the assignations still continued. When Celia Sánchez died in 1980, Fidel was bereft.

In 1980 he married Dalia Soto del Valle, the mystery woman with whom Fidel had shared his intimate life since 1961. As if reinforcing the myth that the Revolution was his only mistress, Castro imposed such a low profile on her that Brian Lattell, a CIA analyst, says that "(she) and her sons might as well have been consigned to a witness protection program, so elaborate are the security precautions that surround them". She never attended any of his public appearances (unless in disguise) and did not accompany him on official functions, diplomatic receptions, or foreign trips. During the latter, his mistresses included Juana Vera and "Pili" Pilar—both interpreters—and Gladys, a Cubana airline flight attendant.

All told, his many liaisons, relationships, and two marriages produced 9-12 children. He was coy about it. Asked in 1993 how many children he had, Castro replied, "Less than a dozen... I think." (Wikipedia and Juan Reynaldo Sanchez, his bodyguard, tally nine and ten, respectively.) Like their mothers and his siblings, some are with him, some against him and some have come to terms with the status quo.

Raúl, on the other hand, is a dedicated family man. He married Vilma Espín in 1959 and had four children: Mariela Castro, Alejandro Castro Espín, Déborah Castro and Nilsa Castro. Vilma died in 2007. He has not remarried.

* * *

Before we left Sancti Spíritus, Rosie and Richard showed us their new pride and joy, a 2016 Chinese-made 4-door SUV with all the trimmings. The gauges and labels were either in script or a Roman rendition of Mandarin. At least the numbers were Arabic. I laughed at the Chinese lack of sensitivity for their Cuban export market, however small. Richard laughed too but was just happy he could get the car. He only took it out on special occasions.

At Sancti Spíritus we bid goodbye to the Carretera Central, deviating south to Trinidad, Cienfuegos and the Bay of Pigs. Roy decided to taxi to Trinidad, 76 km away on the coast. Due to the noise, he hadn't slept at all and had only slept fitfully the previous nights—and he was still recovering from the flu. The ride in the old Chevy taxi didn't really help. The diesel fumes only aggravated his condition. It was to be Roy's last ride in a Cuban taxi.

23

La Pata

Tina, George, Brenda and I set off for Trinidad at 8 am with a tail breeze. Now off the Carretera Central, there was even less traffic. We encountered rolling hills as we neared the Sierra del Escambray. Thankfully, the weather wasn't too hot and the 75 km ride down to the coast was a pleasure.

I'd finagled about 100 toothbrushes from my dentist, Lance Bailey, and nearly as many ballpoint pens from my lawyer, Mark Goodman, a college roommate, to give away as gifts during the ride. These articles were small and light enough to carry on our bikes. They brought smiles to everyone's face. Ballpoint pens cost nearly $15 CUCs at dollar stores; everyone wanted one. I'd exhausted my supply long ago, but Roy and Brenda had nearly forgotten their stash. So they set about distributing with alacrity. Brenda gave one passer-by with a young boy a toothbrush and asked him how many kids he had. When he answered that he had five, she gave him four more.

Handing out toothbrushes to kids. Credit: R. H. Miller.

At the little town of—I think—Crucero, I paused to wait for the others. A UK-made, perfectly restored 1950s Ford Zephyr caught my eye. It seemed so out of place in this undistinguished village, especially after what I saw next. A large truck with a big cargo box behind the cab pulled off the road one-hundred feet in front of me. It quickly gathered a crowd. No signs identified it. People—even kids—with jars, buckets, plastic containers, large bottles, anything that would hold liquid ran to its rear and crowded, not bothering to queue up. A window at the back opened up and people held their containers up to a woman who began taking them, filling them up with something and handing them back. When a kid struggling with a full five-gallon container passed by me I asked him what was being given away. "Beer," he said.

This little town had no store. It made me wonder how they got groceries. At least they got free beer, thanks to Fidel.

Free beer being handed out in Cruzero. Credit: R. H. Miller.

Eight kilometers before Trinidad, we entered the Valle de Los Ingenios, one of the most beautiful landscapes in all of Cuba. The valley was the center of colonial-era sugar production, which created the wealth that built Trinidad. The industry was totally destroyed during the wars of independence, and afterward moved north and east into Matanzas Province.

Dozens of 19th-century sugar mills, warehouses, slave quarters, manor houses and a fully functioning steam train remain.

Valle de los Ingenios outside of Trinidad. Credit: R. H. Miller.

I stopped to wait at the far top edge of the valley to share the wonders of the view with Tina, George and Brenda, and to lead them into the city. A small oriental man with a day pack, walking in the opposite direction, stopped to ask directions. I tried my *ni hau* and *konichiwa* on him but he turned out to be Korean. With virtually no supplies, nearly no Spanish and even less English, the Korean was attempting to walk across Cuba. I marveled at the boundlessness of the human imagination.

Trinidad, on Cuba's south coast, was the fourth of seven cities founded by Diego Velázquez in 1514. Its cobbled streets are laid out in a modified radial pattern. Much of the architecture is neoclassical and baroque with Moorish allusions. The developmental hiatus after the loss of much of the sugar industry following independence allowed Trinidad to fossilize; a beautiful stagnation reinforced when the Carretera Central was built farther north in the 1930s bypassing the town and nearly making it irrelevant. In the 1950s, tourists discovered Trinidad and President Batista passed a preservation law recognizing the town's historical value. Fidel Castro declared Trinidad a national monument in 1965 and restoration of its historic core begun. It was made a UNESCO World Heritage Site in 1988.

Trinidad Plaza Mayor. Credit: R. H. Miller.

With so many tourists, accommodations in Trinidad can be difficult to obtain. Our B&B, on first impressions, did not impress. Its location on a run-down dirt street was not reassuring. Even more foreboding was the B&B Tina, George and I had been relocated to. Untethered dogs ran wild and children used the street to relieve themselves. However, the interiors and rooms were nice and comfortable. Our hostess prepared 2 lb. lobsters for us accompanied by a mediocre Cuban white wine that was nonetheless made delicious by its unique provenance.

The night was noisy at both locales. Our next-door neighbor was recently widowed and took to drinking and playing loud music well into the night. Tina finally had enough, got dressed and, out on the porch yelled, "Ció!" followed by an entreaty in English to quiet down. The music immediately stopped. Roy and Brenda weren't so lucky. The source of their music and noise was widespread along their street. While our hostess, María Eugenia, had a quiet word with her neighbor the following day, Roy and Brenda's host told them that Cuba was a noisy place at night, there was nothing he could do about it and for them to get used to it.

Trinidad was the end of the road for Roy and Brenda. A scheduling conflict required their return to the US so, eschewing a taxi—Roy had had enough diesel fumes to shorten his life—they made arrangements to take a bus back to Havana. Meanwhile, we all enjoyed a day playing tourist in Trinidad.

The Plaza Mayor has been restored to beyond a pristine state. Close by a high school was holding math classes. We crowded the windows to look in while the students glanced back at the tourists. Walking around we encountered a man rebuilding a box spring mattress, a recycling art unknown in the US. Off another spur street, another man was rolling cigars at a desk kiosk adjacent to a café and gift shop. George bought one of his handiworks and smoked it right there, Cuba having few restrictions on smoking in public.

Box spring repairman in Trinidad, one of about 200 legal self-employment categories.
Credit: Tina Cobos.

Cuban music has enjoyed a tremendous creative burst under Castro, akin to the flowering of Russian literature under the Soviet Union. Perhaps adversity is the mother of great art. Bike journeys are not conducive to late evening musical entertainment, exhaustion being the better part of temptation. Nonetheless, we were able to sample a couple of Cuban *conjuntos*. At Trinidad's Plaza Menor an acoustic foursome, two with homemade instruments, created a sound that belied their humble appearance. Understated and subtle, they nonetheless drowned out all other sounds and gathered a crowd hesitant to disperse.

Conjunto quartet at Trinidad's Plaza Menor. Credit: R. H. Miller.

We bought one of their CDs after being reassured that the recording had been professionally made. Back in Havana we'd bought another CD from a six-man electric band that had impressed us. They'd even played my request, *Cuando Salí de Cuba*, a sad song about exile. Back in the US the CDs turned out to be big disappointments. On both, the first 4-5 cuts were Revolutionary propaganda, paeans to Socialist heroes and the new society. One even managed to scan and rhyme 'Comandante Ernesto *Che* Guevara' into a couplet, albeit a long one. But those compositions were a far cry from the *Internationale*, which at least stirs the soul and inspires to action. After those first few cuts the CDs became garbled and unplayable.

Trinidad had been the original landing site for the Bay of Pigs invasion, chosen for its proximity to the Escambray Mountains and its reputed antipathy towards Castro and his revolution. But whatever antipathy existed in the 1960s we were unable to discover now.

The following day we bid goodbye to Roy and Brenda. They were enjoying a breakfast of scrambled eggs and nearly raw bacon, a Cuban preference the Smiths didn't take to. We took final pictures all around and headed out to Cienfuegos, 83 km away.

For lunch we stopped at a roadside open-air café offering fresh squeezed orange juice. The bartender, looking at the size of my bike's sprockets, asked how many speeds it had. "Twenty-seven," I answered, adding, "Its low gear is so low, it can coast uphill."

He liked that. We got to talking. He commented that, "Obama meeting with Raúl wasn't Nixon meeting with Mao. Still, everyone is really happy. Only North Korea left, but it's a tough nut."

A group of disheveled, scantily-clad, hairy characters talking loudly in English rode in from the direction of Trinidad. They were riding rusty, dodgy single-speed cruiser bikes with 3-gallon plastic kitty-litter buckets for panniers that were overflowing with their trip possessions. I was reminded of the Joad's Model-T in the Grapes of Wrath when they were heading for California and was about to yell, "Call if you find work!" when Tina engaged them.

They said they were going to ride across Cuba. They'd hitchhiked on a boat and had been dropped off at night near Trinidad, implying that their visit was undocumented—though they wouldn't elaborate. The bartender advised them to get a visa or they'd be jailed. We found out later when we reached Havana that they'd been deported.

The entry to Cienfuegos funneled us directly to the Prado, a grand avenue with a pedestrian mall down the center. The Prado runs from the main highway connector up north down to the magnificent Bahía de Cienfuegos, one of Cuba's major ports. Declared a UNESCO World Heritage Site in 2005, money has poured in to revitalize the neoclassical buildings fronting the Prado. On September 5, 1957 naval cadets and officers from the Cienfuegos Naval Base (with some funding from the CIA) staged a revolt against the Batista regime, one of the many uprisings on the island that were independent of Castro's July 26 Movement. Batista bombed the city and his troops recaptured it by nightfall.

It was easy finding our B&B along the logically numbered, grid-patterned streets. But we were again faced with musical B&Bs, being shuttled to three of them in total. Our final hostess served us a freshly-caught marlin dinner in a small dining room next to the 3rd story rooftop patio with a view of all Cienfuegos. She was well-off enough that she'd applied for a tourist visa to visit the US. Somehow, the Cuban government had approved the trip; but the United States declined her visa, suspicious that she might remain.

It made no sense to me. Cubans who arrive illegally in the US are automatically granted asylum. However, in this case, a Cuban who applies to travel legally is denied entry because she might remain, *in spite of the fact that the Cuban government doesn't think she'll remain in the US*. Go figure.

* * *

On March 2 we left Cienfuegos for Playa Girón—landing beach and headquarters of Brigade 2506 back in April 17-19 of 1961 during the Bay of Pigs invasion. The 94 km was flat all the way, albeit treeless at the start.

At Horquitas, site of the Brigade's deepest incursion, irrigated fields lined both sides of the road. It is one of the richest agricultural areas on the island with a lush and varied selection of crops. One giant irrigation pump was debouching a two-foot diameter torrent into an irrigation ditch. The heat was already oppressive and the temptation too great. I asked the attendant if we could douse ourselves in the clear, cool cataract. He was only too delighted to comply. Each of us in turn soaked ourselves in the concrete-lined ditch under the torrent.

Once we entered Matanzas Province, the surroundings became wild, shady and beautiful along a narrow paved byway. We were entering the Zapata swamps.

Even before the invasion, Castro had been attempting to create a tourist destination out of the Bay of Pigs area. The unfinished accommodations in Girón had served as the holding cells for the captured *brigadistas*. The invasion and its aftermath added a historical draw to the beach, fishing and diving attractions. Nonetheless, we encountered no tourists. About ten kilometers before Girón, Cubanacan, the government tourist bureau, had built *El Carbonero*, an attractive roadside *palapa* bar. Besides the bartender and a *miliciano*, we were the only ones there.

I suspect *El Carbonero* is located right at or very close to San Blas, the small town where Brigade 2506 made its last stand on its eastern front—the battle that Eli César wrote about in his book *San Blas: Ultima Batalla en Bahía de Cochinos*, and the invasion's second biggest engagement after the Battle of the *Rotonda*. If so, the government has changed its name to Bermejas. San

Blas, like the Battle of the *Rotonda*, was a heroic stand for the Brigade, one where the Castro casualties were much higher than the Brigade's, but one they also lost.

George and Tina along the road to Playa Girón. Credit: R. H. Miller.

Though I managed to photograph the *miliciano* from afar, he wouldn't let me take a close-up. I entreated him saying that Obama was coming and we were now friends. He was engaging and friendly but said he'd get in trouble. The bar only offered pop and beer—in spite of advertising fruit juices—but it did have coconut trees adjacent. The bartender got us three coconuts and in no time had macheted them open and stuck a straw in.

After downing the juice, Tina asked for the machete. She wanted to try her hand at opening a coconut. When she almost sliced her finger off, the bartender took over. After we'd downed the fourth coconut's water, he split it open for us and showed us how to eat the soft layer of sweet mucus atop the coconut meat. Afterward she dug out the coconut meat and fed a rickety little dog that had come up to beg.

We encountered no feral dogs in Cuba. Cuban dogs are loved, well behaved and well trained, so this little dog was an exception. The bartender said it'd been abandoned somehow and he was resisting adopting it. Had we not been on bikes and the dog so small, it would have followed us until it became ours.

Playa Girón is a quiet, small, relatively new town of a few hundred people laid out along a single road. The buildings are located on about one-third-of-an-acre or larger lots, suburban-style. At the time of the invasion it was even smaller, inhabited by *campesinos* who scratched out a living making charcoal and fishing.

For George, Girón was the end of his ride. The delay at the start had pushed him too close to his departure date. He would take a taxi to Havana on the morrow. Meanwhile, he plopped down in a rocking chair and napped until dinner. Our B&B hostess, Yunaiky, was unable to cook for us that night due to a prior engagement. Instead, she recommended a *paladar* just down the street. One of its specialties was crocodile steak.

Without a sign and no way to identify it, we decided to take a pedi-taxi there. It turned out be only half-a-block distant. We all laughed, including the good-natured driver who took great pride in his conveyance having added a rear view mirror, a plastic *Virgen de la Caridad del Cobre*, an odometer and other decorations to his dashboard. One CUC settled the bill. He concluded with, "Call me if you want a ride back," to which we all had another good laugh.

Outside, the *paladar* was just another pastel-colored nondescript house. In the back, a large area had been enclosed by a smartly-built, tall and tight wattle fence, with a palm frond roof. About ten tables graced the tastefully enclosed outdoor space that was decorated to perfection. The waiter, servillete over his forearm, recited the menu while I translated. We all chose the special, a trifecta of shrimp, fish and lobster. I asked him about the croc (which he'd failed to mention), and he said yes, they served it. But he couldn't officially announce it because it was a protected species. I was sorely tempted to try it. Dinner was accompanied by fresh sweet potato chips, yucca fritters, *congrí*, salad and 2 bottles of excellent white wine—all for $20 CUCs each.

The following morning we bid farewell to George and rode towards the Brigade 2506 landing site. Along this stretch of coast, only two locations have sandy beaches suitable for amphibian landings: Playa Girón and the inside of Bahía de Cochinos itself, especially Playa Larga at its head, where the two invasion landings took place. In between, the coast is rocky, razor-sharp dead coral with a three-to-four foot vertical rise from the water.

"Beach" between Playa Playa Girón and Playa Larga. Not a good place for an amphibious landing. Credit: R. H. Miller.

The Playa Girón beach is now dominated by the Cubanacan resort, Villa Playa Girón, a resort whose reviews include the following: "a grumpy, fat trollop behind the reception desk," "watery beer served in tiny plastic cups with a huge head," "cocktails of cheap rum and sugary soda," "holiday camp disaster zone," "restaurant's buffet is pathetic." I could go on. But the real insult is the series of concrete walls separating the "resort" from the rest of the world. Around the resort's hinterland, a semi-circular wall isolates it; the only entrance is through the manned gate. Mark Moxon, a travel blog writer, describes the rest:

> "But the designers of the Hotel (sic) Playa Girón were obviously not content with simply closing off the perimeter and the rocky coast, because some mud fool has built a concrete wall across the mouth of the pleasant crescent-shaped beach, only 50m or so off shore. This means that when you sit there on the beach, all you can see dead ahead is a wall of mouldering concrete grot, stained with green streaks and crumbling gently into the sea. I idly wondered if the locals were

433

worried that someone else might try to invade the beach and these were their defenses. If so, they've surely succeeded in deflecting future attacks; it's hard to see why anyone would want to reclaim this small part of holiday hell."

We stopped to take pictures at the west entrance to town. The billboards proudly touting Castro's victory were in tatters. Along the pleasant ride to Playa Larga we encountered teams of machete-wielding foliage cutters keeping the Zapata jungle from taking over the road—the road along which Armandito's Second Battalion had retreated after their stand at the Battle of the *Rotonda*; the road along which *El Chino* had run to Girón headquarters to beg for ammunition and reinforcements from Pepe San Román; the road long-since paved after those fateful three days, but now carrying almost no traffic.

The road maintenance crews caught our eye because they were dressed in a traditional Cuban garb of khakis, knee-high putees, belt-hung machetes and straw hats. When we saw a mower by himself, Tina stole a telephoto shot of him which he did not try to stop—they were, after all, uniformed personnel.

Roadside weed control along the Playa Girón-Playa Larga road. Notice traditional dress with high putees. Credit: Tina Cobos.

As the road veered north along the Bay of Pigs itself, diving centers and modest Cubanacan resorts dominated, the latter all fenced. I expected to enter the village of Playa Larga in due time, get a glimpse of the beach where Armandito and the 2nd Battalion landed, and perhaps even see the hulk of the *Houston* still beached off in the distance. And yes, perhaps Playa Larga was what was surrounding us as we pedaled ahead. But before I knew it, there we were: at the junction of the Girón, Jagüey Grande and Buenaventura roads.

This was the *rotonda*, where the great battle of the Bay of Pigs invasion had been fought. Except that it was no longer a roundabout; it was a giant Y. In the center stood a concrete monument to the Castro dead. I pulled over and mulled the scene.

The intersection just north of Playa Larga that was once La Rotonda; now just a Y, with monument to Castro casualties in the center. Credit: R. H. Miller.

"No roundabout!" I gasped.

By eliminating the roundabout, might Castro be hoping to obliterate any vestiges of that defeat? Flowers surrounded the modest stelae, a couple dozen or so of the dead's names inscribed upon it. Without a roundabout, traffic had no chance to pause; no chance to contemplate what had transpired here on the night of April 17th, 1961.

But *I* needed to pause. I was traversing terrain of endless emotional upheaval.

Adjacent to the road junction, along the Jagüey Grande spur, a fenced CUC (or dollar) store offered a few items. We stopped for lunch. The attendant hadn't heard of the Battle of the *Rotonda*. A small sign on the side wall commemorated the 50th anniversary of the Bay of Pigs. It read: "Girón, first great military defeat of Yanqui imperialism in Latin America." Alongside, a now-famous picture of Fidel jumping off a tank, presumably to take control of the operation on the spot, limbs nerdily but engagingly splayed, black horned-rim glasses on his face, showed his commitment to turn back the invasion and save his revolution from defeat.

I'd hoped to see more. After sharing tuna and peanut butter sandwiches washed down with two liters of Spar OJ, we moved on. Perhaps some vestige of Cachorro's mission lay ahead along the Playa Larga, Palpite, and Jagüey Grande causeway.

The nineteen men of Cachorro's 1st Parachute Battalion had been dropped somewhere along both sides of the road up ahead. Their job had been to blow up the culverts and bridges on the causeway, and so delay the Communist troops and tanks from counter-attacking the invading forces. But they'd been late and the drop hadn't gone well.

The forests gave way to open wetlands with shoulder-high bog grass, impossible territory upon which to operate or hide—or give chase. Now I understood why Castro's militia bided their time waiting for the paratroopers to come out on their own, and why *El Cojo* Vera was able to escape alone and on foot. Along the way many smaller, albeit identical concrete monuments to Castro's dead peppered the road's verges. I was surprised at how far towards Jagüey Grande they extended. Were those deaths inflicted by Cachorro's detachment, by aerial attacks, by friendly fire, or where they deaths incurred during one of the Castro forces' retreats from wounds suffered closer to the *rotonda*?

By the time we reached the derelict sugar refinery, Central Australia, where a big billboard with Castro's face announced "Jagüey Grande: Secure Rearguard of Girón," we were ready for a break. Castro's headquarters had been at the sugar mill—it having the only working phone for miles around— during the little war. Immediately up the road we arrived at the tourist bus complex where we'd stopped for lunch on the bus ride to Baracoa three weeks previously. It had been one of the best meals we'd had *and* they served fresh-squeezed orange and pineapple juice, a treat we couldn't pass up.

Billboard on road (causeway down which the Castro forces attacked Brigade 2506) from Playa Larga to Jagüey Grande announcing "Secure rearguard of Girón," a reference to Fidel Castro's headquarters at Jagüey Grande. Credit: R. H. Miller.

When the chef saw us, he came out to shoot the breeze. I asked him if he remembered me from the bus stop ride three weeks before. He said, "No."

So I told him, "I don't remember you either."

He quipped, "So, there we are. We have something in common: We don't remember each other." We both laughed. Cubans, like the Irish, like word play.

Then he said that he did remember me; I was the only "Cuban" in a bus-full of tourists, identifiable because I'd engaged him in repartee.

* * *

We found Ileana's B&B in Jagüey Grande right away. Ileana was a stout, older woman who'd have been hard-pressed to run a B&B by herself, especially one with three stories. She'd found a creative way around the hiring restrictions the government imposed. She had two "employees." They only "worked" when she needed them and she didn't "pay" them. At the end of a guest's stay, Ileana would recite a sob story about how hard the girls worked, how little she could afford to pay them, how poor Cuba was and, if the guests had it in their hearts, would they mind giving the girls a $10 CUC tip—but of course, it was completely voluntary.

The girls gave me the impression that Ileana was a bit of a scammer, but a good sort nonetheless. She had a great sense of humor: "Fidel and Raúl are riding in a plane. Fidel pulls out a $20 CUC bill and confides to Raúl, 'If I throw out this bill from this plane, the Cuban who finds this $20 CUC bill is going to be a very happy Cuban!' Raúl answers that he's got a better and cheaper idea: Throw out two $10 CUC bills and there'll be two happy Cubans. Then the pilot pipes up, "I've got an even better idea: Throw both of you out the plane and there'll be 11 million happy Cubans.'"

I commented not to let the local CDR hear her tell that joke. She responded, "Things have improved. They'll no longer kill you for that, you'll only disappear."

The ride up to Matanzas city on Cuba's north coast was long but not too hot. The city is spread around an 11 kilometer-deep bay, one of Cuba's most important seaports. Oil tanks and tankers line its western entrance. Our B&B was on its eastern shore, right on the bay, with a delightful set of tunneled steps out in the back yard leading down to a coral grotto in the water.

Only 98 kilometers remained to Havana, a distance easily tackled in one day. However, I wanted to visit some old family haunts along the way, so we broke the ride up into two days, choosing to luck to find a B&B in Guanabo, a centrally-located town along the Playas del Este, the Varadero-for-Cubans beach resorts. We hit the gossip jackpot.

Julio César, our host, had been in the tourist business since the 1990s, playing cat-and-mouse with the government while trying to make an honest buck—in the legal, grey or black market, depending on how the regulations *du jour* dictated. He started out running a taxi for tourists that at times was legal, at times not. He got to know the local cop and his rounds, who in turn befriended or avoided him. It cost Julio César a stint in jail.

He began his B&B business when they and *paladares* were first made legal. But then Castro had second thoughts. Without actually outlawing them, he increased taxes and regulations to such a degree that it put many out of business. Julio César said taxes went up to $330 CUCs per month irrespective of the number of clients or the B&B's income. In addition, B&Bs couldn't hire anyone for anything. Now he can, though there are complexities, the state being concerned over "exploitation" of labor.

In spite of the recent labor reforms that incentivize people off government employment and into self-employment, Julio César says the government is terrified of small and medium-sized enterprises. Permitted categories include auto body repair, computer programming (in a country woefully short of computers), hair cutting and beauty shops, gardeners, nannies, dog trainers, shoemaking, home repairs, selling music CDs, manicurist, selling religious items and medicinal herbs, photographer, tire repair, and such, totaling nearly 200 enterprises with concomitant taxes ranging from 25 to 50% and employment restrictions that require a lawyer to interpret. One Cuban-American economist, sarcastically dismissing the changes because they do little for the economy, only lessen the state's burdens, wagged that now Castro allows Cubans to sew buttons on shirts for money—without being thrown in jail. Of course, the new entrepreneurs disagree. They're thrilled at the changes, but will probably soon feel shackled when they can't build on their success.

The fear of medium-sized businesses isn't just ideological aversion to profits ("making more money than necessary") and exploitation ("making the best [ab]use of a resource"). Julio César suspects old-fashioned fear of competition is at the root of it.

Raúl and his late wife, Vilma Espín, have three daughters. One is married to a general whose public persona is so behind-the-scenes that Julio César couldn't recall his name. The general is not a politician and doesn't wish to draw attention to himself. However, he is the architect of most of Cuba's successful mid- to large state enterprises, such as the Caracol Dollar/CUC stores, and the foreign joint ventures. His military, family and commercial positions endow him with unrivaled power; power which in Julio César's informed opinion he will not easily give up, but will continue to wield behind the scenes.

When Raúl's term is up in 2018, Julio César expects vice-president Miguel Mario Díaz-Canel Bermúdez, 56, to succeed, but not in any meaningful way. Raúl's second-in-command, José Ramón Machado

Ventura, 85, is expected to continue wielding power by leading the Party. But Julio César expects Raúl's son-in-law general to wield the real power.

Our host served us a very special dinner of lobster and marlin. As a side dish, he made *the* meal from the 'special period' when the USSR fell apart: cabbage sautéed in butter with pepper and bits of bell pepper. It was actually delicious, but back then it was the only food available. Except, that is, for what he called a "Communist breakfast:" sugar water and bread followed by cutting cane in the fields.

In conjunction with President Obama's Cuba thaw at the end of 2014, Cuba and the US concluded a spy swap. Five Cuban spies were released in exchange for Alan Gross, an American aide worker convicted of bringing satellite and computer equipment to members of Cuba's Jewish community without the permit required under Cuban law. Julio César told us that the five returned spies, in their report before Cuba's Central Committee of the Communist Party, dropped a quiet and unexpected bombshell.

Having spent years in the US, they'd grown accustomed to the benefits of freedom and choice. In their debriefing they urged greater reforms for Cuba and increased personal initiative for the people. Julio César said that the recommendations were taken with a grain of salt, but he believes they made an impression. After all, their credibility was impeccable: the five spies were dedicated enough to pursue their work with enthusiasm and, unlike many Cuban baseball players who've defected, came back to Socialist Cuba willingly.

* * *

Boca Ciega, the town where my immediate and extended families' beach houses had been located, was only blocks away from Guanabo. We visited with Julio César and his family over many cups of sweet Cuban coffee, traditionally brewed *with* sugar, before we headed out.

Guanabo and Boca Ciega run seamlessly into one another; but while Guanabo was alive with activity, Boca Ciega was eerily dead. Guanabo has commerce; Boca Ciega seems to continue being a beach house community—as it was in my family's time—but now for middle-level bureaucrats, I surmised. Moreover, this was the first week of March—still winter. And while we'd experienced very hot temperatures in the interior and along the south coast, Cuba's north coast and the Florida Straits can be windy and relatively cool in winter.

Once I located the strand, instinct took me right to our old house. It had been painted blue and was now four separate apartments each with a cyclone fence gate. It had been well-maintained. Tina wanted to knock on a door but I preferred not to, mostly from my natural reserve, but also because my memories of Boca Ciega primarily revolved around the beach, wandering the streets with my cousins, concocting harmless escapades and hanging out at my extended family's compound, which I now sought out.

Author's nuclear family's beach house in Boca Ciega, 2016. Credit: R. H. Miller.

I realized instantly that we must have passed right by it without recognizing it. And in fact, that was the case. The Fitzgerald-López compound had been green and open, two stories high, and provided beach apartments for perhaps ten nuclear families. Now it was fenced and pastel yellow, its identity an unrecognizable mix of functions. But the original high-walled handball courts by which I was able to identify it, hadn't been altered. The convenience kiosk across the street where I'd bought a *malta* and plantain chips had disappeared. I found it profoundly ironic that Socialism had atomized society to such a degree, and that Castro's crimeless society required so many fences.

Author's extended family (Fitzgerald-López) beach compound in Boca Ciega; now surrounded by tall block wall. Credit: R. H. Miller.

We walked the one block to the shore and across the boardwalk over the coastal dunes. The beach had that lonely wintry, windy, seaweed-strewn look about it. No one was there. Low, choppy surf, its apron lapping far inland, stroked the shallow forebeach. I took pictures without people, for my sisters mainly, walked back to our bikes and rode on to Havana.

* * *

The Playas del Este are separated from Havana by Havana harbor, a 5-6 kilometer-long bay with a narrow entrance and three bulbous pods for termini. In 1957-58 President Batista built a tunnel under the harbor entrance connecting old Havana with the iconic Morro Castle and Guanabacoa. Bikes, pedestrians and motorbikes are not allowed. However, a cyclo-bus runs periodically to carry bikes, bikers and pedestrians.

Alternatively, a small—it held only about twenty passengers—rattle-trap pedestrian and bike ferry connects both shores of the bay, its route about a mile deep inside the harbor. Rattle-trap is a charitable description. The no-bigger-than-a-Lake Powell-house-boat-rental had no seats, no bathroom, no lifeboats or bulkheads—but it did have overhead straphangers. The ferry's eastern terminus was not easy to find, the approach winding through poor neighborhoods on marginal dirt and potholed roads with no signs indicating its location. We stopped every block or so to ask directions. The ferry terminal was a nonedescript concrete building about the size of a small American fast-food joint. A Guanabacoa bike club preceded us, planning to ride the length of the Malecón. We queued up to get on. Just past the pre-loading entry door, three *milicianos* sat at a table: Cuba's version of the TSA (Transportation Security Authority). Only a mentally handicapped terrorist would target this vital piece of infrastructure.

I figured the security screening was a make-work formality. The Cuban bikers were waved through and actually told to hurry up so as not to delay the ferry's punctual departure. While the ferry attendant was also motioning us forward, one of the *milicianos*, a female, couldn't pass up this opportunity. She insisted on having us remove panniers, handlebar and trunk bags, and remove our hydration back-packs—and empty them all to check for dangerous contraband. I complied slowly.

When she got to my Gillete Twin Trac II razor she held it up, examined it and said, "I have to confiscate this."

I could picture her hairy legs luxuriating under its Lubastrip as she swathed it across her shins. I didn't care that it cost more than $3 a blade in the US, I wasn't about to give it up easily. It was my last blade and I resented her arbitrary exercise of corrupt power. I told her I had a difficult time nicking my Adam's apple with it, and what could I do, threaten the pilot with a close shave? I was about add, 'I can't hijack the ferry to Cuba; I'm already here!' but thought the better of it.

She responded, "Regulations are regulations."

So I asked to see her supervisor. She thought about the request for a scant second and responded that she was going to let me through as a personal favor *because she was nice*. I thanked her and kowtowed before she got to my Swiss Army knife, Leatherman tool and mustache scissors. We were free to board the ferry.

The ride across Havana harbor took five minutes. We landed in front of the Russian Orthodox Church, a beautiful but completely out-of-place structure in old Havana, its snow-white stuccoed exterior topped by multiple crosses of St. Mark.

We'd made it! My bike odometer read 1,185.55 kilometers, Baracoa to Havana. The ride to Tondy's was a leisurely victory lap. We stopped on the Malecón directly across Morro Castle to take pictures. An old-fashioned wrecking ball was demolishing derelict buildings across the street. On the broad Malecón promenade three men had set up a table displaying fishing tackle for sale. They were neatening up their wares when a small, rusty, unrestored old car with four men cruised by and slowed down.

"*Maricones! Flojos! Hijos de putas! Comemierdas!* (Faggots! Limp wrists! Sons of whores! Shit eaters!) They shouted vigorously.

"*Borrachos! Alcohólicos! Ordinarios!* (Drunks! Alcoholics! Uncultured commoners!) The tackle sellers yelled back. Everyone laughed.

Tondy and Tania welcomed us back with hugs, kisses and cold beer. On our last night Tondy treated us to a home-made Cuban nouvelle cuisine meal: oregano-spiced black beans, pork and chicken kabobs trimmed with grenadine-marinated pineapple, yucca con mojo, malanga fritters with a honey-garlic dip, salad, white wine and flan.

* * *

Exit procedures at the airport went smoothly. Money got exchanged; overweight baggage got charged, the unfriendly customs agent waved us through and the plane left on time. Upon landing in Miami, the stewardess' boilerplate announcements, in both Spanish and English, were mostly background chatter. But then, and only in Spanish, came the following: "If this is your first trip to the United States, and you want to stay here, please notify the airline. We will help you with the paperwork."

I was stunned. I didn't expect sanctuary help from the airline, much less a proding to defect.

Apprehensive about US Customs, I had our US Department of the Treasury paperwork indicating our permitted category, our required daily journals, our education proposal and resumés, and our expenditure receipts in hand to present when asked what our business in Cuba had been.

"Where are you coming from?"

"Cuba."

"How was it?"

"Good and bad," Tina responded.

She smiled, said "Welcome home," and waved us through.

EPILOGUE

Our bike journey was originally intended to continue through Pinar del Rio Province to Cuba's west end, about another 200 kilometers, with a final milk-run flight to the Isle of Youth and the Cárcel Modelo, the prison built in part by my grandfather and later occupied at different times for different insurrections by Fidel and Raúl Castro, and my cousins Cachorro and Armandito. However, we were unable to continue the journey because extending our visas proved impossible.

Canadian tourists automatically receive a 90-day tourist card to visit Cuba. Americans only get a 30-day tourist card, with an extension "easily" available, according to guidebooks. Not so; we tried.

For starters, the charter flights for legal US travelers automatically provide the 30-day tourist card with a fixed return date within that time period. Open returns are not available. A tourist card extension requires forfeiting the price of the reserved return flight and buying a new ticket from Cubanacan, the Cuban tourist agency. Additionally, the window of opportunity for an extension is only three days before scheduled departure. Cuban immigration offices are hard to find and keep very idiosyncratic hours. There are always long lines of petitioners. The penalty for overextending a stay lands you in custody until your activities in the country have been investigated.

Finally, there's a classic catch-22 that's nearly impossible to overcome. A petition for a tourist card extension requires receipts from one's lodging accommodations. When I presented these to the immigration officer, she said, "These are not official receipts." When I told Tondy, our host, what had happened, he said the receipt he gave me was from a receipt booklet provided by the government and used to determine tax assessments—it was as "official" as it got. I tried once more but was unable to overcome the receipt hurdle.

Pinar del Rio Province is a contrast to the rest of the island. It is Cuba's tobacco growing region. The Cordillera de Guaniguanico, with a high point of 2,300 feet, spans its length. It is a modest range, unique for its *mogotes*, giant, hairy, limestone warts, reminiscent—in a much smaller scale—of the *tepuis* of Venezuela. As a boy, Cachorro once set out on horseback with a buddy to climb a *mogote*. But when they got to the base of one, they looked up and exclaimed, "It's perfectly vertical!" and turned back.

In the late 1990s, modern rock climbing hit the Viñales valley, heart of tobacco and *mogote* country, with both Cubans and foreigners putting up routes—in spite of a paucity of technical equipment. As lifelong rock climbers and mountaineers, Roy, Tina and I wanted to check out the Cuban climbing scene. But it was not to be. In 2011 the Cuban government outlawed all climbing in the Viñales valley.

There was one other objective I had in the valley of Viñales, now a National Park and UNESCO World Heritage Site. The *Finca el Rosario* was confiscated from Chuchu Aisa's family (part of Tita Faget's clan and mentioned in chapter 6 as a then-future operative in the CIA's infiltration program). The estate is now a country house for the exclusive use of the Castro family. Fidel uses it for hunting and fishing trips. Inside the extensive grounds there is a seven-bedroom mansion where Fidel entertains guests. It is completely surrounded by trees but has a view of the sea. Since I had the directions for how to get there, I wanted to at least pass by the entrance as innocently as possible and try to get a glimpse without being arrested.

Altogether, Fidel Castro has 13 personal properties—all confiscated from previous owners—in Pinar del Rio Province. In next-door Havana, where his main residence is located, he has 18 personal properties—again, all confiscated. As if those were not enough, he has 35 more homes, and hunting and fishing lodges scattered throughout the other provinces, the Isle of Youth (3) and the cays of Cuba.

If, in the future, confiscated property claims are ever entertained by a more liberal regime, my family will be there. Not because we need the money, but because it's the right thing to do.

* * *

When we landed in Miami after our flight from Havana, Martica, my Venezuelan cousin, and her son Julio and daughter Marta Julieta picked us up at the airport.

My mother, Ana María, had two brothers slightly older than herself. One of them, Robert (after whom I'm named) emigrated from Cuba in the 1940s and settled in Caracas, Venezuela where he married Lya, a *Venezolana*. They had many children, who in turn, also had many children who have all prospered. Uncle Robert sent his youngest daughter, Martica, to the US for her high school years to learn English. She lived with my immediate family in Arizona while attending a Catholic girls' school run by nuns. Lya Rita, Uncle Robert's oldest daughter, became a lawyer and rose to become the first woman cabinet member in President Luis Herrera Campins' administration. Although she did her best, the Campins administration grew more unpopular as its term ran its course.

Uncle Robert Fitzgerald, brother of Ana María (the author's mother), who immigrated to Venezuela in the 1940s. His children and grandchildren are now trying to immigrate to the US. Credit: R. H. Miller

Venezuela's much touted social contract had begun showing signs of stress. Carlos Andrés Pérez, elected to ameliorate a widening poor/rich divide through neo-liberal economic policies, ended up, in the short term, exacerbating them. In 1992 Lieutenant Colonel Hugo Chávez led a coup against the Pérez administration. The coup failed and Chávez was imprisoned, but Pérez soon ended up being driven from office. Two years later Chávez was pardoned. In 1998 he ran for president and won. By the end of his first year in office, he'd overhauled the constitution and launched his Bolivarian Revolution.

One month before Stephen Cox, *Liberty* magazine's editor, commissioned the article which gave birth to this book, my sister Naná, in Phoenix, Arizona, got a call from my cousin Martica, in Caracas. After catching up on family gossip, Martica opened a new chapter in the family's chronicle. She requested that we hire a US immigration lawyer to begin the

447

long, costly and convoluted process of gathering their lives and delivering themselves from Hugo Chávez' 21st Century Socialism.

Martica and Lya Rita had been out shopping one day in Caracas when two masked men accosted them, held them at gunpoint and demanded they empty their bank accounts at the nearest ATM. After complying, they went to the nearest police station to report the crime. To their utter astonishment, the officer that filed the report was one of the men who had kidnapped them. Terrified, they nonetheless continued the charade, fearful of possible repercussions if the officer suspected he'd been identified.

As if that experience wasn't bad enough, it happened twice more. These "express kidnappings," as they've been labeled, are becoming more common. After nearly ten years of waiting, Martica finally got her US residency green card.

Her son Julio was luckier. While attending the Thunderbird School of International (now Global) Management, he met Kelly, an American girl, got married and landed a job as a Latin American securities analyst for Morgan Stanley. He now resides in Miami.

Martica's daughter, Marta Julieta, is still struggling to escape Venezuela. A talented fashion designer, she worked for Prada and Alexander Wang, New York fashion firms, on a work/study visa until it ran out while she was undergoing the necessary steps for legal US residency. She then applied for a scholarship to pursue an MBA degree on a renewed student visa (both of which she got). We're all hoping her green card comes through before her MBA does.

Lya Rita, the lawyer and ex-cabinet minister, is still in Caracas, living on little more than bread, noodles, tuna fish and whatever becomes available in the rapidly dwindling Venezuelan food supply after sometimes entire days of waiting in lines to buy whatever little is on offer. With a 2016 inflation rate of 480%, and projected to reach 1,600% in 2017, her prospects look dimmer every day.

Although news report analyses of Venezuela's shortages and inflation rate are usually attributed to the drop in crude oil prices in 2014, the real culprit is the Chávez-Maduro mismanaged socialist policies. As of August 2016, those policies have now affected Castro's Cuba.

After the implosion of the USSR in the early 1990s and the subsequent "special period"—a euphemism for the loss of Soviet subsidies—in Cuba, Venezuela stepped in to provide new subsidies. With oil running at over $100 per barrel at the time, Chávez believed he could afford to become

Castro's patron. Venezuela provided about 50% of Cuba's oil at very favorable prices.

In return, Castro sent Cuban doctors to Venezuela. Nicknamed *siete-mesinos* (seven-monthers, or premies, a reference to premature babies, the belief being that they're not ready for 'prime time' or are trained too quickly), Venezuelans tend to shun them in preference for Venezuelan doctors whenever they're facing an invasive operation.

But then the fracking revolution happened, and oil prices plummeted in late 2014. They are nowhere near recovery. Raúl Castro announced in August of 2016 a new energy rationing policy reminiscent of the "special period" due to a 20% reduction of Venezuelan oil imports. Both fuel consumption and electricity will be reduced by 28%. No word on whether Castro will cut back on his doctor exports.

* * *

We were due to spend a week in Miami—since the 1960s a free suburb of Havana—visiting and interviewing family and friends I hadn't seen in nearly 20 years.

Six years previously, commissioned to write a review of Juanita Castro's bombshell book, *Fidel y Raúl Mis Hermanos*, I called my aunt Tita up to ask a favor. Juanita Castro had left Cuba through Mexico, but then she'd made her way to Miami where she settled down. Wanting to keep busy and be productive, she'd opened up a small pharmacy in Little Havana to support herself. In the hyper-ideological atmosphere of the Cuban exile community, she had to keep a very low profile.

Some hated her just for her family name. No one knew of her efforts to help people escape, much less her CIA connections. I asked Tita to go to Juanita's pharmacy and take the measure of her. What was Juanita Castro like? At first Tita wasn't quite sure what I wanted her to do. Perhaps I was too dense to realize that facing a Castro, for Tita, after all she'd been through—her son Armandito's war, imprisonment, and infiltration; her brother-in-law's double imprisonment and descent into despair; her own exile and tribulations—might be an unwelcome shock to an old lady. But Tita agreed to do it.

When I called her back she told me that Juanita had retired. With the release of her book and the ensuing fame and notoriety it generated, Juanita had to get out of the public eye.

Tita had turned 94 just before our trip to Cuba. She'd always opposed it, warning me that Cuba was much more dangerous than all the recent media reports about wonderful tourist experiences. She was now bedridden and wandered in and out of sanity. Cuca, her sister, was in great physical health but lived in a happy place all of her own. *Las Viejas*, as they were affectionately referred to, were being cared for by Dunia, Tondy's sister.

Alina, Tita's daughter, and MariCris, Cuca's daughter, had their hands full finding additional help to spell Dunia. The house was a beehive of activity with Dunia performing her duties; Alina and MariCris interviewing care-giver applicants; a Cuban doctor-turned-nurse until he could pass the Florida medical boards to practice in the US checking up on the *viejas*. Our arrival also coincided with a visit from Lauristela, Armandito's widow, whom I hadn't seen in years. Armandito had died on August 5, 2008. His lack of boundaries had killed him: he ate himself into diabetes and morbid obesity.

We were lucky to find Tita in one of her lucid moments, though not lucid enough to recall her English. I gave her the highlights of the trip, recounted finding my grandmother's grave (her aunt), told her I was dedicating this book to her and Armandito, held her hand and told her I loved her. She died a month later, at 10:15 am on May 4, 2016.

* * *

Alina provided an introduction to *La Casa de la Brigada*, headquarters of the Bay of Pigs veterans' association and museum; while MariCris introduced me to her ex-husband, Carlos *Cachorro* Manuel León Acosta. Although my sister Naná had once met him, I hadn't.

Cachorro greased the skids for me by calling up *El Chino* and vouching for me, this on top of Alina's phone introduction of me as Armandito Lastra's cousin. Cachorro told me to remind *Chino* that *Chino* was the first man he'd ever slept with (referring to *Chino's* sharing his *colchoneta* with Cachorro in the leonera at El Príncipe). When I told *Chino*, he said Cachorro got it backwards: "That it was he, *Chino*, who had slept with Cachorro."

La Casa de la Brigada, headquarters and museum of the Bay of Pigs veterans' association, Miami, Florida, 2016. Credit: Carlos León.

Humberto 'El Chino' Díaz Argüelles, Battle of La Rotonda combatant and President of the Bay of Pigs Veterans' Association. Credit: R. H. Miller.

Humberto *El Chino* Díaz Argüelles, candidate for president of the veterans' association, was happy to meet with me. After touring the museum, *El Chino* sat down with me for a 4-hour interview. The *Brigadistas* have always been leery of journalists. At first, immediately after their return, they were told to keep mum by the CIA for a variety of reasons. So the Bay of Pigs story was told by the foreign press from interviews with the Castro government. As the famous quip goes, "History is written by the victors."

It took another six months for *Life* magazine to come out with an accurate account of the invasion and aftermath. By then, first impressions had coagulated in the public's mind, and the subsequent assassination of President Kennedy nearly eliminated any further curiosity about the Bay of Pigs. In spite of Haynes Johnson's (1964) and Peter Wyden's (1979) excellent books on the affair, most people had bought Castro's version that the US had illegally tried to invade Cuba with mercenaries.

Chino was a big, muscular man, even in his early 70s. Cachorro told me he'd been quite an athlete when he was young. *Chino* was open and transparent, even offering up an opinion on Ted Cruz, who was then running for the Republican nomination for president, and on Cruz' dad, who was born in Cuba. The Cruzes had had the temerity to show up at the *Casa de la Brigada* knowing nothing about it or the veterans' association and not even showing any curiosity. Ted Cruz wasn't about to get *Chino's* vote. He dismissed Trump with a snort. During our visit and before we parted, *Chino* introduced me to every veteran that walked into the Casa.

Chino won the election for president of the veterans' association and, busy as he was, continued providing follow-up interviews via email.

I cannot begin to add up all the hours I spent interviewing Cachorro, in person, on the telephone and via email. Balding, bearded, with intense eyes, he is average-sized and keeps himself fit. MariCris had never introduced us before; they'd had a tempestuous affair and short marriage, but had continued to remain in contact. Here's how she summed things up:

"Carlos and Armandito were friends since forever. Carlos' grandfather (last name Acosta) was mayor of Marianao, where my dad's family lived; his mother went to kindergarten with my uncle Ricardo, and my paternal grandfather used to say Carlos' grandmother was the most beautiful woman in Marianao (he said this out of earshot of my grandmother, who was very jealous). So I knew Carlos and his family always. We started going out when I was 19 - 1969. His sister Bibi and I were then (and still are) best friends. My dad (Pillo) died in May of 1978; he and Carlos loved each other but I barred Carlos from the funeral. I was a bit bitchy. Carlos finally signed the divorce papers in September 1978."

To further complicate matters, MariCris' husband doesn't take to Cachorro, while their son idolizes him. But the exes retain the greatest respect for each other.

Cachorro, in turn, introduced me to Bay of Pigs veterans Mario Martinez Malo and Roberto Mancebo, both of whom contributed to this book. With the remaining veterans beginning to die of old age, Momentum Miami and the Miami World Cinema Center began recording interviews with the survivors in 2011.

Carlos 'Cachorro' León Acosta, on right, with Carlos Manuel Varona, Brigade 2506 veteran and son of Antonio de Varona, Prime Minister of Cuba from 1948 to 1950 and later President of the Senate. Carlos Varona was one of the 19 paratroopers dropped along the Playa Larga-Jagüey Grande causeway with Cachorro to blow up culverts and bridges. The two fought over a moldy baloney sandwich they'd found in the swamp. Source: Carlos León collection.

One day, after the turn of the 21st Century, Cachorro got a call from one of Castro's ex-militiamen in Cuba. The man had served as a guard at one of the prisons he'd been held at. The guard had gone on to university and acquired, of all things, a degree in economics. When he called Cachorro, he'd already retired from a professorship at a Cuban university. He called to apologize for what had happened and for his behavior as a guard. He'd marveled at how the prisoners treated the guards: with a lack of rancor, with respect, and even with friendship. He'd been very impressed. Castro had described them as selfish mercenaries, worms, thieves, traitors—and worse. He'd found the descriptions totally wrong and, in retrospect, wished he'd treated them better.

While writing this memoir, I'd send Cachorro drafts of each chapter for commentary and corrections. He had read very little on the Bay of Pigs, and didn't discuss it much with the other veterans in spite of being very active in the organization. Hell, they'd shared the experience together; there wasn't much to discuss. In one phone interview with him, he told me that *El Cojo* Vera, his commander during the 19-man demolition operation and the second in command of the 1ˢᵗ Paratroop Battalion—the paratrooper who'd escaped capture by just walking away after the Brigade's defeat—had been killed in Cuba during an infiltration operation. After reading in the manuscript that Vera was alive and living in Miami, he called him up and re-connected with him.

It seemed as if the past was resurrecting itself and seeking him out. He was invited out to dinner once to meet an "interesting character." Always game for a free meal, especially at Versailles, Miami's toniest Cuban restaurant, and intellectual conviviality, he accepted. The interesting character's name didn't mean anything to him, even after the guy asked Cachorro, "So, you were in the Bay of Pigs operation?"

The character drew Cachorro out until Cachorro was recounting and critically reviewing the operation from both a political and military perspective. Cachorro does not tend to guardedness (at least with me). At some point in the discussion it came out that the "interesting character" had been a CIA operative and infiltrator prior to and during the Bay of Pigs invasion. He'd also been involved in some of the plans to assassinate Fidel Castro. The man had been present at *Che* Guevara's capture in Bolivia in 1967 by the Bolivian army. He had pleaded for Guevara's life, requesting that he be extradited and face justice for his many crimes. But the Bolivian government demurred. Guevara was summarily shot and the "interesting character," Félix Rodríguez, witnessed it. The last photo of Guevara alive is with Rodríguez, who now has Guevara's Rolex watch.

Cachorro's embarrassment didn't extend to turning down *torrejas en almibar* for desert; but it was profound. He felt as if he'd been lecturing Eistein on Relativity.

Another time while writing this book Cachorro realized that he'd never thanked Jim Donovan for setting him free. He told me he was going to call him right away and do so. I reminded him that Donovan was dead. He answered that it didn't matter; he'd thank his family.

* * *

The Cuban Revolution was not a revolution seeking "social justice," like the French and Russian Revolutions of the 18th and 20th centuries had sought. Instead, it had more in common with the American Revolution of 1776. The American Revolution was fought for what one might label, "technical reasons": taxation with representation, free trade, no housing of British soldiers in American homes without due process, and other such "technical" issues. The equal distribution of wealth was not among them.

The main complaints against Fulgencio Batista were that he'd usurped power illegally and that he ruled as an authoritarian. His regime was riddled with graft, abuse of power, rent-seeking and neglect of duty. The primary demands of the many and various revolutionaries seeking to overthrow him were the restoration of the Constitution of 1940 and free and honest elections—nothing more. There were no demands for free medical care, nation-wide literacy or agrarian reform any more than usual in any society. The bits about social justice, racial discrimination, wealth inequality, lack of education and such were items added to the mix after Castro's victory by Castro. Of course these issues had some validity, especially in an absolute sense, but virtually none in a relative sense. And they were issues that appealed after the Revolution had gained power, when everything seemed possible. But they were not why the Revolution was fought.

Patrick Symmes, in his book *The Boys from Dolores*, puts it another way:

> *"The revolution against Batista was largely a phenomenon of…the middle class, the professionals and technocrats, the engineers and lawyers. People like Fidel Castro. It was a revolution of lawyers and dentists. These were the people in Cuba who could literally afford to rebel, to risk things in pursuit of the better instincts of Cuban nationalism and democracy."*

Hawaii Senator Daniel Inouye once commented that Batista "has been described by some as the worst tyrant in the Caribbean." But those that survived the brutal regimes of Rafael Leonidas Trujillo in the Dominican Republic, François *Papa Doc* Duvalier in Haiti, or the Cubans who live under Fidel Castro's tyranny might dispute the senator from Hawaii. "He was no better or worse than any of Cuba's previous presidents," was Tita's assessment of Batista.

Fidel Castro was determined to install a Marxist regime in Cuba. To in any way allude to his intentions before he'd consolidated power would have led to his overthrow—just look at the number of presidents, prime ministers, revolutionary commanders, judges, soldiers, media and industrial enterprises that he purged. In a 1975 interview, Raúl Castro confirmed that it was Fidel who first introduced *him* to Marxism, back in 1951 when Fidel had given him Engel's *The Origin of the Family, Private Property and the State*. Raúl read it twice and experienced something of a Pauline conversion.

In 1958, Cuba had the second highest GDP in Latin America, a phenomenal achievement for such a tiny country, especially considering that Cuba was the last country in the hemisphere to gain independence—only 56 years earlier. It was ahead of several European countries in development, including Spain, Portugal and Greece. According to PBS' American Experience,

> *"Cuba ranked fifth in the hemisphere in per capita income, third in life expectancy, second in per capita ownership of automobiles and telephones, first in the number of television sets per inhabitant. The literacy rate, 76%, was the fourth highest in Latin America. Cuba ranked 11th in the world in the number of doctors per capita. Many private clinics and hospitals provided services for the poor. Cuba's income distribution compared favorably with that of other Latin American societies. A thriving middle class held the promise of prosperity and social mobility."*

In 1959 the economy began to fall apart. In 1960, the confiscations went into overdrive. In 1961, the mass arrests of dissidents became a reality.

Surely there were better ways to perfect Cuba than to kill, rob and drive away its most talented members. Over the course of Castro's—so far—57-year Revolution, Cuba's GDP per capita dropped to 12th in the Western Hemisphere (2011 numbers). Some economists dispute these numbers because per capita income is so low. And without a market economy, accurate GDP is difficult to measure.

Additionally, Cuba is a welfare state; not just in the traditional sense of providing safety nets for the poorest, but also because it depends on handouts from sponsor states. Prior to 1959, Cuba was self-reliant. Afterward, it became dependent first on the Soviet Union, then on Venezuela and now on the United States. *Yes, the United States—in spite of the embargo!*

One of the primary sources of foreign exchange in Cuba is family remittances, to the tune of $2.5 billion annually (2014 figures; probably more now). Some of the money, indirectly, comes from US taxpayers.

Here's how it works: Cuban refugees are automatically granted asylum in the US and are provided with food stamps, heath care and a stipend, i.e. welfare. Some of this is sent back to family in Cuba. With Cuban hustle, many refugees get jobs but continue to collect benefits. The remittances give a whole new definition to Cuba being a "welfare" state—dependent on the

US dole. Many Cuban refugees who came to the US in times past recognize the problem and are urging the US government to change the automatic acceptance rule for Cubans and apply normal asylum procedures to present-day Cuban immigrants.

The thinking is that these asylees are "economic" migrants as opposed to "political" refugees, a sentiment shared by many in the Obama administration. Regina Anavy, in her book, *Out of Cuba: Memoir of a Journey*, disputes this line of reasoning saying:

> *"When you are talking about a state-centralized economy and a political system that does not allow dissent or reward individual effort, is there a difference between an economic and a political reason to leave? Seems to me...that those who leave for economic reasons today are also casting a political vote with their feet."*

As to life expectancy, Cuba's much touted longer life expectancy than the US—79.07 years vs 78.74 years (2016)—is nothing to crow about. One third of a year longer is less than half a percentage point increase in longevity, and certainly no rationale for Castro's atrocities. Cuba ranks 38th in the world in life expectancy. Some would attribute the trivial gains to hard work and caloric deprivation, proven life-lengthening regimens. Yet we saw plenty of chubbiness during our bike ride. Cuba's obesity rate is 21.5%. Weight gain tends to be a natural reaction post caloric deprivation. Perhaps Cubans' overweight problem is an overcompensating isostatic reaction to the "special period" in the 1990s.

Today Cubans in exile and inside Cuba want change. But they no longer try to achieve it through force. The days of Brigade 2506 and Alpha 66 are over. Nearly all Cubans are dedicated to non-violent change. The only Cubans using force to impose their will today are the members of the Castro regime.

* * *

Fidel (Hipólito Casiano) Alejandro Castro Ruz died on November 25, 2016 at the age of 90. Though he outlived my mother both in absolute terms—she was 78—and in relative terms—by sixteen years, he did not—in absolute terms—outlive Tita, who died at the age of 94. It was a tiny but immensely satisfying—albeit posthumous—symbolic victory for an old woman over the 20th century's deadliest ideology.

Acknowledgments

As a family memoir—which this book is—it's presumptuous to attribute to only one author. During the course of the writing, many family and non-family members contributed facts and fiction (sometimes the latter), in effect, co-authoring; and participated as content editors and critics. But it was up to me to conceive of the idea, configure a framework, compose the sentences and choose the words. Though I very much enjoy writing, it is a slow and tedious process for me. Writing creatively is for me a one-to-two paragraph production per day, with revisions of the previous day's one-to-two paragraphs. This book took about two years to write over the course of about ten years.

Does anyone ever read the Acknowledgements? I always do, though rather perfunctorily. At this point I'll resort to boilerplate prose by assuming all responsibility for any errors and omissions (though it'd be lots more fun to blame my cousin-in-law Cachorro, my sister Naná, my cousin MariCris, and especially my aunt Tita and cousin Armandito, who are no longer with us and can't complain for blaming them).

I cannot prioritize the most important individuals to whom I'd like to extend a thank you. Some seemingly minor ones were nearly as important as the more existential ones. So I'll just dive in:

Tina Cobos, my lover and consort, for her unconditional support, boundless enthusiasm, and unedited honesty. As my editor of first resort, she was my guinea pig for holding a reader's attention, always my first priority in prose. She nipped some of my extravagant flights of fancy (and aborted takeoffs) and eased the burden on subsequent editors. As a biking companion, she turned trouble into fun and fun into ecstasy.

Howard Miller, my late father, for living a life full of reason, adventure, and accomplishment (writing included) as if there were no other choice. He was an inspiration in the realization that we are each of us in the driver's seat of life and can go anywhere we choose.

Ana María Miller, my late mother, for her encouragement, if not in all of my adventures, at least in my attempts to write, and for her endowment of roots and wings. As a central character in this memoir, she was indispensable. I wish she were here to read it, add to it, set me straight and fine-tune accounts.

Two editors deserve at least four sheaves of paper, a couple of cartridges of printer ink and a brand new Roget's Thesaurus for having profoundly inspired and nurtured my writing. Martha McDonald Reinke, ex-lover, adventure companion, talented hack, one-time real estate editor for the *Phoenix Business Journal* and contributor to the *Mini Storage Messenger*, admired my early efforts to compose stuff. It was under her aegis that I published my first paying article. Though I have no idea what she's been doing since we broke up, she saw my potential when it was just a fancy.

Stephen Cox, Professor of English at the University of California San Diego, publisher and editor of *Liberty* magazine and author, has been encouraging and correcting my writing for many years, *and* publishing most of my article submissions to *Liberty* magazine. Though he has at times been so supportive, I fear he must be desperate for material since, like Groucho Marx, I question whether any magazine that publishes me is worth writing for.

Anita Hatch-Miller, my sister, for being my number two editor, always arguing about grammar, caviling about accuracy, criticizing beyond the call of duty, and her intense involvement—and of course, for her contributions as translator and artist. Only one year apart in age, some sibling rivalry intruded. With the first few chapters she gravitated towards nitpicking, correcting grammar and avoiding any positive comments other than, "it's fine." But as the chapters kept coming, either the grammar improved or she got caught up in the narrative, because she turned complementary. The praise became so lavish, I deflected responsibility by saying that the story was so compelling, "it wrote itself." By the next chapter she retorted that "the chapter read itself." She could give no higher compliment.

Armandito Lastra Faget and his mother Tita Faget, both of whom this book is dedicated to, and without whom there would be no book, were indispensable; not only for the extensive interviews they submitted to (actually just regular catching-up family conversations and visits) but for their service to their countries. Armandito, of course, fought for freedom and justice (yes, it's a cliché, but a profoundly true one, and one that ought never to be minimized); Tita, more indirectly, taught Spanish to many American Peace Corps volunteers. She was a bulwark of support to her son while in prison; to my grandmother while alone in Cuba; to my mother in exile, dementia and demise; and to me as a second mother.

Carlos León Acosta, aka *Cachorro*, my fourth ex-cousin-in-law, with whom I talked nearly every day, sometimes multiple times, while writing the second part of this book was more than indispensable. His modesty belies his wisdom. I thank him for his unstinting efforts to liberate Cuba and to keep a high standard of objectivity and probity in past and continuing Cuban controversies. But more than the accomplishment of this book, I'm grateful for his friendship and love.

My companions on the bike ride across Cuba, Roy and Brenda Smith, and George Yen for being a part of this project. George, a college roommate, hosted Tina and I when we cycled the perimeter of Taiwan. Without his help, that trip would have been nearly impossible without a professional guide. I hope that in some part I repaid that debt by taking him to Cuba.

But I especially want to thank Roy Smith, mentor, inspiration, hero, sometime writer and fellow adventurer. As a fat teenager obsessed with nothing in particular, I was taken under Roy's wing: he made a mountaineer out of me, a skill that broadened into other adventurous pursuits and, more importantly, the realization that I could achieve anything to which I set my heart and force of will. Roy's lifelong experience as an adventure educator, along with mine, provided the legal underpinnings for our Cuba bike trip. He and Brenda also had the good graces and humor to play ideological foil to my anti-Castro, radical libertarian perspective thereby enriching all of us.

This book could never have been written without the help, recollections and insights of the Brigade 2506 veterans. Humberto *El Chino* Díaz Argüelles, president of the *Casa de la Brigada*, kindly deigned to meet with me and provide his broader perspective. Roberto Mancebo, Armandito's *hermano* and my *tocayo*, provided a hand-drawn map of the battle of the Rotonda and many anecdotes and facts about that battle. Mario Martinez Malo kindly lent me the unpublished monograph of his account of the battle of the Rotonda and submitted to a phone interview.

MariCris Casanueva and Alina Lastra, my cousins and the daughters of *las viejas,* Cuca and Tita, provided photographs, documents, information and valuable gossip throughout the writing process and added hospitality and eye candy while in Miami. I must thank Chuchu Aisa for his one important insight into Armandito's turn against the Castro regime; Lauristela Ortiz, Armandito's widow, for putting up with me and for the many anecdotes she provided about her man, and her daughter, Lori for photos; Luis R. Luis, for his account of Castro's entry into Havana; Jorge, Tania & Dunia Thondike, very distant, shirt-tail relatives for their hospitality in Havana and Miami. Johnny Fitzgerald, my cousin, for help in obtaining visas and verification of facts concerning his father John Fitzgerald, my mother's brother.

I want to thank my cousin Martha Fitzgerald for her hospitality in Miami, and for reading parts of the manuscript (and her delicious food, yum!); Julio and Martha Julieta Polanco, her son and daughter, for their hospitality while we were in Miami—and their support in this endeavor.

There are two more humans and three entities without which our trip to Cuba would not have been possible. And it is the two humans that were instrumental in getting the entities to respond: Barbara Yarrow and Chris Wuehrmann, both formerly at Yavapai College in Prescott, Arizona where I taught for ten years, supplied us with letters of sponsorship for this project, thereby allowing us to obtain a US Treasury Department permit for travel to Cuba. Roy Smith, whom I've already thanked, requires additional thanks for obtaining letters of sponsorship from Prescott College in Prescott, Arizona where we both attended and taught; and from Bloomsburg University in Pennsylvania where Roy ran their Outdoor Adventure Program for many years.

Finally, Lance Bailey, DDS and Mark Goodman, LLD donated about one hundred toothbrushes and ball point pens to us to distribute as good-will gifts during our bike ride in Cuba; Joe Schallan, forensic librarian, for research help; Steven Irwin and Jeff Hatch-Miller, for computer techy help; and Alejandro Ramos, my publisher at *Cognitio Books & Apps*, for recognizing the merit in this work and sheepherding it through to completion—thank you guys!

Author contact information:

Robert H. Miller

1740 Oregon
Prescott, AZ 86305

roberthowardmiller@gmail.com

Bibliography

Alfonso, Aristides. "Las Villas y Mansiones de Fidel Castro." Cubaeuropa.

Alonso, Araceli. *Out of Havana: Memoirs of Ordinary Life in Cuba*. Blue Mounds, Wisconsin: Deep University Press, 2014.

American Experience. "Fidel Castro Timeline: Post-Revolution Cuba 1958-1976." PBS.

American Experience. "Fidel Castro. People & Events: Pre-Castro Cuba. PBS. December, 2004.

Anavy, Regina. *Out of Cuba: Memoir of a Journey*. Cognitio Books & Apps, 2013.

Ayers, Bradley Earl. *The War That Never Was: An Insider's Account of CIA Covert Operations Against Cuba*. Indianapolis/New York: The Bobbs-Merrill Company, Inc., 1976.

Baker, Christopher P. *Havana*. Emeryville, CA: Avalon Travel; Moon Handbooks, 2003.

Batista, Fulgencio. *The Growth and Decline of the Cuban Republic*. New York: The Devin-Adair Company, 1964.

Bovo-Caras, Estevan L. *"We Shall Never Abandon Our Motherland": Museum and Library of the Bay of Pigs Veterans Association Brigade 2506*. Pictorial history, Miami.

Campbell, Brian E. *Brigade 2506: Young, Idealistic, and anti-Castro*. Ohio State University, 2011.

César, Eli B. *San Blas: Ultima Batalla en Bahia de Cochinos*. Miami, FL: Editorial Los Amigos, 2006.

Castro, Juanita *with* Collins, María Antonieta. *Fidel y Raul Mis Hermanos: La Historia Secreta*. Doral, FL: Aguilar, 2009.

Cuban Information Archives. *BOP & 2506*. Miami, FL: Cuban Information Archives Website, 1998-2014.

Dille, John and Flaherty, Tom. "This Was the Bay of Pigs: The Men Who Fought Tell the Eyewitness Story of the Tightly Planned Battle in Which Everything Went Wrong and Reveal the Shocking Miscalculations that Produced the Fiasco." *And* "Washington Searches Its Memory for the Answers," *Life*. May 10, 1963.

Eire, Carlos. *Waiting for Snow in Havana*. New York, London, Toronto, Sydney, Singapore: The Free Press, 2003.

Encinosa, Enrique. *Heroes del Escambray*. Futurodecuba.org. From *Escambray: La Guerra Olvidada*. Editorial SIBI, 1988.

Fernandez Barrios, Flor. *Blessed by Thunder: Memoir of a Cuban Girlhood*. Seattle, WA: Seal Press, 1999.

Foreign Claims Settlement Commission of the United States; Claim No. CU-0285, Decision No. CU-5960. Washington, D.C., November 17, 1970.

Foster, Kevin. *Cycling Castro's Cuba: The Tour de Cuba*. Kaweah Commonwealth, CA: Pisces Publications, 2004.

Jimenez, Guillermo. *Las Empresas de Cuba 1958: Enciclopedia Económica de Cuba Republicana*. Miami: Ediciones Universal, 1995.

Johnson, Haynes. *The Bay of Pigs: The Leaders' Story of Brigade 2506*. New York: W.W. Norton, 1964.

Jordan, Rosa and Choukalos, Derek. *Cycling Cuba*. Melbourne, Oakland, London, Paris: Lonely Planet, 2002.

Linklater, Andro. *Owning the Earth: The Transforming History of Land Ownership*. New York, London, New Delhi, Sydney: Bloomsbury, 2013.

Lynch, Grayston L. *Decision for Disaster: Betrayal at the Bay of Pigs*. Washington & London: Brassey's, 1998.

Martinez-Malo, Mario. "Bay of Pigs Veterans Interviews on Vimeo." Momentum Miami, Miami World Cinema Center, July 28. 2011.

Martinez-Malo, Mario. *La Batalla de la Rotonda*. Miami: Self-published monograph, 2006.

Matos, Huber. *Cómo Llegó La Noche*. Barcelona: Tusquets Editores, 2002.

Miller, Robert H. "Waiting for Fidel." *Liberty*, April, 2007.

Miller, Robert H. "Inside the Castro Family." *Liberty*, April, 2010.

Miller, Robert H. "Fidel Castro Agonistes." *Liberty*, November, 2016

Ministerio de las Fuerzas Armadas Revolucionarias, Estado Mayor General, Republica de Cuba. [Indictment and Sentence of Brigade 2506]. La Habana, Republica de Cuba. 7 Abril, 1962.

Norwich, John Julius. *Sicily*. London: John Murray, 2015.

Pérez-Cisneros, Donovan, John B. & Koenreich, Jeff. *After the Bay of Pigs: Lives and Liberty on the Line*. Miami: Alexandria Library, 2007.

Pérez-Cisneros, Pablo. "Sobre el Castillo del Príncipe y los Presos de la Brigada 2506." *Penúltimos Dias: Historia y Archivo*, Abril, 2011.

Persons, Albert C. *Bay of Pigs: A Firsthand Account of the Mission by a U.S. Pilot in Support of the Cuban Invasion Force in 1961*. Jefferson, N.C. & London: McFarland & Co., Inc., 1990.

Phillips, David Atlee. *The Night Watch*. New York: Ballantine Books, 1977.

Prellezo, Lily *with* Basulto, José. *Seagull One: The Amazing True Story of Brothers to the Rescue*. Gainesville, FL.: University Press of Florida, 2010.

Quirk, Robert E. *Fidel Castro*. New York & London: W.W. Norton, 1993.

Rasenberger, Jim. *Brilliant Disaster: JFK, Castro, and America's Doomed Invasion of Cuba's Bay of Pigs*. New York, London, Toronto, Sydney: Scribner, 2011.

Remigio, Arnaldo. *Girón: The True Story of Three Days of Bloody Combat (by a Cuban Army Paramedic), AKA The Betrayal of the Eagle: Battle Diary of the Bay of Pigs and AKA Sixty to One: The other side of the Story of the Bay of Pigs Invasion; The Combat Behind the Lines of Castro's Forces.* Unpublished MS.

Roach, Mary. *Grunt: The Curious Science of Humans at War.* New York: W.W. Norton, 2016.

Robinson, Linda. "The Price of Military Folly—JFK, the CIA and Cuban Exiles: A Disaster Called the Bay of Pigs," *U.S. News & World Report,* April 22, 1996.

Rodriguez, Félix I. & Weisman, John. *Shadow Warrior: The CIA Hero of a Hundred Unknown Battles.* New York: Simon and Schuster, 1989.

Rúiz, Leovigildo. *Diario de Una Traición: Cuba 1961.* Miami, FL: Lorie Book Stores, 1972.

Sánchez, Juan Reynaldo *with* Gylden, Axel. *The Double Life of Fidel Castro: My 17 Years as Personal Bodyguard to el Líder Máximo.* New York: St. Martin's Press, 2015.

Santovenia, Emeterio S. & Shelton, Raul M. *Cuba Y Su Historia.* Miami: Cuba Corporation, Inc., 1966.

Schumpeter. "The Imperial CFO," *The Economist.* June 18, 2016.

Shackley, Ted, Chief of Station JMWAVE. *Dispatch: Report No. 282: Report of Negotiations of Families Committee as told by Ernesto Freyre, Secretary of the Committee.* CIA, 04/25/62.

Smith, Wally & Barbara. *Bicycling Cuba.* Woodstock, Vermont: Backcountry Guides, 2002.

Spufford, Francis. *Red Plenty: Industry! Progress! Abundance! Inside the Fifties' Soviet Dream.* London: Faber & Faber Limited, 2010.

Symmes, Patrick. *The Boys from Dolores: Fidel Castro's Schoolmates from Revolution to Exile.* New York: Vintage Books, 2007/8.

Szulc, Tad. *Fidel: A Critical Portrait.* New York: Avon Books, 1986.

The Cuban Revolution. www.Cubaverdad.net/revolution.htm

The Economist. "Somalia: Most Failed State." September 10, 2016.

"Timetable History of Cuba: After the Revolution." historyofcuba.com

Tupy, Marian. "Cuba's Literacy ate, Life Expectancy Nothing to Lionize." Reason.com, April 19, 2016.

Valladares, Armando. *Against All Hope*. New York: Alfred A. Knopf, 1986.

Vidal, Guillermo Vicente. *Boxing for Cuba: An Immigrant's Story*. Golden, CO: Fulcrum, 2007.

Vila, Dr. Herminio Portell. *Nueva Historia de la República de Cuba*. Miami, FL: La Moderna Poesía, Inc., 1986.

Wells, Laura. "He 'foiled' a CIA hit on Castro involving a poisoned wetsuit, sent top Nazis to the gallows and saved a US U2 pilot downed over the USSR: Family reveals incredible life of Bronx lawyer immortalized by Tom Hanks in 'Bridge of Spies.'" *Daily Mail.com*. October 16, 2015.

Wyden, Peter. *Bay of Pigs: The Untold Story*. New York: Simon & Schuster, 1979.

Young, Warren. "Door to Freedom: A Quiet Lawyer's Eloquent Patience," *Life*. January 4, 1963.

About the Author

Robert H. Miller grew up in Cuba, learned English in Mississippi, attended high school and college in Arizona, and did post-graduate work at the University of Colorado, Boulder, specializing in primatology and archaeology with an emphasis on the evolution of civilization. He participated in the multi-disciplinary and multi-institutional project to search for the origins of the domestication of corn in Mesoamerica, excavated early man sites in northern Arizona and was a producer for Spirit Expedition Films on their Inca Royal Road project.

Miller has taught at Prescott College and Yavapai College and has published many articles in *Liberty*, *The Denver Post*, *The Phoenix Business Journal*, *River Runner*, *Canoe*, *The Arizona Republic*, *Rock & Ice*, *American Atheist*, *Essays in the Philosophy of Humanism*, *Salka Wind*, *Outerlocal*, *The Alpinist*, on Cuba, Latin America, economics, politics, history, philosophy, adventure and book reviews, and contributed to *Papers on the Archaeology of Black Mesa*, Arizona, edited by George J. Gumerman and Robert C. Euler, Southern Illinois University Press, 1976, as the photographer.

An accomplished outdoor enthusiast in rock climbing, mountaineering, survival, mountain biking and kayaking, he has also taught those skills at Outward Bound, Challenge Discovery, Prescott College and Yavapai College. He is the author of *Kayaking the Inside Passage: A Paddler's Guide from Olympia, Washington to Muir Glacier, Alaska*, Countryman Press, 2005, and a contributor to Why We Boat, Vishnu Temple Press, 2017.

Additionally, Miller has been a house designer and builder, specializing in masonry and cabinetry. In his retirement he likes crossing countries by foot and bicycle, and climbing *via ferrate*. He lives in Prescott, Arizona.

Made in the USA
San Bernardino, CA
16 August 2017